# Points of Departure

# Points of Departure

*Samuel Weber between Spectrality and Reading*

Edited by Peter Fenves,
Kevin McLaughlin,
and Marc Redfield

NORTHWESTERN UNIVERSITY PRESS
EVANSTON, ILLINOIS

Northwestern University Press
www.nupress.northwestern.edu



Printed in the United States of America

10 9 8 7 6 5 4 3 2 1

Library of Congress Cataloging-in-Publication Data

Names: Fenves, Peter D. (Peter David), 1960– editor. | McLaughlin, Kevin, 1959– editor. | Redfield, Marc, 1958– editor. | Weber, Samuel, 1940– honouree.
Title: Points of departure : Samuel Weber between spectrality and reading / edited by Peter Fenves, Kevin McLaughlin, and Marc Redfield.
Description: Evanston, Illinois : Northwestern University Press, 2016. | Papers from an International conference held at the Chateau de la Bretesche, Missillac, France, on July 4–7, 2010. | Some papers translated from French or German.
Identifiers: LCCN 2016031996 | ISBN 9780810133761 (pbk. : alk. paper) | ISBN 9780810133778 (cloth : alk. paper) | ISBN 9780810133785 (e-book)
Subjects: LCSH: Weber, Samuel, 1940– | Literature, Modern—History and criticism. | Critical theory. | Philosophy, Modern.
Classification: LCC PN94.2 .P645 2016 | DDC 801.950905—dc23
LC record available at https://lccn.loc.gov/2016031996

## CONTENTS

# ACKNOWLEDGMENTS

This volume would not have been possible without the generous support of the Albert and Elaine Borchard Foundation, which provided the funds both for an international conference at the Château de la Bretesche, Missillac, France, on July 4–7, 2010, and for the translation of the essays that were originally written in French and German. We are particularly indebted to Dr. Janna Beling, co-director of the Borchard Foundation Center on International Education. The editors also would like to thank Professor Patricia Easton and Lisa Flores-Griffith of Claremont Graduate University for their time and effort in making this volume a reality. The volume editors are grateful to the editors of Northwestern University Press for their unwavering support and encouragement in bringing this project to completion.

We are especially thankful to Pierre Alferi-Derrida, who, as representative of the Derrida Estate, granted us permission to include "Vous voulez rire!" in the volume.

# Points of Departure

Introduction

✦

# The Layout

Peter Fenves

The contributors to this volume understand the work of Samuel Weber as an opportunity, including an opportunity to transform the standard understanding of what it means for an opportunity to arise. According to the standard understanding—which gives rise to associated concepts such as *opportunism*—an opportunity is a favorable condition in which an otherwise unattainable goal can be realized, and the question whether an opportunity is seized or lost depends on whether the goal is accomplished or missed. Weber's work disputes this understanding of an opportunity, and nowhere more succinctly than at the end of *Targets of Opportunity*, where he sketches a concept of the opportune situation that can be seen to guide the broad scope of his work. Analyzing an argument that Walter Benjamin pursues in his early interpretation of Friedrich Hölderlin's "Blödigkeit" ("Timidity" or "Frailty"), Weber writes of the "moment of opportunity" that it is "not to be 'seized' but rather traversed: it is a 'port' or 'portal' (lexical root of op*port*unity), which leads not to an ultimate goal but to a multitude of 'carpets.' "[1] According to a common expression in English, "opportunity knocks," and Weber, characteristically attentive to the inter- and intralinguistic resonances of certain words and phrases, hears the sound of opportunity in its lexical root. The "port" in *opportunity* opens up an opportunity to alter the standard concept of opportunity, so that it is no longer understood in terms of starting and ending points but is, instead, saturated by intermittent points of departure.

In the passage quoted above, Weber, following customary practice, translates the German word *Gelegenheit* as "opportunity." The word does not appear in Hölderlin's poem, but Benjamin introduces *Gelegenheit* into his "aesthetic commentary" in order to encompass the semantic range of two cognate terms: *Lage*, which is generally translated as "situation," and *gelegen*, which is often rendered as "opportune" but suggests the act of having laid something down. The something in this case is the very space through which the poet enters into life. Here are the opening five lines of "Blödigkeit," in which the poet encourages himself to overcome the "timidity" or "frailty" that would make him shy away from life and thus from his own poetic existence:

Sind denn dir nicht bekannt viele Lebendigen?
Geht auf Wahrem dein Fuß nicht, wie auf Teppichen?
Drum, mein Genius! tritt nur
Bar ins Leben, und sorge nicht!
Was geschiehet, es sei alles gelegen dir!

Are not many lively ones familiar to you?
Doesn't your foot tread on the true as on carpets?
Then, my genius, only now tread
Nakedly into life, and care not!
Whatever happens, everything is laid out for you! [2]

Thus translated, these lines suggest that the poet surmounts his own timidity or frailty by recognizing the situation in which he finds himself. The situation can be called "opportune" insofar as it allows him to be who he is: a poet in the act of making poetry. Understood in this way the concept of opportunity that emerges in the opening lines of Hölderlin's poem is at once different from the standard concept and yet limited in its application—different because it erases the distinction between auspicious condition and final goal, yet limited because the erasure of this distinction applies only to poets who, by virtue of their vocation, traverse the space of "the true." Benjamin extends the scope of Hölderlin's transformation of the concept of opportunity by showing that the "situation" of which the poet speaks is nothing less than the "Wahrheit der Lage," or "truth of the situation" in general.[3] As Jacques Derrida notes at the beginning of the fictive "interview with a passing journalist" that is included in this volume, "the thinking of location or of place" can be considered the "major *topos*" of all Weber's books.[4] And in tracing out the topology or topography of Hölderlin's late poem, Weber both follows and departs from Benjamin's commentary: he follows Benjamin by reiterating the intimate relation between "laid out" (*gelegen*) and "opportunity" (*Gelegenheit*), but he departs from Benjamin's commentary by emphasizing, above all, the *plurality* of the "carpets" that Hölderlin compares with "the true." Although Hölderlin's use of the plural in the case of "carpets" is easily overlooked, it is, for Weber, no small matter. If one can identify the crucial characteristic that "the true" has in common with carpets, it is probably this: instead of being a means to an end, carpets, like "the true," are media. The subtle yet forceful discrepancy between the plurality of carpets and the singularity of "the true" not only casts doubt on the notion of the "truth of the situation" *in general*; it also suggests a generalization of the situation laid out in the poem, such that it no longer applies only to the poet—or, conversely, the position of the poet in relation to "the people" is pluralized in light of the multiple carpets. Opportunity is thus equalized in a certain sense; more precisely the structure of the "opportune" situation requires the categories of multiplicity and singularity, while at the same time excluding the principle of self-identity. The poem refuses to say whether the once "frail" poet survives his entrance into life; that is, it does not say whether the poet remains identical to himself—and thus remains "the" poet—as he strides upon the carpets-like space of "the true." This refusal amounts to a gentle denial.

Consonant with the emphasis on the multiple-singular structure of the situation of the poet that Weber, guided by Benjamin's commentary, rediscovers in Hölderlin's poem is a practice of translation that owes a debt to Hölderlin and Benjamin, among many others. The practice is particularly evident in Weber's unexpected translation of the root term under consideration here, namely *Lage*, which, as noted earlier, is generally translated as "situation." Just as Weber notices the "port" in *opportunity*, so he directs attention to the "lay-" root in *Lage*. One of the striking features of the German verb *legen*, like its English counterpart, is its indeterminacy with regard to the categories of action and passivity. The verb encompasses both act and sufferance, doing and undergoing. Adding a specific direction to the categorial indeterminacy of the German-English verb, Weber translates *Lage* as "layout." It is the outward-directedness of any given situation that makes it "opportune," and this outwardness does not so much oppose inwardness as suggest—in German, the verb would be *nahelegen*—the unwrapping of a scene in which the line of demarcation between action and passivity, or actors and audiences, remains in flux. In this regard it is no accident that the subject matter of Weber's dissertation is a scene of unwrapping, where, guided by Balzac's *Peau de chagrin*, the structure of the narrative is laid bare.[5] Similarly working with and around a lyric poem in the final section of *Targets of Opportunity* Weber does not emphasize the theatrical character of the layout, but it is nevertheless apparent in his analysis of the poem and its commentary, where the image of the poet striding upon "the true" is refracted through Hölderlin's and Benjamin's theories of tragedy and *Trauerspiel* (mourning play). Opportune situations, thus "layouts," are irreducibly theatrical—not events in the purity of their occurrence but stagings and scene settings in which the temporal criteria distinguishing enactment from repetition are eroded in the same stroke as the categorial distinction between acting and sufferance.

In choosing *layout* as the translation of a cardinal term in Benjamin's commentary, Weber brings out a decisive dimension of the opportune situation: its relation to technology, or better yet, to cite Weber's translation of the German word *Technik*, its relation to "technics."[6] *Layout* is often used with reference to certain moments in the process of production. Weber works with this aspect of the English term and discovers a corresponding German word in Benjamin's commentary, namely *Muster* (pattern or exemplar). As Weber notes, however, the *Muster* about which Benjamin writes cannot be understood in terms of representation or replication, whereby the pattern or exemplar would provide the blueprint for the ensuing product: "This pattern, although exemplary, is not representational but 'arbitrary,' hence determined not through its content but through its context: its spatial disposition, its layout."[7] Even though Weber does not lay emphasis on the "technical" character of the layout, an alternative concept of technology or "technics" can be seen in this brief description. Instead of being understood as goal-directed action that aims to control an object, the layout is characterized by contiguity and contingency—so much so that the "exemplary pattern" does not govern the production process but rather reproduces, with unforeseeable differences, its contingent conditions and contiguous arrangements. With remarkable concision Weber thus sketches the concept of technics under consideration in a broad spectrum of his writings, most especially in *Mass Mediauras*. The layout is not the basis of a product, distinct from nature by virtue of human intentionality, which is directed toward its goals as weapons are directed toward their targets; rather it is a reiteration of the opportune situation that by its very nature—every opportunity is necessarily only a possibility—cannot be installed, regulated, or otherwise manipulated.

✦

The final section of *Targets of Opportunity* thus recapitulates some of Weber's major lines of inquiry, from the precise reading of certain literary and critical texts, through an exacting practice and theory of translation, to the broad fields of research signaled by the concepts of media, theatricality, and technology. But there is a further reason to emphasize Weber's analysis of the concept of opportunity in the introduction to this volume. His work is stamped by a series of opportune situations that brought him into dialogue with some of the most far-reaching, controversial, and consequential thinkers in the second half of the twentieth century. In the early 1960s Weber began the project of translating the culture-critical essays of Theodor Adorno, whose voluminous work, beyond *The Authoritarian Personality*, was largely unavailable in English. His early interest in the Frankfurt School of Social Research brought him into contact with Herbert Marcuse, who encouraged him to send the drafts of his translation to Adorno himself. Around the same time Weber attended Paul de Man's seminar on Heidegger's *Sein und Zeit* (*Being and Time*), and in the course of their subsequent discussions de Man highly recommended the work of a young French philosopher, Jacques Derrida. Weber's engagement with the thought of the Frankfurt School brought him to the University of Frankfurt, where he completed the translation of and influential introduction to Adorno's *Prisms*, the opening essay of which, "Critical Theory and Society," has been a persistent point of reference for English-language discussions of cultural criticism since its publication in 1967.[8] And shortly afterward Weber became a *wissenschaftlicher Assistant* (scholarly assistant) at the Institute for Comparative and General Literature that Peter Szondi had only recently established at the Free University in West Berlin.

The reason to draw attention to the opportunities Weber traversed during these years is not to provide notes toward a future biography. Nothing is more antithetical to the direction of his thought than the notion of individual life that informs standard practices of biography, which tend to take as their subject the supposedly successful or unsuccessful individuals who sometimes seize and sometimes miss the opportunities that would define them. This antagonism to the protocols of biographical criticism can be seen, for instance, in his brief reflection on the idea of "the lively ones" (*die Lebendigen*) in the concluding section of *Targets of Opportunity*, where he shows that, for Hölderlin and Benjamin, this idea is incompatible with featureless conceptions of individuated life that direct much of what is considered biography. Whatever else may be said of "the lively ones," they do not move along a rectilinear path from birth to death, punctuated by goals attained and opportunities missed. Weber's contestation of standard biographical practices is most evident, however, in his extensive engagement with the founding texts of psychoanalysis. Weber began to study psychoanalytic theory in the context of his early involvement with the Frankfurt School, but his studies led him back to the texts of Freud and thus soon brought him to Lacan, who had famously proclaimed a "return to Freud" in opposition to versions of ego psychology that were promoted, for instance, by certain members of the Frankfurt School. Whereas the governing imperative of standard biographical practices can be described as the demand for rectilinear continuity, even when gaps appear in the record of the subject's ongoing activities, the primary motifs guiding the studies of Freud and Lacan that Weber published in the 1970s are those of the fracture, the fissure, and the pause.[9] The point of drawing attention to the course of Weber's studies is not to show how he seized the opportunities that came his way but rather to indicate the fractured character of the situations he traversed. Some of those situations can be designated by proper names such as Marcuse with de Man, Adorno with Derrida, and Szondi with Lacan. Others are better designated by common nouns, such as *critical theory* with *rhetorical reading*, *psychoanalysis* with *deconstruction*, and *philological analysis* with *media theory*. All of these situations came under discussion at an international conference that was held at Château de la Bretesche in Missillac, France, in July 2010, where many of the essays in this volume originated. The aim of the conference was to sketch out various lines of research that intersect with Weber's work. The volume is accordingly entitled *Points of Departure*. As I explain below, the volume is subtitled *Samuel Weber between Spectrality and Reading* because the essays that resulted from the conference are primarily directed at questions of spectrality, theatricality, and media, on the one hand, and those of reading, language, and mediation, on the other.

✦

In the central chapter of *The Legend of Freud* Weber undertakes a careful reading of Freud's inquiry into the dynamics of humor, *Der Witz und seine Beziehung zum Unbewußten* (*Jokes and Their Relation to the Unconscious*), paying particular attention to the manner in which, as a result of the translator's effort to produce a continuous and tractable exposition, the standard English translation tends to miss what occurs in Freud's text. What the translation misses could be called the wit of Freud's text in its relation to his concept of the unconscious. *The Legend of Freud* identifies the missing element with laughter, which, according to Weber, poses difficulties to the analysis and comprehension of *Witz* by "introducing what might be called a *discontinuous temporality*" into its structure: you must laugh in order for the joke to have been the joke it is.[10] The introduction of a destructuring element into the structure of an utterance or outburst from which no speech can be fully protected is the final essay of this volume: a fictive interview invented by Derrida under the title "Vous voulez rire!," which begins with an epigraph drawn from the chapter of *The Legend of Freud* under discussion here. The imperative *Vous voulez rire* would be translated literally as "You'll want to laugh," but its sense is more accurately captured by the colloquial phrase "You've got to be kidding." For Derrida the element of disbelief lies primarily in the stance of sovereignty. And in the context of the fictive interview, Weber's work *cum Witz*—exemplified by his inquiry into "the meaning of the thallus"—becomes an opportunity for Derrida to discover a degree of "passing" in whatever self-consciously presents as journalism.[11] The previous essays in the volume are less obviously combative, but they similarly register the always differential and often polemical force of Weber's work. In preparation for Derrida's essay the volume is divided into the two sections indicated above: first a group of five essays organized around questions of spectrality; then a group of five essays that revolve around corresponding questions of reading. The central essay in the volume, written by Weber, addresses spectrality and reading in equal measure, as he places *Hamlet* in a medial position, "between Benjamin and Carl Schmitt." The phrase Weber draws from Shakespeare's play for his title, "For O, for O, the Hobby-Horse Is Forgot," despite and because of its repetition of the unreadable O, breaks what he calls the "binary machine code," thus opening up an opportunity as "anticipation and a prophesy, beyond anything that its speaker could have intended."

The initial contribution to the first section, Dragan Kujundžić's "Ghost Scriptum, or Nothing to Play With," is closely connected to the issues under discussion in Weber's essay and thus functions as a second introduction to the volume as a whole. Situating Weber's analysis of Shakespeare's play in relation to Derrida's invocation of the Ghost of Hamlet at the beginning of *Specters of Marx*, Kujundžić opens up a broad reflection on spectrality in the context of what Weber has called, following Benjamin, "post-Reformation nihilism." The subsequent essay in the volume, Béatrice Jongy-Guéna's "Postmortem

Automediality and the Ghosts of Cyberspace," is also concerned with "post-Reformation nihilism"—more exactly, with a contemporary mode of mediality in which a virtual life is sustained on the Internet regardless of the mortal status of its subject. Jongy-Guéna begins with an inquiry into the complex legal questions engendered by postmortem virtuality, in which self-identity is maintained in video tombstones and similar forms of automediality. While discussing the legal ramifications of postmortem virtual identity, Jongy-Guéna undertakes a critique of the purported "survival" promised by these new practices of self-assertion, emphasizing that virtual life too is as subject to time as the very medium of alteration. Nikolaus Müller-Schöll similarly draws on Weber's writings on theatricality to launch a vigorous critique of spectator theory, including Jacques Rancière's recent promotion of the so-called active spectator. As Müller-Schöll argues, it is more productive to continue the line of thought proposed by Benjamin and developed in Weber, wherein the spectacle is not installed for the benefit of the spectator; rather the audience—distinct from the spectator—constitutes a community that, because it is never "there" but always only "coming," eludes all forms of representation. Among the starting points for Müller-Schöll's "Unrepresentable Audience" is the idea of epic theater as it emerges in Bertolt Brecht's work and Benjamin's corresponding commentaries. The same is true of Astrid Deuber-Mankowsky's contribution, "Signal and Mandatary," which revolves around Benjamin's sketch of "the destructive character" and takes its point of departure from Weber's analysis of the crucial feature that the destructive character and epic theater share in common: gestural interruption. Accounting for the historical figures whose outlines are recognizable in Benjamin's essay—which extend from a banker to Brecht—Deuber-Mankowsky shows how the destructive character, like epic theater, creates paths of thought and thus makes it possible for there to be futures that are not simply reinstallations of the present. From the perspective of those who are fully invested in the reinstallation of the present, epic theater and the destructive character represent more or less vague threats, which elicit the kind of anxious questions expressed in the title of Marc Crépon's essay, "Protection from What and for What?" Extending a line of thought that Weber develops in his analysis of what Benjamin described as the "mythic connection" between death and guilt, Crépon draws attention to a recent French law that allows for infinite detention and, by so doing, separates sanction from guilt. The state presents itself as a spectral agent that protects against death and that accordingly punishes for the purpose of protection. Crépon closes the first section of the volume by drawing attention to the organizing theme of Weber's most recent writings: the possibility of a "politics of singularity," which, circumventing the dialectic of universality and particularity, "would have as its responsibility the invention, against the tide, of a step sideways, of a gap or a difference."

The essay that opens the second section, Isabelle Alfandary's "Destinies of 'The Purloined Letter,'" begins by identifying a characteristic feature of

Weber's engagement with the work of Derrida and Lacan: instead of taking sides in their fierce and now famous debate concerning the "truth" in Edgar Allan Poe's story, or alternatively, instead of seeking to establish peace between the opposing factions, Weber genuinely mediates the difference between Derrida and Lacan; that is, in Alfandary's words, he fosters an "intertwined understanding, where each work is always already read in its conceptual intersection with the other." This, for Alfandary, constitutes the "Weberian method," and it governs her intricate analysis of how Lacan's reading of Poe's story, like Derrida's, does not assert but rather problematizes truth. Just as Alfandary's essay enacts a form of the intertwining of understanding in two late twentieth-century readings of Poe, so Susan Bernstein's essay, "The Other Synesthesia," is concerned with the intertwining of sensation and the emergence of a corresponding "community of the arts" in one of Poe's outstanding readers in the previous century, namely Charles Baudelaire. Taking her point of orientation from Weber's critique of the concept of friendship proposed by Giorgio Agamben, which speaks of a certain synesthesia but also implies an originary moment of total unification and perfect legibility, Bernstein argues that the entanglement of sensation in Baudelaire's work cannot be encompassed by standard concepts of synesthesia, above all because it circumvents and subverts any suggestion of synthesis. As befits a volume that concludes with Derrida's reflections on the eruption of *rire* (laughter) in *lire* (reading), Bernstein places laughter—alongside "citations, syncopations, sobs, waves, tremors, quaking"—among those forms of utterance or outburst that "structure the spasmodic dislocation of the other synesthesia." Kevin McLaughlin's contribution to the volume, "Parting with the Self," complements Bernstein's essay by locating a certain potency or dynamism—here called "poetic force"—that fosters the event of "spasmodic dislocation." Drawing on Weber's insight into "an 'I' defined by singularity," which emerges from his inquiry into Benjamin's attempt to locate the furthest limit of art as the "medium of reflection," McLaughlin shows how Hölderlin's hymn "Friedensfeier" ("Celebration of Peace") thwarts and thus circumvents the antinomies of Kant's *Zum ewigen Frieden* (*Toward Eternal Peace*), which are themselves generated by a conception of the "I" as a wild particularity that must submit itself to the universal regularity of the law: the poem thus celebrates the capacity of language "to resist the effort to designate things and to make it into an instrument of mastery." Whereas McLaughlin's contribution to the volume culminates in an inquiry into "Celebration of Peace," Marc Redfield's essay "The 'Cultured Nazi' and the Cut of the Shibboleth" attends to the mass spectacle of global warfare. Weber's account of capitalist culture sets the stage for Redfield's close reading of Quentin Tarantino's film *Inglourious Basterds*, which he contrasts with Jonathan Littell's novel *Les Bienveillantes* (*The Kindly Ones*). Redfield argues that a fascination with Nazism in mainstream Western English-language culture plays a major role in managing anxieties about the dislocating power of mediation, including and especially mediation by a globalized English, and Tarantino's film "not only pays tribute to the law of the linguistic shibboleth but also reenacts the Nazi flight from language to 'blood.'" Peter Szendy's "Loose Words, or Arche-Reading" closes the second section by extending the concept of reading even further—indeed extending it so far that reading is set loose from writing. At issue in Szendy's reflection is the act of reading what has never been written. Working with Thomas Hobbes's ambiguously dismissive definition of prophecy, "Loose Words" emphasizes the intimate relation between "arche-reading" and prophecy, wherein something is read or said in advance of what is written or done. "Let us risk saying," Szendy concludes, as he recalls concepts of reading at work in the texts of Weber, Benjamin, and Derrida, "that the prophetic arche-reading is what *opens* all reading."

The layout of the volume reflects, in sum, the multiple opportunities for reading, research, and reflection that emerge in the course of Weber's work. The volume concludes with two interviews. The second of these interviews, "Screen Memories," was conducted on the occasion of the commemoration of the fiftieth anniversary of the Peter Szondi Institute for Comparative and General Literature at the Freie Universität in Berlin. In conversation with Irene Albers and Sima Reinisch, Weber describes the volatile early years of the Institute, in which he began to develop and expand his characteristic mode of analysis. It was at the Institute that Weber first encountered Derrida, as he briefly recounts in "Screen Memories." The scene of their original misrecognition is a motif to which Derrida repeatedly returns in the fictive interview he invents with a "passing journalist."[12] Leaving all kidding aside—and thus commensurate with the imperative *Vous voulez rire*—Derrida proceeds to read Weber's name. In German *Weber* means "weaver," and Derrida describes his effect in precisely this manner: Weber "is" the weaver of textiles in general and nets in particular. Because he knows how to weave (this knowledge is "technics" par excellence), he similarly knows how to unravel texts and networks alike. To this closing stroke of wit one may add, in light of Weber's reading of the poem with which this introduction began, that Weber is the weaver of the "carpets" that Hölderlin likens to "the true" and associates with the singular time-space in which "everything is opportune for you." This is what we, to reuse Szendy's concluding phrase, "risk saying."

## Notes

1. Samuel Weber, *Targets of Opportunity: On the Militarization of Thinking* (New York: Fordham University Press, 2005), 130.
2. Friedrich Hölderlin, *Sämtliche Werke: Frankfurter Ausgabe*, ed. D. E. Sattler (Frankfurt am Main: Roter Stern, 1975– ), 14: 99–100; my own translation.
3. Walter Benjamin, *Gesammelte Schriften*, ed. Rolf Tiedemann and Hermann Schweppenhäuser (Frankfurt am Main: Suhrkamp, 1972–91), 2: 114.

4. Derrida, "Vous voulez rire!," 212 in this volume.

5. The dissertation was published as Samuel Weber, *Unwrapping Balzac: A Reading of "Le Peau de chagrin"* (Toronto: University of Toronto Press, 1979).

6. See, for instance, Samuel Weber, *Mass Mediauras: Form, Technics, Media* (Stanford: Stanford University Press, 1996), 51.

7. Weber, *Targets of Opportunity*, 130.

8. Theodor W. Adorno, *Prisms*, trans. Shierry Weber Nicholsen and Samuel Weber (1967; reprint, Cambridge, Mass.: MIT Press, 1981).

9. Samuel Weber, *Rückkehr zu Freud: Jacques Lacans Ent-stellung der Psychoanalyse* (Berlin: Ullstein, 1978); translated as *Return to Freud: Jacques Lacan's Dislocation of Psychoanalysis*, trans. Michael Levine (Cambridge, U.K.: Cambridge University Press, 1991); Samuel Weber, *Freud-Legende: Drei Studien zum psychoanalytischen Denken* (Olten: Walter, 1979); translated as *The Legend of Freud* (Minneapolis: University of Minnesota Press, 1982).

10. Weber, *The Legend of Freud*, 89.

11. See ibid., 65–83.

12. For an account of Derrida's first encounter with Weber—to which both Derrida and Weber refer in the closing contributions to this volume—see chapter 13, note 4. Derrida began writing an essay on Weber's work at the invitation of Simon Morgan Wortham, who was editing a volume of essays that was eventually published as *Experimenting: Essays with Samuel Weber*, ed. Simon Morgan Wortham and Gary Hall (New York: Fordham University Press, 2007). The transcription of the French text for this volume was prepared by Emilie Marie-Louise Cappella and carefully reviewed by Brigitte Weltmann-Aron.

*Spectrality (Theatricality, Media)*

Chapter 1

# Ghost Scriptum, or Nothing to Play With

Dragan Kujundžić

> The appearance of the language-system begins to resemble its *apparition*, not as intermediary but as *intermedium*.
>
> —Samuel Weber, "Saussure and the Apparition of Language" (1976)

That the world we live in and the places where we work have undergone profound changes under the pressures of globalization and virtualization is nothing new to the readers of Samuel Weber. In *Institution and Interpretation: Expanded Edition*, Weber has convincingly argued and analyzed the diminishing of the sovereign nation-state under these pressures, together with the transformation of the fields and disciplines of knowledge attending such sovereignty. Such changes in the modes of tele- and technocommunications, a persistent line of inquiry in Weber's work, emerge "not as possibility to be realized and actualized, but as the dynamic tendency of a network of links, out of which a knowledge emerges as nodes of clusters and connections, which in turn are always subject to transformation by further exploration or developments of the network or networks." What has been for a while now, or perhaps from the very beginning, a passionate intellectual trajectory tied to the name of Samuel Weber is an inquiry into this passage, transition, or movement from *work* to *network*. This transition, well under way, as Weber argues in the same essay, challenges "what was formerly regarded as a university of reason" to reconfigure itself "in light of virtualization" to a location or place where it will be, or Weber emphasizes, "*has to be* in more places than one." Such a university would "keep itself open to the future."[1]

In this place where we are gathered to honor Weber, are we not entitled to ask: Who would be better placed to write about these dislocating transformations of knowledge (or who is in more places than one) than Weber? The question is of course purely rhetorical. More than anyone I know, Weber is, in several places, locations, and disciplines at once, places we know, that seem familiar, places that he de-familiarizes, and locations that he opens up or invents by his transformations, a veritable *Passagenwerk*, the work of passage from work into network. We are thus all entangled in his web.

Let us note that Weber's work entails explicitly a plea for a *net* (synonymous with *web*), for example in the chapter "Networks, Netwear and Narratives" in *Targets of Opportunity*: "Is it possible to conceive of a 'movement' that would *net*, rather than *network*, one which would leave room for the question that, for Benjamin at least, follows the end of every story—'And what happened next?' Or must that question always be targeted by a preemptive answer?"[2] (That last question by Weber, in his own writings, needless to say, is only rhetorical and is decided and answered in favor of the *net* or the *web* in advance.) As Jacques Derrida says in "Vous voulez rire!," which is dedicated to the work of Weber, "What is a paradigm in general, the Stranger asks himself when facing Younger Socrates. . . . After which comes the immense and famous discussion around the paradigm of the weaver (υφαντης, *Weber*, if you prefer) and the art of weaving. . . . I would like to describe SW not only as an artist weaver (royal politics, etc.), who knows how to stitch together, analyze, etc., but *I* would like to unravel the way in which SW is absolutely singular in that paradigm."[3]

To use the title of his essay on *Hamlet*, to which I will return, Weber is "hic et ubique," here and everywhere else, or, as he himself proposes to translate this Latin expression used by Hamlet, "here and wherever."[4] Such multiplications of spatiality follow or surround Weber like a web wherever he goes. After his lecture on Walter Benjamin and *Angelus Novus* at the University of California, Irvine, some fifteen years ago, in a multilingual banter that ensued between Weber and Derrida discussing how to translate *network* into French, it was concluded that in his lecture Weber turned "reason," in French *raison*, into *réseau*, a network. Weber himself operates like an electronic web, a resourceful *réseau*, his email address after all being sweb21.

In the concluding chapter to *Theatricality as Medium*, in an interview session with Simon Morgan Wortham and Gary Hall, Weber was asked about the "style" that pertains to "his own writing," precisely in terms of a perceptive attention to dislocation staged by and elaborated in his writing: "In your recent work on theatricality as medium, you comment on the way in which the writing of Jacques Derrida explores its own 'theatrical quality as a "staging."' But what of the performance or performativity that attends your own writing? What of its own 'taking place'? Does this open up or open onto a different sort of 'theatrical/theoretical' space or (dis-)location?" This is what Weber had to say in response: "Certain impulses have come to me precisely from the encounter with *different* cultures and languages: first German, then French, both always interacting with certain (American) English. Perhaps this is the reason why a certain 'intensity' did not develop in the way it has in Derrida's writing, an aspect he has described as his 'monolingualism.' If you are asking about this kind of difference, then it is surely not simply a 'deliberate strategy' on my part, but something that my experience—trajectory—imposed on me."[5]

Thus finding Weber "here and everywhere," *hic et ubique*, in the passage-works of the web and difference, translates in his own idiom as an understated response that is formed in his encounter with and demand from the Other. Such comings and goings point to an ethical element that Weber would probably be too modest to avow (when placing his own significant ethicopolitical gesture in a footnote, for example) but is encapsulated in his footnoted comment on translation of *hic et ubique* into English as "wherever," in close proximity to the colloquial "or whatever": "By concluding an assertion with the phrase 'or whatever,' the speaker disclaims responsibility for the assertions just made. In contrast to such a disclaiming function, *hic et ubique* points to a difficulty of assuming responsibility for words whose effects cannot be ambiguously localized—*but it does not attempt to avoid that responsibility.*"[6] Operating in the passages toward the Other, in a dislocating force of translation, in the time-place, to again use Hamlet's words, "out of joint," Weber articulates and *mediates* a singular voice of responsibility. Such responsiveness and ability to respond to and welcome the Other ("Certain impulses have come to me precisely from the encounter with *different* cultures and languages") also open up a space mindful of the future. The only future we have, the future of and with the Other.

As Derrida writes in "Vous voulez rire!":

> The Weberian technique . . . his inimitable signature, of his deconstructive style as much as his argumentative writing style . . . puts to work an extreme attention to the letter of several languages, through a passage that translates but also invents in the very transfer. . . . But, another remarkable trait, Weber precisely invents *his* idiom by traversing several languages at once, he *plays* (for he always plays) between several languages. He travels from one language to the other, not in order to discover there blissful, virgin, intact islands between continents, but in order to call forth from the abyss still unknown linguistic landscapes, *unheimlich* archipelagoes, semantic straits and isthmuses propitious to explorations but also to the most unheard-of contaminations.[7]

To this dimension of the "Weberian technique" Derrida avows a debt: "What is unique and precious for me, among other things, in all that I owe Sam Weber, is to live in more than one linguistic culture at once, the German, English and French; he is 'chez lui—at home' everywhere, and *I* am learning to follow him."[8]

The interpellation by which the Other summons has already been announced in the words by Weber quoted above: *the future*, *difference*, *response*, and *responsibility*. They are marks of this interpellation. The topic of justice, being-with the other, "a politics of memory, of inheritance, and of generation" (Derrida) impose themselves, precisely, from the sensibility to the time "out of joint," from a certain sensibility that is *hic et ubique*. In *Specters of Marx* Derrida, writing about *Hamlet* and the same scene that Weber has commented upon, where Hamlet encounters the Ghost, proposes that the source of the ethical announces itself from the difference at the heart of the living: "Without this *non-contemporaneity with itself of the living present*, without that which secretly unhinges it, without this responsibility and this respect for justice concerning those who *are not there*, of those who are no longer or who are not yet *present and living*, what sense would there be to ask the question 'where'?"[9]

That is why a certain mournful predisposition is not dissociated from an affirmation and an affirmative anticipation of the future, from saying yes to it: "The desire for memory and the mourning of *yes* set in motion the anamnesic machine. And its hypermnesic acceleration. The machine reproduces the living, it doubles it with its automaton."[10] A certain gramophony, technicality, and mediality attend to any yes and affirmation of Being, says Derrida in *Ulysse gramophone* while discussing that the telephone comes "before the act or the word," and he adds, "And as my friend Sam Weber has reminded me, a Dasein accedes to itself only on the basis of the Call (der Ruf), a call which has come from afar."[11]

A certain coming and going perceived at the very heartbeat of the living present, a split between the respect for and the specter of the inheritance and the coming of the future, fissures the present "as such" and responds to both the living and the dead, to what may be still to come in the name of the immemorial past. It is a responsive thing to do and a responsible place to be:

> This question *arrives*, if it arrives, it questions what will come in the future-to-come. Turned toward the future, going toward it, it also comes from it, it proceeds *from* [*provient* de] the future. It must therefore exceed any presence as presence to itself. At least it has to make this presence possible only on the basis of the movement of some disjoining, disjunction, or disproportion: in the inadequation to self. . . . What stands *in front* must also precede it like its origin: *before* it. Even if the future is its provenance, it must be, like any provenance, absolutely and irreversibly past.[12]

The protection and respect accorded life will have come thus from respect to a unique and a singular that are divided between their past and their future, a singular as an iteration and repetition. ("The word 'specter' is the perfect anagram of 'respect.' I since discovered that another word is also the perfect anagram of these two, which is 'scepter.'"[13]) A live presence is also something like a ghost, a specter who or that watches me and is thus also a *spectator*, coming and going, a ghost who comes and goes, who is to come and who is the future, to put it in French, *revenant qui vient, qui est à-venir*. "This justice carries life beyond present life or its actual being-there, its empirical or ontological actuality: not towards death but toward a *living-on* [*sur-vie*] namely a trace of which life and death would themselves be but traces and traces of traces, a survival whose possibility in advance comes to disjoin or dis-adjust the identity to itself of the living present."[14] In every *revenant* there is something of a *survivant.*

Let me repeat as a reminder that it is in a dislocated coming and going that we have first encountered Weber, on the way someplace else, turned toward the difference of the Other, the ghost, the *hic et ubique*, and toward the future. I have introduced a concept of spectrality and the reworking of the ontological that Derrida dubbed *hauntology*: "*Staging* [italics added] of the end of history. . . . Repetition *and* first time: this is perhaps the question of the event as question of the ghost,"[15] in order to underscore the mediatic and theatrical always at work in any "question of being" or ontology.

In *Institution and Interpretation: Expanded Edition*, Weber claims, "*Iterability irritates*: which is to say, it excites, impels one to leave the confines of the familiar and the consoling; it troubles, confuses and confounds, producing precisely the effects that the Cartesian method was designed to eliminate." He goes on to elaborate how Descartes sought to exclude from the cogito memory, forgetting, temporality, but forms of repetition and recurrence come to "*haunt* the Cartesian, modern, bourgeois subject: the other as excluded but necessary duplication of the Self."[16]

In *Mass Mediauras*, in the chapter "After Deconstruction," Weber addresses precisely this fissure or difference, "the ghostlike manifestation of iterability," which is both followed by deconstruction and traced by it, making it an exemplary reading strategy for the mediatic. Deconstruction traces the passage between an *apparatus* and an *apparition*, by which "self-sameness, in order to be constituted, emerges out of repetitive comparison and in order for something to be there, it must therefore pass through the element of heterogeneity, or otherness, in order to be constituted as the same. . . . Seen in this perspective—which Derrida calls differ*a*nce—iterability splits the mark into a past that can never be fully rendered present and a future which is always about to arrive. . . . What is called the present is the *coming-to-pass of the future*."[17] The past comes—back from the future, such is the logic at work or network woven by deconstruction, a *hauntology* always already at work, in the very workings of the world. "The spectral logic is de facto deconstructive logic," says Derrida in "Spectrographies."[18]

In *Mass Mediauras*, in the chapter "Upsetting the Setup: Remarks on Heidegger's 'Question after Technics,'" Weber points out the strategy by which Heidegger attempts to ward off the heterogeneity of the technical only to find himself "led elsewhere, in another direction, toward poiesis. . . . Because of this uncanny, duplicitous, ambivalent singularity, the questing after technics never arrives at the stable acquisition of knowledge. Or at least it cannot be measured in terms of cognition."[19]

The mediatic thus dictates another logic of space, spatiality, and temporality, one that allows no pretechnical appearance of Being, but a being always already dis-located in the moment of appearance, split between the having been in the past and the going to the future in the movement of singular iterability. "The 'there is' ['*il y a*'] or 'that there is something rather than nothing' belongs, perhaps, to the experience of the event rather than the thinking of being. The coming of the event is what we cannot and must never prevent, another name of the future itself."[20] The technological and mediatic that are always at work wherever experience is constituted (whenever something is felt, comes to pass, is recorded, memorized, experienced) thus require another account of being. What *is*, to paraphrase Derrida from *The Politics of Friendship*, need not necessarily *be*. The question "To be, or not to be?" may not be the most important question to ask, or does not necessarily pertain to Being, says Derrida in *Specters of Marx*, invoking *Hamlet* yet again. It is the spectral that precedes being: "This other, this specter of this other regards us, concerns us: not in an accessory way, but within our own identity."[21]

Yes, we are, like Weber, *all over the place*, *hic et ubique*, changing vantage points, coming and going, between texts and analytic situations, "Catching Up with the Past," "Going(s) On," to use the titles of chapters from his book *Mass Mediauras*, a *hic et ubique* on the move. But we are never far from Weber and the very practical, experiential situatedness of this analysis, moving back and forth and in between temporality, technology, spectrality, and "our own" contemporary time and space. Let me give just one example, still on the topic of coming and going. The globalizing forces of capital and media make the "subject" more and more prone to the feeling of isolation and abjection. The contemporary media play at this displacement by attempting to stage a sense of consoling, soothing sameness of programming, a repetition of the same, familiarity of the seen. Indeed, as Weber points out in the chapter "'War,' 'Terrorism,' and 'Spectacle': On Towers and Caves" from *Theatricality as Medium*, the media make a great effort to "support such identification" and make images "clearly localizable, self-contained, and meaningful." This would be the ideology in the image at work. But such ideological consolidation is pitted against a structural displacement at the very point of its origin. The spectacle is always (*hic et ubique* several times again) "once here and elsewhere," divided between the not just now and the now that is not just there. "At the same time, the spectacle plays to spectators who are similarly neither here nor there, or—which amounts to the same thing—here and there at once."[22] In Weber's *Targets of Opportunity* the move from work to network, now attached to a technomilitaristic machine, coupled with targeting, operates as a theater of war, "a network of netwar," to assuage collective guilt by inventing an enemy and doing away with it, and thus seemingly consolidating the structural displacement at the origin of a networked community. However, all such acts of targeting are violent since they consist of a "denial of indebtedness to an alterity without which nothing could be identified, no aim taken, no target hit."[23]

The collusion of the technomedia and war is no secret. There is a buck to be made there, and the mediatic is attached to the war machine and shares in its profits. First the camera shows up, and then the bombers. An anecdote from the siege of Sarajevo during the war in the former Yugoslavia is illustrative: "A neighbor, who is, say, a Serb, to another, who is a Muslim, as a curse: 'May your house appear tonight on CNN!'" In his essay "Wartime" in the collection *Violence, Identity, and Self-Determination*, Weber points out, "The fact that a Bosnia or a Rwanda is possible in the glare of the TV screen is what renders Freud's psychoanalytic approach to the question of violence as pertinent today as it has ever been."[24]

For a while now the analysis of wars in *Theatricality as Medium* has been a location where one could most often find Weber at work and network. A certain nihilistic turn to itself from the very interiority of modernity has been the site of Weber's most patient analyses. This nothing turning onto itself and forming a mediatic stage of which the recent mediatic instantiations are only offspring of mediatic off*shoots* Weber located in the figure of *allegory* as deployed by Benjamin in his book, the title of which has been translated as *The Origin of the German Tragic Drama*. In the wake of, vigilantly following, and thus at times preceding, extending, and bringing about its living-on, the work of Derrida, particularly his attention to the concept of spectrality and iterability, Weber deploys the concept of allegory as found in Benjamin and his own versions of iterability and spectrality, which, in his more recent works, appear translated under the names "theatricality" and "Benjamin's-abilities." It is to these two concepts that I now turn.

Analytic traces of the encounter between Weber and Benjamin are strewn throughout his opus. Weber has emerged as the most insistent, systematic, and simply brilliant analyst of Benjamin's oeuvre today. One should give this its due assessment. In order to give minimal justice to the concepts of allegory and theatricality in Weber and Benjamin, I will have to leave aside for now Weber's magisterial analysis of Benjamin's "The Work of Art in the Age of Technical Reproducibility," for example, in *Mass Mediauras*, and will only note that Weber was the first to alert us to the mistranslation of this title ("Reproduction") and to insist on the *ability* in "Reproducibility." The notion of allegory as found in Benjamin has been deployed in various critical contexts and interpretive junctures. In *Targets of Opportunity*, for example, the genealogy of modernity encapsulated by the concept of allegory is brought to bear on the concepts of war, work, and network. In the aftermath of the Reformation and the Counter-Reformation, the path to redemption formerly available through the "good works" of the Catholic Church has been supplanted by the *sola fides*, faith only of the Lutheran reformation. In his book on the *Trauerspiel*, Benjamin examined this challenge to the Christian soteriological narrative, the *Heilsgeschichte*, claims Weber, which was replaced by a theater staging death and destruction, the allegorical "mourning play." The allegory of the "mourning play" appears at the moment when, as Weber quotes in his essay "Allegory and Theatricality in Benjamin," "the secularizing (*Verweltlichung*) of the Counter-Reformation gained force in both religious confessions, [and] religious inclination," but "religious inclinations still did not lose their weight: it was only that the century refused them a religious solution, in order to impose or demand a worldly one in its place."[25] Thus Christian Europe bars the transcendental narrative from occurring, and only faith, *sola fides*, a radical immanentism, folds back on itself in a profound self-referential abyss in which nothing gets to be "represented" since it is nothing that formed the core of this immanentist fold. But it does get to be staged. "Walter Benjamin designates throughout his text that 'natural history' refers to a movement of perdition rather than progress, a 'fallen' creation that is doomed to finitude and mortality without any perspective of meaning that would transcend such limitation."[26] The outcome of the Reformation unleashed forces by which the transcendental was turned onto itself as radically immanent and thus opened a nihilistic void at the heart of the Christian world. This void, precisely as *nothing* to play with, appears in Weber's and Benjamin's analyses as the very stage on which a profound multiplicity (since immanent and permutable allegorized meanings) vies for "expression." A stage movement, mise-en-scène, has become literally a movement over the abyss, mise-en-abyme. What is expressed is founded on these spectral, nihilistic boards, where no resurrection is possible but only contact between life and death and thus a multiplication of ghosts and specters, of which Hamlet's father is just the most emblematic instantiation: Hamlet was a student in Wittenberg.

The baroque allegory, the story of the Fall, thus ushers in a crisis in both earthly and divine modes of representation:

> What the baroque consequently rejects is any admission of the limitation of immanence and it does so by emptying transcendence of all possible representable content. Far from doing away with transcendence, however, such emptying out endows it with all the more powerful force: that of the vacuum, of the absolute unbounded other, which, since it is no longer representable, is also no longer localizable out there or as beyond. The otherness that is no longer allowed to remain transcendent therefore reappears this side of the horizon, represented as a cataract, abyss, or fall. Or, even more radically, as *allegory*.[27]

Instead of the sovereign who borrows his transcendence from God (the path to such transcendence, we should remember, has been foreclosed by the radical immanentism of the *sola fides*), and whose legitimacy is shattered, the political space emblematized by the *Trauerspiel* is inhabited by a plotter, a schemer, and the political space opened up to a certain ambivalence and theatricality. "It is this medium, in all of its avowed inauthenticity—which Benjamin links to a spatial simultaneity of the stage—that replaces the faltering eschatological medium of Christian *Heilsgeschichte*."[28] The outcome of the European religious wars leaves something like a car wreck, floodlit with the lights of emergency vehicles, while a plotter directs the traffic around it and tells the gawkers, "Move on, there is *nothing* to see." But like a fleet of emergency vehicles, what is ushered in by this crisis of sovereignty is a staging of an emergency, an accident, a ruin, a theater of wars and targets of opportunities, all staging a profound nothingness at work as a network, displayed or staged as an (emergency, state of exception) vehicle of political expediency. "In short, what you see in the *Trauerspiel* is all you are going to get: all and nothing," Weber concludes in "Allegory and Theatricality in Benjamin." In the theatrical site of the German baroque drama (but in Benjamin and Weber this has also been diagnosed as a genealogy of modernity by now), "the sight of these [theatrical] images is intended to compensate for the emptying of the world. But they remain allegorical 'masks,' and hence the world they 'reanimate' is the world of the living dead, of ghosts and ghouls, rather than of the resurrected."[29]

Thus the theatrical medium of which German *Trauerspiel* gives not "artistically" significant examples but examples crucial for the genealogy of modernity and mediality, becomes emblematic of the post-Reformation nihilism at work—or network—in the tormented body of the Christian world. "Through its staging of suffering, murder, and death in the mourning play, this rhythm, which marks the recurrence of the 'fall' rather than the coming of resurrection, endows the baroque network with relative stability and, indeed endurance. But it is a stability and endurance of a shared guilt rather than the expectation of salvation." This guilt, Weber points out in his analysis of the genealogy of network and netwar, "serves to isolate the other as enemy, which is to say a potential target to be hit and shunted aside, *beseitigt*."[30]

In the crisis of sovereignty an intriguer appears on the stage of history. In his essay "Taking Exception to Decision: Walter Benjamin and Carl Schmitt" in *Benjamin's -abilities*, Weber writes, "The intriguer exploits the mechanism of human action as the result of forces over which there can be no ultimate control, but which precisely for that reason can be made a subject of probabilistic calculations."[31] In American political parlance and the crisis of a democratically elected presidential sovereignty, that would be a recent denomination of a politician as a "maverick" or a "decider." "For the intriguer, . . . the exercise of power as manipulation of others must be its own reward. In the absence of the Work (since the Reformation elimination of 'good works' resulted in the elimination of Work tout court), virtuosity is all that is left. Anyone who thinks otherwise might well ponder the fate of Wotan, his family, and the nation that followed in their footsteps."[32] Thus what appeared as an analysis of an obscure genre and plays that no one reads or stages anymore, even at the time Benjamin wrote the book on the *Trauerspiel*, turned out to be a reflection on the very forces of nihilistic destruction related to the "death of God" and the void filled with the technomediatic virtuosity and prowess, not unrelated to the situation we currently find ourselves in, perhaps first of all in the United States.

Benjamin thus understood and tried to ward off by his writing the forces that, unleashed by the aesthetic ideology of the German tragic drama and coupled with the forces of technology, would soon spell destruction on a global scale. ("The only hope available to the baroque is to . . . slow if not abolish the irresistible pull toward a catastrophic terminus."[33]) Such was Benjamin's analysis of Kafka, in whose stories he was the first to discover, in the minute and imperceptible tremors of Kafka's narratives, the echoes of the massive deployment of "the technology of modern warfare." But this reality of Kafka's stories "can virtually no longer be experienced by an *individual*, and that, in Kafka's world, frequently of such playfulness and interlaced with angels, is the exact complement of his era which is preparing to do away with the inhabitants of this planet on a considerable scale. The experience which corresponds to that of Kafka, the private individual, will probably not become accessible to the masses until such time as they are being done away with."[34] The nihilistic void of modernity, staged by the baroque allegory and so subtly and insistently interpreted by Benjamin, only needed its target of opportunity (the private body of Franz Kafka, a Jew, multiplied and massified by means of technical reproducibility) to come to its nihilistic *telos* and end. In Weber's latest book, *Inquiétantes singularités* (Uncanny Singularities, 2013), in a chapter in which he performs a remarkable and necessary critical "adjustment" of Giorgio Agamben's notions of "pure life" and "the camp," "La vie nue et la vie en général" (Bare Life and Life in General), the "massification" anticipated by Benjamin in his essay on Kafka is analyzed in terms of *specific* ethnic *grouping*, now *beseitigt* in the death camps: "Plus généralement, un modèle émergea selon lequel, non seulement la mort mais bien *la mise à mort organisée et systématique de groupes ethniques* fut pratiquée et justifiée par la promotion d'*une vie meilleure* [More generally, a model emerged according to which not only death but *organized and systematic putting to death of ethnic groups* was practiced and justified by the promotion of a better life]."[35] In his essay "Allegory and Theatricality in Benjamin," to remain a bit longer in the vicinity of allegory in the German tragic drama (but now, again, fully aware that it is a genealogy of modernity that Benjamin and Weber are providing), a despotism often depicted in these plays, "less 'Oriental' than 'Western' " (so it is the genealogy of Western modernity), is itself "a desperate reaction to a no win game. The theatrical medium does not so much seek salvation as ward off impending catastrophe through its spatio-temporal, that is, localized suspension on stage. Such a desperate project is therefore predicated upon inevitable and considerable *violence*."[36] The "German mourning play buries itself entirely in the hopelessness of the earthly order," says Benjamin. "The secularized world of the baroque is going towards its end. . . . The baroque mourning play is going nowhere."[37]

For Benjamin and Weber the play that stands as an emblem of the baroque is *Hamlet*. It is in the analysis of this play in " 'Ibi et ubique': The Incontinent

Plot ('Hamlet')" of *Theatricality as Medium* that Weber makes most explicit a connection between iterability, spectrality, and his notion of theatricality. The radical immanence at work in the German baroque play opens up the stage to a melancholic gaze cast on the world where the staging puts in proximity both the live persons, personae, and the dead ones. In *Hamlet* and the German baroque play, and also the new media, the genealogy of which can be traced to these two, "the emphasis on life only underscores the ghostly nature of the screen as well as that of [the] stage: what it brings to life is not simply resurrected, but also embalmed."[38]

The notorious haunting of Hamlet's father's ghost is given a close scrutiny and an original analysis. Weber carefully reads the scenes of swearing and the comic relief (Hamlet to Ghost: "Art thou there, truepenny?") accompanying these scenes in Act I (never before truly read or given a proper accounting) to underscore the splitting of the space of the stage, and a radical spectrality of the play, stemming from the performative force unleashed by the swearing scenes. He points out that Hamlet is forced repeatedly to change his place on the stage in order to swear to secrecy his friends Marcellus, Horatio, and Bernardo. The outbidding of the oath, first in words, then in deed, never satisfying Hamlet, indicates the representational and symbolic void opened up by the Reformation, of which, as I have already indicated, the German tragic play is an allegory. "Note Hamlet's insistence upon all the external trappings of a formal oath: it is not enough for Marcellus to protest, 'We have sworn, my lord, already,' not enough that he has already agreed verbally to Hamlet's injunction 'never make known what you have seen tonight.' Although Hamlet, like Horatio, has studied in Wittenberg, the Protestant mistrust of sacramental ritual seems to extend to the 'faith' that for Luther is supposed to supplant it."[39] The rift between Catholicism and Protestantism staged as the bidding for the "proper" mourning of the father, and as a one-on-one relation between the father and the son (Hamlet the Father speaks *only* to Hamlet the Son, qua ghost or unholy spirit), explicitly related to Luther and Wittenberg, serves in the play, as Benjamin and Weber point out, to underscore the structural forces of representation (or its unraveling) at work in this scene. *Hic* in "Hic et ubique" should also be heard as an echo of *hic est meum corpus* of the Catholic Eucharist, violently rejected by the Lutheran *sola fides* (Wittenberg) as ghostly, phantomatic, spectral, and sentenced to wondering. By placing the Ghost on and beneath the stage, thus putting on display the impossibility of internalizing the father's ghost in the act of mourning (Hamlet's well-known *melancholia*, his incapacity to "introject" the loss), the play, enacting the forces of the religious schism qua a secularized spectacle, spectralizes the stage and makes the plot incontinent. Thus the greatest political rift in modern history, the schism in the Christian church, comes to haunt the very representational space of the play. The stage becomes divided and infinitely di-visible, thus anticipating the workings of the modern media: "The iterable *divisibility* of 'representing' thus contaminates the visibility of the represented. The intended act—here, the oath—is derailed by the fact that it is always already the product of acting."[40]

Everything is on the stage and everywhere else. What is crucial for understanding the workings of the play is the instability of the symbolic order stemming from the incapacity to "properly mourn" the father (the death of God; the sacrifice of Christ; the impossibility of transcendence, the path to which is barred by Luther's *sola fides*, captured for example in the history of religious painting by Hans Holbein the Younger's *The Body of the Dead Christ in a Tomb*, 1522; Holbein being no less than the illustrator of Luther's Bible, 1534), which unhinges the representational space, or the possibility of the plot to begin or end in a homogeneous way required by the metaphysical tradition of Aristotelian dramatic theory. "'Hic et ubique' is as succinct a characterization of the divisible space of a spectral theatricality as is possible, but 'shifting our ground' is hardly going to be an effective response. Not just 'time' is out of joint,' but 'space' as well."[41] The Ghost is everywhere and nowhere, and that contaminates, so to speak, the figures on the stage, in Weber's words, living or dead. The plot leaks spectrality and mediality and requires different interpretive tools for understanding the comings and goings of this play, and subsequently of the modern media stemming from it.

Over the years Weber accorded a remarkably systematic attention to the topic of spectrality and staging and thus the emergence of mediality as they appear in some other literary texts developing or coinciding with literary "modernity." However, *Hamlet* always seems to be the dominant underpinning reference. In his magisterial reading of Sterne's *Tristram Shandy*, for example, Weber is able to discern the ways in which Sterne uproots the generic rules of the novel along lines similar to those by which *Hamlet* appears as a tragedy that fails as a soteriological narrative, staging its own end, and concludes the essay with insights anticipating *Theatricality as Medium*. Weber notes that Sterne's character Parson Yorick fails to constitute itself/himself as a literary character: "Who or what is *Yorick*? Or rather, it would be more appropriate to ask: *how* is, or *was* he? For the story of Yorick never allows us to forget that the subject of the tale is a *ghost* in more ways than one. . . . His name refers back not to a living being, not even to a fictional character, but to a *skull*—and Hamlet's encounter with it."[42] Since Yorick (or *Yorick*, as Weber's use of italics to indicate a quotation and staging is indicative of this referential oscillation or downright voiding and impossibility, poor Yorick!) has not been constituted as a character other than a ghost, he cannot, strictly speaking, die either. We are left with a nihilistic *dance macabre* within the novel, or, authorized by the pun in the title of another of Weber's essays, "Song and Glance," from *Benjamin's -abilities*, a *glance macabre*, the anamorphic sight and site of a skull, an allegorical representation characteristic of the early baroque painting as much as Shakespeare's tragedy, depicted for example in *The Ambassadors* (1533), again by Holbein. In this picture the anamorphically deformed apparition central to the composition is "visible" and thus constituted as "representation," fully as a skull, only when the gaze is leaving the image or the room, in *the last* moment of leave-taking, in an *Abschied*, only at the point of departure and as a partition or emptying out, hollowing (Hol-bein—a hollow bone) of the scene and of the gaze simultaneously staged and canceled out by this image, generating a rhetoric of deadly or rather spectral temporality, "out of joint." Likewise Sterne voids the realm of literary representation or the epic narrative homogeneity of the genre of the novel, since what is being represented is nothing less than the staging of an interruption, a parting, a coming and going: the end of the world.

Yorick's death, in this perspective, is less an "event," introducing a radical break into the continuity of a unique life, than a symptom (or a *phantom*). It confirms what has already begun to emerge, here at the very beginning of the novel: that the death of the hero marks the spot where plot stops and another kind of space begins—neither that of the novel nor that of a tale but rather the uncertain space of a theatrical stage. In this sense the inscribed citation "Alas, poor Yorick" sets the stage for a different kind of telling, which will be more scenic than narrative and in which ultimately "nothing" will be said or shown, with the possible exception of a reading called upon to "hold out to the end of the world."[43]

In Weber's contribution to this volume, "'For O, for O, the Hobby-Horse Is Forgot': *Hamlet* between Schmitt and Benjamin," this staging of the originary repetition of "ultimately nothing" qua spectral *revenance*, a *hauntology* (Derrida), is analyzed as the repetition of the "O": "'O, O.' No binary machine code here but rather a repetition that is also an anticipation and a prophesy, beyond anything that its speaker could have intended." The "O" thus operates in close proximity to *nothing* or *zero*; it is an n+1 or O/0+1 of the play's signification beyond binarism, hovering between a zero and multiplication, haunting in fact any representation or signification with a possibility of this originary voiding, tending toward infinity and *nothing* ("the king, a thing of nothing," for example, in *Hamlet*; King Lear, "an O without a figure"; or T. S. Eliot's "'Is there nothing in your head?' / But / O O O O that Shakespeherian Rag" from *The Waste Land*: anything and nothing that its specter, that is, speaker, could have intended). In "Zero," J. Hillis Miller writes similarly about *Hamlet*, "The O/0 or nothing means 'country matters,' with an obscene pun in 'country.' 'Nothing' or 'O' in such texts represents a feminine lack, absence, or *béance*."[44] And Weber in turn writes, "The 'O, O' also by chance happens to cite the first letter of Ophelia's name, as well as being an exclamation, either of joy or of despair—or of both."[45] Weber and Miller echo here, but with a significant difference, Jacques Lacan's famous but completely erroneous etymology of Ophelia as "O *phallos*."[46] Ophelia in fact derives from ὠφέλειᾰ (*ōphéleia*: help, aid, succor), thus, rather than Lacan's masculinized phallocentric etymology, points to receiving, supporting, maybe even stage directing, like Hamlet himself, but also a character marked by voiding, melancholy, the *melain chole*, black watery abyss repeatedly insisted upon, for example, by Rimbaud in "Ophélie" ("l'onde calme et noire où dorment les étoiles, La blanche Ophélia flotte comme un grand lys," herself a "fantôme blanc," a white ghost, on the long black river, "sur le long fleuve noir"), opened in and by this play. On the other hand, in relation to "O," the name of Horatio points to two directions: in Latin, "the timekeeper" (in Italian *Orazio*, thus related to the play's "time out of joint"), and possibly to the Greek *khora*, χώρα, pointing to space and place as well as the passive "power" to receive (for example, the future of the tragedy that Horatio is to receive, remember, and tell others in the future, as bequeathed to him by Hamlet at the end of the play and as analyzed by Weber in the conclusion of his essay: "The legacy he bestows upon Horatio, this acknowledgement, this 'readiness,' leaves open the possibility of transmission and of tradition without insisting on redemption as its final goal"). Horatio is thus an emblem of time *and* space (out of joint), since *khora*, as Derrida says, "anachronizes being."[47] Hélène Cixous in "Shakespeare Ghosting Derrida," similarly sees the "O" as a figure for the operation of *Hamlet*, particularly relating the Ghost and the "O": "The Ghostest ghost, the lostest ghost, o, o, o, o, oblived, oblivioned. . . . *The Ghost does not arrive*. Poor Ghost. . . . The Ghost with sighs in O, makes bubbles, leaves empty traces in the Shakespearean fabric. . . . O, O, O, O, O—the rest of (Gh)o(st), the letter of the father."[48]

Finally, in the originary repetition of the "O" in the title of Weber's essay, echoing a quote from *Hamlet*, one may hear the beginning of Derrida's *Ulysse gramophone: Le oui-dire de Joyce*, a repetition as an originary affirmation: "Oui, oui, vous m'entendez bien, ce sont des mots français."[49] "O, O," "Oui, oui," an "O" countersigned. It is in this essay that Derrida relates phone calls, telephony, gramophony, and technology, "a call from afar," *rire* and *dire* and *lire* and Samuel Weber. Derrida takes it up in "Vous voulez rire!" as well, as if describing an O of the open mouth bursting with laughter: "This is where Weber's laughter breaks out. Discreetly, as in a Jewish joke, in making fun of himself he tells the truth about all."[50]

Thus in the "O, O" may we not hear "a call" inflected to a horizon (or to its etymology, orizon) other than the Greek onto-teleology, as suggested in Derrida's *Ulysse gramophone*, a difference figured in the faulty telephone connections in Joyce's novel, Leopold Bloom's errant peregrinations, "Elijah, the great operator, the other," hear thus a certain dis-orientation and the *destinerrance*, a departure of or from the Greek onto-teleology and Being (To be or not to be, that is the question?)? Summoned to Other shores, called perhaps by an "Oy, Oy" or an "Oy, vey!" if not *haunted*, and what a haunting ("*Hamlet* between Schmitt and Benjamin"), by an "Oy, gevalt!"?

The literary interpretation of *Hamlet* that perhaps most resembles Weber's is Tom Stoppard's *Rosencrantz & Guildenstern Are Dead*, both the play (1966) and the film that he wrote and directed (1990). The play does not stage *Hamlet* but the very *theatricality* at work in this play. We could say of it what Weber says of *Hamlet*, that "every speech onstage is already an echo and repetition of a 'part' inscribed elsewhere."[51] The play starts with a coin toss. It always turns heads. One should read in this several things discerned in the original: *Hamlet* owes its ghostly, spectral, "spooky" feeling to the repetitions the origin of which is unknown, except maybe that the repetitions are at the origin. The flipping of the coin intensifies this sense of repetition: something has happened; like the coin flips, the two main characters are aimlessly tossed on the stage, and whatever their actions, it will cost them their "heads." Furthermore the coin they flip is a "sovereign," thus inviting the interpretation of its status in the play in the wake of the attention it receives in Benjamin and Weber. (I refer the reader to "Taking Exception to Decision." It is the best assessment of the question of sovereignty in Benjamin and Schmitt to date.) The Beckettian absurdism of *Rosencrantz & Guildenstern Are Dead* makes of the sovereign a coin flip, a flip of the sovereign. The repeated toss that brings back the king ("heads") in his symbolic, spectral guise parodically repeats the return of the ghost that refuses to rest in peace in the original *Hamlet*. This parodic return of the sovereign ghost qua the coin flip, the very motion of iterability and theatricality in play, may be best captured by Weber's interpretive insight that "the baroque play finds a saving grace in its own theatricality."[52]

The plot in *Rosencrantz & Guildenstern Are Dead* is interminably divided by more and more stag*ing* and plott*ing*, beginning with the entrance into (or is it the exit out of?) the play, beginning with the scene of the traveling *stage coach*, and then suddenly transposed into *Hamlet*, forever unsettling the frame of reference, underscored by the inability of the leading protagonists to identify themselves. The following scene starts at the stage of the traveling theater but imperceptibly, like a fold of a Möbius strip, turns into Elsinore, completely confusing exteriority and interiority and delocalizing the frame of reference, *hic et ubique*:

> GUIL (*turning*): What?
> ROS: It was tails.
> *He tosses the coin to* GUIL *who catches it. Simultaneously—lighting change sufficient to alter the exterior mood into interior, but nothing violent.*
> *And* OPHELIA *runs on in some alarm, holding up her skirts—followed by* HAMLET.[53]

The scene is a perfect illustration (and vice versa) of Weber's "The visible plot is suspended by a divisible voice [and multiple framing] emanating from an invisible plot below and before all possible plots or plotting." Their inability to remember the origin of their departure or destiny, split in their identity and temporality, *already living their own death* (Rosencrantz and Guildenstern *are dead* but alive on stage), underscores this ghostly division in the characters of Rosencrantz and Guildenstern. *Rosencrantz & Guildenstern*

*Are Dead* radicalizes or allegorizes *Hamlet* just as Weber makes its theatricality theoretically explicit: in order to come to terms with tradition and the political, one has to learn to deal with specters and ghosts, even or especially those that haunt our most intimate selves. It is not the king that is spectral, but our own predicament is that we are haunted, from the moment we have been sent for, by the ghost of our own existence and every time called, summoned, conjured, or "mimicked" (should I say, allegorized) by the staging of this play. "The emptied world" "becomes the condition of the masked resurrection." "But that resurrection remains a mask, tied to the theater." *Rosencrantz & Guildenstern Are Dead* illustrates the radical theatricalization of the original play's potential, "referring to its medial conditions of possibility."[54]

In *Hamlet and Hecuba: The Intrusion of the Time into the Play*, written in 1956, Carl Schmitt already noticed with some lucidity that Shakespeare's *Trauerspiel* (*Hamlet*) is *unplayable* as a tragedy: in Shakespeare's "so called tragedies," says Schmitt, "we can least afford to ignore the unplayability (*Unverspielbarkeit*) of the tragic."[55] However, he tries to arrest this movement of spectrality and "unplayability" by insisting on grounding the play in an exact referential "historical" reading and by insisting on the direct and unmediated connection between Hamlet and James I, somehow made univocally explicit in "the Mousetrap." His book even includes a "response" to Benjamin's *Origin of the German Tragic Play*, downplaying the power of allegory. I will leave aside this debate and the delayed "response" to Benjamin that is some thirty years late; it deserves a long analysis. We know that Schmitt was sent the book by Benjamin himself with words of admiration and a dedication upon its publication in 1928. I should briefly note, however, that the long delay in responding publicly and to a now dead author says a lot (or could say a lot to Schmitt) about precisely the unavowable forces at work in his own political trajectory, the undigested and nonintrojected historical baggage that *haunts* his "response." A statement in this response that "*Hamlet* is not Christian in any specific sense,"[56] meant as a critical remark to undercut the authority of allegory as interpreted by Benjamin, is nothing but a *Verneinung* of the first order, but one revealing a belated spasm of the very nihilistic void analyzed by Benjamin, which started in the Reformation and later found a mechanically reproduced sacrificial target (to include "the private citizens" Kafka and Benjamin) to fill this void and thus restore itself to a purified unity, in the worst imaginable manner. (If Benjamin's *Hamlet* is not in any way "specifically Christian," than, maybe . . . Jewish?) In Schmitt's response that target is repressed or talked about or to only when it is there no more, while it is there no more precisely with the historically irreversible ideological and political complicity of Carl Schmitt. But there is no stopping the ghosts of history. Just as in *Hamlet*, the repression makes the Ghost return more insistently. That is what Schmitt's response misses in *Hamlet* and in his own address to Benjamin's ghost.

The truth of the play, according to Schmitt, is paradoxically (something he does not quite take into account in its full consequences) in the play within the play staged by Hamlet. "Paradoxically" since such staging precisely qua staging, qua mediality, splits the frame of reference and the truth of the play, inasmuch as the "truth" of his own "response to Benjamin" remains divided by the *décalage*, *nachträglich* haunting. What the play within the play reveals, rather, is that in this play "every place is part and parcel of a *medium*, although never simply in the sense of an interval or transition *between* two fixed points or poles. The medium is what happens when places are haunted by an uncanny divisibility. Medium is the ghost of a place: its haunt." Schmitt's localization of the referential truth of this play solely in the time of Elizabethan England disregards *Hamlet*'s nihilistic forces of modernity splitting the stage, its frame of reference, including a split that affected Germany precisely at the moment when it put itself at the promontory of "the new Europe." "What otherwise is known as 'secularization' becomes, in Benjamin's account, more like allegorical theatricalization. Such allegorical theatricalization cannot simply overcome time and mortality, *but it can temporarily arrest, interrupt, and suspend their progress*."[57]

What is eerily historically "true" in Hamlet is not particular historical references but the capacity to serve as a lure of history and provide an interpretive frame not for resembling but for interpreting and staging it, dare I say deconstructing it, through the ghostly movements of its "disorderly excess," which it also attempts to temporarily arrest. *Hamlet* stages how European history (the history of "the West") *comes to pass*. But thus also in its wake (as in the vigilant encounter with the Ghost) allows for a different history to be imagined or staged, precisely in the horrible immemorial memory of its catastrophic origin (which also includes, relevant and revenant for the encounter between Schmitt and Benjamin in my interpretation, qua Polonius, a *certain* Poland, and the burning traces of her holocaustic ghosts). "The elevation of these corpses upon the stage [at the end of *Hamlet*] reveals what has been known all along but perhaps not fully recognized: that the theatrical stage remains a temporal stage, which comes only in going, and which, in departing, leaves room for what is to come."[58]

Ghost Scriptum: "Ghosts have an affinity for mourners, for those who ponder over signs and over the future."—Walter Benjamin.

## Notes

1. Samuel Weber, *Institution and Interpretation: Expanded Edition* (Stanford: Stanford University Press, 2001), 230, 235.

2. Samuel Weber, *Targets of Opportunity: On the Militarization of Thinking* (New York: Fordham University Press, 2005), 108.

3. Jacques Derrida, "Vous voulez rire!," 232 in this volume. This unfinished text, written as late as 2004, was made available to the author by Marguerite Derrida on July 1, 2010. Marguerite Derrida and ©Succession Derrida 2016 are gratefully acknowledged. Translation by the author and Brigitte Weltman-Aron.

4. Samuel Weber, *Theatricality as Medium* (New York: Fordham University Press, 2004), 388.

5. Weber, *Theatricality as Medium*, 356, 361.

6. Weber, *Theatricality as Medium*, 388, emphasis added.

7. Derrida, "Vous voulez rire!," 226 in this volume.

8. Derrida, "Vous voulez rire!," 227 in this volume.

9. Jacques Derrida, *Specters of Marx*, trans. Peggy Kamuf (New York: Routledge, 1994), xix.

10. Derrida, *Specters of Marx*, 276.

11. Jacques Derrida, "Ulysses Gramophone," trans. Tina Kendall, revised by Shari Benstock, in *Acts of Literature*, ed. Derek Attridge (New York: Routledge, 1992), 273.

12. Derrida, *Specters of Marx*, xix.

13. Jacques Derrida, "Spectrographies," in *Echographies of Television* by Jacques Derrida and Bernard Stiegler, trans. Jennifer Bajorek (Cambridge, U.K.: Polity Press, 2002), 194.

14. Derrida, *Specters of Marx*, xx.

15. Derrida, *Specters of Marx*, 10.

16. Weber, *Institution and Interpretation*, 244, 245.

17. Samuel Weber, *Mass Mediauras: Form, Technics, Media* (Stanford: Stanford University Press, 1996), 145, 138, 149.

18. Derrida, "Spectrographies," 117.

19. Weber, *Mass Mediauras*, 75.

20. Derrida, "Spectrographies," 11.

21. Derrida, "Spectrographies," 86.

22. Weber, *Theatricality as Medium*, 332, 331.

23. Weber, *Targets of Opportunity*, 105.

24. Samuel Weber, "Wartime," in *Violence, Identity, and Self-Determination*, ed. Samuel Weber and Hendt de Vries (Stanford: Stanford University Press, 1997), 89.

25. Benjamin, quoted in Weber, *Theatricality as Medium*, 170.

26. Weber, *Targets of Opportunity*, 174.

27. Samuel Weber, *Benjamin's -abilities* (Cambridge, Mass.: Harvard University Press, 2008), 187.

28. Weber, *Targets of Opportunity*, 104.

29. Weber, *Theatricality as Medium*, 176, 177.

30. Weber, *Theatricality as Medium*, 104–5.

31. Weber, *Benjamin's -abilities*, 191.

32. Weber, *Theatricality as Medium*, 179.

33. Weber, *Theatricality as Medium*, 173.

34. Walter Benjamin, *Illuminations: Essays and Reflections*, trans. Harry Zohn (New York: Schocken Books, 1968), 143.

35. Samuel Weber, *Inquiétantes singularités*, trans. Charles Coustille (Paris: Hermann Éditeurs, 2013), 135.

36. Weber, *Theatricality as Medium*, 179.
37. Weber, *Benjamin's -abilities*, 157, 159.
38. Weber, *Theatricality as Medium*, 181.
39. Weber, *Theatricality as Medium*, 183.
40. Weber, *Theatricality as Medium*, 185.
41. Weber, *Theatricality as Medium*, 185–86.
42. Samuel Weber, "Reading: 'To the Very End of the World,'" *MLN* 111.5 (1996): 830.
43. Weber, "Reading," 833.
44. J. Hillis Miller, "Zero," unpublished ms., 2003; J. Hillis Miller, "Three Literary Theorists in Search of 0," in *Provocations to Reading: J. Hillis Miller and the Democracy to Come*, ed. Barbara Cohen and Dragan Kujundžić (New York: Fordham University Press, 2005), 210–27.
45. Weber, "'For O, for O, the Hobby-Horse Is Forgot," 107 in this volume.
46. Jacques Lacan, "Desire and the Interpretation of Desire in *Hamlet*," trans. James Hulbert, *Yale French Studies* 55–56 (1977): 11–52.
47. Jacques Derrida, *On the Name*, ed. Thomas Dutoit, trans. David Wood, John P. Leavey Jr., and Ian Mcleod (Stanford: Stanford University Press, 1995), 94. The edition includes *Khora*.
48. Hélène Cixous, "Shakespeare Ghosting Derrida," trans. Laurent Milesi, *Oxford Literary Review* 34.1 (2012): 13.
49. Jacques Derrida, *Ulysse gramophone: Le Oui-dire de Joyce* (Paris: Galilée, 1987), 57.
50. Derrida, "Vous voulez rire!," 222 in this volume.
51. Weber, *Theatricality as Medium*, 185.
52. Weber, *Benjamin's -abilities*, 191.
53. Tom Stoppard, *Rosencrantz & Guildenstern Are Dead* (New York: Grove Press, 1967), 34.
54. Weber, *Theatricality as Medium*, 184, 191, 195.
55. Karl Schmitt, *Hamlet or Hecuba*, trans. David Pan and Jennifer Rust (New York: Telos Press, 2009), 40.
56. Schmitt, *Hamlet or Hecuba*, 61.
57. Weber, *Theatricality as Medium*, 187, 191, emphasis added.
58. Weber, *Theatricality as Medium*, 197, 199. The postscript is from Walter Benjamin, *The Origin of German Tragic Drama*, trans. John Osborne (London: Verso, 1998), 193.

Chapter 2

# Postmortem Automediality and the Ghosts of Cyberspace

Béatrice Jongy-Guéna

Can we recover our dead on the Internet? Cyberspace provides a new form of "extraterritoriality" for the subject, to use Kafka's term. The development of sites like Facebook, YouTube, MySpace, Second Life, of blogs, personal websites, and, very recently, of video screens for tombstones that can be connected to a website, poses the question of postmortem representations of the self. As Susanna Egan and Gabriele Hems write, "We live in an auto/biographical age. . . . In every medium, cultures are permeated and increasingly transformed by auto/biographical narratives, productions, and performances of identity."[1] The authors account for a recent phenomenon: the increasing number of autobiographical manifestations falling under the category not of written but of video performance, or new media personal narratives. Researchers have coined the term *automediality* to designate this phenomenon.[2] It is the question of postmortem automediality that this essay is interested in. How do these new technologies modify, in industrialized countries, the notion of the individual and the processes of mourning and memory, in other words, civilization itself?

## The Ghosts of New Technologies

What happens when someone with an online account dies? Often the Internet "goes into overtime"; that is, the digital identity survives the civil identity. The virtual world is also a spectral world. Until very recently, after a death a site like Facebook continued on as it had before. Friend invites were still sent to the defunct user, and comments were posted on his or her wall.

In February 2009 Facebook added a clause to its user policy affirming the right to maintain the data of a user indefinitely after his or her account was closed. This decision caused an outcry, and Facebook removed the clause. Today profiles of the deceased can be viewed only by family and friends. The family is asked to fill out an online form and to provide a death certificate or a press article, as Facebook's privacy policy outlines:

> Memorializing Accounts. If we are notified that a user is deceased, we may memorialize the user's account. In such cases we restrict profile access to confirmed friends, and allow friends and family to write on the user's Wall in remembrance. We may close an account if we receive a formal request from the user's next of kin or other proper legal request to do so.
>
> Limitations on removal. Even after you remove information from your profile or delete your account, copies of that information may remain viewable elsewhere to the extent it has been shared with others, it was otherwise distributed pursuant to your privacy settings, or it was copied or stored by other users. . . . Additionally, we may retain certain information to prevent identity theft and other misconduct even if deletion has been requested. If you have given third party applications or websites access to your information, they may retain your information to the extent permitted under their terms of service or privacy policies.[3]

Internet users' reactions show that some see this policy as a breach of trust on the part of the American company. "Shameful New Facebook Service!" and "Facebook Seeks to Become Real Population!" are just two of the titles of articles addressing this issue.[4] Contacted by the French online journal *Rue89*, a Facebook representative responds, "When we hear that a user is deceased, the profile is placed in 'memorial.' Some parts of the profile are hidden to protect the defunct's private life: the 'status' line is suppressed, the user's memberships to groups to which he/she belonged are removed, and friends only can visit his memorial profile. We encourage users to resort to groups and group discussions to mourn and remember their defuncts."[5]

Facebook will not say how many of its members are placed in "memorial mode." Unless a user informs them, Facebook administrators have no means of knowing about the death of one of their members.

Second Life has implemented a similar policy:

> In your will, you must include the legal (real-life) name of the person who you want to inherit your Second Life account and assets, in the event of your death. . . . You may not transfer or assign your Account and its contractual rights, licenses and obligations, to any third party without the prior written consent of Linden Lab. . . . In general, the support team requires:
>
> Testamentary letter or other appropriate order
> Copy of the death certificate
> Copy of the will
> Copy of a government-issue ID sufficient to identify you.[6]

According to Frédéric Senis of the website *Les Médecins Maîtres-Toile*, personal websites have an infinite life span: "Sites such as Archive.org, with their Wayback Machine or their Google cache, ensure the survival of a website long after its technical death or after it has been updated, as if, somehow, the network had its own memory."[7] The same applies to blogs: after a blogger has died, the data remain accessible. Readers unaware of the blogger's death can continue to post comments.

The question of privacy is relevant here. Personal websites are considered intellectual works and therefore are left to the beneficiaries of their owner's estate. And Facebook? Guillemette Faure, a journalist at *Rue89*, points to the problem in the article quoted earlier: "Who owns the rights to a Facebook account? . . . Is it part of the legacy of the deceased and can it be passed on? Is the privacy of the user protected in death by Facebook's policies? Does the account belong to the company that registered the data? The question remains an open one, according to legal expert Murielle Cahen. Another problem: Facebook is subject to the American legal system. 'It is probable that the French law would apply to the French Facebook,' Murielle Cahen explains, 'but then, implementing the French law would be another issue.' "

One might be surprised to learn that legislators and the public find it reasonable for families to take control of the accounts of deceased users. The Facebook wall works like a memorial without the user's consent. Interactive automediality makes it possible for others to take up a position left unoccupied by the deceased and to erase him or her. One reader of an article explaining this is indignant: "This would mean letting the deceased's families access their blogs and change their contents? By what right? . . . It is not respectful of the deceased's freedom of expression."[8] This reaction identifies an aspect that jurists do not take into account: the creation of a blog results in the production of a new identity and in the affirmation of a singularity that is often in tension with that imposed by family and society. The desire to transform the account into a memorial is thus the recuperation, within the family, of a singularity. "What will you do with me and with all these things that belonged to me?" Louis asks in the play *Juste la fin du monde* by Jean-Luc Lagarce.[9] Families already take possession of the physical body of the deceased, as Kafka sarcastically remarks: "Will they also lay me in the tomb, at the end of a life that their solicitude will have made happy?"[10] Now families can also claim the virtual body.

Some digital platforms have tried to offer solutions to these problems. "Digital executors" enable people to leave passwords and instructions for the trustees of their estate upon their death. "I think that in a few years this will be as natural as writing a 'normal' will or life insurance," affirms Lisa Grandberg, a cofounder of My Webwill. "Just like we have always done, we document our lives by writing diaries, photos and letters. Today, the big difference is that most things are digital and password-protected."[11] My Webwill makes it possible for people to decide whether their online accounts should be deactivated, transferred to someone else, or updated with a final message. Members select two "verifiers" responsible for informing My Webwill of their death and providing a copy of the death certificate. It is possible to subscribe to a lifetime membership.

Other websites specialize in last words. The French website *Après la mort* (After Death) offers to deliver postmortem messages. The service is free and, because the message is encrypted, users have the privacy to write whatever they like; no one can access it, not even the administrator:

> The check-in system is the only way we have to verify your existence, it is necessary that you adapt it exactly to your check-in frequency. . . .
>
> This frequency is determining, this is what verifies your existence, if you do not check in on the chosen frequency, we consider you dead. However, before sending out the programmed message(s), an email will be sent to you every day for three days. Without a check-in from you after these three days, the message(s) will be sent. . . .
>
> At the same time, we send you an email to confirm that the email(s) have been sent to there [*sic*] recipient(s). You gonna tell me "isn't it silly because I will be dead," and you will be right . . . but you never know.[12]

Another, less well-known form of posthumous automediality was developed in the United States and Australia: video screens in cemeteries. Robert Barrows of California registered a patent for Video Tombstone, a headstone equipped with a screen to enable visitors to watch messages from the deceased. In order to avoid interference with an adjacent headstone, Wi-Fi headphones are also provided. Barrows entices potential customers with this advertisement:

> Now you will be able to go into a graveyard, click on a remote control device, and listen to anything the person might have wanted to say before they died. . . . The invention will change a major aspect of civilization. Cemeteries will come alive with stories told through video-tombstones. It will change the way we look at life and death and it will even change the way history is told. When people start recording their own obituaries for playback in video-tombstones, it will force them to examine their lives in ways they may not have even considered before.[13]

Barrows is also the author of *Cemeteries of Lies*, a novel based on confessions made via video tombstones. His enterprise is based on voyeurism, though it is unclear how the video tombstone differs from autobiographical writings published posthumously. What is original according to Barrows, is that now the automediality of strangers becomes available to everyone, as one only needs to insert coins or a credit card into the headstone and to rent headphones. Barrows tells the BBC, "You can go from grave to grave and click on anything that person wanted to say before they died. . . . Imagine how interesting it would be to go to tombstones where you didn't know the person, or historical tombstones to find out what someone had to say."[14] Barrows also envisions using the Internet so that messages can be transmitted long after death. The idea is to produce the impression of a voice from beyond the grave, reviving the practice of mediums.

A different perspective is offered by Anna Gosline in *New Scientist*, who warns, "They might just relate their life stories, or worse: they could confess to lurid indiscretions."[15] Barrow admits, "The video tombstone may also create tremendous controversy and it will also raise some free speech issues, because how can you control what somebody might say from 'beyond the grave,' and will it be truth or lies?"

An inventor in Florida created the Vidstone Serenity Panel, powered by solar energy. The system features a camera and a microphone incorporated into the headstone, enabling visitors to leave messages. This is reminiscent of Facebook's memorial application. Visiting a cemetery becomes an interactive experience between the dead and the living.

These inventions proliferate on the Internet, turning it into a virtual cemetery. One need only enter the YouTube link engraved on a headstone to find online diaries and life stories. These practices signal a narcissistic affirmation of singularity, a staging that has nothing to do with the Foucauldian practices of the self.

## From the Practices of the Self to the Society of the Spectacle

For Foucault the practices of the self "permit individuals to effect by their own means or with the help of others a certain number of operations on their own bodies and souls, thoughts, conduct, and way of being, so as to transform themselves in order to attain a certain state of happiness, purity, wisdom, perfection, or immortality."[16]

What Foucault describes is an *aesthetics of existence* among the Ancients, that is, the search for a principle of life, an *ethics*. The finality of this ethics is to give to other citizens, through exchange and debate, a thought always in motion, fueled by the multiple experiences of life. Foucault described this ethics as an elaboration of the self by the self, a laborious and difficult transformation driven by a constant concern for truth. He notes that, in our philosophical tradition, the precept "Take care of yourself" has been replaced by "Know yourself." The Internet exacerbates this rupture. On the Internet writing is offered without delay, without reviewing what has already been written. The Internet gives birth to a new type of subjectivation, in the Deleuzian sense of "the production of modes of existence or styles of life."[17] On the Internet subjectivity is no longer singular or solipsist; it is multiple and relational. Does interactivity signal the death of introspection? "Serge Tisseron names this desire to communicate about one's inner world 'extimacy,' a term which invites us to focus on some aspects of our private life"[18] Most of the time in these contemporary practices the point is not to have an *ethical behavior* nor to promote *self-creation*, let alone to develop one's citizenship, as stipulated by Antiquity's *hypomnêmata*. The psychological aspect takes precedence over the sociopolitical aspects, as Richard Sennett explains: "Openness to others in the hope of sharing feelings is the modern meaning of *Gemeinschaft*. It operates on the principle that selfhood can be generated through mutual confession and revelation, and under the illusion that experiences of power, inequity, or domination all have a meaning subsumed in psychological categories."[19] Foucault's invention of the self aims toward locating the truth, which is not a psychological or individual truth. The writings on the self have to serve as *exemplum*. Whereas the Ancients tried to share a human experience, today the preoccupation is extricating oneself from any kind of inheritance, familial or social, and flaunting one's uniqueness. Thus contemporary automediality is an extension of what Georg Simmel termed "qualitative individualism," which emerged in the nineteenth century: "All relations to others are but stations on a path leading the Self to him or herself. [The idea is to] convince others of the incomparable reality and individuality of one's world."[20] Literature at the turn of the twentieth century echoes this change, as is shown by Kafka's and Gide's claims of uniqueness and, in *The Notebooks of Malte Laurids Brigge*, by Rilke's desire to have a proper death (*Eigenes Tod*).

Katja Grote rightly notes that the practices of funerary rites changed with the emergence of modernity.[21] Society left the responsibility of the dead to the family. The individual came to be celebrated, especially by the bourgeoisie. Now it is the individual who is in command of his or her death (as he or she organizes his or her own funeral). With a video screen people can plan how they will be remembered. As a result it is not only the size or appearance of the mausoleum that signifies the social rank of the deceased but also the medium chosen to express oneself. To be sure, such a wish is pharaonic. Gary Collison, professor of American studies at Pennsylvania State University, writes, "Cemeteries are places where people try to outdo each other, display their wealth and power. This would certainly be a new way to do that."[22] In Australia cemeteries are already equipped with speaking tombs, generating complaints from those who come to visit neighboring graves.[23] It is as good a way as any to draw attention to one's mausoleum. We are therefore witnessing a double movement: on the one hand, death becomes taboo and is hidden (in large cities one no longer follows the funeral procession); on the other hand, memory is transformed into a spectacle. In both cases death is eliminated.

This is nothing less than a new form of culture, writes Derrida: "Every culture is characterized by its way of apprehending, dealing with, and, one could say, 'living' death as trespass."[24]

> One must go further: culture itself, culture in general, is essentially, before anything, even a priori, the culture of death. Consequently, then, it is a history of death. There is no culture without a cult of ancestors, a ritualization of mourning and sacrifice, institutional places and modes of burial, even if they are only for the ashes of incineration. . . . The very concept of culture may seem to be synonymous with the culture of death, as if the expression "culture of death" were ultimately a pleonasm or a tautology. But only such a redundancy can make legible the cultural difference and the grid of borders. Because every culture entails a treatise or a treatment of death, each of them treats the end according to a different partition.[25]

Making the cemetery a "lively place [*rendre vivant le cimetière*]" with video screens amounts to transforming it into a theater in which the spectacle presented by the deceased might relieve the sense of uneasiness produced by his or her tomb. Such is the modern Narcissus described by Simmel in search of eternal youth and material pleasure.[26] It is the very image promoted by the founder of Vidstone Serenity Panel: the video will "cheer up" those visiting the grave "and help them remember their dearly departed with a smile." Let the spectacle replace mourning and tears! Cemeteries will become the place of a sensational automediality propagated by the web. A (real or imaginary) self is exhibited in the mirror of the screen, as is evidenced by the Lonelygirl15 hoax. The fictitious nature of this 2006 interactive video was not revealed until several months later, ultimately drawing a good deal of attention from media outlets. Lonelygirl15 told the story of a teenage girl on YouTube. As Lee Siegel explains, in this series of videos "private life was enacted as though it were a fabricated performance." Siegel explains why, when it became clear that it was a hoax, the videos were nonetheless favorably received rather than condemned: "People have now come to expect inner life to be performed, rather than disclosed."[27] Perhaps future forms of automediality will entail installing a computer and a webcam in tombs, in case the deceased should like to continue to express themselves, or simply to allow viewers to see death at work, the ultimate performance of the subject.

Commemoration pervades representations of a self that aspires to live eternally, whether on the web or on a tombstone.

## A New Ontology

Georges Gusdorf writes, "In Bergsonian words, autobiography exposes a dialogue between the superficial self, randomly asserted by daily occurrences, and the profound self, vigilance of the depths from which are voiced the values, the constants of the individual being." The writing of the self is the "attempt to seek a unified identity, if always in the mode of 'once upon a time.' . . . I was, therefore I am; I am therefore I will exist beyond myself, when I don't exist any longer. *Et in Arcadia ego*."[28] This is also true for online autobiography. For the blogger as for the diarist, it is often the virtual self that is most authentic. Even on Facebook, where personal notes are more superficial, most users seek to show their "true" self, stripped of trumperies. Samuel Weber writes, "Thus, it is the Romantic heritage of an Absolute Self that continues to dominate the broadcast media, and that seeks today to extend its hold over the very different medium that is the internet."[29] This transcendental "I" sought by Novalis, is it not digital automediality's utopia? The Internet accentuates the aura of the self, as Raymond Martin and John Barresi remind us: "The self is the center of various structured ways humans have of talking about themselves. . . . The self . . . is to 'self talk' what God is to 'religious talk'—an absent presence, which because it can never be revealed always promises more than it can deliver. What it promises—what God as a center of religious discourse also promises—is substantiality, permanence, and luminous meaning."[30] Does putting oneself online amount to affixing one's identity to the web forever? What space is less destructible than the Internet? Libraries burn, paintings deteriorate, but digital data remain, or so we believe. The website Archive.org presents its project thus: "The Internet Archive is working to prevent the Internet—a new medium with major historical significance—and other 'born-digital' materials from disappearing into the past. Collaborating with institutions including the Library of Congress and the Smithsonian, we are working to preserve a record for generations to come." Two tenets of their mission are of particular interest here:

> Reviving dead links: A few services . . . are starting to offer access to archived versions of Web pages when those pages have been removed from the Web. This means that if you get a "404—Page Not Found" error, you'll still be able to find a version of the page.
>
> Looking back: With a "way-back machine"—a device that displayed the Web as it looked on a given date—historians and others would literally have a window on the past.[31]

Does anything ever die on the Internet? *Tomorrow never dies*.

Therefore we can imagine blogs, personal websites, and accounts on social networks like Facebook as empty places that the virtual self, wandering on the web, would come to inhabit from time to time. These sites might be likened to *The Book of the Dead*, the scrolls of Ancient Egypt, which prescribes, "Whoever memorizes this book on earth or has it written in his sepulcher, will leave and return to his grave whenever he wishes without obstacles."[32] Is not automediality characteristic of the postmodern quest for spirituality in an industrialized and secularized world? A technics-generated eternity of immortal cyborgs created by man in his own image.

The postmodernism critic N. Katherine Hayles describes Hans Moravec's 1988 futurist novel *Mind Children* in these terms: "[He] argues that human beings are essentially informational patterns rather than bodily presences. . . . He offers a fantastic scenario in which 'you' have your consciousness downloaded into a computer. . . . 'You' effectively become immortal." There is a difference between the soul and data, but the confusion is not without a reason: "The contemporary privileging of information is reinforced by religious yearnings and beliefs that have been around for a long time and that are resonant with meanings for many people. . . . The virtual subject will in some sense be a cyborg."[33]

Technics would thus offer a substitute for the unknown character of death. The self will control the most uncontrollable, as Weber warned in 1996: "Is the ultimate objective of technics a certitude and a security that is unwilling to leave any place to incalculability and to chance?" And he quotes Heidegger: "The conquests of technics can make the impossible possible. . . . The latter's unconditional domination forces both in advance into a uniformity from which metaphysically there is no escape."[34] This uniformity discussed by Heidegger is at work in postmortem automediality, supported by platforms such as Facebook, "digital executors," and video screen sellers offering standardized products. The individual can customize his or her discourse and image. During the "Automédialité" conference, Robert Folger effectively demonstrated that blogs were a mix of practice of the self (self-fashioning) and subjugation, for the online identity must be ratified by the community—it would not be ratified in real life—and meet bureaucratic standards. One example of this is the form that Facebook members have to complete in their "profile" and "author" sections.[35] Contemporary automediality corresponds to the Heideggerian conception of technics, as described by Weber: "Technics pursues its project of self-securing as the Will to Will by what Heidegger literally calls the 'placing of orders'—*Bestellbarkeit*."[36] Weber underlines the extremely dynamic aspect of modern technics as *Gestell* (emplacement) and observes the evolution of the notion of objectivity: "For that aspect of 'objectivity' that objects to or resists the subjective project of self-securing is progressively reduced as the object is increasingly treated as merely the raw material of objectives to be striven for and reached."[37]

Businesses offering to aid individuals in organizing their funerals throw into relief the bureaucratization of death since the turn of the twentieth century. Further evidence of this turn: inventors of digital headstones advertise their projects on funeral home forums, and the Serenity Panel won the annual award of Most Innovative Product in 2005. The consumerist era casts its shadow even over death. One can imagine the competition among various companies offering ever more sophisticated and expensive products, with greater longevity. Some are already guaranteed for eternity.

But this eternity is an illusion. The virtual self is an "avatar" (a term constantly in use in Internet discourse) exhibiting its metamorphoses. During the fourth congress of the International Auto/Biography Association, Julie Rak stressed the unstable and ephemeral aspect of identities in the cyberspace.[38] On Facebook self-reflection is displaced by ephemeral impressions and passing thoughts. One wishes to capture the self "in the moment." As for blogs, one's virtual existence is constantly under scrutiny. Bloggers are very attentive to the number of visits and comments left on their pages. Contrary to diaries, blogs require activity as evidence of the existence of a fragile, insecure self, disappearing one page at a time. Second Life users always have the possibility to transform their avatar or to get a new one.

For Lacan the self, or subject, is not real; it is but a "moment in discourse."[39] The child discovers his or her physical totality in the mirror. This creates what Lacan calls the "armor" of the subject, an illusion of unity that engenders the ego. Today the screen is the mirror. The postmodern self is fragmented, multiple, dispersed. According to Zygmunt Bauman, the aim is to avoid having a fixed identity: "to refuse to be 'fixed' one way or the other . . . not to wed one's life to one vocation only . . . to forbid the past to bear on the present . . . to sever the present from history . . . the avoidance of being fixed."[40] The computer screen acts as the mirror in Foucault's theory. It has a double nature, between heterotopia and utopia.[41] It is utopian because it is a "placeless place." Indeed "in the mirror, I see myself where I am not." "But it is also a heterotopia, in so far as the mirror does exist in reality, where it exerts a sort of counteraction on the position that I occupy. From the standpoint of the mirror I discover my absence from the place where I am since I see myself over there." Maurice Blanchot notes the affinities between the image and the corpse.[42] The latter is neither the living person nor someone else. Similarly, the image is neither the thing nor another reality. Corpse and image are neither here nor there; rather they belong to an intermediary world. Such is the function of pictures and comments on the blogs and Facebook pages of deceased users; such is the role of video diaries in cemeteries. The disappearance of our virtual self is eminently melancholic. Barthes defines *acedia* as "death without sepulcher."[43] Websites, blogs, and personal accounts remain as a trace of something that no longer exists, just like films screened in cemeteries. On these screens the self is Gracchus the hunter, whose funeral vessel never reaches the afterlife and must continue to sail on "earthly water," restlessly and with no prospect of salvation or annihilation.[44] Apropos this impossibility of death, Blanchot writes of a "dead transcendence": "The dead God has found a kind of impressive revenge in his work. For his death does not deprive him of his power, his infinite authority, or his infallibility: dead, he is even more terrible, more invulnerable, in a combat in which there is no longer any possibility of defeating him. . . . God is dead, which may signify this harder truth: death is not possible."[45] In fact cyberspace is often compared to Limbo. The web appears as a melancholy space of creation, which, according to Agamben, is neither a phantasmatic scene nor the real world but an "intermediate" zone, an "epiphanic place, located in the no-man's-land between narcissistic self-love and external object-choice."[46] Whereas the ongoingness of the Internet can be perceived positively as the eternal survival of the self as digital data, it evokes (unless of course our dream is to be cyborgs) a melancholy odyssey. "There is no third land for human beings," Kafka says.[47] Limbo in Christian doctrine is the anticipation of a utopian third land. Such is the subject's *exterritoriality*. "The existence is an exile in the fullest sense," Blanchot explains. "We are not there, we are elsewhere, and we will never stop being there."[48]

Such practices reveal the plight of a society that refuses to bury its dead and to make room for what is to come.

## Perpetual Burial Plot

When a Facebook user or a blogger dies, there remains an "empty place," to borrow a phrase from Rilke.[49] The orphan virtual self wandering on the web is reminiscent of the ghosts that haunt *The Notebooks of Malte Laurids Brigge*, whose contours have been drawn but never filled in. Leaving an empty place, however, is not the same thing as being absent. The Internet is full of corpses refusing to rot away and leave room for others. When a Second Life user dies, his or her avatar is no longer animated. He or she is frozen like a mortuary statue.

In modern-day cemeteries filmed self-portraits will intermingle, ghosts will be determined never to rest in peace, never to give up their ipseity. But Limbo is the place of stagnation, the melancholy landscape of a past that will not pass. According to the Rhenish mystic Jacob Böhme, "Where you do not live according to your ipseity and your own will is where the angels live, with you and everywhere. Where you live according to your ipseity and your own will is where the devils live, with you and everywhere."[50]

In contemporary Christian society, Weber notes, the self has replaced the soul: "The self is generally conceived of as that which marks the ability of an individual to stay the same over time. In this sense, it is the secular aspect or manifestation of the 'soul.'" Benjamin proposes to renounce this new belief and welcome death, which is the hallmark of our humanity. Weber's comment is illuminating: "But one [of] if not the most significant attribute shared by living beings as individuals is mortality. It is only by participation in something other than themselves, some sort of supra-individual project, community or collective that they can hope to attain a certain measure of 'survival.'" This survival of the individual as well as of humanity is impossible unless one abandons the objective category of sameness (*Gleichkeit*), which designates permanence in time, as opposed to ipseity (*Selbstheit*), according to Paul Ricoeur's distinction. Weber continues: "This paradoxical insistence on the Self as that which must be abandoned signifies for Benjamin: nothing more or less than the acknowledgement of a genuine temporality, which is to say, of time as a medium of alterity and of alteration, rather than one of self-fulfillment as staying the same."[51]

What the present-day Internet offers, virtually, is the preservation of all singularities. A perpetual burial plot. On the Internet there is room. Infinitely? Some Second Life users wish to constitute a sort of wax museum to commemorate the missing avatars.[52] This is to say that they want to create an online cemetery, such as those that exist for Tamagotchi. Real and virtual cemeteries are confused with one another. Digital headstones will function by hyperlinks, thus doubling the guarantee of eternity. Vidstone sings the praises of its product: "Memories can now come one step closer to forever being remembered and not forgotten." Commenting on Sophocles's *Oedipus at Colonus*, Weber warns us against excessive commemoration, which threatens society: "Oedipus proposes to Theseus that he keeps the place of his death and burial secret, confiding it only at the end of his life to 'dem Allerbesten,' who at the end of his life will do the same, keeping the secret and then transmitting it to his successor—'dem Folgenden'—to the next, but not necessarily the 'next of kin.' And this keeping and transmission of the secret place of death—will, Oedipus assures his host, protect his city against all dangers better than any army or host of allies ever could."[53] Commemoration risks stalling society in the past and folding it on itself, thus closing itself off from both the future and from otherness and rendering it unable to evolve and thus doomed to be destroyed. Does Antigone not die of honoring the dead too much? Weber elaborates:

> Oedipus' admonition not to be forgotten in death is very different from the call to be kept alive through memory. Memory of "me dead" excludes all notion of reanimation or resurrection. Death is final for the individual living being, which is why survival is here associated with a secret and inaccessible place that will therefore not even serve as a place of mourning. The object of memory will henceforth be associated with a place that is neither simply empty nor simply full. It is the place of death in life as the irreducible marker of life in its singularity. Only by accepting such singularity, Oedipus' words imply, can the future of the polis be assured. For only such a polis will consider its territory delimited not by walls to keep out the foreigner as enemy, but by limits that serve as a threshold, between land and sea, but also between present, past and future. Like the secret place of Oedipus' death, the threshold that defines the territory of the polis as a limit does not merely enclose it but rather opens it from within to an unknowable future.[54]

The wish of immortality, that is, of bringing time to a standstill, results—in politics—in the bloodiest tyranny, as *Macbeth* and *Richard III* exemplify. The virtuality of the tomb does not prevent the closure of society. A large part of the world's population is excluded by so-called globalization; sites like Facebook bear witness to the consolidation of small communities. They are, as we have seen, passed on to the family. Yet the family is not the most appropriate key to the future. Weber thus analyzes Oedipus's will: "Such a place of death can never be possessed or appropriated, not even by the children of the deceased (here Antigone and Ismene). The secret will thus be passed on not to the blood relatives of the ruler—this perhaps is the negative lesson of the tragedy of Cadmus and his descendants—but to the 'next best' successor, thus acknowledging the discontinuity succession of time for finite living beings."[55]

The family that preserves its deceased's Facebook account or installs digital screens on a loved one's tomb does not bury its dead. It is like Orpheus, who refuses to let Eurydice die because he is fascinated by her image. It is in the invisible sepulcher, hidden from the world, that the individual finds his or her true place. This is where he or she belongs. Oedipus, Weber writes, "had never had a city, a family, a *place* of his own. . . . The place where Oedipus is most at home is the place where he finally ceases to be."[56] It is thus necessary to leave Eurydice to her shadow, of which the all-encompassing web will take care.

In contrast to God, websites are not immortal. They are the proprietary holdings of corporations. One day Facebook, Second Life, and others will no longer exist. In this new polytheistic system one must know how to choose one's God and entrust one's memory to whoever seems to have the longest life span. As for blogs and personal websites, they depend on their hosts, and therefore their days are numbered. Further, they are sometimes removed for other reasons during the lifetime of their author. When they cease to be updated, they are no longer found by search engines, and they disappear into the ether of the web. If the dead always have an heir, that heir will be in the same position as the one keeping the secret of Oedipus's sepulcher. The successor can keep his or her word and keep it hidden, or be unfaithful to it and reveal to the spectators where it is.

The contemporary self is fragmentary, illusory, and fictionalized.[57] The Internet reinforces this crisis by multiplying virtual identities. Martin and Barresi wrote in 2006, "It is as if all of Western civilization has been on a prolonged ego trip that reality has finally forced it to abandon. If this interpretation is plausible, then what happens next may be a new phenomenon in history, a kind of dark night of the 'soul.'"[58] One may wonder whether, with the emergence of these forms of postmortem automediality, this night of the soul—that is, of the self, which for Weber is the secular manifestation of the soul—has not already begun. Will we start to see people buried with their computer and an Internet connection in order to continue updating their personal account and pages even in death? In the United States and Australia families have started to order tomb screens, and if they do not proliferate, it is likely due to the fact that everyone is waiting for their neighbor to make the first move. Doubtless this threshold of decency will be crossed, violating what

Heidegger, quoted by Weber, calls "the mystery of being and the inviolability of the possible."[59] Let us hope, therefore, that everyone will remember to write their digital testament and choose, like Oedipus, *den Allerbesten*. And that they will follow the example of his tomb, as reiterated by Weber: "The secret of this place resides in the way it leaves room for what is to come."[60]

**Translated by Antoine Traisnel**

## Notes

This essay seizes upon the impulse of a seminar held by Samuel Weber under the title "Spectator and Witness—Traces of the Other in *Society of the Spectacle*. The Philosophical-Psychoanalytical Margins of a Culture of Spectating and Remembering," one of a series of seminars organized by Hans-Peter Jäck called "On the Politics of the Other." October 4–6, 2002, in Frankfurt am Main. The text deals with this impulse—to conceive of spectators as witnesses—in relation to current research discussions, above all those in German-speaking theater studies and performance theories. An excerpt has been published in German and English in the volume *Ungerufen: Tanz und Performance der Zukunft*, edited by Sigrid Gareis and Krassimira Kruschkova (Berlin: Theater der Zeit, 2009). I presented an extended but still preliminary version as my inaugural lecture at the University of Hamburg in January 2010 and as a keynote at the conference "Theatre and Audiences: Sharing the Creative Process" in Liège in September 2012.

1. Susanna Egan and Gabriele Hems, "Autobiography? Yes. But Canadian?," *Canadian Literature* 172 (2002): 5–6.

2. Jörg Dünne and Christian Moser, *Automedialität: Subjektkonstitution in Schrift, Bild und neuen Medien* (Munich: Fink, 2008), 7–16.

3. https://en.wikipedia.org/wiki/Criticism_of_Facebook.

4. Cédric, "Le nouveau service de Facebook qui fait honte!," *Autour du web*, October 28, 2009, http://www.autourduweb.fr/nouveau-service-facebook-deces-necrologique/. [Unless otherwise specified, translations from French are mine.—Translator]

5. Guillemette Faure, "Qu'est-ce qui arrive aux comptes Facebook après la mort?," *Rue89*, January, 21, 2009, http://rue89.nouvelobs.com/-83923.

6. "Linden Lab Official: Death and Other Worries outside Second Life," Second Life, last updated February 12, 2016. http://wiki.secondlife.com/wiki/Linden_Lab_Official:Death_and_other_worries_outside_Second_Life.

7. "La mort d'un site: Le commencement de l'absence de fin ou le début des ennuis?" Available at http://www.medecins-maitres-toile.org/.

8. Arosmik, "Propriété numérique en Corée: Et après la mort?," *Agora Vox*, May 21, 2010, http://www.agoravox.fr/actualites/international/article/propriete-numerique-en-coree-et-75195.

9. Jean-Luc Lagarce, *Juste la fin du monde* (Besançon: Les Solitaires intempestifs, 2005), 45.

10. Franz Kafka, *Journaux, Lettres à sa famille et à ses amis* (Paris: Gallimard, 1984), 346.

11. http://www.pressreader.com/canada/the-starphoenix/20100309/282041913298133.

12. "Explanations on the Service," *Après la mort*, 2003, http://www.apreslamort.net/explications.php. [In English on the website.—Translator]

13. "The Video Enhanced Gravemarker," R. M. Barrows, 2006, http://www.barrows.com/.

14. "Video Diary from Beyond the Grave," *BBC News*, July 8, 2004, http://news.bbc.co.uk/2/hi/americas/3876351.stm.

15. Anna Gosline, "High-Tech Messages from the Grave," *New Scientist*, July 8, 2004, http://www.newscientist.com/article/dn6119-hightech-messages-from-the-grave.html.

16. Michel Foucault, "Les Techniques de soi," in *Dits et écrits* (Paris: Gallimard, 2001), 4: 785.

17. Gilles Deleuze, *Pourparlers* (Paris: Minuit, 2005), 156.

18. Sébastien Biset, "Pratiques culturelles émergentes et automédialité," in *L'Automédialité contemporaine*, ed. Béatrice Jongy (Dijon: Abell, 2008), 152.

19. Richard Sennett, "Destructive Gemeinschaft," in *Beyond the Crisis*, ed. N. Birnbaum (Oxford: Oxford University Press, 1977), 185.

20. Georg Simmel, *Philosophie de la modernité* (Paris: Payot, 1989), 1: 300.

21. See Katja Grote, *Der Tod in der Literatur der Jahrhundertwende* (Frankfurt am Main: Peter Lang, 1996).

22. "Video-Enhanced Grave Marker," *Wikipedia*, May 2012, http://en.wikipedia.org/wiki/Video-Enhanced_Grave_Marker.

23. See Haley A. Lovett, "Are Talking Tombstones a New Way to Mourn or an Annoyance?," *Finding Dulcinea*, May, 18, 2009, http://www.findingdulcinea.com/news/technology/2009/may/Are-Talking-Tombstones-a-New-Way-to-Mourn-or-an-Annoyance.html.

24. Jacques Derrida, *Apories: Mourir-s'attendre aux "limites de la vérité"* (Paris: Galilée, 1996), 52.

25. Derrida, quoted in Samuel Weber, "A Different Partition" (unpublished ms., 2009), 1.

26. Simmel, *Philosophie de la modernité*, 1: 268.

27. Lee Siegel, *Against the Machine: Being Human in the Age of the Electronic Mob* (New York: Spiegel and Grau, 2008), 49, 51.

28. Georges Gusdorf, *Lignes de vie* (Paris: Odile Jacob, 1990), 1: 299.

29. Samuel Weber, "Medium, Reflexivity and the Economy of the Self," in *L'Automédialité contemporaine*, 46.

30. Raymond Martin and John Barresi, *The Rise and Fall of Soul and Self: An Intellectual History of Personal Identity* (New York: Columbia University Press, 2006), 264.

31. https://archive.org/about/.

32. *The Book of the Dead*, 1550–1500 BC, Musée du Louvre, chapter 1.

33. Katherine Hayles, "The Condition of Virtuality," in *The Digital Dialectic*, ed. Peter Lunenfeld (Cambridge, Mass.: MIT Press, 2000), 72, 73, 92.

34. Samuel Weber, *Mass Mediauras* (Sydney: Power Publications, 2006), 53, 54.

35. Robert Folger, "New Kids on the Blog? Subjektkonstitution im Internet," in Dünne and Moser, *Automedialität*, 292–93.

36. Weber uses the definition in the 1954 edition of *Webster's Unabridged Dictionary*: "the assigning or appointing of a definite place" (*Mass Mediauras*, 71).

37. Weber, *Mass Mediauras*, 53–54.

38. Julie Rak, "The Digital Queer: Weblogs and Internet Identity," *Biography: An Interdisciplinary Quarterly* 28.1 (2005): 12–13.

39. Martin and Barresi, *The Rise and Fall of Soul and Self*, 256–57.

40. Zygmunt Bauman, *Postmodernity and Its Discontents* (Cambridge, Mass.: Polity, 1997), 89.

41. Foucault uses *utopia* in its strict etymological sense, as "a place that doesn't exist"; *heterotopia* indexes the real space where all the other real places are "represented, contested or inverted." Michel Foucault, "Des espaces autres," in *Dits et écrits*, 2: 1575.

42. Maurice Blanchot, *The Work of Fire* (Stanford: Stanford University Press, 1995), 348.

43. Roland Barthes, *Comment vivre ensemble*, ed. Claude Coste (Paris: Seuil/Imec, 2002), 57.

44. Franz Kafka, *Œuvres completes: Récits et fragments* (Paris: Gallimard, 1980), 2: 455.

45. Maurice Blanchot, "La Lecture de Kafka," in *La Part du feu* (Paris: Gallimard, 1949), 15.

46. Giorgio Agamben, *Stanze* (Paris: Rivages, 1994), 58.

47. Kafka, *Journaux*, 531.

48. Blanchot, "La Lecture de Kafka," 17.

49. Rainer Maria Rilke, *Die Aufzeichnungen des Malte Laurids Brigge* (Frankfurt am Main: Insel, 1982), 26.

50. Jacob Böhme, *Confessions* (Paris: Fayard, 1973), 196.

51. Samuel Weber, "Drawing—The Single Trait," (unpublished ms., n.d.), 1, 23. This essay was subsequently published in *Techniken der Übereinkuft: Zur Medialität des Politischen*, ed. H. Blumentrath et al. (Berlin: Kulturverlag Kadmos, 2009), 79-98.

52. http://www.memoirevive.tv/blog/actus/avatarmort/. Published January, 12, 2008. This website is now defunct, and no entry for this date is available at www.archive.org.

53. Weber, "A Different Partition," 22.

54. Ibid., 22–24.

55. Ibid., 24.

56. Samuel Weber, *Theatricality as Medium* (New York: Fordham University Press, 2004), 146.

57. See Béatrice Jongy, *L'Invention de soi au tournant du siècle: Rilke, Kafka, Pessoa* (Frankfurt am Main: Peter Lang, 2011).

58. Martin and Barresi, *The Rise and Fall of Soul and Self*, 305.

59. Weber, *Mass Mediauras*, 54.

60. Weber, "A Different Partition," 24.

Chapter 3

# The Unrepresentable Audience

Nikolaus Müller-Schöll

## No Relationship between Actors and Audience

It begins with an end. The last notes of solemn music are heard. A flourish. Then applause. Two hands, feet, and then the man belonging to them push through the curtain at the rearmost end of the stage. Bit by bit his cast members follow, then they all stand before us: three women, three men. Clad in casual clothing. A frozen smile on their faces. Slowly, as if hindered by an invisible hand, they walk to the front and gradually let us grasp the fact that they are not doing anything more than all other actors at the end of their evening's work. The ensemble of another performance stands in front of us, actors who have their work for today behind them and now, in front of us, are commenting on what they do: the completed performance, their roles in it, their work conditions, the life in hotels, always surrounded by colleagues, their acting, their salaries, subsidies, and us.

For sixty minutes the director Ivana Müller, producing in Amsterdam and Paris, born in Zagreb, lets the six performers stage this show, a minimalistic performance that exhibits the rules of its production.[1] But as simple as what we see here may seem, the thoughts that produce it are multifaceted. As in encounters with contemporary conceptual art, the little we see gives us a lot to think about. And, at the latest, this thinking begins when the actors start talking about "us." We, the audience, are the people to whom they bow down. But when they describe us, when they mention the familiar faces that look at them from among us, we realize: it is not us who they mean. Having come to the performance to see one of the most original ensembles of the current performance scene, we have in actual fact become the observed. For the six people on the stage we are nothing more than the performers of an audience, representatives of the mass of applauding we have just heard, whom they are talking about when they look at us, but who, represented by us, are present only as absentees.

*Playing Ensemble Again and Again* is the name of a performance that lets us contemplate a twofold double representation: of the actors, who are not what they seem to be, and at the same time also of ourselves, the spectators, who are not regarded as that which we really "are." Convened under a title that contains the invocation of a community, of a played *ensemble*, ultimately nothing other than the framework of the theater is performed for us. The purpose of this framework, even in the most radical of illusionary theaters, is the dissolution of illusion, the transition from performance to reality. Only that which usually appears as reality—the bowing down of the actors in front of the audience—is staged here as a performance. And that the performance that is otherwise rescinded in the transition had already ended as everything was beginning. On display before us is, strictly speaking, the convergence of a community characterized by showing and watching, in which a beholden ensemble of actors observes and comments upon a beholding ensemble of spectators. Comparing the stage to a tableau, its processes with a dance of pictures, ultimately with a movie, we see here, so to speak, its closing credits played in slow motion—and realize: we are in the wrong movie; we represent others, just as the actors are conversely the actors of another movie. *Playing Ensemble Again and Again* leads us to suspect something like a law that leads actors and audience to converge in performances. It is a law of reciprocal misjudgment, the convergence of at least two films that are running at the same time but that will never be able to align themselves, unless in a short moment of perfect illusion. Following on from Lacan's famous adage on the relationship of the sexes to one another, one could say *il n'y a pas de relation entre les comediens et les spectateurs*. There is no relationship between actors and audience.

## Omitted Omissions

What Müller's scenically applied research suggests, among other things, is a rethinking of those theories of the audience that, in the course of the "performative turn," entered German theater research from American discussions of the 1960s, where they were considered a substantiation of the "discovery of the spectator," which, according to a standard work, could be observed from the turn of the twentieth century.[2] Whatever became of the observer theory developed on the path from New York to Europe is made clear by casting glances at a translation of one of Richard Schechner's central texts. At a prominent point in his much read book *Performance Theory*, Schechner presents a diagram that vividly illustrates an expansion of the concept of theater within the realm of performance. In the shape of an onion, in layers encircling and overlapping one another, we find the following concepts: *Drama*, possibly an underlying written play; *Script*, the constitutional course of the evening's events; *Theater*, the staging as it is presented by the actors during the evening's performance; and *Performance*. Performance thereby encompasses everything that occurs between the first spectator entering the theater and the last spectator leaving it. Performance must thus exist *between* actors and audience, requires their mutual appearance. In Schechner's diagram the outermost layer of the onion is not, as are all the others, drawn as a continuous line but rather is interrupted by gaps.[3] I interpret this to mean that performance is never fully determinable precisely because of the fact that is constituted only in the interplay of actors and audience. Performance is evaded by the ever singular, always different, never fully formalizable act of encounter.

Reprinted in the commendable collection *Texte zur Theorie des Theaters* (*Texts on the Theory of Theater*), edited by Christopher Balme and Klaus Lazarowicz at the beginning of the 1990s, Schechner's diagram is modified in a marginal yet highly significant way: the outermost layer is drawn as a continuous line.[4] This modification could have occurred by chance; however, this chance is characteristic of the German understanding and history of American performance and of the concept of performance in Germany. An idea molded in the eighteenth century, the idea of a crowd of spectators who are to be more or less unified—the "audience"—takes the place of an ever changing, never quite controllable diversity of spectators.[5] This "audience" is comparable with the audience in front of which Müller's performers bow as they in fact stand in front of us, in front of others than those to whom they are addressing themselves. In past decades this abstract entirety has slid into the role of the subject of the performance and has become the foundation of theories that have sought anew to formalize that which eludes formalization and to make it the basis of a new metatheory. In contrast Schechner's performance theory—at least as it is sketched in the diagram—would mark the end of such a metatheory.

## The Medial Boundary of Spectator Theories

That which Schechner merely hints at ought to be explored further. If the spectator today has "practically, but perhaps more aesthetically become the central issue of theater, its practice and its theory," [6] perhaps this is because, at the end of the day, theater and theory content themselves with a series of platitudes when thinking about the audience. Wilmar Sauter pinpoints the quintessence of this when he says that the "audience is allocated a constitutive role in theater" and explains that it is the "a[udience]" that is "above all the receiver in the process of theatrical communication. Theater is performed for the spectator; a theatrical event is not conceivable without the a[udience]."[7] This corresponds to an idea in other texts, according to which the minimum prerequisite for theater is that somebody says something and somebody else watches and listens. Upon careful reflection, these two *state-of-the-art* defining ideas give rise to many questions: What are we talking about when we talk about the "audience"? *Which* spectators is theater performed for, or rather which kind of performance is associated with the spectators evoked here? Who is the *other* here, listening and watching? And what does theatrical communication even mean in this context?

If one takes a glance at theories founded on such premises, one realizes that the audience evoked in such theories—and in the reception theories dealt with in literary studies—is often taken as a pretense for the replacement of a complex structure with a structure that is less complex. Discussion about the production or the performance is replaced by a discussion about audience comprehension. Statements about the audience prove to be self-declarations about the writer or disguised statements about the market. The audience is ascribed the role of a God in a negative theology, which one can constantly allude to, because, in line with his vocation, this God of course cannot be positivized and cannot step forward to contradict the words that are put in his mouth.

Last but not least, one of the problems pertaining to the current discourse surrounding the spectator is that we avoid the question about whether a *human* spectator is even needed in order for theater to take place. This question is not just a question about whether theater can be performed in front of God, in front of an animal, a plant, a stone, or a mirror, but rather a question about the medial foundations of theater.[8] If it is the case that there is no form of human utterance that, due to its linguistic constitution, has not always implied a certain kind of theater, produced theater—in the sense that one is already in a scenic or medial constellation—then the question of the spectator appears to be futile in the way that it positivistically and empirically abridges the question of the experience of alterity through media and for this reason fails to recognize it. Then it is not the empirical spectator, it is also not the "ego" claiming to be the spectator that we need to consider within the concept of the audience but rather the fact of being subjected to the order of the other on the basis of the uncircumventable medial foundation of every human utterance. Strictly speaking, *audience* refers to the theatrical constitution preceding any production and any performance. However, if we try to comprehend the audience in this way it is impossible to think of, because it is always one step ahead of this thinking, constraining it, dictating and negotiating its rules. Having said that, it is within this thinking thinkable only as that which eludes thinking, always differently, always singularly, and at the same time always in a pluralistic way.

## The Spectator in Contemporary Performance Theory

Contemporary performance theory describes the constitutive role of the audience or of spectators as "a jointly responsible part of a whole," signatories to a "theatrical pact," activated participants or "spectators," "absolute rulers over all possible semioses without another, superordinate goal to follow."[9]

The interesting thing about these definitions is that, at best—to use the title of an essay by Jacques Rancière—they propagate an "emancipated spectator."[10] Rancière wishes for an end to the philosophical tradition of viewing the spectator from lofty intellectual towers as someone who watches and speaks ignorantly, is alienated, has a false awareness and bewitched senses. He would also like to see an end to the practice of trying to tear the spectator from his supposedly passive onlooker demeanor and turn him into an actual agent. Instead of this the spectator should be able and allowed to see what he sees from his singular position in order to do or to think what he wants. Rancière advocates the abandonment of the assumption that a performance is the result of a process of cause and effect, that the artist communicates something that the spectator then receives. He posits the active spectator—whose actions are constituted in watching, observing, selecting, comparing, interpreting, combining, and composing—against those dichotomies handed down in worn patterns of describing the stage, oppositions between watching and knowing, appearance and reality, activity and passivity: oppositions that Rancière sees as incarnate allegories of inequality. The spectator is the distanced observer and active interpreter of the performance. Rancière opposes the notion of a community in the theater with an idea according to which everybody translates and associates what they see with their own intellectual adventures. In this way the spectator becomes similar to the others, shares with them the ability to associate and disassociate, but nothing more. Every spectator is the protagonist (*acteur*) of his own story and simultaneously spectator to it.

What is striking about this point of view and others like it is that it is not able to provide an answer to the question of why this manner of spectatorship should occur in the theater, of all places, and not on the street, in public squares, in cafés or train stations. Furthermore it relinquishes qualitative differentiation and, with it, any kind of critical view of the stage. It is not without reason that Rancière invokes his own experience of the political patronization of workers via intellectuals and the underestimation of their own, other kind of intellectualism, to which his attention was attracted during his examination of nineteenth-century sources. As honorable as this source study and the resulting about-face of a leftist avant-gardist may be, what he maps out, under the pretext of egalitarianism, as the ideal of the emancipated spectator still appears to be naïve. He portrays a position of nonreflective liberalism in the field of theater that loses sight of the fact that equality in the face of unequal economic and cultural capital is not brought forth by awarding everybody equal rights or setting everybody the same boundaries. In practice he forgets that the spectator in contemporary media—including the theater—is the object of a permanent manipulation. What the "pact" model forgets is the inequality of the contracting partners. At the moment of purchasing theater or movie tickets, we know far less in comparison to the producer of the performance or the film about what we are letting ourselves in for, much less what kind of long-term consequences our attendance might entail. During the theatrical pact of the performance we attend, we know just as little, at the moment of assent, about why we will have granted our approval of this contract, which, as is true of all contracts, will not come into completion until some time in the future.[11] If it is carried to excess, the trust that was the foundation of our pact, the belief that we would receive what we had hoped for or what we were promised, will be shattered. However, this disappointment generally only concerns obvious provocations, presentations not living up to our viewing expectations, viewers being overwhelmed or underchallenged, an unexpected message, or violations of good taste. This hardly ever applies to the structural handling—that aspect of *nolens volens*—that can be referred to as a *politics of representation*: all of the stipulations, institutionalized and put in place by the production, that are already there even before the first spectator has entered the room and that will stay there long after he has left—in a manner of speaking the apparatus, within which the encounter between actors and spectators then takes place. This apparatus combines the intratheatrical sequence of events with the social, economic, political, and historical conditions that play into every supposedly free and equal encounter in the theater or in performance, and which in this manner endow actors and onlookers with power and influence over the direction of the encounter to a greater or lesser extent, in manifold ways.[12]

Just as it is blind to the stipulations set by the relative apparatus and the *nolens volens* manipulations that accompany them, liberalistic theory is blind to anything in the theater that is *not communicative* or that *communicates in a different way* from that which an idea of communication based on the model of transmitter-message-receiver could ever dream of. There is probably no other theoretician who captures this difficult aspect better than Walter Benjamin, whose entire oeuvre was in many ways dedicated to the salvation of this idea of a different kind of communication in the artistic process.

## Requiem for the Receiver: Walter Benjamin's Translator Essay

Much discussed in recent decades, "The Task of the Translator" was completed by Benjamin in 1921 as the preface to his translation of Baudelaire's "Tableaux parisiens" and begins with the famous apodictic denial of any regard for the viewer, listener, or reader when examining art:

> In the appreciation of a work of art or an art form, consideration of the receiver never proves fruitful. Not only is any reference to a certain public or its representatives misleading, but even the concept of an "ideal" receiver is detrimental in the theoretical consideration of art, since all it posits is the existence and nature of man as such. Art, in the same way, posits man's physical and spiritual existence,

> but in none of its works is it concerned with his response. No poem is intended for the reader, no picture for the beholder, no symphony for the listener.[13]

Benjamin talks of literature, of the visual arts and music—but not of theater. Could he have added that no theater is intended for the audience? No performance intended for the spectator?

In order to find answers to these questions we first of all need to examine what it is that Benjamin is giving us to think about in these sentences. During the course of the essay it becomes sketchy, yet within the context of his thinking about language, vividly comprehendible. Benjamin repeatedly seizes on the opening passage during his essay, continues it and deploys it in his contemplations on the nature of translation. In this way he asserts that a poem is essentially neither communication nor utterance, and its translation, if its aim is to serve a reader who does not understand the original, can only go awry. Although he leaves the question of how the essence of a good translation constitutes itself open, he determines that a poor translation is to be defined as "the inaccurate transmission of an inessential content."[14] The poor translation translates only what is external to the poem—its communication message (*Mitteilung*)—but not its essence. This external content can be expressed only imprecisely, as in its rendering it is ultimately forced to refrain from any references or connotations, inherent in every word, that are in excess of the poem's message or denotation. Finally, Benjamin contrasts the poor translation with an understanding that displaces the order of original and translation in equal measure. In Benjamin's essay the original proves to already be a translation, and, then again, the translation always portrays a variation in the sense that it renders something audible and legible that had never been written in the original. The translation presents the same thing in a different way and in this difference hints at an alteration already present in the original.[15] Benjamin presents this alteration as that which asks for the translation and enables it, but which at the same time prohibits it and renders it impossible. His term for this alteration in the original is *translatability*, deployed by him as a variant of *communicability*. *Translatability* signifies the potential of the original to be different and to always mean something other than what it seems to be or what it appears to be to any specific observer or reader.[16]

In this way we would have in principle arrived at a conception of the work of art that is the spitting image of Rancière's. Rancière writes that players and spectators encounter one another in the theater via a third party that does something at the moment of their encounter which neither is able to control sovereignly. Together with Benjamin and in view of the poem, one could describe this third party as the translatability of the poem, as its principal potential to be translated and thereby to always be understood differently. Benjamin nonetheless draws entirely different conclusions. Whereas Rancière deduces that an ever different interpretation of the effects can and—in the interest of the equality of the emancipated spectators—*must* take the place of the search for the cause of the effects, Benjamin maintains that, in spite of the impossibility of adequate perception and interpretation, there is something that needs to be kept hold of in a work of art that, even if it remains forever indeterminable, still demands not to be forgotten: "One might, for example, speak of an unforgettable life or moment even if all men had forgotten it. If the nature of such a life or moment required that it be unforgotten, that predicate would not imply a falsehood but merely a claim not fulfilled by men, and probably also a reference to a realm in which it *is* fulfilled: God's remembrance."[17] According to Benjamin, there is a quality in every work of art that has nothing to do with communication, exchange, or message but rather leads to the work of art and constitutes it without being totally absorbed within this constitution. Even if an other, a medium is required to bring this constitutive quality to apparition, it remains in the apparition, in the medium, forever precarious; it is that which extends the interpretation beyond every single interpretation and turns it into a *reading*. It demands new interpretations over and over again.

## Infinitely Numerous Finite Readings

For the form of *reading* that one might think of in this context, a practice of reading could be drawn upon, that, in an almost unsurpassable radicalism, has called the foundations of understanding into question because it emanates from the assumption that, in relation to the method of its observation, every object must be conceded the right to object, indeed the right to co-formation. Emanating from these literally abyssal thoughts, it is theoreticians like Paul de Man, Werner Hamacher, Carol Jacobs, J. Hillis Miller, and Samuel Weber who have shown us that reading is the center of interpretation as it is the center of the institutions that are based upon interpretation (institutes, faculties, universities), an act that does not let itself be formalized in any way.[18] The interpretation of a text is based on its reading, indeed on an imperative of reading: one has to read. But exactly that on which the interpretation would like to be based refers *in* and *in excess of the interpretation* to the fundamental doubt about the legibility of any text whatsoever, a kind of doubt that—briefly and allusively formulated—likewise arises out of the text-character of the text itself as out of the ever different, ever singular ways of reading. In other words, this fundamental doubt arises out of the communic*ability* of what a text approximately communicates,[19] as well as out of reading as a medium of intermediation that never stays purely external to that which is conveyed. The communicability of the texts as well as the mediality of the act of reading are forgotten where texts are reduced to theses, where one model of reading and meaning among many is privileged at the expense of all others. However, a different kind of reading begins with doubts about legibility, a kind of reading that conceives of the text as a mise-en-scène, as the result of a compromise between different interests, brought about and restricted by the time and place of its transcription as well as its reading. Every reading thought about in this way signifies the opening of a chance for tendencies repressed in such compromises, for that which cannot express itself in a certain historical situation or, rather, cannot assume a role.

It is only when one conceives of texts as mise-en-scènes—and this is suggested by the theoreticians mentioned as well as by many others—that productions, conversely, can be thought of as texts, without theater studies immediately seizing upon the long prevailing notion of theater as a mere continuation or implementation of literature on a stage, and in this respect explorable by literary means and methods of interpretation or, ultimately, as one component of literary studies itself. Carried over into considerations of performances, the analyses of productions or merely of their single elements—for example, the histrionic gesture, the particular behavior in a scene or a sequence of consecutive scenic configurations—a dual underlying assumption arises out of the insight into the mediality of reading. Every theatrical event is essentially infinitely interpretable. Every reading is essentially interminable. In other words, both assumptions arise out of the fact that performances, like texts, are, to use a formulation of Benjamin, barely discernable from "configuration[s] pregnant with tensions."[20] Where, in spite of their dual infiniteness and interminability, a description is undertaken, an interpretation attempted, it is inevitably bound to an excess that one might mistakenly be tempted to label *subjective* because it is by no means to be legitimated or only within the context of a *politics of reading*. It remains untenable and unsubstantiable and thus opens up one's reading to other readings to come.

At this point it could seem as if I am speaking in favor of an ultimately relativistic practice of interpretation, perhaps in turn for the form of emancipated spectatorship advocated by Rancière. However, the point is, essentially, to reveal the prerequisites of established practices of interpretation and thereby to allude to the entrenchment of interpretation, reading, and critique within a domain that one would have to ascribe to ethics in the classical categories. With Benjamin and against the greater part of contemporary theater, media, and performance theory—that practice of exegesis, dictated to by its object—it is a call for something that, using a phrase coined by Emmanuel Levinas, can be conceived of as a reading of the "trace" of the other.[21] Precisely because he has always preceded me at the moment of my analysis, or rather at the moment of my interpretation, the other predetermines an infinite task as well as my inevitable failure to accomplish it. Reading the traces (and not signs or messages) of the other leads to a process of interpretation that, on the one hand, must proceed according to the rules of traditional hermeneutics but that, on the other, must necessarily transgress these rules because their prerequisite—the *ex ante* presentation of the knowledge of the other, the horizon of meaning that I share with him—has ceased to exist. A limitation of knowledge must be kept in mind that results from the never completely deducible difference of the other, from the difference of time, place, and history. The imperative of understanding during the process of interpretation must revert to an imperative of not understanding. Elaborations on this paradox or aporia are perhaps best in reference to theories of the witness.

## The Spectator as Witness

In an entry in his exile diary, his *Arbeitsjournal* (work journal), from October 5, 1945, Brecht records a conversation with Lion Feuchtwanger, who tells him that the news agency AP has asked him to write weekly reports about the Nuremberg Trials, which he has refused. "i'm not good at that kind of thing," Brecht quotes Feuchtwanger and adds his riposte: "then do it as well as you can, it is you who has been summoned. . . . speak poorly, stutter, let yourself be gagged, but appear in the arena."[22] The conversation juxtaposes two positions of witness testimony that give food for thought. Feuchtwanger's declination seems to be carried by two considerations, which Brecht pits against each other. One obvious consideration asks the question of whether or not he, the novelist, the author of historical narratives, is a *good* correspondent. Here one could see a gesture of modesty obscuring other, less honorable motives, such as the vanity of the author who does not want to concern himself with a genre he considers to be beneath him or the laziness of a person who does not want to spend his time following a trial. The other consideration pertains to the question of whether or not he would be a good witness. Feuchtwanger appears ambivalent on this point. "i'm not good at that kind of thing" seems to imply that he could bear witness but that others would do it better. At this point Brecht launches the answer that separates witness testimonial from the question of ability, elegance, and adequacy in order to remind Feuchtwanger of a responsibility that can be translated into the context of my deliberations on the audience. The witness may be a false, a deficient, indeed a completely unsuitable spectator and listener; his knowledge may be insufficient, his perception distorted, his language faculty constricted. Nevertheless the lonely, singular, and irreplaceable experience remains, which only he can report about and for which he has a responsibility that nobody can take off his hands. The same can be said for the chronicler, critic, or reader of the events that take place between himself and the production at the moment of performance. His testimony, like what remains of the fleeting theater, is irreplaceable.

The testimony of the spectator is laden with all of the problems, aporias, and paradoxes of witness testimony in general, with which Jean-François

Lyotard, Giorgio Agamben, and Jacques Derrida have extensively dealt in recent times. At a prominent point in his book *The Differend: Phrases in Dispute*, Lyotard discusses the assertion of a denier that there can be no evidence for the existence of the gas chambers—and therefore of the "Final Solution"—because only somebody who had seen them as deathly with their own eyes could bear witness to them.[23] Agamben portrays the paradox of witness testimony in the figure of the "Muselmann" described by Primo Levi and others, the paradox of a prisoner who has more or less given up, is more dead than living, is unable to be spoken to, and who, avoided by his fellow inmates, waits for death. This person on the threshold of human and nonhuman, mute, displaced, inscribes a gap in all testimonies. He, in whom one claims to have seen the integral witness of Auschwitz, cannot speak, whereas every witness who can speak has nothing to say.[24] Whereas these positions run the risk of orienting themselves on a model of witness testimony as proof or knowledge—albeit *modo negativo* because they view not-speaking as one part of the ability to speak (Lyotard), or because they situate witness testimony, for example, at the nonplace of articulation in the shape of a caesura or a remainder (Agamben)—Derrida places his "fundamental axiom" that witnessing is not proof at the core of his reflections on witness testimony.[25] The deciding prerequisite for the affinity between spectator and witness followed here makes it seem expedient to incorporate Derrida's elaborations, albeit in an extremely truncated form, into my reflections on a different notion of the audience.

In his essay "A Self-Unsealing Poetic Text: Poetics and Politics of Witnessing," Derrida develops the aporias and paradoxes of witness testimony first of all and ostensibly in view of Paul Celan's poem "Aschenglorie," which ends with the lines "No one / bears witness for the / witness" but goes much further than this, becomes more elementary, more fathomless in view of "that steering towards the other." "Every time I speak or indicate my interest to the other," writes Derrida, "I bear witness." If we talk about testimony, we are at the same time, according to Derrida, talking about a tangible action—which can be illustrated by referring to a court scene—just as we are talking about speaking to the other in general. This speaking is per se subject to the possibility of its own obliteration. As a "condition of possibility" this speaking is intrinsically inscribed with an uncertainty that is at the same time also its condition of impossibility:

> When testimony seems to be secure and thus becomes a theoretically provable truth, when it, in the moment that it takes place, solidifies as information or fact, as a process of proof, i.e. as a firm conviction, it runs the risk of losing its value, its meaning or its status as testimony. But this is to say—and this is always the same paradox, always the same paradoxopoetic matrix—that from the same moment in which it is secured as theoretical proof, testimony is no longer secure *as*

> testimony. In order to be secure as testimony, testimony cannot and may not be considered to be absolutely secure, as absolutely certain and reliable in the orders of a knowledge of it as such.[26]

Testimony emerges from a promise or a pledge, from an "I assure that I was or am mentally present at this or that event and you must believe me because I have obligated myself to tell you the truth. Believe me, you have to believe me." Bearing witness can therefore be designated a performative; it belongs to a performative-pragmatic order and not a theoretical-constative one. Witness and addressee do not have or no longer have direct access to the object of testimony, which is why the performative act of testimony must answer to the performative act of "I believe you." By speaking of a one-off and irreplaceable experience, the witness invokes an untranslatability. On the other hand, if this were a given in the strict sense of the word, the witness could no longer bear witness. Thus we again find the structure of *iterability*, inherent in speaking. In order to appear *as* a one-off, the one-off must come to light in a translatable or, more generally speaking, repeatable way. In particular Derrida underlines the set of problems that arise from the exigency of the "as," or rather from the "as such." From this he educes that with which he precedes his deliberations: that "each responsible testimony" includes "a poetic experience of language." This poetic experience seems to constitute itself in the fact that testimony as event must establish its own poetics, that, resembling a poem, it must appear as "a poetical," as a "singular act which refers to a singular event and is linked to language by an inimitable, that is to say inventive connection."[27] If testimony is bound to an appearance, by the same token it must not be allowed to submerge itself within the appearance, within the discourse of bearing witness. Witnessing can occur in ways other than the purely discursive—via the body, an indentation. But having said that, it cannot occur entirely without discourse. Opening the order of the "as such" does not mean that it must appear "as exactly this," as a witness bearing testimony. Paradox: the necessary act of *bearing witness to* is not necessarily bound to *something* being attested to. This means there is a kind of testifying that is, in its core, a lie or perjury but that is nevertheless testifying. It seems to me that one could conceive of this purely logically deduced deconstitution of testimony as a renouncing within the utterance process, afformatively accommodating and at the same time deforming and enfeebling the "performative." The spectator as witness relinquishes himself in this sense and his relinquishing is, beyond all verisimilitude, that which lingers as the remainder of the fleeting event of encounter in the theater arena. Summarized in a different way: the spectator as witness is simultaneously the guarantor of truth and the representative of its incompleteness, its withdrawal.

If, on the one hand, the foundations of our contemporary theater discourse—for example, the obdurately repeated talk of the supposed copresence of actors and spectators that sets theater apart from film, television, and other reproductive media—are eroded to this extent, the ascertainment of the spectator as witness will, on the other hand, constitute his irreplaceability in a new way. Irreplaceable is he who bears witness. This activity, signaled by testimony or oath, is necessarily discursive; this means that it is the concomitance of singularity and repetition, inasmuch that it must, accommodating its singularity, let itself be repeated in order to be able to be addressed at an other and a future. Bound to discourse, the witness cannot be replaced by technology, such as a video or film camera. As Derrida points out elsewhere, these yield a kind of proof that needs to be interpreted. Using this kind of technology, the facts can only allude tautologically to their own existence, are assembled together as a narrative and drawn toward fiction.[28] From the trace to its presentation an activity is required that must be misappropriated where the talk is of authenticity or the immediacy of the event in its recording. In contrast, it needs to be emphasized, the irreplaceable quality of the testimony is nothing more than the incomprehensible trace of an irreducibly elapsed presence, which simultaneously perpetuates and betrays the testimony.

## Some Conclusions

If, based on the reflections outlined here, a theory of the audience has proved to be more or less impossible, we would still have to cling to the utopian potential described in a notion of performance that does not develop from the stage but rather between the stage and the auditorium. This potential cannot, however, be separated from the utopian societal ideas out of which it arises. If one asserts the suspension of the separation of actors and spectators, as Brecht does in his vision of a coming society (in his "learning plays," *Lehrstücke*), without this coming society already being present it quickly reverts to an ideology that is represented in other domains with sentences like "We're all in the same boat"—sentences that suppress the fact that in every boat there is a captain, an engineer, and perhaps also idle guests who travel along, sailors with differing amounts of capital, varying levels of power, and dissonant interests. What remains today of the utopia of mutually produced performance is, in this way, not so much its actual upholding as a shift in theatrical codes and institutions under the aegis of an assertion of another kind of playing with different structures. In many cases the alteration of codes has helped bring interests to light that were hitherto unheard of and unseen on stages. For example, older and newer works from the field of performance art—such as works by René Pollesch, Laurent Chétouane, and Wanda Golonka and by groups such as Vivarium Studio, Rimini Protokoll, and Nature Theater of Oklahoma—question the supposedly merely technical preconditions of traditional stage practice: the dialogue between characters, the role, the division of theater buildings into parts to be played upon and others not to be played upon, the arrangement of players and spectators within the space, or the traditional play with illusion.[29] In their works it becomes apparent that a sovereign male heterosexual subject or individual has been at the center of traditional theater as well as at the center of Western theory. By using different modes of speaking, of understanding one's role on stage, of interaction between players and spectators, and by creating a new understanding of the space, they have exposed the dispositif of traditional theater in theater and have made it recognizable as a historical dispositif based on the marginalization of the woman, of the nonacting other, of the effeminate man, of non-sense, and, more generally, based on a logic of opposition that is also characteristic of the strict division of players and spectators in the theater and theory of the eighteenth century. Paradoxically enough, traditional theater had to forget precisely these preconditions of a shared language, a shared space, a shared time, and a shared "walking under the unthinkable" that theater stands for in the most radical theater theories of modernity.[30] On the other hand, with the name *performance*—in the sense of *performance art*—as well as with the various collective nouns that have arranged this new heterogeneity on the stage, a reversal has often taken place that turns outbreaks out of the old order into a new order, establishing a new ideology. Today such a new ideology can often be found where one encounters so-called immersive theater or theater practices dedicated to enabling a "collective experience" or "collaboration," which in fact turn out to be another version of neoliberal structures, comparable with the so-called web society or social networks: the players enjoy a freedom that is given within the framework of more or less hidden orders, which, not least, include the obscuration of these orders. Thus the current reality of the proposition of an emancipated audience lies in its utopian potential to turn against ideologies of performance,[31] as well as against every other institutionalized form of theater. As an unrepresentable audience the unrepresentable community of spectators and listeners, each singular and always different, points to a coming theater, the possibility of which inaugurates a contemporary theory only where this theory defies theater's false presentations.

It remains to make one last observation. Schechner's concept of performance allows the performance to end when the last spectator has left the theater. But is this really the end? When does theater end, and when does it begin? If a more precise inspection of that which constitutes a spectator leads to the detachment of the notion, in which A plays B while C looks on, from the physically present spectator who is as such addressable only in a mediated manner and, reversed, the detachment of his perception—inasmuch as that perception's turn to witness testimony is irreducibly separated from what is testified by way of a temporal and spatial divide—from its putative presence or sensory certainty, then the result is, if nothing else, the unsettling of the certainty of the ending of the performance. Would a stipulation of performance by way of the spectator not ultimately lead us to a conception of that which pertains to performance as being something essentially illimitable? This modification would by all means allow us to conceive of an experience supposedly familiar to every spectator as a component of the theater, an experience of the fact that we are capable of formulating what we have seen in words only later, weeks or years later, and sometimes, comparable with one of the primeval scenes of psychoanalysis, only once it has repeated itself in a different way, in a different place, and at a different time. I began with an end that was in fact a beginning. In this way these reflections on the ending of the theater—which is sometimes just the beginning—offer an opportunity to conclude.

**Translated by Lydia White**

## Notes

1. Ivana Müller, *Playing Ensemble Again and Again*. I am referring to the staging of May 23, 2009.
2. Cf. Erika Fischer-Lichte, *Die Entdeckung des Zuschauers: Paradigmenwechsel auf dem Theater des 20. Jahrhunderts* (Tübingen: Francke, 1997).
3. Cf. Richard Schechner, *Performance Theory*, 2nd ed. (London: Routledge, 1988), 70.
4. Cf. Christopher Balme and Klaus Lazarowicz, *Texte zur Theorie des Theaters* (Stuttgart: Reclam, 1991), 391.
5. For a critique of the audience see Søren Kierkegaard, *Eine literarische Anzeige* (A Literary Review) (Gütersloh: Gütersloher Taschenbücher Siebenstern, 1983), esp. 93ff. It is upon this treatise that Heidegger later founds his examination of the word *man* in *Being and Time* and Benjamin his examination of the bourgeois public sphere in his theories of the theater and the media of his time. Cf. Müller-Schöll, "Theatrokratia," in *Das Theater des "konstruktiven Defaitismus": Lektüren zur Theorie eines Theaters der A-Identität bei Walter Benjamin, Bertolt Brecht und Heiner Müller* (Frankfurt am Main: Stroemfeld, 2002), 19–44.
6. Hans-Thies Lehmann, "Vom Zuschauer," in *Paradoxien des Zuschauens: Die Rolle des Publikums im zeitgenössischen Theater*, ed. Jan Deck and Angelika Sieburg (Bielefeld: transcript, 2008), 26.
7. Wilmar Sauter, "Publikum," in *Metzler Lexikon Theatertheorie*, ed. Erika Fischer-Lichte, Doris Kolesch, and Matthias Warstat (Stuttgart: Metzler 2005), 253. The addition in brackets is by Müller-Schöll.
8. On the question of humanity to be discussed in this context, see Martin Heidegger, *Die Grundbegriffe der Metaphysik: Welt—Endlichkeit—Einsamkeit*, 2nd ed. (Frankfurt am Main: Vittorio Klostermann, 1992); Jacques Derrida, "'Eating Well,' or the Calculation of the Subject: An Interview with Jacques Derrida," in *Who Comes after the Subject?*, ed. Eduardo Cadava and Jean-Luc Nancy (London: Routledge, 1991), 96–119.
9. Some of the theoretical approaches that I don't discuss in detail are collected by Florian Malzacher, "There Is a Word for People Like You: Audience," in Deck and Sieburg, *Paradoxien des Zuschauens*, 43–54. However, during discussions of

the approaches he assembles, he arrives at appraisals with which I cannot affiliate myself.

10. Cf. Jacques Rancière, *Le spéctateur émancipé* (Paris: La Fabrique éditions, 2008), 7–29.

11. See, in detail, Nikolaus Müller-Schöll, "Im Zeichen der Teilung: Wanda Golonkas *An Antigone* und Lars von Triers *Dogville*," in *OB?SCENE: Zur Präsenz der Absenz im zeitgenössischen Tanz, Theater und Film*, ed. Krassimira Kruschkova (Wien: Böhlau, 2005), 143–61, esp. 151–60.

12. Cf. Joachim Gerstmeier and Nikolaus Müller-Schöll, eds., *Politik der Vorstellung* (Berlin: Theater der Zeit, 2006).

13. Cf. Walter Benjamin, "The Task of the Translator," in *Illuminations*, trans. Harry Zohn (New York: Viking, 1968), 69; Christiaan Hart Nibbrig, *Übersetzen: Walter Benjamin* (Frankfurt: Suhrkamp, 2001); Alfred Hirsch, *Übersetzung und Dekonstruktion* (Frankfurt: Suhrkamp, 1997).

14. Benjamin, "The Task of the Translator," 70.

15. By using the term *alteration* I mean to hint at what Derrida calls *différance*: see Jacques Derrida, "Différance," in *Margins of Philosophy* (Chicago: University of Chicago Press, 1982), 1–28.

16. On the notion of translatability, see Jacques Derrida, "Des Tours de Babel," in *Difference in Translation*, ed. J. F. Graham (Ithaca, N.Y.: Cornell University Press, 1985), 180; Rodolphe Gasché, "Saturnine Vision and the Question of Difference: Reflections on Walter Benjamin's Theory of Language," in *Benjamin's Ground: New Readings of Walter Benjamin*, ed. Rainer Nägele (Detroit: Wayne State University Press, 1988), 92; Müller-Schöll, *Das Theater des "konstruktiven Defaitismus,"* 152–57; Samuel Weber, *Benjamin's -abilities* (Cambridge, Mass.: Harvard University Press, 2008).

17. Cf. Benjamin, "The Task of the Translator," 70.

18. See Paul de Man, *Allegories of Reading: Figural Language in Rousseau, Nietzsche, Rilke and Proust* (New Haven, Conn.: Yale University Press, 1979); Paul de Man, *The Rhetoric of Romanticism* (New York: Columbia University Press, 1984); Werner Hamacher, "Unlesbarkeit," in *Allegorien des Lesens* (Frankfurt am Main: Suhrkamp, 1979); Lindsay Waters and Wlad Godzich, eds., *Reading de Man Reading* (Minneapolis: University of Minnesota Press, 1989); Carol Jacobs, "Kleists *Style*," in *Kleist lesen*, ed. Marianne Schuller and Nikolaus Müller-Schöll (Bielefeld: transcript, 2003), 11–37; J. Hillis Miller, "Gesetzgebung in der Literatur: Das Beispiel Kleists," in Schuller and Müller-Schöll, *Kleist lesen*, 181–208; Samuel Weber, *Institution and Interpretation* (Minneapolis: University of Minnesota, 1987).

19. For more details on this problem, which can only be hinted at here, see Werner Hamacher, *Entferntes Verstehen* (Frankfurt am Main: Suhrkamp, 1998).

20. Cf. Walter Benjamin, "On the Concept of History," in *Illuminations*, 262; see also an analogous note in the epistemological convolute N of the unfinished "Arcades Project" in Benjamin, *Gesammelte Schriften*, ed. Rolf Tiedemann and Hermann Schweppenhäuser (Frankfurt am Main: Suhrkamp, 1974–91), 5: 595.

21. For the concept of the trace, see Jacques Derrida, "Freud und der Schauplatz der Schrift," in *Die Schrift und die Differenz*, 4th ed. (Frankfurt am Main: Suhrkamp, 1989), 302–50. See also Emmanuel Levinas, *Die Spur des Anderen: Untersuchungen zur Phänomenologie und Sozialphilosophie*

(FreiburgAlber,1983); Emmanuel Levinas, "Vom Sein zum Anderen—Paul Celan," in *Eigennamen: Meditationen über Sprache und Literatur* (Munich: Hanser, 1988), 56–66. In relation to this see also Emmanuel Levinas, *Antlitz und erste Gewalt: Ein Gespräch mit Hans-Joachim Lenger über Phänomenologie und Ethik*, in *Lévinas Ethik im Kontext,* ed. Christian Kupke (Berlin: Parodos, 2005), 11-24.

22. See Bertolt Brecht, *Arbeitsjournal* (Frankfurt am Main: Suhrkamp, 1974), 2: 472, translated here by Lydia White.

23. Jean-François Lyotard, *Le Différend* (Paris: Minuit, 1983).

24. See Giorgio Agamben, *Ce qui rest d'Auschwitz* (Paris: Rivages, 1999), 103–6.

25. See Jacques Derrida, "A Self-Unsealing Poetic Text: Zur Poetik und Politik des Zeugnisses," in *Zur Lyrik Paul Celans*, ed. Peter Buhrmann (Copenhagen: Text und Kontext, 2000), 158.

26. Derrida, "A Self-Unsealing Poetic Text," 169, 150.

27. Derrida, "A Self-Unsealing Poetic Text," 150.

28. See Jacques Derrida und Bernard Stiegler, *Echographies de la télévision: Entretiens filmés* (Paris: Galilée, 1996), 52.

29. See Nikolaus Müller-Schöll, "Theater of Potentiality: Communicability and the Political in Contemporary Practice," *Theatre Research International* 29.1 (2013): 1–15; Nikolaus Müller-Schöll, "De la rébellion contre l'institution au théâtre, hors de soi: Le *freies Theater* depuis 2000," in *Mises en scène d'Allemagne(s)*, ed. Didier Plassard (Paris: CNRS Éditions, 2013), 104–19; Nikolaus Müller-Schöll, "Poverty of Experience: Performance Practices after the Fall," in *The Idea of the Avant-Garde*, ed. Marc James Leger (Manchester, U.K.: Manchester University Press, 2014), 75–79.

30. Cf. Nikolaus Müller-Schöll, "Brecht, Hölderlin und der Einbruch des Realen," in *Orte des Unermesslichen: Theater nach der Geschichtsteleologie*, ed. Marita Tatari (Zürich: Diaphanes, 2014), 109–24; Nikolaus Müller-Schöll, "'Unter Undenkbarem wandelnd . . .': *Ödipus von Sophokles nach Hölderlin von Müller* im Raum von Mark Lammert inszeniert von Dimiter Gotscheff am Hamburger Thalia-Theater," in *Ödipus, Tyrann*, ed. Ortrud Gutjahr (Würzburg: Königshausen & Neumann, 2010), 165–178.

31. For an examination of this ideology, see Nikolaus Müller-Schöll, "Nonperformatif et medium partagé: William Forsythe, Wanda Golonka," *Théâtre/Public* (December 2008), 68–70.

Chapter 4

# Signal and Mandatary in Benjamin's "The Destructive Character"

Astrid Deuber-Mankowsky

## A Kind of Portrait Sketch, a Kind of Happiness (*Glück*)

On October 28, 1931, Walter Benjamin wrote from Berlin to Gershom Scholem in Jerusalem that for a year his "closest contact" had been with a young man by the name of Gustav Glück. (*Glück* means "happiness.") At the time Glück was the director of the foreign division of the State Credit Society (Reichskreditgesellschaft); Scholem would find a "kind of portrait sketch of him—to be taken *cum grano salis*—in 'The Destructive Character,' " which Benjamin had already sent to Scholem.[1] *Cum grano salis*: with a pinch of salt—that is, with judgment, not precisely literally, with an addition, a supplement.

The short text appeared a month later in the feuilleton of the *Frankfurter Rundschau*. It is only one and a half pages in length, but all the same this text seems to cause a certain discomfort. Scholars tend to avoid it. Already the title of the text, "The Destructive Character," which was published two years before Hitler came to power, seems to push it into dangerous proximity to extreme political positions, an anarchistic futuristic or, even worse, right-wing and fascistic position. Or one could suppose a proximity to the contemporary postrevolutionary belief in "the new man," *den neuen Menschen*, in the young Soviet Union.

But there is something different going on. The text needs to be understood as an intervention against a certain concept of the teleological and apocalyptic and at the same time against a Marxist promise of salvation. It questions a concept of history that is itself in a deep sense ahistorical and incongruent with the essence of time itself. It is a critique Benjamin formulates with regard to, for example, dialectical materialism. This was a point at issue in his discussions with Bertolt Brecht. What Benjamin is exploring in this short text, which is in fact embedded in further philosophical considerations on the ongoing changes of the conditions of humanity—caused as well by the upcoming technologies and mass media as well as by the appearance of the masses—is nothing less than an understanding of how change has to be understood in a situation in which tradition is not guaranteed anymore. Far from gnostic political theories, for example that of Carl Schmitt, which was developed as a remedy for the contemporary chaos, Benjamin tries to develop a positive approach to the concept of change and transience as a moment of time and temporality itself. For Benjamin redemption is neither liberation from materiality and the flesh nor a leap out of time into immortality. It resonates with a happiness that, as he will put it in "Theses on the Philosophy of History," "is thoroughly colored the time to which the course of our own existence has assigned us."[2] This convergence of happiness and temporality is what already linked the name of his friend Gustav Glück (Happiness) with the experience that is thought through in "The Destructive Character." The text is "a kind of portrait sketch of the friend," a taking stock of the situation of the author, and thereby a taking stock of the current condition. Furthermore Benjamin takes his personal experience as a point of departure for a reflection on the nature of time itself.

In 1931 conditions were characterized by a further intensification of the economic and political crisis. As he wrote to Scholem in July 1931, Benjamin saw civil war on the horizon, and at the beginning of October he soberly predicted the victory of the National Socialists; the communists had not found the necessary contact with the masses and the "possibility of revolutionary action."[3] The report he gives to Scholem is just as succinct as it is accurate: "The economic order of Germany provides as firm a footing as the high seas and emergency decrees collide with each other like the crests of waves. Unemployment is about to make revolutionary programs just as obsolete as economic and political programs already are. To all appearances the National Socialists have actually been delegated to represent the unemployed masses here."[4]

In this time of political and economic intensification, Benjamin's thinking went through what he described four years later as a "process of total cataclysm": "The mass of images and thoughts originating in the distant past—when my thinking was purely metaphysical, even theological—had to undergo [this process] so that they could nourish my current disposition with all the force they contained."[5]

The hymn Benjamin sings to the destructive character in his short text is also an indication of the tensions that accompanied this "total cataclysm"—that is, the revolution of the mass of images and thoughts originating in theological thinking—and rendered its actualization possible. Without letting go, without forgetting, no change is possible. Destruction is thus revealed as an aspect of time itself, as a condition of living and a condition of history.

Unlike the creator, the destroyer, Benjamin writes in "The Destructive Character," is young and cheerful, always blithely at work. "Destroying rejuvenates,"[6] he asserts, alluding to Nietzsche's apologia for forgetting. As Nietzsche puts it in his famous second *Untimely Meditation*, "On the Uses and Disadvantages of History for Life," "Man must possess and from time to time employ the strength to break up and dissolve a past in order to live."[7] Destroying, as Benjamin puts it, "cheers, because everything cleared away means to the destroyer a complete reduction, indeed a rooting out, of his own condition." Benjamin names this destroyer "Apollonian." Its harmony comes from insight into the necessary fateful destruction (*Vergängnis*) of the world, from which it follows that the world must be examined for its worthiness to be destroyed. For the destructive character it constitutes "the great bond embracing and unifying all that exists."[8]

The destructive character wishes to leave no trace; indeed—as Benjamin intensifies the point by citing Brecht's 1926–27 *Reader for City-Dwellers* conceived of "for gramophone records [*Schallplatten*]"—he "obliterates even the traces of destruction"; he is not interested in being understood; he does not seek comfort, is without "casing [*Gehäuse*]"; he is the enemy of the "étui-man" and knows only one watchword: "make room."[9] The destructive character initially appears as a counterpoint to the collector, his life a counterpoint to that bourgeois style of life that is oriented toward possession, preservation, security, and duration, which Benjamin had so vividly depicted in his recollections of childhood, *Berlin Childhood around 1900*. The first sketches of these recollections originated only a half year after the publication of "The Destructive Character" and were written while he was residing in Ibiza April through July 1932. A countersketch, in the end, to the West Berlin life of a bourgeois intellectual that Benjamin, himself a passionate collector, had led until 1929.[10] On April 17 he wrote to Scholem about that life, "The most advanced civilization and the most 'modern' culture not only are part of my private comforts but are also in fact the means of my production. That is, it is not within my power to relocate my productive base to Berlin east or north. (I would be able to emigrate to Berlin E. or N., but only to do something different from what I do here.)"[11] In this passage Benjamin plays on his relation to the left and, in particular, to the Communist Party. Berlin East and Berlin North were the workers' sections of the city. He tries to convey to his friend in Jerusalem that he makes his life—a life anchored in the nineteenth-century bourgeoisie—along with the knowledge and the memory of his generation, into the medium of writing that knows its debt to "materialism," but he does not want to give up or renounce this life and its history precisely because they are part of his "means of production."

What interests him is not to find a new, communist promise of salvation but to pinpoint the historical node where the bourgeois world in which he was born perishes and another world—characterized by mass movements, technical media, and economic and political crises—takes its place. The tensions that result from this attempt to bridge two eras and a class divide by employing his own life as a medium of literary production determine the short essay on the destructive character. The first sentence is "It could happen to someone looking back over his life that he realized that almost all the deeper obligations he had endured in its course originated in people who everyone agreed had the traits of a 'destructive character.'"[12]

Someone who looks back on his life usually has a reason for it. Often this reason is not pleasant (*glücklich*). It is recorded that Benjamin was occupied with thoughts of suicide from the summer of 1931 to his fortieth birthday, in July 1932.[13] In the corresponding diary entries he gives exhaustion as a reason for concentrating on the past rather than the future, "on the assumption that what lies ahead of me is not worth making much of a fuss about." He was tired of the struggle for money, tired of "aspects of [his] personal life"—his divorce from Dora Kellner-Benjamin had occurred a year prior and had left him homeless and without financial resources—tired and dissatisfied with the "methods" that he saw people of his "situation" and his "kind" choosing "to assert control over the hopeless situation of cultural politics."[14]

In the essay's opening sentence it is a "shock" that interrupts the one absorbed in looking back on his life and returns him to the present. Shock arises with the recognition, "perhaps by chance," that "almost all the deeper obligations he had endured" came from people "who everyone agreed had the traits of a 'destructive character.'" What triggers the shock? Proximity to people whose destructive character everyone agreed on? Or the recognition that the destructive character acts in the service of history and life, and thus the new or revaluation of the destroyer that accompanies this recognition? Benjamin writes that the stronger the shock, "the better [the] chances of representing the destructive character."[15] The combination of shock and recognition recalls the function of the retarding interruption of the dramatic action in epic theater, with which Benjamin was intensively occupied at the time. In his letter to Scholem on July 20, 1931, he writes that Brecht's *Versuche* (*Essays*) were the only "poetic or literary essays" that he championed as a critic "without 'public' reservations." He gives as a reason that a part of his development came about in confrontation with these writings because they, "more rigorously than any others, give an insight into the intellectual context in which the work of people like myself is conducted in this country."[16]

Samuel Weber has pointed out that the effect of amazement that is triggered in the audience by the interruptions of dramatic action according to Benjamin's portrayal of epic theater is designated as shock in his later texts.[17] In "Little History of Photography"—which appeared in three installments of the *Literary World* in September 1931, only a few weeks prior to the publication of "The Destructive Character"—Benjamin also designates the effect of the ever decreasing size of the camera with its always decreasing exposure time as shock; the camera is ever readier to "capture fleeting and secret images." Taking up the study of epic theater composed in early 1931, Benjamin writes that one must confront this effect with the becoming-writing of photography in order to grasp it through the "literarization of the conditions of life."[18] Furthermore shock—along with moments of fleetingness and repeatability, of proximity and being-in-movement—is a component of the mass perception that Benjamin claims (*reklamiert*) for the age of technological reproducibility.

In epic theater—whose forms, for Benjamin, correspond to the "new technological forms, cinema as well as radio"—the multiple interruptions of the action lead to a multiplicity of proffered gestures, which thereby transform the audience, according to Benjamin, into amazed (*staunende*) spectators who become interested in discovering the conditions in which they live—or, put better, which do *not* let them live—in order to change them. It must be emphasized here that Benjamin does not secure any sort of automatism, but he conceives of these gestures in opposition to the "rule of the masses grounded in reflexes and sensations." Initiation into a form of perception whose measure would be the "organization of the hearing-masses," as well as initiation into the "position [*Stellungnahme*] of responsible collectives"—instead of a form of perception merely having "an effect on individuals' nerves"[19]—would, for Benjamin, be the sole political means to counteract a development culminating in the National Socialists' becoming the "de facto" (as Benjamin wrote to Scholem) delegates of the masses of the unemployed.

If the representation of the destructive character proceeds in a manner "gesturally" similar to that of epic theater, then it is evident that the destructive character *represented* is not the same as the one with whom Benjamin begins his characterization at the start of the text. Representing, for Benjamin, is not expressing but, as he notes in a diary entry from the same time, "a making real, a process that subjects thought to the profoundest modifications—much as running toward a goal is not just the expression of a wish to reach it, but a making real, a process that likewise subjects the wish to profound modification."[20]

The representation places the destructive character—his conduct and action, his cheerfulness, his selflessness, composure, and destruction—in relation to the "tensions of the political and social environment," which, Benjamin writes to Scholem on July 31, 1931, "no one, least of all a writer, can ignore in his work."[21] In this regard the portrait of Gustav Glück, like gestures in epic theater, may serve as initial material, but it is in no way the result. For, as Benjamin already concluded in his 1919 manuscript "Fate and Character," character, like fate, "can be apprehended only through signs, not in itself."[22] In accordance with this earlier conclusion, the representation of the destructive character is accompanied by its methodological literarization.

The destructive character—regarding whom, as Benjamin writes, everyone agreed—becomes, in his representation, an arrangement of signs; he thus functions as a "signal."[23] Therefore, as Benjamin writes in reference to the opening sentences, just as the "triangulation sign [*trigonometrisches Zeichen*] is exposed on all sides to the wind, so he [the destructive character] is exposed to idle talk." Unlike the creator who seeks solitude and needs distance, "the destroyer must be constantly surrounded by people, witnesses to his efficacy."[24] He seeks proximity, and the fact that he thus becomes an object of gossip is unavoidable. The destructive character does not place any value in being understood. Rather he demands misunderstanding, as Benjamin puts it in a subtle comparison, much like oracles, which he also designates as "destructive institutions of the state."[25]

Interruption, mortification, making still, holding in, placing a caesura—all these concepts that Benjamin had introduced earlier, in *Elective Affinities*, the book on German tragic drama (*Trauerspiel*), and so on—to place aesthetics, cognition, and critique in a new relationship, also determine the representation and reappraisal of the destructive character. Benjamin takes up the concepts of shock and gesture in order to redetermine the relation of aesthetics, cognition, and critique under the conditions of the aesthetic forms of epic theater that correspond, according to him, to the new technical forms of radio and cinema.[26] The destructive character is manifestly devastating, but he is not annihilating. As Benjamin explains in "Little History of Photography" concerning the perception of the masses under conditions of technical reproduction, the destructive character is always in motion. He knows no distance and no calm (*Ruhe*) and converts singularity into fleetingness and repetition.

As Benjamin emphasizes once more, the destructive character sees nothing permanent, but he sees "ways" everywhere: "Where others encounter walls or mountains, there, too, he sees a way. . . . But because he sees a way everywhere, he has to clear things from it everywhere."[27] What the destructive character therefore creates are ways (*Wege*). Ways of thought (*Denkwege*). Ways of transmission. Ways out.

The representation of the destructive character—just as Benjamin writes in his text on epic theater—accentuates not what is to come but the "incommensurable, singular." Whoever writes for epic theater represents the attitude (*Haltung*), as Benjamin equivocally formulates it, that "it can happen this way, but it can also come about in an entirely different manner."[28] Like the destructive character, who therefore "always stands at a crossroads," the writer of epic theater sees ways everywhere.

As Weber has shown, the gestural decomposition of the progression of action and of the story holds the future open by refusing utopian designs and concentrating on the here and now. It is anti-eschatological and anti-apocalyptic. The place of this open future—one that cannot be reduced to a present that is still to come—can thus be nowhere other than here and now, in this instant (*Augenblick*), in this moment, in this being-there (*Dasein*).[29] It is a kind of happiness (*Glück*), as Benjamin defines it in the early manuscript "Fate and Character": happiness is "what releases the fortunate man from the embroilment of the Fates and from the net of his own fate," what releases him from his past; happiness is what makes it possible to conceive of a "path of liberation" out of an order that is constituted by the concepts of misfortune and guilt.[30] Once again one recalls Nietzsche's emphasis on the healing effect of forgetting and his description of happiness: "He who cannot ensconce himself on the threshold of the moment [*Augenblick*] and forget all the past, who cannot stand balanced like a goddess of victory without growing dizzy and afraid, will never know what happiness is—worse, he will never do anything that will make others happy."[31]

## The Mandatary

Who was Gustav Glück, whose name means "happiness"? In what sense is "The Destructive Character" a "kind of portrait sketch if him"?[32] We know little of him from Benjamin. There does not exist a single letter from or to him.[33]

Gustav Glück was born in Vienna in 1902 and was thus ten years younger than Benjamin. He came from an assimilated, educated, haut-bourgeois Vienna family that had converted to Protestantism. His father was a well-known art historian and museum director; until 1931 he led the painting gallery of the Kunsthistorisches Museum in Vienna. In 1938 he emigrated with his wife first to London and then to the United States. Gustav's elder brother, Franz Glück, was also an art historian and a famous collector and, after the war, director of the Historical Museum of the City of Vienna. Franz stayed with his wife and children in Vienna during the war and survived. Gustav's sister was an actress and moved in theatrical circles; she emigrated to London.

After finishing his schooling in the early 1920s Gustav left Vienna for an apprenticeship in a bank in New York. In 1926 he returned to Europe via Paris, where he met Franz Hessel, and lived for the next few years not in Vienna but in Berlin. There, due to his professional competence as well as his cosmopolitanism and linguistic proficiency, he was able to achieve an enviable career quickly: in 1928, at the age of twenty-six, he became the director of the foreign affairs division of the Reichskreditgesellschaft in Berlin. An inscription in Benjamin's book on German tragic drama, dating from this time, reads as follows: "This dedication Saint Gustav Glück / Your harborage on this page / October 1928 Walter Benjamin."[34] Glück was amiable, educated, optimistic, cheerful, international, and eloquent. He was friends with Hessel and with Karl Kraus and belonged to Brecht's inner circle.

In the letter to Scholem from July 14, 1931, Benjamin names Glück, in addition to Ernst Bloch, as among those close to him with whom he wished to analyze Scholem's critique of his essay on Kraus and his use of the "materialist method." Glück was "not a writer," Benjamin said, but a "senior banking official," but he knew Kraus and his writing and took an "active part in the genesis of the Kraus essay."[35] As for Benjamin, the conversations with Glück were so important that he dedicated the essay on Kraus to him. Benjamin included Glück, Scholem, Bloch, Egon Wissing, and Ernst Schoen in the will that he composed on July 29, 1932, the date of his planned but unrealized suicide. In 1936 he sent Glück and his brother, Franz, a copy of *German*

*Men and Women*. And—as Scholem conjectured in a letter to Hannah Arendt from December 16, 1945—he left a portion of his unpublished writings with Glück when he emigrated.

In 1933 Glück was hired by an American bank. He traveled often but maintained his residence in Berlin until 1938, when he moved to London to be the director of the European office of Chemical Bank. He emigrated to Argentina in 1942 and was engaged there as a cofounder and secretary of the Comité Austricaco, a federation of bourgeois and communist Austrian émigrés. In 1946 Glück returned to England and, in 1947, to Vienna, where he was the director of the Austrian Länderbank before finally moving to Frankfurt am Main as a member of the board of directors of Dresdner Bank, where he was associated with the circle at the Institute for Social Research.

Glück's father and brother were passionate and well-known collectors. In 1982 the Glück library, Franz's collection, comprising more than twenty thousand volumes, was acquired by the German Literary Archive in Marburg. Gustav dealt with his inheritance differently; he was neither a collector nor a "creator." The few letters that Benjamin exchanged with Franz—using Gustav as an intermediary—concerned book collecting. With this background in mind, one sees the profundity of Benjamin's contention that the destructive character is a "kind of portrait sketch" of Gustav Glück. The man ten years his junior not only provided a link to Brecht's circle of friends; he himself came from an haut-bourgeois family and arranged contact for Benjamin with his brother, the collector and dealer.

The destructive character is a "mandatary," Benjamin wrote in the notes for his essay, for he does not destroy for his own sake.[36] A mandatary acts on assignment. Among the actors in epic theater, some appear as "mandataries of greater powers that remain in the background."[37] The destructive character acts as the mandatary of history; for him, what is at stake is that he "does not live for an instant [*Augenblick*] without an historical assignment."[38]

Against this backdrop it is no longer particularly astonishing that the destructive character "stands in the front line of the traditionalists."[39] While some people "pass things down to posterity, by making them untouchable and conserving them," destructive people pass them down "by making them practicable and thus liquidating them." In the notes Benjamin adds, "make them citable." Here, as Burkhardt Lindner correctly observes, the "simple opposition" between the collector and the destructive character begins to dissolve: "We come across a deep complementarity of both figures, because, for Benjamin, handing down does not transmit the untouchable and unchangeable, but that which is produced anew by every generation."[40] Thus the collector is also concerned with a renewal, though a renewal of what is past: "To renew the old world—this is the deepest drive in the collector's wish to acquire new things."[41] This sentence occurs in a "A Talk about Collecting," which Benjamin wrote under the title "Unpacking My Library" and which appeared in the July 1931 edition of the *Literary World*.

## Mass Movements, Shattering of Tradition

The conditions of the time, as Benjamin would summarize it four years later in Paris in "The Work of Art in the Age of Its Technological Reproducibility," were determined by a "violent shattering of tradition." For Benjamin they represent the reverse side of what he designates as the "present crisis and renewal of humanity." All three—the shattering of tradition, crisis, and renewal—stand in the "closest relation to the mass movements of our day" and thus, at the same time, to the media of the masses: film, radio, mass media, the big city.[42] Precisely those media that Benjamin so lucidly interpreted and placed in their political, social, and aesthetic context.

As Weber points out, Benjamin was not born a media specialist and did not study media techniques. He was concerned with questions of philosophy, aesthetics, literature, and art. And even if his relationship to academic and institutional knowledge remained problematic, he would not have been able to describe the radical singularity of the new media of the twentieth century if he had not been so well acquainted with the history of philosophy and aesthetics. For a break to be radical, as Weber argues, there must exist a differentiated relationship to that from which one departs.[43] Benjamin's virtuosity in the interpretation of the aesthetics and politics of mass media required, according to Weber, a distinguished understanding of old media.

Benjamin was conscious of this and consciously called upon his recollections of his Berlin childhood and his connection with the culture of the nineteenth century in order to register and describe the changes in the twentieth century with even greater seismographic precision. The tensions growing from this are nowhere clearer than in the concept of the aura and in the thesis of its historical decay or, perhaps, of its necessary ruination.[44]

With the aura Benjamin takes up a concept that he had already developed in 1931 in "Little History of Photography" to designate the medium of a form of perception destined to disappear. That same year he wrote "The Destructive Character." In the same letter to Scholem in which he describes "The Destructive Character" as a "kind of portrait sketch" of Glück, he writes that "Little History of Photography" has arisen as "prolegomena and paralipomena" for the Arcades Project. This was the project Benjamin had been pursuing since 1927 to describe the phantasmagorias of and write the prehistory of the nineteenth century. In the same letter he indicates that he is judging a sound-film competition for which he has to read and evaluate approximately 120 sketches every week.[45]

This temporal span, from the first arcades and photographs at the beginning of the nineteenth century, from which Benjamin developed his concept of the aura, to the origination of sound film proper at the beginning of the 1930s, designates the temporal space that is treated in the image of the destructive character. Benjamin introduced the aura as the medium that lends to the gaze of people in portrait photographs up to around 1850 "fullness and security . . . even as it penetrated that medium."[46] In a second attempt, in the essay on the work of art and in "On Some Motifs in Baudelaire," he formulated the definition that was to become famous.[47] This definition of aura was connected to his assertion that the photographs of the French photographer Eugène Atget, who had primarily recorded city views of Paris bereft of people, sucked "the aura out of reality like water from a sinking ship."[48] If the childhood photograph of Kafka, in which the child in his "shoreless [*uferlos*] sadness" threatens to drown in the midst of the props that surround him, is the occasion for the introduction of the aura to describe the difference from early photography, the photographs bereft of people appear to be a remedy against this sea of sorrow that distorts the gaze upon the present.

Peter Bürger recalls Habermas's remark that Benjamin was "always ambivalent concerning the loss of aura."[49] What could make this ambivalence more apparent than an image in which aura must be sucked like water from a sinking ship so that the gaze upon reality can once again become possible? If Atget's images, as Benjamin writes, disinfect the dingy, indeed "stifling atmosphere generated by conventional portrait photography in the age of decline," they at the same time allow the "shoreless sadness" Kafka's photograph transmits to the viewer to appear in a new light.

The effect of Atget's images is not only to render the gaze free for the present but also to render the gaze free for the aura itself. For Benjamin the salutary effect of Atget's photographs is that they distance the viewer from his environment and from himself. This distance (*Distanz*) is indeed no longer that remoteness (*Ferne*) from which the people portrayed in early photography appear to gaze at the viewer; it is the effect of a self-alienation that Benjamin calls a "salutary estrangement between man and his surroundings."[50]

From this distance one can recognize that the destruction of the aura that manifests in the "shoreless sadness" of Kafka's childhood photograph has technical *and* social causes: the technical ground is the introduction of faster (*lichtstärkere*) lenses, which drove aura out of photography; the social ground is the "degeneration of the imperialist bourgeoisie,"[51] which drove aura from reality. The confrontation with these social and technical grounds finally allows us to gaze at the aura without distortion. It presents itself to this gaze as "a strange weave of space and time: the unique appearance of distance, no matter how close it may be. While at rest on a summer's noon, to trace a range of mountains on the horizon, or a branch that throws its shadow on the observer, until the moment or the hour takes part in their appearance—that is what it means to breathe the aura of those mountains, that branch."[52] With the decline of aura, the human being is banished from the center of the world. The historical turn that introduces the fall of the auratic age concerns not only the becoming-other of the world but also concerns how the human being appears and positions herself within the world. The famous comparison of the optical unconscious, first discovered by the camera, with the instinctual unconscious, discovered in psychoanalysis, is thus not least an indication of the sickness that technology inflicts upon man by showing him that he is no longer master in his own home.[53]

"Cast off [*abgesprengt*] and godforsaken,"[54] gazes little Franz Kafka, gaze human beings, into the world in late portrait photography. These are the people not seen in Atget's images. With the decline of aura, they have lost their connection to the world.

In "Little History of Photography," Benjamin calls the first people to be reproduced "still untarnished—or, put better, without inscription," members of the emerging bourgeoisie.[55] The person who disappears along with the aura from the center of the image is thus historically situatable. He is the untarnished bourgeois. He could have belonged to the circle of German people whose handwritten letters Benjamin commented upon and, in 1936, sent from Switzerland to National Socialist Germany under the pseudonym Detlev Holz. The twenty-seven letters, appearing for the first time from 1931 to 1932 in the *Frankfurter Zeitung*, originated between 1783 and 1883.

The people in late portrait photography who look "dispersed and godforsaken" into the world are the heirs of the bourgeois epoch; they are those who remain after the world whose center they once occupied has perished.

The portrait is frozen in a pure pose; the situation in the atelier with the requisites of the imperial bourgeoisie—with flash and an artificial twilight produced by retouching and gum printing supposed to replace the aura—is the essence of the empty position in which spirit is no longer present. Benjamin interprets the rigidity of the pose as an expression of the "impotence of that generation in the face of technical progress."[56] This makes clear not only the weight that he places on the penetration of technology for overcoming crippling impotence but also how difficult this overcoming and turning toward the present must be for those who, like Benjamin, are the progeny of that generation.

There is a portrait photograph of Benjamin and his brother, Georg, that unintentionally recalls Kafka's childhood image and Benjamin's description of it. It probably dates from 1902 and shows the children dressed as Tyroleans, with walking sticks in their hands, their gazes directed into the distance outside of the image, in front of the scenery of an Alpine landscape. The lost childhood image of Benjamin which he described in his memoirs, *Berlin Childhood around 1900*, in the piece titled "Mummerehlen," must resemble Kafka's image even more closely:

> Wherever I looked, I saw myself surrounded by folding screens, cushions, and pedestals which craved my image much as the shades of Hades craved the blood of the sacrificial animal. In the end, I was offered up to a crudely painted prospect of the Alps, and my right hand, which had to brandish a kidskin hat, cast its shadow on the clouds and snowfields of the backdrop. But the tortured smile on the lips of the little mountaineer is not as disturbing as the look cast

> down upon me from the child's face, which lies in the shadow of a potted plant.[57]

From the "shoreless sorrow" only the mussel remains as a memory of the water and the sea. It is the counterimage to the scene that is framed by the aura: "I, however, am distorted by similarity to all that surrounds me here. Thus, like a mollusk in its shell, I had my abode in the nineteenth century, which now lies hollow before me like an empty shell. I hold it to my ear."[58] Here Benjamin vividly describes how, with the decline of the world of the nineteenth century, he lost his proverbial home, and at the same time describes how intimately familiar this world, condemned to perish, was to him from his childhood—and how deeply familiar the feeling of melancholy was to it. It almost seems as if the collector, whom Benjamin sees as caught in the process of dying out, repeats this scenario exactly, at least if one shares Benjamin's observation that, for the collector, "ownership is the most intimate relationship that one can have to things. Not that they come alive in him; it is he who lives in them." He concludes his talk on collecting, "Unpacking My Library," with this sentence: "So I have erected before you one of his dwellings, with books the building stones; and now he is going to disappear inside, as is only fitting."[59]

✦

Benjamin's depiction of the destructive character and of the antagonistic imbrication of creation and demolition occurring within it, of collecting and dissolving, renewing and conserving, death and life, corresponds in its foundations to Nietzsche's second *Untimely Meditation* and to the reflections on the relationship of eros and the death drive that Freud revised in his 1932 edition of *New Introductory Lectures on Psychoanalysis*. Benjamin was familiar with and valued the 1920 treatise *Beyond the Pleasure Principle*. Of course he could not have known of the new edition of the lectures at the time of the composition of "The Destructive Character"; however, he would have agreed with Freud's thesis that phenomena of life proceed from the "concurrent and opposing action of these two"—of the erotic drives, which "always seek to combine more and more living substance into ever greater unities," and of the death drives, "which oppose this effort and lead what is living back into an inorganic state."[60]

Insight into the political and social conditions of the time presupposes, for Benjamin, insight into the temporality of existence (*Dasein*)—into the historicity of perception and of technology. For just this reason the writer of epic theater puts an accent on the "incommensurable, singular" and not "on the grand decisions that lie on the vanishing points of expectation."[61] As Weber emphasizes with Benjamin, for the writer of epic theater it is a matter of the here and now.

**Translated by Catherine Diehl**

## Notes

1. Walter Benjamin, *The Correspondence of Walter Benjamin, 1910–1928*, ed. Gershom Scholem and Theodor W. Adorno, trans. Manfred R. Jacobson and Evelyn M. Jacobson (Chicago: University of Chicago Press, 1994) (cited henceforth as Corr.), 386; *Gesammelte Briefe*, ed. Christoph Godde and Henri Lonitz (Frankfurt am Main: Suhrkamp, 1995–2000) (cited henceforth as GB), 4: 62.

2. Walter Benjamin, *Selected Writings*, ed. Michael W. Jennings, Howard Eiland, and Gary Smith (Cambridge, Mass.: Belknap Press, 1996–2003) (cited henceforth as SW), 4: 389; *Gesammelte Schriften*, ed. Rolf Tiedemann and Hermann Schweppenhäuser (Frankfurt am Main: Suhrkamp, 1974–89) (cited henceforth as GS), 4: 397.

3. Corr., 381; GB 4: 47.

4. Corr., 382; GB 4: 53.

5. Corr., 486; GB 5: 89.

6. SW 2: 541.

7. Friedrich Nietzsche, *Untimely Meditations*, ed. Daniel Breazeale, trans. R. J. Hollingdale (Cambridge, U.K.: Cambridge University Press, 1997), 75; Friedrich Nietzsche, *Unzeitgemäße Betrachtungen* 2, in *Sämtliche Werke: Kritische Studienausgabe*, ed. Giorgio Colli and Mazzino Montinari (Berlin: de Gruyter, 1980), 1: 269.

8. SW 2: 541; GS 4: 397.

9. SW 2: 541–42; GS 4: 396.

10. On Benjamin's position as an intellectual between the fronts, see Irving Wohlfarth, "Der 'destruktive Charakter': Benjamin zwischen den Fronten," in *Links hatte noch alles sich zu enträtseln*, ed. Burkhardt Lindner (Frankfurt am Main: Syndikat, 1978), 65–99.

11. Corr., 377; GB 4: 25.

12. SW 2: 541; GS 4: 396.

13. See Gershom Scholem, *Walter Benjamin: Die Geschichte einer Freundschaft* (Frankfurt am Main: Suhrkamp, 1975), 223–26.

14. Cf. Corr., 355; GB 3: 479–80, 488–91; SW 2: 469; GS 6: 422.

15. SW 2: 541; GS 4: 396.

16. Corr., 380; GB 4: 45.

17. Samuel Weber, *Benjamin's Abilities* (Cambridge, Mass.: Harvard University Press, 2008), 107.

18. SW 2: 527; GS 2: 385.

19. GS 2: 5, 521, 527, 528.

20. SW 2: 471; GS 6: 425.

21. Corr., 380; GB 3: 44.

22. SW 1: 201; GS 2: 172. On the relation between "The Destructive Character" and the earlier "Fate and Character," see also Wohlfarth, "Der 'destruktive Charakter,'" 68.

23. SW 2: 542; GS 4: 397.

24. For the hidden allusions to Karl Kraus and the Kraus essay, see Wohlfarth's elaborations.

25. SW 2: 542; GS 4: 397.

26. Cf. GS 2: 524.

27. SW 2: 542; GS 4: 397.
28. GS 2: 525.
29. Weber, *Benjamin's Abilities*, 105.
30. SW 1: 203; GS 2: 174.
31. Nietzsche, *Untimely Meditations*, 62; Nietzsche, *Kritische Studienausgabe*, 1: 251.
32. Corr., 386.
33. I would like to thank Wolfgang Glück, the son of Franz Glück, who allowed me to read through the letters that Gustav Glück wrote to Franz from 1917 to 1948. They represent an important source for a better understanding of the relations that joined Benjamin and Gustav Glück.
34. Hartmut Wizisla, "'Plaquette für Freunde': Widmungen für die ersten Leser," in *Walter Benjamins "Deutsche Menschen,"* ed. Hartmut Wizisla and Barbara Hahn (Göttingen: Wallstein Verlag, 2008), 45–57, quotation at 49.
35. Corr., 376; GB 4: 23. See Christian Schulte, *Ursprung ist das Ziel: Walter Benjamin über Karl Kraus* (Würzburg: Königshausen & Neumann, 2003), 55. See also GS 2: 1092.
36. GS 4: 999. [In the relevant sense, *mandatary*—translating the German *Mandatar*—means one "to whom a mandate, charge, or commandment is given." Henry C. Black, *A Dictionary of Law* (St. Paul, Minn.: West, 1891).—Translator]
37. GS 2: 525.
38. GS 4: 1000.
39. SW 2: 542; GS 4: 398.
40. Burkhardt Lindner, "Der destruktive Character," in *Benjamin-Handbuch: Leben–Werk–Wirkung*, ed. Burkhardt Lindner (Stuttgart: Metzler, 2006), 452–53, quotation at 453.
41. SW 2: 487; GS 4: 390.
42. SW 3: 104; GS 7: 53.
43. Weber, *Benjamin's Abilities*, 95.
44. Cf. SW 3: 103–4, 105–6; GS 7: 353, 355.
45. Corr., 385; GB 4: 61, 62.
46. SW 2: 516–17; GS 2: 374. Benjamin already mentions the concept of aura in the "Hashish Protocols" in March 1930, though without defining it methodologically. There he writes under the key phrase "statements . . . on the nature of aura": "Everything I said on the subject was directed polemically against the theosophists. . . . First, genuine aura appears in all things, not just in certain kinds of things, as people imagine. Second, the aura undergoes changes, which can be quite fundamental, with every movement the object possessing the aura makes. . . . On the contrary, the characteristic feature of genuine aura is ornament, an ornamental halo, in which the object or being is enclosed as in a case. Perhaps nothing gives such a clear idea of aura as Van Gogh's late paintings, in which one could say that the aura appears to have been painted together with the various objects" (SW 2: 327; GS 6: 588). The concept is already mentioned in the *Elective Affinities* essay (SW 1: 348; GS 1: 192). Beauty cannot appear, Benjamin writes, "in an aura of transparent clarity." Aura is used here in the literal sense of the medium of air that can have varying consistencies, be it transparent or veiled. In this regard "atmospheric degradation" plays an important role in the history of painting, as Benjamin also suggests in the course of his text (SW 2: 514; GS 2: 374).

47. Cf. SW 3: 104–5; GS VII, 355; SW 4: 338; GS 1: 647.
48. SW 2: 518; GS 2: 378.
49. Quoted in Peter Bürger, "Benjamins Kunsttheorie: Möglichkeiten und Grenzen ihrer Aktualisierbarkeit," in *Schrift Bilder Denken: Walter Benjamin und die Künste*, ed. Detlev Schöttker (Frankfurt am Main: Suhrkamp, 2004), 165–85, quotation at 179.
50. SW 2: 519; GS 2: 379.
51. SW 2: 517; GS 2: 377.
52. SW 2: 518–19; GS 2: 378.
53. Cf. SW 2: 511–12; GS 2: 371.
54. SW 2: 515; GS 2: 376.
55. SW 2: 512; GS 2: 372.
56. SW 2: 517; GS 2: 377.
57. SW 3: 391–92; GS 4: 261. I am using the edition of *Berlin Childhood around 1900* edited by Adorno (GS 4: 235–304). The textual basis for this is a text printed in the *Unterhaltungsblatt* of the *Vossischer Zeitung* on May 5, 1933, under the title "Mummerehlen." Benjamin shortened the text substantially in the final handwritten copy of 1938; see GS 7: 691n9. [As he explains in the opening lines of the text, Benjamin mishears "Muhme Rehlen" (Aunt Rehlen) as "Mummerehlen." See GS 3: 410n40 for more information on the linguistic resonances of the German term *Muhme*.—Translator]
58. SW 3: 392; GS 4: 261. Anja Lemke provides a good commentary and lucid interpretation of "Mummerehlen" in *Gedächtnisräume des Selbst: Walter Benjamins 'Berliner Kindheit' um 1900* (Würzburg: Königshausen & Neumann, 2005), 76ff.
59. SW 2: 492; GS 4: 396.
60. Sigmund Freud, *New Introductory Lectures on Psycho-Analysis and Other Works*, vol. 22 of *The Standard Edition of the Complete Psychological Works of Sigmund Freud*, trans. James Strachey (London: Random House, 1964), 107.
61. GS 2: 525.

Chapter 5

# Protection from What and for What?

Marc Crépon

"Protection from what and for what?" Though it may not seem so, this question is borrowed from Samuel Weber, whose text "La faute, la mort et les 'traits unaires'" ("Breach, Death, and 'Unary Traits'") is threaded through with this question.[1] At a time when there is no sovereign political state that does not claim its right to ensure, and to determine how to ensure, the protection of its citizens and that is not ready to compromise the principles upon which its legitimacy was founded, this phrase might sound like a *provocation*. The measures taken *in the name of security* by governments after the events of September 11, 2001, call forth a reflection that finds, in any case, an immediate echo on both sides of the Atlantic. And it is certainly not by chance that, emphasizing to what extent "the raison d'être of the modern state" has, in order to become protective, now ceased to be "directly or overtly eschatological or redemptive," Weber refers, by way of a footnote, to the law adopted on February 25, 2008, by the French Parliament and defended at the time by the former minister of justice Rachida Dati—a law ordering the "detainment for security of criminals judged dangerous."

## 1.

Before offering a reading of "La faute, la mort et les 'traits unaires,'" I will, by way of introduction, linger for a moment on this example. In her critical book *Libertés et sûreté dans un monde dangereux* (*Liberties and Security in a Dangerous World*), Mireille Delmas-Marty summarizes the 2008 law's objective: to allow "a condemned prisoner to be held in detention, after the completion of his sentence, for a period of one year, indefinitely renewable."[2] The pronouncement follows a whole series of measures and laws adopted since September 11 not only to respond to the "terrorist threat" but also to extend the response to all supposed dangers threatening the "security" of citizens and to protect them from all individuals or groups of individuals identified, located, and controlled by police and judicial authorities *as* the incarnation of this insecurity. At the same time, this statute goes a step beyond that by upending the protection on display—or rather by the tangled confusion of security and insecurity—so that everything advanced and proposed *in the name of* protection is also and unfailingly a threat. And what is this step? It consists in breaking up relations among *guilt*, *responsibility*, and *sanction*.

If it is true that "detainment for security," understood as the deprivation of liberty, remains a sanction (which its name tends to mask), and if it is true that it prolongs this sanction indefinitely beyond the term served, then the law said to be of "detainment for security" signifies that there is no need to be guilty again, to commit a new transgression (*faute*) in order to be sanctioned.[3] It is enough that the authorities can suppose that the detainee could be made guilty again by virtue of criteria that the authorities themselves retain the power to define and adapt—all of which the notion of "dangerousness" (*dangerosité*) confusedly recovers—in order for a sentence to be prolonged. Thus the sanction does not depend on the commission of a civil breach (*faute*). It is no longer the *proof* of guilt but the *suspicion* of dangerousness that leads to sanction. From such a reversal the consequences are actually considerable. The first is that the sanction is the product of a phantasm of "absolute security": it allows for the illusion of a life that can be protected, in an exponential way, from all danger, as if risk could be eliminated. It is this phantasm, this illusion that inverts the relation between a breach (*faute*) or crime and protection. Until then it was understood that the law could prevent crime only by threat of punishment—and such a threat worked only according to the efficacy of its dissuasion, which, it was admitted, could not be total. There were, there would always be criminals, men and women subjected to the laws they broke. The law was therefore supposed to protect citizens from criminals in two ways: through fear of sanction it remained for the most part *dissuasive*; it punished those not restrained by this fear and who were found guilty of an offense (*un délit*). The law thus understood was meant to suppress not the *possibility* of crime but its *impunity*, and it was always only after the fact that it was applied. It was not called upon, in its severity, its harshness, its eventual *cruelty* (because all deprivation of liberty is cruel), to *anticipate* the crime but to come after it.

The second consequence of the reversal that detaches dangerousness from guilt concerns precisely this cruelty. There will always be some violence overlooked as a reminder that when the law punishes, it is *cruel*. Not to speak only of capital punishment and the corridors of death in which the condemned crouch for decades, nor even of those extreme cases that are the camp at Guantánamo and Abu Ghraib prison and so many other detention sites all over the world famous for the atrocities committed there, *all* imprisonment is *cruel*. As so many accounts and films have shown, starting with Jacques Audiard's *Le prophète*, there is no prison in the world in which incarceration is not cruel—and there are very few sovereign states, including the great democracies that profess respect for the rights of man, in which the conditions of detention are not inhumane and disgraceful, whether the cruelty results from promiscuity with other detainees, from the brutality of surveillance, or from any other form of insecurity. Any analysis must therefore take as its point of departure this principal assertion: detention is a *cruelty* authorized by society. And when this same society or its representatives demand enforcement of the law, a crackdown on sentencing, when they demand, propose, or decide on still and always more repression, it is also this cruelty that society is demanding in the name of justice, and all the more so if the repression is supposed to be preventative (at the cost of a contradiction in terms).

Herein lies the paradox: the exponential dream, illusion, or desire of a life protected, ultrasecured, sheltered from all those men and women who *might* present a danger (the "crazies," the possible repeat offenders, the "pedophiles," the presumed "terrorists") is a *demand* for cruelty. Politicians, short on legitimacy or votes, are not mistaken: they must exhibit to a public always hungry for vengeance and make known to potential voters-avengers that they know how to show themselves as intractable with all these potentially dangerous elements. They have to convince us that a little legitimate cruelty does not scare them. And it is in this way that what is decried *in the name of protection* becomes a source of insecurity. In other words (those of Freud), to which I will return, there is thus *perhaps* no demand for protection that is not inhabited by the death drive.

## 2.

Before turning to the death drive, we need to look more closely at "La faute, la mort et les 'traits unaires.'" Recall Weber's great lines, foremost that which also refers to his "Towards a Politics of Singularity: Protection and Projection." At the end of a long genealogy he ends up at the following question, which I have borrowed for the title of my essay: "If, as I have sought to show elsewhere, *protection* is really the project that defines the nation-state in modern political theory and often also in its practice, then this presupposes a question that is rarely asked even though it informs most conceptions of politics: protection *from* what and *for* what? I suggest that the beginnings of a response can be found in the essentially Christian notion of original sin understood as a *fortunate fall* [une *chute bienheureuse*]" ("La faute," 147). This genealogy consists in starting from Genesis, that is, from the creation of man in the image of God, from a man created in order to go forth and multiply and spread across the earth—a man especially to whom life is given in the Garden of Eden, *but not yet death*. One must set out, therefore, from "life without death," from a life understood as pure generation in order to understand how death comes about. It is this coming about that holds Weber's attention, not only because it refers initially to a life unaware of death but also because mortality appeared as the ultimate consequence of a "deliberate human action," and as that action is an act of disobedience, death is a punishment. Death comes to sanction the violation of the divine prohibition from tasting the fruits of the tree of knowledge of good and bad. It is why death cannot be separated from the genesis of guilt. Man became mortal because he committed a transgression of the law. At the same time, the law itself seems to have had no reason for being other than to make the imputation of guilt and death justifiable: "Death is not simply introduced into human life: it is justified as punishment for transgression. Man becomes mortal because he becomes guilty following his deliberate actions, by which he knowingly violated divine law" (Weber, "La faute" 146). Thus follows the second stage of this genealogy, the closest to the biblical text, which leads us directly to the definition of the project of the nation-state *as protection*, with neither the reasons for nor the object of the nation-state being yet specified. To assume that disobedience to the law would effectively be the cause of finitude and, thus, the justification for death, obedience would have to have, as a symmetrical reason, the possibility of making amends for the wrong (*faute*) and canceling out the punishment. Actions that attest to obedience open the door to the resurrection of the dead. Thus the Fall becomes a *felix culpa*.

It is in this fortunate Fall—in this possibility of an action that saves from death—that Weber perceives the beginnings of a response to the question I have chosen to take up here: "Protection *from* what and *for* what?" This question puts us on the path of an intrinsic relation between *our* demand or *our* desire for "protection" and all the other causes of mortality presented to *us*. The function of the modern state would be to protect us from death, or more generally still to guarantee *our* security against every form of destruction. It would take the entire vocation and justification of what I have elsewhere called "collective necessity" to assure the community of a "being against death."[4] Such a function in any case determines the horizon of what is expected of it but also the reproach that one is always inclined to address it with: that of not doing enough or of doing nothing, of not acting efficiently or of remaining impotent, a reproach that always returns to the same assessment or sentiment of abandonment, as we saw again not so long ago with the black tide that invaded the Gulf of Mexico's shores and the accusations made against government authorities and more notably against President Obama, as if it were self-evident that he should have the knowledge and the capacity to stanch the flow of oil.

But the genealogy must be pushed still further. The state not only transforms redemption into protection through obedience to the law; it also inherits the task of warning against and punishing the law's transgression. Or rather it does not separate one from the other. Far from contenting itself with protecting, it also punishes: it punishes to protect and protects in punishing, or at least in brandishing the threat of punishment. But *who* is it protecting, exactly? What or who is designated by this "us," the use of which becomes, we have seen, overblown as soon as we speak of protection? Is it life—life in opposition to death? What life, *the life of all*, *all* life? But death is not only the opposite of life; it is also the opposite of birth—and all birth, in its essence, calls for protection. If it is true that the modern form of the state is that of the nation-state, then this opposition is all the more inherited and, with it, concern for those whose birth gives them a particular right to *protection* against death. Weber summarizes the meaning and range of the word *nation* here in a formula that concentrates in it all the elements of an original analysis of the most secret impulses behind the power of this nationalism that never hesitates to give death, to punish by supreme chastisement in the name of protecting the "native-born": "The nation fascinates and persists as the virtual fulfillment of the Promise of Nativity, and it is this in the last instance that informs and defines its demographic 'biopolitics'—from whence the importance of one's place of birth, which determines the right to citizenship. Because a Nation-state that claims to be providential must also be localizable. Borders and walls, fences and enclosures are erected and defended to demarcate the 'native' from the 'foreign' and to protect life against death" ("La faute," 149).

And it is true, as Weber reminds us, that all ambivalence toward this protection arises because it protects against the essentiality of death by giving itself the right to mete out death. The price of its affirmation of the sacred character of life is its capacity to take life. Put in another way, it only opposes the death drive by authorizing itself to be cruel. The death penalty is thus exemplary of what seems to constitute, in the final analysis, the culmination of this genealogy: "Without guilt [*faute*], no redemption. Without law, no safety. Without punishment, no law. Without death, no life" ("La faute," 150).

## 3.

But why this genealogy? Why this long detour through the genesis of the modern state? Weber's text is, as his so often are, elliptical, and between this long detour through the Bible and what follows is a complex and minute reading of Benjamin's essay "Fate and Character," itself elliptical.[5] It is up to the reader to tie the threads together. We should also keep in mind the hypothesis suggested by Weber himself in his reading: "La faute, la mort et les 'traits unaires' " is inscribed in the philosophical project of thinking politics otherwise by proposing what he calls a "politics of singularity"—which should begin by freeing itself of the *felix culpa*'s gravity and consequently of a certain bond with death and guilt. Understood in this light, the analysis of Benjamin's text would have no other purpose than to propose, between the lines, certain elements so as to begin to respond to the following questions: Is all politics devoted, in essence, to salvation, redemption, or atonement for wrongdoing (*faute*)? If not, what is the alternative?

This is why the point of departure of Weber's reading consists in recalling the arguments deployed by Benjamin in favor of the "radical separation" of character and destiny (fate). If it is indeed true that destiny is distinguished—and here is a first bridge to what came earlier—by "its constitutive relation to 'guilt' [*faute*],"[6] then to separate destiny from character comes back to liberate character (which the notion of the "unary trait" allows us to clarify) from wrongdoing (*faute*) and guilt. In the same way, if binding destiny to transgression (*faute*), as do Benjamin and Weber, returns to anchor it in the juridical domain, it will fall to this other politics to invent another relation not only to law but, more essentially still, to the constitutive relation of law to death—that is to say, also to the death penalty, even where it is abolished—and to cruelty. One consequently conceives the question at the horizon of these reflections, which are all—Benjamin's question, Weber's question, and the question inspired in us by their reading—superimposed. If an alternative politics is at stake, understood as a "politics of singularity," then how does this other politics relate to the drive to power, to the death drive, and to cruelty?

The question presses all the more in that what links destiny to transgression (*à la faute*), unlike to character, is the *mortality of the living*. All difficulty here rests—as in that other, very similar text by Benjamin, "Critique of Violence"[7]—on the difference or contradiction between living and life, between the naturalness of life, identical to itself, and the mortality of the living, or still more between the exculpation of the former, as Weber writes, and the charge brought against the other. Death is not a property of life but the punishment of living in its *singularity*. Can singularity escape the weight of this punishment and thus the weight of destiny? Can it be thought on a different horizon? In his study Weber, reading Benjamin, multiplies the mediations in this direction. From the Aeschylean hero that constitutes one of these mediations, in Franz Rosenzweig's interpretation of the tragic hero's silence,[8] we are reminded that the hero's aspiration (*Zug*) distances him from the juridical-legal order of law in order to draw him into "the more elusive, more indeterminate area of *Gerechtigkeit*, a justice no longer based on commensurability, on *guilt* [*faute*] as *misfortune*."

But it is obviously the introduction of the concepts of character and trait (*Zug*) that participates most in this rupture. One thus understands that the strategy of the analysis relates it to a game of chess in the sense that the game, in order to end, consists in advancing one's pawns and moving one's pieces, turn by turn, with a certain objective in mind. First advance, first move: to show that if character is revealed by its "traits," these traits do not arise from nature; they do not constitute the determinations of any essence. Their power is to be "detached," "removed," "replaced." Without overreaching here, it is probable that recognizing this constitutes the first condition of a "politics of singularities." From the game's outset this both frees "character" from all appropriation or instrumentalization, always "deadly" (*mortifères*), that would pull it over to the side of a characterization of individuals as much as of peoples or of all other notions of community, whether political, ethnic, religious, social, professional, academic, or other—and orients it more toward *disidentification* or *disappropriation*, which Weber's reading of Genet's play *The Balcony* at the end of "La faute, la mort et les 'traits unaires'" leaves us pondering: "The word *Zug*, which, as has already been noted, is the nominalization of the verb *ziehen*, to pull or to trace, does not therefore suggest only movement, but often the transition from stasis to movement, a change often brought about by an external force, or at least a force that is not entirely internal, and hence, not entirely 'natural' (in the usual sense of that word). . . . In conjunction with 'character,' a *Zug* then becomes a 'trait,' but a trait that can at any moment be withdrawn by being detached from its current location" ("La faute," 159–60).

For Weber, as for Benjamin, this is what makes the radical singularity of character—and what also gives it a comic dimension. The result is the following paradox: it is not identification that makes singularity, but *disidentification*—which is without a doubt to say that there is no character and thus no singularity except in the production of a gap, the marking of a difference, the invention of a deviance. In other words, it is always about an *invention*, perhaps even of an "idiomatic invention." This is what the subsequent text conveys by lingering on the notion of genius and stipulating that it must be understood less as a quality that one would have from birth—which would give it the weight of destiny and lead it into the tragic nets of guiltiness: the misfortune and transgression (*la faute*) of being born—than as the capacity to engender, to give birth to something independently of (or separate from) that birth. I must cite here the very beautiful passage from Benjamin's "Fate and Character" that Weber's analysis in "La faute, la mort et les 'traits unaires'" takes up: "While fate brings to light the immense complexity of the guilty person [*la personne livrée à la culpabilité*], the complications and bonds of his guilt [*sa faute*], character gives this mystical enslavement of the person to the guilt context [*dans l'horizon de la faute*] the answer of genius. Complication becomes simplicity, fate freedom. For the character of the comic figure is not the scarecrow of the determinist; it is the beacon in whose beams the freedom of his actions becomes visible."[9]

Of "genius" one therefore ought to hold onto not only "its divisibility, its separability, its inability to stay with and be absorbed by an integrated ego," Weber elaborates, but especially and magnificently the way it brings together Hölderlin's voice with Benjamin's and returns us to the point at which we began, all the while leading us toward the end: it must "step *unprotected* into life" (emphasis added). It is tied to destiny and to all the relations this implies, including that which links it to death, by the fact that it "frees itself" from it—by the fact, in other words, that it no longer lives beneath death's domination or bound to its commands. With the singular trait (*le trait unique*) Weber thus moves through its exposition (which is also that of life), its movement, and its detachment—and therefore to the question of whether these can give rise to a politics. It is significant that it is at this precise moment of the text that Weber reveals the motive he had until then kept secret: "to explore how a 'politics of singularity' might be thought."

## 4.

This leads us to Freud and guilt—and, by this secret means, to death and cruelty. The question I would like to ask is thus the following: What is there of the "death drive" and of "cruelty" in this "politics of singularities"? How can this other politics—a politics relieved of the weight of transgression (*faute*) and guilt but not necessarily, for all that, of *the responsibility for death*—confront the death drive and cruelty? Perhaps the answer to this question demands that we return to the "without" of the absence of protection that characterizes progress in life and the invention of character? Before arriving at these ultimate repercussions I would like to return to the final developments of "La faute, la mort et les 'traits unaires' " without which the very title of the text would be incomprehensible. The nearly last movement of the text (before a conclusive reading of a scene from *The Balcony*) is Lacanian. Weber translates the Benjaminian character trait first into Freud's "singular trait," understood as a pole of identification, and then into its Lacanian interpretation in the form of the "unary trait" (*trait unaire*). But why this call to the unary trait? Because it permits us to understand singularity as a "*differential* but fully *relational* notion, a trait or trace" ("La faute," 170, emphasis added). It defines, Weber writes, "a process by which the subject—which includes the political subject—occupies an irreducibly ambivalent place" (170).

I am unable to dwell at length on these references (Freud, Lacan, Genet) or to follow the text in its elliptical but particularly significant detour through a reading of Kafka, to which Benjamin was also no stranger. It is time to attempt to answer the questions posed earlier, those concerning wrongdoing (*faute*) and guilt, death and dying, protection and exhibition, unsurpassable cruelty and political (or ethicopolitical) responsibility. The relation of destiny to death is known: it is the price that must be paid for transgression (*faute*)—and because it happens thus this same destiny makes possible, authorizes, and even legitimates cruelty. Civilization protects itself from the death drive by instituting a legitimate recourse to violence that can extend all the way to the death penalty. Our legal relation to death is therefore divided between the death we might be tempted to inflict if law did not forbid it (the pleasure-desire of murder, which Freud makes in *Totem and Taboo* one of the three primitive drives, along with incest and cannibalism) and the death we incur (or risk submitting to a substitute) if we violate the law that forbids us from inflicting it. Death is thus at one and the same time that from which we protect ourselves and that from which the threat, under all legal forms, protects us. *Our* fate is to be trapped in this double *bind*.

Can we escape? Is this what we would be entitled to expect of a "politics of singularity"? Whatever the case, in the logic of fate, death is taken up in the guilty individual's being *face-to-face* with the law that punishes him, with "coercion" and its expiation—and it is up to each person to *deal with it.* To the degree that the law protects, it abandons he who adapts to it or transgresses it in the anguish of his mortality. Guilt encloses each in a privileged if not exclusive relationship to *his* own death. It is why the possibility always slips in, in all the interstices, both of a murderous consent that puts a spotlight on others' *guilt* and of the desire to see them punished, condemned, executed, lynched.[10] The rapport between death and guilt also signifies that in the name of the state's protective essence and the demanded security, one can caution, encourage, or even desire legal violence, the "cruelty of power," which culminates in so many places and so many circumstances in the death of others. What the genealogy of the protector state sketched above legitimates, in the last resort, is the always possible relation to the death of such determinate others (exemplified not only by war but also by so many repressive laws and, everywhere that it is upheld, in China as in the United States, the death penalty) and to the cruelty of which they could be the object, a cruelty that consists in justifying if not wishing for death—which can be called, after Camus, a "murderous consent." The determination of others as "targets," their designation as "enemy," or still more the claimed indifference to their vulnerability and their mortality are the variable motivations that can extend well beyond the nation-state's frontiers and interests. All forms of belonging, of religious or political communal solidarity, of limited fraternity, exclusive and always potentially murderous, are implicated here. Which is why this consent is imposed as a dimension of existence *that must be reckoned with.* And there will always be some illusion, just as some denounced Freud at the beginning of *Thoughts for the Times on Death and War* (1915), of claiming exception from the heights of "culture" and imagining that it is always the business of others. Is this another way to think the weight of destiny?

If this is the case, then a "politics of singularity"—one that could manage to escape a confrontation with death and guilt in order to "escape" destiny—would have to confront the weight of its consents, even where they are inherited, upheld, and repeated. This in any case is the hypothesis with which I will suspend this reading. At all lines of demarcation and on all fronts this politics to which nothing is given in advance and for which nothing can be either programmed or calculated—this politics would have as its responsibility the invention, against the tide, of a step sideways, of a gap or a difference. This would imply shattering, in a singular way each time, the circles that divide and circumscribe the relation to the other's death, knowing that the abysses hollowed out between the vulnerability and mortality of those on both sides are so many criminal flaws (*failles*) in *our* belonging to the world.

**Translated by Denise Davis**

## Notes

1. Samuel Weber, "La faute, la mort et les 'traits unaires,'" *Les cahiers philosophiques de Strasbourg* 27 (2010): 139–74. Subsequent references to this source are cited parenthetically in the text.

2. Mireille Delmas-Marty, *Libertés et sûreté dans un monde dangereux* (Paris: Seuil, 2010), 7.

3. [I have translated *faute* by a number of words, including *breach*, *wrongdoing*, *transgression*, and *offense*, depending on the context.—Translator]

4. See Marc Crépon, *Vivre avec, la pensée de la mort et la mémoire des guerres* (Paris: Hermann, 2008).

5. Walter Benjamin, "Fate and Character," in *Selected Writings Vol. 1 (1913–1926)*, ed. Marcus Bullock and Michael W. Jennings (Cambridge, Mass.: Belknap, 1996). [The title of this essay has also been translated as "Destiny and Character," a translation Weber prefers because *destiny* preserves the relation to the original German *schicken*, "to send," from which the word *Schicksal* (destiny) is formed.—Translator]

6. [Weber renders Benjamin's *Schuld* as "guilt"; the French text of Weber's essay in turn renders "guilt" as *faute*.—Translator]

7. Walter Benjamin, "Critique of Violence," in *Selected Writings Vol. 1*.

8. Franz Rosenzweig, *The Star of Redemption*, trans. William W. Hallo (New York: Holt, Rinehart and Winston, 1971).

9. Benjamin, "Fate and Character," 205–6. Weber's own translation of Benjamin's text is helpful here: "While destiny unrolls the enormous complexity of the guilty and indebted [*verschuldeten*] person, the complication and bonds of their guilt, character reacts to the mythical enslavement of the person in the guilt-nexus by giving the response of genius. Complication becomes simplicity, fate freedom. For the character of the comic person is not the scarecrow [*Popanz*] of the determinist: it is the beacon [*Leuchter*: chandelier] in whose rays the freedom of his deeds becomes visible" ("La faute," 27). See "Drawing—The Single Trait," in *Techniken der Übereinkuft*: *Zur Medialität des Politischen*, ed. H. Blumentrath et al. (Berlin: Kulturverlag Kadmos, 2009).

10. From this point of view, one could never say enough about how much the western, with all the demands for justice it stages, is exemplary of this complex relation between the fascination with the law and the "death drive" that makes of the former the last refuge of cruelty.

*Interlude*

Chapter 6

# "For O, for O, the Hobby-Horse Is Forgot"

## *Hamlet* between Schmitt and Benjamin

Samuel Weber

This is surely not the first and probably not the last reading that will seek to approach Shakespeare's *Hamlet* from the dual perspective of Carl Schmitt and Walter Benjamin. However, Schmitt and Benjamin will serve here as points of departure, from which I will follow a trajectory for which I must take full responsibility, however unoriginal it may finally seem.

But why start with Schmitt and Benjamin rather than with some of the many other readers and critics of *Hamlet*? For two reasons. First, as Peirce writes, one has to start somewhere, and that somewhere will always not be somewhere else. Nor can it ever be complete. But this does not eliminate the task of justifying one's choice of starting points, of "origins," if you will. So here is my second and more significant reason: both Schmitt and Benjamin situate *Hamlet* in a historical setting that strikes me as particularly relevant for anyone reading, seeing, or hearing *Hamlet* today. For this reason Schmitt and Benjamin provide a basis for reflecting on what this play might signify some four centuries after it was written, without seeking to ignore or destroy its historical specificity by creating a sense of false proximity. Historical texts are precisely historical in and through the distance and difference that separate them from the time of their "reception"—or rather, as I would prefer to say, of their "encounter." We *encounter* such texts by moving both toward them and away from them, as the word *counter* suggests (although more clearly in its German equivalent, *gegen*). Such an ambivalent movement does not necessarily make actual contact with the play—we remain separated from it, at least as critics—but rather approaches it precisely by preserving and experiencing its irreducible distance from us. The upshot of that experience is not, as academic critics generally suppose, "knowledge" as much as it is "feeling," which consists neither in grasping nor even in touching but rather in a process of *being touched* and altered in the absence of any direct contact. If these distinctions seem obscure, they will hopefully be somewhat clarified during the course of this essay.

Let me begin by juxtaposing two remarks of the writers I have just mentioned. First Schmitt, from his book *Hamlet or Hecuba: Time Breaks into the Play*: "European Literature has created three great symbolic figures: Don Quixote, Hamlet and Faust. Of the three, one—Hamlet—has already attained the status of myth. All three are remarkably readers of books and thus intellectuals, so to say. All three have been thrown off their spiritual paths. With respect to their origins and provenance: Don Quixote is a Spaniard and a pure Catholic; Faust is German and Protestant; Hamlet stands between them, in the midst of the split that has determined the destiny of Europe."[1] Let me just observe, parenthetically, that on the day I have begun writing this text, January 13, 2012, the rating agency Standard & Poor's has announced that it is downgrading the credit status of all the Eurozone members with the exception of Germany, the Netherlands, Finland, and Luxembourg. However topical and perhaps aleatory this fact may seem, I want to suggest that the current and ongoing financial crisis that threatens European unity also underscores the continuing cleavage between the predominantly Protestant (largely Northern) and Catholic (largely Southern) European countries. In short, even in a domain as apparently (but deceptively) remote from our concerns as that of political economy, the "split" to which Schmitt refers continues to mark contemporary Europe, as well as the countries and cultures that developed out of it.

If this is so, the relevant questions then become: In what exactly does this split consist, and what bearing does it have on Shakespeare's play? And it is here that the work of Benjamin can be helpful. So let me finally come to the passage from his writing that I want to use as a kind of second epigraph for this essay. It is drawn from *The Origin of the German Mourning Play*, in which a number of relatively brief but extremely suggestive remarks concerning *Hamlet* are inscribed. The following sums up at least one central aspect of the title figure, as Benjamin construes it:

> One time at least the age succeeded in conjuring up the human figure that speaks to the split between neo-classical and medieval illumination through which the Baroque construed the melancholic. But it was not Germany that accomplished this. It was Hamlet. The secret of his person is enclosed in the playful but therefore also precisely calculated traversal of all stations of this intentional space, just as the secret of his destiny is enclosed in events that are *entirely homogeneous* with this his attitude. *Hamlet alone is for the mourning play a spectator by (and of) the grace of God [von Gottes Gnaden]; but he can be satisfied not in what their play brings to him, but strictly and solely in his own destiny*. His life, as the exemplary object given to his mourning, gestures before its extinction toward Christian providence, in whose bosom his mournful images turn into blessed existence. Only in a life of this princely sort can melancholy, by encountering itself, be redeemed.[2]

If the passage quoted from Schmitt is relatively simple and straightforward in its generality, the same hardly holds true for the remarks just quoted. They require "unpacking," especially for anyone who is not absolutely conversant with the book from which it is drawn. In *The Origin of the German Mourning Play* Benjamin describes the German baroque *Trauerspiel* as a response to what can be called—although he does not use these terms—a historical crisis of Christian salvational history (in German, *Heilsgeschichte*), which Benjamin associates in general with the Reformation and in particular with its German Lutheran version. Luther's devaluation of "good works" as a path to salvation and his concomitant emphasis on "faith alone" as the way to grace are both the symptom and the articulation of this crisis, which results in the splitting of the Western Church into Catholics and Protestants. For Benjamin, Luther's discrediting of "good works" affects not just the sacraments administered by the Church but all "work" as such, that is, all purposive-intentional acts and activity. The background for this "attack on good works" as well as its ramifications remain largely implicit in Benjamin's analysis, but since they are crucial for his analyses let me try to elaborate them. What is put in jeopardy by the Reformation, and what is then combated by the Counter-Reformation—which, Benjamin insists, is not limited just to the Catholic Church but is at work wherever worldly institutions are to be legitimated in any way whatsoever—involves not just the relation of the "immanent" fallen world to an other-worldly "transcendence," these being the categories that Benjamin uses and that are therefore echoed by virtually all of his readers. Rather what is involved is something far more earthly and "immanent," if one will, for it concerns the relation of life to death, or rather the way this relation is conceived. Prior to the Reformation a Christian culture had imposed itself in Europe that was based on what can be described as a certain onto-theological subordination of death to life. Since before the Fall, life, issuing directly from the Creator, existed without death, death could be construed, from Genesis on, as something secondary: namely as the result of human transgression. And therefore death could also be construed as subject to alteration by human action, by "good works," especially once the transcendence of life over death had been demonstrated by the birth, crucifixion, and resurrection of the Savior. This expectation of a possible salvation of singular, guilty, and therefore mortal living beings could, up until the Reformation, therefore be considered to fall within the purview of ordinary human experience. This expectation formed the historical-theological basis of what Schmitt would later call "the principle of representation," in which he located the distinctive political significance of the Catholic Church.[3] "Representation" in his use of the term (in German, *Repräsentation*, not *Vorstellung* or *Darstellung*) entailed a certain valorization of the empirical world of appearances—a selective, hierarchized valorization, to be sure, but one that could provide access to a meaning that would transcend the limits of a merely mortal, and guilty, existence.

It is precisely this access, however, that the Lutheran Reformation calls into question and that is also in question in Shakespeare's *Hamlet*, both in the play as such and in the title figure who gives the play its name. But it is a name that already is as split as the world it inhabits: split between the deceased king and "young Hamlet," his son. To which a third must be added: for in addition to the king and his son there is also the title of the play. All three are inseparable, and all three are distinct. And it is in the space of this distinction that many of the problems the play deploys play themselves out.

But it is not just a space; it is also, and perhaps above all, a time. A time that is famously—one hesitates to quote the phrase, so overworked has it become—"out of joint." If I have quoted it despite a certain aversion to imposing such "saws" upon readers—something I will, alas, have to do more than once in this essay—it is because I want to try to read this phrase as a point of departure that will hopefully enable us to move in a somewhat less belabored, less familiar direction.

Hamlet pronounces the words at the very end of Act I, after he has seen and spoken to the Ghost and then sworn his companions to secrecy. The famous words are framed, and in a way that has been largely eclipsed by the words themselves but which deserves attention. Hamlet bids his companions, Horatio and Marcellus, to go inside together:

> Let us go in together.
> And still your fingers on your lips, I pray.
> The time is out of joint. O cursed spite
> That ever I was born to set it right.
> Nay, come, let's go together. (I.v.194–98)[4]

"Let's go together": Hamlet's injunction frames the celebrated phrase, in which he both defines the challenges that confront him and also regrets that he must confront them at all. For if "the time is out of joint," it is precisely this disjointedness that will complicate any such "going together," much less the individual effort "to set it right." And yet he recognizes this as his destiny: after his encounter with the Ghost, and despite the various doubts that will assail him as to the Ghost's true nature, what he can never doubt is that, demon or not, in the Ghost he has met his destiny.

The problem, of course, is finding out just what that destiny entails. And this will be infinitely complicated by the very thing it seeks to "set right" and that prevents the world from being "jointed" in a transparent manner. The burlesque scene that follows the encounter with the Ghost, where Hamlet attempts to get Horatio and Marcellus to swear on his sword that they will not speak of what they have seen, does not so much represent as perform this quandary, in the threefold split already suggested by the name Hamlet: the Ghost echoes Hamlet's injunction to "swear" each time he tries to get his companions to perform the oath, and the Ghost echoes it from under the floorboards of the very stage on which *Hamlet* the play is being performed. It is as if the out-of-jointness of the time is somehow intimately related to the fictional representational and yet real performative space of the scene, of the stage. The theatricality of the scene thus intrudes upon the scene itself, mocking for an instant, but repeatedly, its effort to represent actions and persons taken to exist outside of the theater.

It is therefore not just the time that is out of joint but the space as well, divided into performative and representational space, each impossible to separate from the other but also impossible to unify with the other. In this, its constitutive disjuncture, the theatrical space reflects and communicates with the historical period in which it takes place. For one of the times that is out of joint is the epoch that finds itself torn between Reformation and Counter-Reformation, as the long reign of Queen Elizabeth approaches an uncertain end. In the last years of the reign of Elizabeth the question of royal succession was anything but an abstract question of doctrine: it involved the building of opposing factions that affected even the theater company to which Shakespeare belonged. As a supporter of the earls of Southampton and Essex, and following the execution of the latter, of James, Shakespeare's theater was directly affected by the struggle for power. And of course questions of heritage and inheritance, both public and private, political and domestic, legitimate and illegitimate, are also at the heart of the play. Finally, perhaps in part as a result of the uncertain outcome of these struggles, time itself is easily perceived as being a medium of utter contingency and unpredictability, which therefore threatens the very notion of meaning itself. Hamlet, who would like to flee the out-of-joint chaos of Denmark and return to his studies in Protestant Wittenberg, finds himself exposed precisely to this aspect of time, whose "joints" no longer join—a family, a state, a couple—but rather separate irrevocably, and this despite or because of the new king's presentation of his wife and Hamlet's mother as his "imperial jointress" (I.ii.9). "Out of joint" here must be understood as literally as possible: the "joint" or juncture no longer joins, for the body politic or familial that it might have been expected to support is now exposed to utter contingency—or worse, to the arbitrary will of unprincipled individuals.

In a world dominated by the ever-uncertain aleatory will of such individuals, Hamlet's initial response is to assert, albeit negatively, his own individuality, by invoking the first-person singular: "O cursed spite / That ever *I* was born to set it right." An experience of time that could have been the medium of a continuous transmission has instead become radically discontinuous. Not so much in the political domain, for the Danish monarchy was not hereditary, but in the private, familial one. Here again, however, the convergence of public and private, political and domestic, underscores not just the equivocation of the world out of joint but also the ambiguity of what could be required to "set it right."

In what could such "setting right" consist? How is it to be determined? The message that the Ghost imparts to Hamlet seems clear enough:

> If thou has nature in thee, bear it not,
> Let not the royal bed of Denmark be
> A couch for luxury and damned incest.
> But howsomever thou pursuest this act,
> Taint not thy mind nor let thy soul contrive
> Against thy mother aught. Leave her to heaven,
> And to those thorns that in her bosom lodge
> To prick and sting her. (I.v.81–88)

Upon closer inspection the Ghost's injunction is clearer about what Hamlet should *not* do than what he should: "bear it not," "Let not," "Taint not." And in conclusion to these three "nots," only one positive command, in parting: "Adieu, adieu, adieu. *Remember me.*"

As Hamlet will do in his response, the Ghost ends his speech by invoking the first-person singular, this time in the reflective, accusative form: "Remember *me.*" But just who is this "me" that is to be remembered? For long after Hamlet will be plagued by uncertainty, vacillating between the Catholic and Protestant versions of just who or what the Ghost really is, and therefore just who or what is to be remembered—or forgotten. In Protestant theology ghosts were taken to be demons, to come from Hell, and thus not to be followed in any way, shape, or form. The Catholic conception of ghosts, by contrast, construed them as sent from Purgatory, hence as redeemable. And this is also how the Ghost introduces himself to Hamlet:

> I am thy father's spirit,
> Doom'd for a certain term to walk the night,
> And for the day confin'd to fast in fires,
> Till the foul crimes done in my days of nature
> Are burnt and purg'd away. (I.v.9–13)

Although Hamlet seems at first convinced, he then wavers before finally, as a result of the king's reaction to "the mousetrap," abandoning all doubt as to the Ghost's authenticity. But no matter how he evaluates the veracity of the Ghost, what will remain decisive from this initial encounter onward is that there is a "me" that demands to be "remembered." From this point on, Hamlet's destiny will be inseparable from the question of memory, his and that of others: in the first place Gertrude, but also in different ways Claudius and Ophelia, but perhaps most of all by those who will come after he is gone. *Hamlet* is a play about the vicissitudes of memory, a few of which I will now attempt to explore.

Hamlet's immediate response to the Ghost's parting words is to echo his command three times:

> Remember thee?
> Ay, thou poor ghost, whiles memory holds a seat
> In this distracted globe. Remember thee?
> Yea, from the table of my memory
> I'll wipe away all trivial fond records,
> . . . And thy commandment all alone shall live
> Within the book and volume of my brain,
> Unmix'd with baser matter. (I.v.95–104)

If Hamlet is to remember the Ghost, his story and his injunctions, explicit and implicit, the initial site of that memory is "this distracted globe." "This"? Again one feels called upon to ask: Which "this"? Where is it? Or, as Hölderlin will put it two centuries later, in a poem dedicated to the goddess of memory, "Mnemosyne": "Was ist dies?" (What is *this*?) Just what does the demonstrative pronoun *this* demonstrate here? To what does it point?[5] What seems absolutely decisive, and not just here, is that there be such a pointing to a specific, individualized place—to a "this" and not to a "that"—but also that the "thisness" of the place thus pointed to should turn out to be ambiguously overdetermined, yet in ways that are anything but simply arbitrary.

In "this" case, then, the "this" points us to a "globe" that can be read in at least three ways, all of which interact with each other: (1) the "globe" of Hamlet's head, bodily organ that is generally understood as seat or site of memory; (2) the world at large, which, for the England of Shakespeare's time, is already in the process of emerging as a unified "globe," to be conquered through maritime power (as Schmitt emphasizes);[6] (3) and finally as the Globe Theater in which the play was performed, site of Shakespeare's theater company. No wonder Hamlet describes the globe as "distracted." But its distraction is not simply the result of the interaction of its multiple meanings and referents. The globe is distracted for other, perhaps more profound reasons. For the only way Hamlet sees open to him if he is to fulfill the command of the Ghost is to abolish all other memories, which are construed as mere distractions. If the Ghost enjoins Hamlet not just to remember but to "remember me," for Hamlet this is tantamount to forgetting everything else in order, as it were, to "save" that "me" from contamination—for instance, by "all trivial fond records" or by "all saws of books, all forms, all pressures past / That youth and observation copied there." In short, all previous experience has to be expunged if the "me" is to be remembered purely for itself, "unmix'd with baser matter."

In order to concentrate on the matter at hand, on the Ghost's command, all other memories—and presumably thoughts—have to be eliminated from the "globe" where nevertheless "memory holds a seat." Memory, in short, presupposes forgetting, and for Hamlet this means of everything that is not "me," that is, the person whose ghost Hamlet encounters.

But separated from everything that is not himself, how can that "me" be remembered? At first Hamlet seems to have a simple and straightforward response to this problem. Early in Act I Horatio, in conversation with Hamlet, recalls having seen his father once. "'A was a goodly King," he observes. But Hamlet replies, correcting Horatio, "'A was a man, take him for all in all" (I.ii.186). And it is indeed the king's "manly" qualities that Hamlet subsequently invokes to demonstrate his incomparable superiority to his brother, Claudius. But this notion of "man . . . all in all" is precisely called into question not just by the king's death, which demonstrates his vulnerability, but also by the Ghost's own admission to Hamlet of the many "sins" that his murder no longer allowed him to repent or atone for:

> Cut off even in the blossoms of my sin,
> Unhousel'd, disappointed, unanel'd,
> No reck'ning made, but sent to my account
> With all my imperfections on my head. (I.v.76–79)

Hamlet is not insensitive to this aspect of man, which is perhaps intensified by the fate of his father. In a conversation with Guildenstern he confesses to a highly ambivalent experience of man: "What a piece of work is a man, how noble in reason, how infinite in faculties, in form and moving how express and admirable, in action how like an angel, in apprehension how like a god: the beauty of the world, the paragon of animals—and yet, to me, what is this quintessence of dust? Man delights not me—nor woman either" (II.ii.303–9). Of course Hamlet again invokes his private experience of man: "and yet, to me . . . Man delights not me—nor woman either." What is out of joint is thus the general conception of man as descended from God and the experience of man as "quintessence of dust"—caught in sinful mortality without hope of salvation and hence without meaning or pleasure.

But it is in the experience of theater—of the theater of the day—that the disjointedness of man and of time converge in a manner that bears directly on Hamlet's own dilemma. In a discussion with Rosencrantz about the visiting Players, Hamlet, son of the murdered king, inveighs against the practice recently in vogue in London theaters of having children play in a manner that figuratively at least murders their elders—and calls their own future into question: "What, are they children? Who maintains 'em? How are they escotted? Will they pursue the quality no longer than they can sing? Will they not say afterwards, if they should grow themselves to common players—as it is most like, if their means are no better—their writers do them wrong to make them exclaim against their own succession?" (II.ii.343–49).

The fashion that encourages children to deride the very practices and institutions they use and exploit, eventually putting their own future in jeopardy, is like an allegory of time in the force field of Reformation and Counter-Reformation, when the succession of sin and guilt followed by grace and redemption is fundamentally perturbed and rendered uncertain—and with it, the survival of institutions. This dethrones not only the sovereign king, or rather takes away his legitimacy, but it also menaces the author in the theater, as the following dialogue makes clear:

> ROS. There was for a while no money bid for argument unless the poet and the player went to cuffs in the question.
> HAM. Is't possible?
> GUILD. O, there has been much throwing about of brains.
> HAM. Do the boys carry it away?
> ROS. Ay, that they do, my lord. (II.ii.352–57)

This ostensibly totally "distracted" discussion, which is almost always eliminated from actual performances of the play, nevertheless brings Hamlet—both the figure and the play—back to the question they in fact have never left: that of the fate of memory and forgetting in a time that is out of joint:

> HAM. It is not very strange; for my uncle is King of Denmark, and those that would make mouths at him while my father lived given twenty, forty, fifty, a hundred ducats apiece for his picture in little. Sblood, there is something in this more than natural, if philosophy could find it out. (358–64)

The "something in this" that is "more than natural" has to do with the disjunctive convergence of private and public, familiar and political, in a response to temporal contingency that apparently leaves room for nothing but idolization of the present moment and the figures that dominate it.

At which point the Players arrive. What they will perform will of course pick up this motif of disjointed time and inconstant memory with respect to human mortality, when the Player-King announces his approaching death to his Queen, who responds that she will remain ever faithful to his memory. Were she to act otherwise, she asserts, "a second time I kill my husband dead / When second husband kisses me in bed" (III.ii.179–80). To which the Player-King responds:

> I do believe you think what now you speak;
> But what we do determine, oft we break.
> Purpose is but the slave to memory,
> Of violent birth but poor validity
> . . . . . . . . . . . . . . . . . . . . . . . . .

> Most necessary 'tis that we forget
> To pay ourselves what to ourselves is debt
> . . . . . . . . . . . . . . . . . . . . . . . . . . . . . . . .
> Our wills and fates do so contrary run
> That our devices still are overthrown:
> Our thoughts are ours, their ends none of our own. (181–208)

The last line returns us, indirectly, to Benjamin's description of Hamlet as a "Spectator through the Grace of God" who is interested not in the play of events but "strictly and solely in his own destiny." But what if the lesson of Hamlet's "own destiny" was that it could never be simply his own? And this in the dual sense: first, of not simply deriving from his intentions, projects, or acts, and second, of not simply being accessible to his knowledge? The behavior of his uncle and mother demonstrate to Hamlet the extent to which action and intention have become separated in the time out of joint. But he goes on to make of this experience his "own destiny" as well, the erroneous killing of Polonius being the most flagrant example, followed by his apparent inability to avenge his father. And yet his murder of Polonius only continues his no less murderous strategy against Ophelia, presumably as a surrogate for the vengeance he is prohibited from taking against his mother.

What triggers this strategy, it seems, is when Ophelia acts to confirm his own intention of forgetting everything unrelated to remembering the "me" of the Ghost, for it is only when she seeks to return to him certain "remembrances of yours" that Hamlet responds with violence, denying that he ever gave her anything to remember in the first place. Such deliberate "forgetting" then returns a bit later, when Hamlet and Ophelia sit together at the performance of "the mousetrap." Hamlet once again obsesses about the disjuncture of memory, time, and pleasure:

> HAM. What should a man do but be merry? For look you how cheerfully my mother looks and my father died within's two hours.
> OPH. Nay, 'tis twice two months, my Lord.
> HAM. So long? Nay then, let the devil wear black, for I'll have a suit of sables. O heavens, die two months ago and not forgotten yet! Then there's hope a great man's memory may outlive his life half a year. But by'r lady a must build churches then, or else shall 'a suffer not thinking on, with the hobby-horse, whose epitaph is, "For O, for O, the hobby-horse is forgot." (III.ii.123–33)

The final sentence, placed in quotation marks, has been historically glossed but remains enigmatic as far as its interpretation is concerned. However, since it condenses at least one consequence of the disjunctive relation of time and memory that marks the world and destiny of Hamlet, an attempt to read it is unavoidable. The hobbyhorse was a masked costume worn by dancers in the popular Morris dance, which the Puritans opposed and finally banned from the celebration. But it is not simply the "hobby-horse" that is in play here but also the popular expression to which it gave rise, for the phrase "O, O, the hobby-horse is forgot" is put in quotes in the Second Quarto. Hamlet cites a generally current phrase that increasingly appears to have detached itself from its historical referent to signify a certain form of habitual forgetting. Here the forgetting is quoted as an epitaph, anticipating Ophelia's death and Hamlet's guilt in provoking it. The "O, O" also by chance happens to cite the first letter of Ophelia's name, as well as being an exclamation, either of joy or of despair—or of both. The survival of the phrase, isolated from its original or referential context, performs textually the isolation that Hamlet seeks to impose on his memory of the ghost of his father. But it is also a vocative, perhaps calling out to the very person from which, once again, Hamlet is separating himself, reducing her name to a mere letter, a cipher of itself and a sign of obliteration: "O, O." No binary machine code here but a repetition that is also an anticipation and a prophesy, beyond anything that its speaker could have intended. For the "hobby-horse" remains the sign of a mask or a costume that mingles the animal with the human, mortal life with its hoped-for transcendence.

When Hamlet places himself in the position of a child with respect to Ophelia—"Lady, shall I lie in your lap?" (III.ii.110), he acts out the familial relation that he can only reject by humiliating the woman he has loved and perhaps still does, but who now serves only as a surrogate for the mother he is forbidden to punish:

> HAM. Is this a prologue, or the posy of a ring?
> OPH. 'Tis brief, my lord.
> HAM. As woman's love. (III.ii.147–49)

Instead of taking up the promise of salvation through reproduction (as in the Sonnets), "woman's love" for Hamlet only confirms the contingency of time and the definitiveness of mortality.

The time that is out of joint is thus the promised time of redemption from sin and guilt that founders on the experience of isolated individuals, which in turn is the correlative of the isolation of memory. Instead of reconfiguring time, such isolated memory—Freud will later call it "screen memory"—contributes to the isolation of the "I" and the "me," of the first-person singular, from all other persons, first, second, and third. This sense of isolation is the destiny not just of Hamlet but of the singular living being in post- and Counter-Reformation culture. Which is to say, the destiny of what can be called "Western modernity."

And here we come to the last point I wish to discuss. As mentioned at the outset, Benjamin sees in Hamlet the achievement of what the German baroque mourning play could never bring off: the overcoming of melancholy through self-absorption. And it is an overcoming that Benjamin insists is fundamentally Christian: "Only Shakespeare was capable of striking a Christian spark [*den christlichen Funken zu schlagen*] from the baroque rigidity of the melancholic."[7]

But in what sense can a "spark," *eine Funke*, be truly *christlich*? Schmitt denies it, and I think with good reason.[8] For it is not a spark that joins what is irrevocably out of joint: a *ray* might do it, or a *wave*. But not a spark. For a spark is instantaneous, discrete, cut off from its source and instantly extinguished. It has little to do with the continuum of the divine as expressed in the trinity of Father, Son, and Holy Ghost.

However, Benjamin may not be wrong in using the figure of the spark to describe a certain overcoming of melancholy through its performance, but only if we read Hamlet as more than just a spectator, even one by the grace of God. For as a spectator Hamlet is also a performer and, even more, a stage director. But the "awareness" that he gains at the end of his performance does not point to his salvation—or to his damnation, its negative but dependent alternative. It points to an afterlife that will not be that of Hamlet the person, or even Hamlet the character, but Hamlet the name. Not, however, as a proper name but as what Hamlet himself calls a "wounded name" (V.ii.349), which will survive only in the story to be told, in the play that has just been read or seen or heard. Thus Hamlet's last gesture is to wrench the poisoned goblet from Horatio's hands so that he may execute Hamlet's last will and testament. Which reads thus:

> Give me the cup. Let go, by Heaven I'll ha't.
> O God, Horatio, what a wounded name,
> Things standing thus unknown, shall I leave behind me.
> If thou didst ever hold me in thy heart,
> Absent thee from felicity awhile,
> And in this harsh world draw thy breath in pain,
> To tell my story. (V.ii.348–54)

The story that will convey and preserve Hamlet's "wounded name" is one that will be left "behind me": it will exceed and survive that first-person singular, preserved not in persons but in "things," "things standing thus unknown."

What Hamlet leaves behind is not a linear or legitimate succession, not a continuity of intention or of meaning, but only things that can be told, heard, seen, and read, but that for all that will remain forever unknown.

Perhaps it is this Unknowable that Benjamin mistook for the spark of Christian Providence, when he referred to the way Hamlet's "life, as the exemplary object given to his mourning, gestures before its extinction toward Christian providence, in whose bosom his mournful images turn into blessed existence."[9] The only bosom that can be found in *Hamlet* is that of poor Ophelia, and in it there is no transformation of mournful images into blessed existence—but rather the contrary, as the discussion of the Gravediggers suggests.

However, the passage generally held to be the one to which Benjamin gestures, in this network of gesturing, can and should be read quite differently. It comes as Hamlet is preparing for the duel with Laertes. Hamlet acknowledges a sense of foreboding but refuses Horatio's suggestion to avoid meeting Laertes: "Not a whit. We defy augury. There is special providence in the fall of a sparrow. If it be now, 'tis not to come. If it be not to come, it will be now; if it be not now, yet it will come. The readiness is all. Since no man, of aught he leaves, knows aught, what is't to leave betimes? Let be" (V.ii.215–20). Again, here at the end of my essay, another saw: "Readiness is all." But how is it possible to be ready for what cannot be anticipated? For what cannot be known: "Since no man, of aught he leaves, knows aught." Hamlet assumes his destiny, which consists not just in the *recognition* of the opacity of a singular, mortal existence—his own but also that of others—but in its acknowledgment. Acknowledgment, however, is neither knowledge nor belief. It is an equivocal acceptance, since from the start Hamlet has been tempted by suicide as a way of avoiding the conflict. But taken together with the legacy he bestows upon Horatio, this acknowledgment, this "readiness" leaves open the possibility of transmission and of tradition without insisting on redemption as its final goal. Instead of redemption there is only another story to be told, a story of a wounded name, but no formula as to how that name might be healed.

The wounds of the name do not heal without leaving scars. But those scars constitute the marks and traces of another story, always to be retold, and whose sequence responds to the challenge of a disjointed time.

Thus Hamlet—in all three senses of the word—joins forces with Benjamin, albeit not with his discussion of the mourning play but rather with that of the storyteller. At the end of the story, as distinct from the novel, there is always the question: And what happened next? The listeners may remain without counsel, but they are left with curiosity.

Is this why we return, over and over again, to *Hamlet*? In search not of knowledge, but in the hope of discovering another story?

It is this alone, perhaps, that makes Benjamin's remark, that "Hamlet alone is for the mourning play a spectator by (and of) the grace of God [*von Gottes Gnaden*]," finally readable. For if "melancholy encounters itself" in the "mournful images" of his life, it is precisely as theatrical images given to others to see, to read, and to hear. But what they say to those others is nothing other than the sigh of hope and despair in which mourning acknowledges its own demise: "O, O, the hobby-horse is forgot." And no Church will be built that can safeguard its memory.

## Notes

1. Carl Schmitt, *Hamlet oder Hekuba: Der Einbruch der Zeit in das Spiel* (Stuttgart: Klett-Cotta, 1985), 54, my translation.

2. Walter Benjamin, *Ursprung des deutschen Trauerspiels* (Frankfurt am Main: Suhrkamp, 1974), 136–37; Walter Benjamin, *Origin of the German Tragic Drama*, trans. John Osborne (London: Verso, 1994), 157–58, translation modified.

3. Carl Schmitt, *Roman Catholicism and Political Form*, trans. G. L. Ulmen (Westport, Conn.: Greenwood, 1996), 8 and passim.

4. References to *Hamlet* are from *The Arden Shakespeare*, ed. Harold Jenkins (London: Methuen, 1982).

5. That Shakespeare was attentive to the resources of such demonstrative pronouns is clear from the final couplet of Sonnet 74, written some ten years later: "The worth of that, is that which it contains / And that is this, and this with thee remains."

6. Schmitt, *Hamlet oder Hekuba*, 66ff.

7. Benjamin, *Ursprung des deutschen Trauerspiels*, 137; *Origin of the German Tragic Drama*, 158, translation modified.

8. Schmitt, *Hamlet oder Hekuba*, 63.

9. Benjamin, *Ursprung des deutschen Trauerspiels*, 136–37; *Origin of the German Tragic Drama*, 157–58, translation modified.

*Reading (Language, Mediation)*

Chapter 7

# Destinies of "The Purloined Letter"

Isabelle Alfandary

Reader of Jacques Derrida and Jacques Lacan, whose work he came to read generously both together and apart, Samuel Weber sought early on to think through the singular constitutive terms of each body of work, as well as the terms of debate that set their two strains of thought against one another. In *Return to Freud*, originally published in German in 1978 and dedicated to the thinking of Lacan, Weber articulated the terms of a complicated yet seminal relationship. Seeking neither to defend nor to reconcile them, he pointed out where their differences lay and the effects of their misunderstandings. Weber thus advanced a timely and illuminating reading of the work of Derrida and Lacan that largely contributed to an intertwined understanding, where each work is always already read in its conceptual intersection with the other. This Weberian method of bringing together the literary text and those critical exegeses aimed at displacing (dis-locating) it inspires this essay.

Poe's "The Purloined Letter" is a text caught from the start in the nets of intertextuality: the narrator announces on the first page, even before the arrival of the prefect: "For myself, however, I was mentally discussing certain topics which had formed matter for conversation between us at an earlier period of the evening; I mean the affair of the Rue Morgue, and the mystery attending the murder of Marie Rôget."[1] As Derrida has pointed out, the story is a weaving of interwoven texts ("'The Purloined Letter' is the text, the text in the text"),[2] which is the reason for my own attempt at reading Lacan's "Seminar on 'The Purloined Letter'" together with the response it drew from Derrida. These texts, connected in that they respond to one another, follow from Poe's text, itself read, at least by Lacan, in Baudelaire's translation. Lacan's reading of Poe was also influenced by a critical text by Freud's contemporary, Marie Bonaparte, a text that Lacan read and to which he responds without ever citing, as Derrida rightly pointed out. I begin by emphasizing the power of the critical summons constituted by the short story's text. In "The Purloined Letter," Lacan wrote, "the narration effectively doubles the drama with a commentary."[3]

The very nature of the letter calls for commentary, and few literary texts have elicited so much critical response. The destiny of "The Purloined Letter," of the letter in and of itself, gives reason for pause. The signifier—which is not, for Lacan, literally identified with the letter but is inseparable from it—summons the subject in that the signifier calls the subject to respond. In the chapter of *Return to Freud*, titled "The Rise and Fall of the Signifier," Weber implicitly warns against the temptation to identify the letter with the signifier and the error to which such an identification would lead.[4]

"The Purloined Letter" gave rise to three successive psychoanalytic studies: Joseph Wood Krutch's *Edgar Allen Poe: A Study in Genius* (1926), Bonaparte's *Edgar Poe: Étude psychanalytique* (1933), and Lacan's "Séminaire sur la 'Lettre volée' " (1966). Bonaparte's idea of a Poe rendered impotent by the fact of his fixation on the maternal object, an idea we can qualify, along with Derrida, as "psycho-biographical,"[5] is taken up from the diagnosis offered by Krutch. But even if we follow Shoshana Felman in giving Bonaparte credit for her attempt to depart from Krutch's naïvely clinical reading by engaging a reading that sidesteps both the effects of reception and the recognition of the story's being the work of a neurotic, the singularity of the literary text is nonetheless fundamentally missing in Bonaparte as in Krutch.[6]

Bonaparte's analysis proceeds from a conception she formulated in an earlier work, which she quotes in *The Life and Works of Edgar Allan Poe: A Psycho-analytic Interpretation*: "Works of art or literature profoundly reveal their creators' psychology and, as Freud has shown, their construction resembles that of our dreams."[7] Her reading of Poe never acknowledges this initial bias. The conception of fiction as a disguise for the activity of the unconscious relies on a deterministic model that takes no account whatsoever of the work of the negative that writing represents, and it misrecognizes all forms of the drive's becoming. Bonaparte's reading is biased; it knows in advance what it is looking for.

In his own commentary Derrida unexpectedly reads between the lines of Bonaparte's dogmatic and indefensible text, as if to save the princess from the oblivion into which she has fallen beneath the pen of Lacan and to direct certain of her critical gestures against Lacan, notably the sensitivity she demonstrates toward the narrator.[8] The reading Derrida proposes, as we will see, is not without reservations. In Derrida's commentary, as well as in Lacan's and even in Poe's text, Barbara Johnson remarks, "it is the *act of analysis* which seems to occupy the center of the discursive stage; and the *act of analysis of the act of analysis* which in some way disrupts that centrality."[9] As limited as it is, Derrida's rehabilitation of Bonaparte is reinscribed in the context of his critical reading of Lacan's commentary.

The notion of "reading through," elaborated by John Cage to designate his practice of basing his poetic writing on the reading of modernist texts, can be applied to the critical history of "The Purloined Letter." Poe's text has been modified by the effect of the succession of commentaries that now accompany it. This critical phenomenon reveals one of the letter's characteristic traits: it is not original. The *first* letter is no longer; it never was. The letter in the short story is unreadable and unread—which is why Lacan designates it as "pure signifier,"[10] theoretically pure of every signified. The letter is always already contained in the movement of reading—as interpretation, manipulation, rewriting. It is contingent, practically indifferent, secondary, and not second—the effect of being recovered.

## A Letter Has No Existence Except as Part of a Chain

Because the letter, as Lacan suggests in the first paragraph of the seminar he dedicated to it, is taken up in what he calls "the signifying chain," it is a link in a chain that assures connection. It is in this purpose that its value lies: "My research has led me to the realization that repetition automatism (*Wiederholungszwang*) has its basis in what I have called the *insistence* of the signifying chain. I have isolated this notion as a correlate of the *ex-sistence* (that is, of the eccentric place) in which we must necessarily locate the subject of the unconscious, if we are to take Freud's discovery seriously."[11] Thus, from the start, the purloined letter is called upon to be read as inscribed in a chain. A letter has no existence in itself, for itself. Its value is only in the dimension of the address, only in the measure of its being addressed without taking its measure or knowing its trajectory in advance.

Before entering into the heart of the subject Lacan justifies his claim, his detour through the literary text. The purloined letter is by far not the only letter, the only space of inscription, on the signifier's route. The psychoanalysis of a subject is similarly an occasion for the unveiling of a "route." Why turn to fiction and not to clinical case studies? The interest of such a detour through what Lacan calls a "story" resides in the power of a trajectory's illustration and demonstration in the space of fiction. Fiction here is a *pure* space, a space of purity understood in the way that Kant uses the word: pure of all interference, uniquely capable of offering to view the circuit ("the circuit of the room")[12] of a signifier isolated from and created by all pieces. Fiction allows what the clinical case prohibits: to be constituted as an object lesson, an example.

> That is why I have decided to illustrate for you today a truth which may be drawn from the moment in Freud's thought we have been studying—namely, that it is the symbolic order which is constitutive for the subject—by demonstrating in a story the major determination the subject receives from the itinerary of a signifier.
>
> It is this truth, let us note, that makes the very existence of fiction possible. Thus a fable is as appropriate as any other story for shedding light on it—providing we are willing to put the fable's coherence

> to the test. With this proviso, a fable even has the advantage of manifesting symbolic necessity all the more purely in that we might be inclined to believe it is governed by the arbitrary.[13]

The tortuous formula with which Lacan defends his turn to Poe is nonetheless clear. The power of exposition of what Lacan calls a "fable" is rooted in the way it manifests as necessary what is conventionally taken to be arbitrary. Fiction manifests and props up as arbitrary what the psychoanalyst designates as "symbolic necessity."

In a note in *Positions*, Derrida admits to being very "interested" in the "Seminar on 'The Purloined Letter.' "[14] Having read Lacan's text judiciously and attentively, he critiques its logic of illustrating a truth.[15] Derrida's reproach of Lacan concerns the singular nature of fiction, the conditions of narration reduced to the lone and poor term *story* (*histoire*).[16] Lacan does, however, interrogate the dramatic and structural dimension of the embedded narrative, notably when he describes the "triple subjective filter" through which the first scene is conveyed.[17] Derrida is thus seen to be relatively unfair when he argues that the "Seminar" is concerned only with the "content of this story, what is justifiably called its history, what is recounted in the account, the internal and narrated face of the narration." What ensues is a series of refutations: point by point, Derrida reproves Lacan in lectures that he judges erroneous or simplistic. The philosopher distinguishes between the "narrating narrator and a narrated narrator" and challenges the category of "general narrator" accepted by Lacan. Separating planes of narration from those of fiction, Derrida takes up what he calls "a problem of framing, of bordering and delimitation."[18] Reader of Lacan, reader of Poe, he complicates the Lacanian reading, refines it. Poe's text is not the only object of Derrida's commentary, then; it offers him a way of engaging in dialogue and controversy with Lacan.

Derrida opens his essay "Le Facteur de la verité" by contesting what he refers to as the exemplary status of truth in fiction: "Truth would play a piece: lifted, by the philosopher or the analyst, from within a more powerful functioning." In his critique he challenges the posture of the analyst-reader of the literary text: "The denuding of this *Stoff*, the discovery of the semantic material—such would be the end of analytic deciphering. . . . Exhibiting, denuding, undressing, unveiling: the familiar acrobatics of the metaphor *of* the truth. And one just as well could say the metaphor of metaphor, the truth of truth, the truth of metaphor." What Derrida objects to is the idea that the text would be "coordinated with its naked truth. . . . When Freud intends to denude the original *Stoff* beneath the disguises of the secondary fabrication, he is anticipating the truth of the text."[19] This reproach addressed to Freud seems fully applicable to the Lacanian logic of subjective truth as mandate.

Yet the truth in question in the Lacanian text is problematic and provisional: it is the truth of the existence of the unconscious and its singular translation into the experience of the interpretive wager that the psychoanalyst makes on the subject. The signifying chain theorized by Lacan is no more hypostatized than it is anticipated because it does not fall under any type, the letter being by definition in Lacan's sense infrasignifying (*infra-signifiante*). The illustrative function of fiction that Derrida emphasizes when he cites Freud on the subject of the literary work ("Wir besitzen ein interessantes Zeugnis dafür") does not entirely do justice to the treatment of the short story in the seminar because Lacan is playing the text's game; he lets himself be played by it.

Derrida's critique revolves around what he calls the misrecognition of the context of the "map [*carte*], the functioning or fictioning, of Poe's text, of this text and its links to others, let us say the *squaring* [*carrure*] of a scene of writing played out in it."[20] Despite the slight reserve that Derrida expresses on the subject of Lacan-the-reader, the verdict falls decisively: Lacan's is "a profoundly traditional reading" of a literary text. In support of his thesis the philosopher cites the psychoanalyst: "It is this truth, let us note, that makes the very existence of fiction possible."[21] Between this truth and the Truth, Derrida, although a reader of scrupulous sensitivity, takes a leap. I would like to try to defend the opposite thesis. What truth are we actually talking about in Lacan? "[A] truth which may be drawn from the moment in Freud's thought we have been studying."[22] Far from being a matter of truth, the whole truth, it is a question of a truth, the Freudian truth, that of the existence of the unconscious brought to light by Freud, inseparable from the conditions of its deconstruction in the precise sense understood by Derrida in his reading of Freud. If, as Derrida claims, "truth inhabits fiction" in Lacan,[23] it is the truth of an existence, that of the unconscious, that is at issue insofar as the unconscious is what emerges from the order of the signifier. The truth, for Lacan, is related to the unconscious of which it is a product, "precisely in what the truth that it bears, that of the unconscious, owes to the letter of language—that is, to what I call 'the signifier.' "[24] Not by chance is fiction the space of verifying Freudian truth; fiction is the space in which the signifier operates, a symbolic space, free of interference from any other order.

The message of "The Purloined Letter" has already reached the recipient (*destinataire*). It becomes indifferent inasmuch as it fulfills a function that, even once accomplished, does not at all exhaust its fate. The letter has a structure of infinity, even if its circulation is not de facto infinite: its effects are multiplicative in the intersubjective system that takes it up. The Lacanian distinction that sets the function of the message against the destiny of the letter is crucial. The message is operative (Lacan says "functional"); the letter is performative, effective. The letter does not signify in itself; it comes to signify. It literally makes a sign.

Lacan does not neglect the message properly speaking but declares that it detaches itself from the letter. The narrative drive of the short story depends on the message remaining unknown to the reader as well as to the principal protagonists. Of the letter's text the reader knows nothing, which does not, however, affect the letter's functioning. On the contrary the letter is valued in that it circulates, is taken up, purloined, replaced.

"His lynx eye immediately perceives the paper, recognizes the handwriting of the address, observes the confusion of the personage addressed, and fathoms her secret."[25] Despite the three gazes that structure the diegesis, whatever their degree of intentionality and perspicacity, there is no total point of view on the letter; there are only partial, more or less penetrating points of view. As Dupin notes of the Parisian police, and this in spite of efforts to recover it, the letter remains unfindable: "That *place entailed blindness*." Gaze and blindness, dialectically linked, are a function of the subject's position in relation to the letter, of its position of subjection to the letter's order. The letter produces effects of infirmity, inhibition, even of "imbecility," as Lacan insinuates of the king. Despite an uncommon talent for clairvoyance, Dupin owes his ability to decipher to his eccentric situation (vis-à-vis the letter's itinerary: "from the place where he is [*il est*]" he can see only insofar as it does not concern him, only so long as he is not made the emissary of the purloined letter, the analyst, except as the letter is "*en souffrance* with us in the transference." Being paid, suggests Lacan, is, for Dupin, about his "withdraw[al] from the letter's symbolic circuit."[26] Unlike Bonaparte, for whom he had but little esteem, Lacan sees in Dupin the figure of the analyst. The verb the prefect refers to in his initial request is *consult*: "upon G's saying that he had to consult us, or rather to ask his opinion of my friend about some official business which had occasioned a great deal of trouble."[27]

The letter missing from its place escapes: it escapes from its author in that he parts with it at the moment of sending it and is himself constituted by this same dispossession; the letter escapes its recipient (*destinataire*) in that it is susceptible to infinite reappropriations, the purloined letter being one of its numerous possible diversions. The letter can at any moment escape its possessor, who never possesses it except in being able to destroy it. Yet even though the letter is destroyed—it is possible that Dupin, however otherwise unduped, is deluded on this point—its journey is not finished; it continues to produce more or less calculable effects in that it continues to be missing in the different places it has successively occupied. When Dupin finally gets hold of it, he figures out from its appearance the destructive plan, a plan he had manifestly abandoned: "as if a design, in the first instance, to tear it entirely up as worthless, had been altered, or stayed, in the second."[28] This is what authorizes Lacan to maintain that even in a thousand pieces the letter continues to be: "But whereas it is first of all the materiality of the signifier that I have emphasized, that materiality is *singular* in many ways, the first of which is not to allow of partition."[29] Weber argues that Lacan "is concerned with the principle by which the signifier is radically separated from its materialization."[30] The singular survival of the letter is due to the effect of immaterial inscription that it acquires in its circulation: "Cut a letter in small pieces, and it remains the letter that it is." For this reason the letter comes under the category of the uncountable: "But as for the letter itself, whether we take it in the sense of a typographical element, of an epistle, or of what constitutes a man of letters—we commonly say that what people say must be understood *à la lettre* (to the letter or literally), that *a letter* is being held for you at the post office, or even that you are well versed with *letters*—never that there is (some amount of) *letter* [*de la lettre*] anywhere, whatever the context, even to designate late mail."[31]

The letter is a sign of an absence. Its being is negative: "This is why we cannot say of the purloined letter that, like other objects, it must be *or* not be somewhere but rather that, unlike them, it will be *and* not be where it is wherever it goes."[32] When Dupin asks for what he calls "an accurate description of the letter," the prefect answers, "'Oh yes!'—And here the Prefect, producing a memorandum-book, proceeded to read aloud a minute account of the internal, and especially of the external appearance of the missing document." The minute description of the missing document is itself missing: "No sooner had I glanced at this letter, than I concluded it to be that of which I was in search. To be sure, it was, to all appearance, radically different from the one of which the Prefect had read us so minute a description. . . . But then the *radicalness* of these differences, which was excessive; the dirt; the soiled and torn condition of the paper."[33] What confirms Dupin's intuition is, against all expectation, "the *radicalness* of these differences": the discrepancy between the described letter and the real letter, between other clues, serves, in the eyes of Dupin, as proof. Like the Saussurean sign, the letter is two-sided, one side being inseparable from the other—except when they are held apart for reasons of pure abstraction.

## The Book, Destiny of the Letter

> At Paris, just after dark one gusty evening in the autumn of 18—, I was enjoying the twofold luxury of meditation and a meerschaum, in company with my friend C. Auguste Dupin, in his little back library, or book closet, *au troisième, No. 33, Rue Dunôt*, Faubourg St. Germain. For an hour at least we had maintained a profound silence; while each to any casual observer, might have seemed intently and exclusively occupied with the curling eddies of smoke that oppressed the atmosphere of the chamber. For myself, I was mentally discussing certain topics which had formed matter for the conversation between us at an earlier period of the evening.[34]

In the last pages of "Le Facteur de la vérité" the philosopher reads this scene as a scene of writing, or archiwriting (*archi-écriture*), in a library offered as the future to come (*l'a-venir*) of the letter, in a silence inhabited by internal conversations. "Everything begins 'in' a library: in books, writings, references. Therefore nothing begins. Only a drifting or disorientation from which one does not emerge." For Derrida this scene is anoriginary (*an-originaire*), a scene of pure self-difference, "an affair of writing, and of writing adrift, in a place of writing open without end to its grafting onto other writings."[35]

The letter is inseparable from the writing that composes it. Its metonymic doubles in the text are legion, from the books in the minister's library leafed through one by one to the prefect's check and the notebook in which he records his description, the writing case (*escritoire*) from which Dupin takes the letter that he did not write, the writing table beside which the minister is seated.

> Certainly; we opened every package and parcel; we not only opened every book, but we turned over every leaf in each volume, not contenting ourselves with a mere shake, according to the fashion of some of our police officers. We also measured the thickness of every book-*cover*, with the most accurate admeasurement, and applied to each the most jealous scrutiny of the microscope. Had any of the bindings been recently meddled with, it would have been utterly impossible that the fact should have escaped observation. Some five or six volumes, just from the hands of the binder, we carefully probed, longitudinally, with the needles.[36]

In this scene of writings that coincides with the search of the minister's apartments, the reader is presented with a fait accompli of the articulation between the book and the letter in the form of the sheet, the page. A book is, after all, only a letter multiplied, a transplanting of letters that "took." Literature as a whole is damaged in "The Purloined Letter." The book, right up to its most sensual materiality ("jealous"), is scrupulously inspected by the police. Of course, it takes a wrong turn, but however wrong it is, this route puts the reader on a secondary but irrevocable interpretive path, that of the link between the letter and the book, a link materialized by the binding. The destiny of every letter could well be the book: literature.

At least two scenes involving signatures can be found in the text: one in which Dupin is in a position of recipient (*recipiendaire*) in an act of signing, the payment scene,[37] and one in which he is the signatory. After the minister leaves the letter on the table, a "fac-simile" is slid into the purloined letter's place and position by Dupin. If the letter is missing from its place (which is in any case the condition of its circulation), its place is not left vacant but is occupied by substitutes that gesture toward it and become so many literary traces of its passage.

> "I confess, however, that I should like very well to know the precise character of his thoughts, when, being defied by her whom the

Prefect terms 'a certain personage,' he is reduced to opening the letter which I left for him in the card-rack."

"How? Did you put any thing particular in it?"

"Why—it did not seem altogether right to leave the interior blank—that would have been insulting. D—, at Vienna once, did me an evil turn, which I told him, quite good-humoredly, that I should remember. So, as I knew he would feel some curiosity in regard to the identity of the person who had outwitted him, I thought it a pity not to give him a clue. He is well acquainted with my MS., and I just copied into the middle of the blank sheet the words—

—Un dessein si funeste,
S'il n'est digne d'Atrée, est digne de Thyeste

They are to be found in Crébillon's 'Atrée.' "[38]

Through the typographical indentation and the dashes that precede the Crébillon citation, the page of the short story becomes the facsimile of the purloined letter. The outside of the letter bears the minister's counterfeit seal—one notes in passing that the purloined letter is the occasion of a self-address—his signature applied by way of mistake, whereas its inside bears Dupin's signature, whose handwriting, we are assured, was known to the minister. As Derrida rightly notes, Dupin and the minister share the same initial "D," answering to "D." The citation, retranscribed at the moment of concluding, constitutes an unexpected increase of hermeneutic activity—proof that the letter, whatever its destination, never finishes questioning its readers.

## The Logic of Destiny

Lacan's reading of the oral word that concludes the short story emphasizes the dimension of destiny as an effect of the letter: "The audacious creature is, of course, reduced here to the state of imbecilic blindness in which man finds himself in relation to the wall-like letters that dictate his destiny."[39] The tragic play from which the Crébillon citation is quoted allegorizes the position of not-knowing in which the subject fatally finds himself in relation to the signifier. Yet destiny in the sense that Lacan understands it is not at all a matter of mysticism; it is instead a matter of logic. The letter can be discovered only if one situates oneself at its level. "But he perpetually errs by being too deep or too shallow, for the matter in hand," professes Dupin of the prefect, thunderstruck by the reunion with the precious document. Dupin remembers a child's game, whose name resonates in the ears of the fable reader: "even and odd."[40] "Odd" is, moreover, the adjective Dupin echoes in the prefect's discourse even before hearing about the ins and outs of the affair:

> "The fact is, the business is very simple indeed, and I make no doubt that we can manage it sufficiently well ourselves; but then I thought Dupin would like to hear the details of it, because it is so excessively odd."
>
> "Simple and odd," said Dupin.
>
> "Why yes; and not exactly that either. The fact is, we have all been a good deal puzzled because the affair *is* so simple, and yet baffles us altogether."
>
> "Perhaps it is the very simplicity of the thing which puts you at fault," said my friend.
>
> "What nonsense you do talk!" replied the Prefect, laughing heartily.
>
> "Perhaps the mystery is a little *too* plain," said Dupin.
>
> "Oh, good heavens! Who ever heard of such an idea?"
>
> "A little *too* self-evident."[41]

The affair is simple like a child's game. Dupin, whom Lacan compares to the narrative position of the analyst within the cure, understands the prefect to the letter: the two signifiers he scans are "simple" and "odd," the very words of the man who comes to find him, the words Dupin delivers out of the blue but that he, the prefect, curiously objects to when he hears them in the mouth of Dupin. I note in passing the affinities between the detective story as a genre and psychoanalysis in view of the enigmatic and encoded character of the Freudian unconscious. The prefect does not hear himself speak any more than the king sees the letter sitting under his nose. That there be any acknowledgment of receipt, the subject must offer proof of a negativity that takes the form of an interception by a third. The idea that guides Dupin is the one the prefect breathes to him and that he misrecognizes as his own. In refusing to acknowledge his own words, or more exactly, by refusing to recognize his place as witness ("Who ever heard such an idea?"), and in departing with a great laugh, which Dupin will remember, the prefect is the subject of the letter without knowing it.

It remains to be seen how an idea as right as it is improbable, that of simplicity, comes to the prefect, an idea he unconsciously submits to the only character capable of hearing what is *inaudible* within this word and within whose hands he puts his own fate and that of the letter. Similarly we might ask about the manner by which the prefect intuited the minister's logic. How did this unthought (*im-pensé*) of the minister's thought, mathematician and poet of his state, which Dupin brings to light, how could this thought make its way to him? The prefect, insofar as he is included in the circuit of the letter, is the depositor of its knowledge, of the effects of knowledge that are coextensive with him, of the effects of the subject that set off the signifying chain. "Simplicity," as Dupin names it, a term he again and without completely knowing it picks up from the prefect ("simple"), is deduced from a context that the minister did not produce by himself—the context imposed by the letter. What Dupin himself fails to see in all letters is the possibility that the key to the enigma was breathed to him by the prefect, proof if he needed it that the letter dupes even nondupes. If the party game is the paradigm of Dupin's thought, it is because it allows, within the conditions of intersubjective relations, learning from the other, seeing his logic at work so as to be able to identify it—even unconsciously: to win against the other, one must play like him.

> "There is a game of puzzles," he resumed, "which is played upon a map. One party playing requires another to find a given word—the name of town, river, state or empire—any word in short, upon the motley and perplexed surface of the chart. A novice in the game generally seeks to embarrass his opponents by giving them the most minutely lettered names; but the adept selects such words as stretch, in large characters, from one end of the chart to the other. These, like the over-largely lettered signs and placards of the street, escape observation by dint of being excessively obvious; and here the physical oversight is precisely analogous with the moral inapprehension by which the intellect suffers to pass unnoticed those considerations which are too obtrusively and too palpably self-evident. But this is a point, it appears, somewhat above or beneath the understanding of the Prefect. He never once thought it probable, or possible, that the Minister had deposited the letter immediately beneath the nose of the whole world, by way of best preventing any portion of that world from perceiving it."[42]

At issue here is the transfer of a knowledge that does not know itself or the inscription of a rule following the structure of the chain. "He never once thought it probable, or possible," does not want the minister to say or even to know the thing, but that this knowledge does not know itself as such, that it is a knowledge liable to be spoken without knowing it: this is exactly the meaning that Lacan attributes to unconscious knowledge.

## The Letter's Trajectory

The letter is not possessed; it is the letter that possesses us: "There must be a very odd *noli me tangere* in this sign for its possession to, like the Socratic stingray, make its man so numb that he falls into what unequivocally appears in his case to be a state of inaction."[43] It is there, the meaning of its rapture. The letter binds/reads (*lie/lit*) not only the subject to whom it is addressed but even him between whose hands it passes, whether he wants it or not.

The letter is charged with a destiny that it spreads through language without anyone paying attention: the one who receives, is he not called recipient (*destinataire*)? The English language is no less charged, though differently oriented, calling "the recipient" (*destinataire*) by a declension on the root applicable to the sender (*envoyeur*): *addressee/addresser*. Around the address is bound the system that Lacan calls "intersubjective," that Derrida pins down in "the metaphor of the mail," that Dupin qualifies as "relation" when he holds forth on the weakness of mathematical reason. Destiny conceives the itinerary as determination, according to Lacan, who even speaks of "law": "It is the law specific to this chain which governs the psychoanalytic effects that are determinant for the subject."[44]

The letter calls the subject into being, a subject whose title is plainly justified as an effect of the address. The subject of the unconscious that Lacan elaborates based on his reading of "The Purloined Letter" is the subject of the address. The subject is conceived in the Lacanian theory of the signifier as an effect of address, an address whose effects are so incalculable that one might be tempted to call them *destiny*:

> To *purloin*, says the Oxford English Dictionary, is an Anglo-French word—that is, it is composed of the prefix *pur-*, found in *purpose*, *purchase*, and *purport*, and of the Old French word *loing, loigner, longé*. We recognize in the first element the Latin *pro-*, as opposed to *ante*, insofar as it presupposes a back in front of which it stands, possibly to guarantee it or even to stand in as its guarantor (whereas *ante* goes forth to meet what comes to meet it). As for the second, the Old French word *loigner* is a verb that attributes place *au loing* (or *longé*), which does not mean *au loin* (far off), but *au long de* (alongside). To purloin is thus *mettre de côté* (to set aside) or, to resort to a colloquialism which plays off the two meanings, *mettre à gauche* (to put to the left side [literally] and to tuck away).
>
> Our detour is thus validated by the very object which leads us into it: for we are quite simply dealing with a *letter* which has been *detoured*, one whose trajectory has been *prolonged* (this is literally the English word in the title), or, to resort to the language of the post office, a letter *en souffrance* (awaiting delivery or unclaimed).[45]

This etymological reflection leads Lacan to interpret the path of the letter. Taking as his point of departure "this truth . . . that makes the very existence of fiction possible," where "truth here reveals its fictive ordering,"[46] he draws on the sense of the letter in the double meaning of the term: he scrupulously follows its narrative trajectory and adopts the contours of its etymological signification. The sense of the letter is to be taken to the letter: "But how are we to take the letter, here? Quite simply, literally [*à la lettre*]." [47] The notion of "the instance of the letter," developed in an article of the same name included in the *Ecrits*, is inspired by the unclaimed letter (*la lettre en souffrance*) and inferred from the reading of Poe's tale. Lacan's teaching has been presented under the patronage of fiction ever since "Seminar on 'The Purloined Letter' " appeared as the first essay of the *Ecrits*, offering to readers "an easy entryway into my style . . . even though that means taking it out of chronological order."[48]

## Truth and Chance of Determination

The question of the staging (mise-en-scène) of truth is taken up by Derrida in his reading of Lacan.[49] We can't help but hear in this definition a concept whose fundamental place in the metaphysical edifice is known. Despite what Derrida suggests, the Lacanian truth differs from this metaphysical truth in that the figure of the barred big Other, such as it is elaborated in the recently published seminar on desire and its interpretation,[50] deprives the Truth of truth, otherwise said to be foundational. Derrida's ironic question, "But is truth an example?,"[51] can be heard literally (*à la lettre*) in Lacan's theory of the signifier. The truth of a subject is the product of an overdetermination that Lacan qualifies as symbolic. This has to do with the necessary position in which the letter, by dint of its circulation, places the subject, the place in the round (*la ronde*) where it takes up its turn: "We see separate out from the real a symbolic determination which, as faithful as it may be in recording any partiality of the real, merely produces all the more clearly the disparities that it brings with it."[52] From this point of view the truth of the subject is the effect of chance, which becomes a necessity for it in its encoded inscription. Derrida himself, champion of the fight against the Lacanian reference to truth that he judges suspect, nevertheless recognizes in "Le Facteur de la vérité" that if there is "a Lacanian *doctrine* of the truth," it is heterogeneous.[53] Does Lacan not read Poe's tale as a place where "the sign and being [are] marvelously disjoint"?[54]

Lacan draws the notion of "signifying overdetermination" from Freud's theory of the unconscious. The symbolic determination that receives its order (as ordinance and as syntactical agent) from the course of the letter does not determine the Real; this would be an absurdity or a belief. Rather the affect overdetermines it in its effects for a given subject: "But these laws are precisely those of symbolic determination. For it is clear that they predate any real observation of randomness [*hasard*], as is clear from the fact that we judge whether an object is apt or not to be used to obtain a series (always symbolic, in this case) of random throws according to its obedience to these laws—for example, whether or not a coin, or this object admirably known as a 'die' [*dé*], qualifies for this function."[55] Without contradicting Mallarmé, Lacan suggests that the throw of the dice presupposed by the letter is of the nature to affect chance.

One of Derrida's principal critiques of Lacan concerns the letter's proper and circular itinerary, which he calls "the law of its itinerary." What the philosopher doubts is how perfectly fine-tuned it is: "This readequation (the truth) therefore indeed implies a theory of the proper place, and the latter implies a theory of the letter as an indivisible locality: the signifier must never risk being lost, destroyed, divided, or fragmented without return." Derrida exaggerates this trait to make his argument, for Lacan doesn't maintain that the letter is actually indestructible; he says only that, even destroyed, "its itinerary doesn't end." However, Derrida sees in what he takes for a dogmatic principle a curiously idealistic conception of the "materiality" of the signifier, the word *phone* being, according to him, the guarantee of indivisibility: "*This 'materiality,' deduced from an indivisibility found nowhere, in fact corresponds to an idealization.* Only the ideality of a letter resists destructive division."[56]

At play in the dispute provoked by Derrida is what he is inclined to consider the randomness of destination. To the regulated destiny of the Lacanian letter is opposed the Derridean *destinerrance*. The questions to be answered are whether the letter has a proper place and whether the letter returns toward what Derrida names its *oikos*, its familiar dwelling. To Lacan, Derrida opposes the thesis according to which "the lack does not have its place in dissemination." Contesting the final proposition of Lacan's seminar, he proposes a counterformula: "[A] letter can always not arrive at its destination." "Can always not" must be heard as follows: "Not that the letter never arrives at its destination, but it belongs to the structure of the letter to be capable, always, of not arriving." It is the consistency of the symbolic order that Derrida calls into question when he reads this principle as a metaphysical belief, bordering on a mystifying superstition. As with the truth, the destination is a question left hanging. In one of the last sentences of "Le Facteur de la vérité" Derrida tends to back off somewhat from his first assertion: "[A] letter does *not always* arrive at its destination, and from the moment that this possibility belongs to its structure one can say that it never truly arrives, that when it does arrive its capacity not to arrive torments it with an internal drifting." For Derrida reaching the destination would be a particular case of the incalculable becoming of the letter. What he calls "its structure" is due to the writing of which it is a product. Yet the effects of writing that Derrida attempted to bring to light are incalculable, effects that he calls at the end of his analysis of Poe's tale "effects of indirection."[57] As the product of being dispatched, the letter opens up all possibilities. To the implacable law of the signifier Derrida's analysis opposes the differential and undecidable logic of writing.

Insofar as it circulates the letter has no proper place. From its dispatch to its open reception, it is in motion. It doesn't stop. From this point of view it is true that the conclusion drawn by Lacan might surprise: "While he has succeeded in putting the letter back on its proper course, it has yet to be made to reach its address. And that address is the place previously occupied by the King, since it is there that it must fall back into the order based on the Law." In Lacanian theory the letter only ever arrives at its destination in the symbolic field, in its articulation with the imaginary round (*ronde*). The destination is not understood in the Real—that makes no sense—because it is the nature of the Real that "whatever upheaval we subject it to, [it] is always and in every case in its place." On this point the Derridean argument does not contradict the Lacanian thesis: to not arrive at a destination can also be a possible destination of the letter. Given the negativity from which it is produced, even if it happens to return to its place, the letter does not annul either the itinerary or the intersubjective effects (of) "its round" (*que "sa ronde"*).[58]

**Translated by Denise Davis**

## Notes

1. Edgar Allen Poe, "The Purloined Letter" (1844), in *The Fall of the House of Usher and Other Writings* (London: Penguin, 2003), 281.
2. Jacques Derrida, "Le Facteur de la vérité," in *The Post Card: From Socrates to Freud and Beyond* (Chicago: University of Chicago Press, 1987), 493. [This essay appears in English in several versions. All quotations and page references are from Alan Bass's translation in *The Post Card*. Bass leaves the title in French.–Translator]
3. Jacques Lacan, "Seminar on 'The Purloined Letter' " (1966), in *Ecrits: The First Complete Edition in English*, trans. Bruce Fink (New York: Norton, 2006), 7.
4. Samuel Weber, *Return to Freud: Jacques Lacan's Dislocation of Psychoanalysis* (Cambridge, U.K.: Cambridge University Press, 1991), 47–49.
5. Derrida, "Le Facteur de la vérité," 444.
6. Shoshana Felman, "On Reading Poetry: Reflections on the Limits and Possibilities of Psychoanalytic Approaches," in *The Purloined Poe: Lacan, Derrida, and Psychoanalytical Reading*, ed. John Muller and William Richardson (Baltimore: Johns Hopkins University Press, 1988).
7. Marie Bonaparte, "Selections from *The Life and Works of Edgar Allen Poe: A Psycho-analytic Interpretation*," trans. John Rodker, in Muller and Richardson, *The Purloined Poe*, 101.
8. Derrida, "Le Facteur de la vérité," 459.
9. Barbara Johnson, "The Frame of Reference: Poe, Lacan, Derrida," in Muller and Richardson, *The Purloined Poe*, 213.
10. Lacan, "Seminar on 'The Purloined Letter,' " 10.
11. Lacan, "Seminar on 'The Purloined Letter,' " 6.
12. Poe, "The Purloined Letter," 21.
13. Lacan, "Seminar on 'The Purloined Letter,' " 7.
14. Jacques Derrida, *Positions*, trans. Alan Bass (Chicago: University of Chicago Press, 1981), 112n44.

15. Derrida, "Le Facteur de la vérité," 426.
16. Derrida, "Le Facteur de la vérité," 427.
17. Lacan, "Seminar on 'The Purloined Letter,'" 12.
18. Derrida, "Le Facteur de la vérité," 427, 429, 431.
19. Derrida, "Le Facteur de la vérité," 414, 415.
20. Derrida, *Positions*, 112n44.
21. Derrida, "Le Facteur de la vérité," 426; Lacan, "Seminar on 'The Purloined Letter,'" 7.
22. Lacan, "Seminar on 'The Purloined Letter,'" 7.
23. "In truth, the truth inhabits fiction like the master of the house, as the law of the house, as the economy of fiction" (Derrida, "Le Facteur de la vérité," 426).
24. Jacques Lacan, "*On a Purpose*" (1966), in *Ecrits*, 305.
25. Poe, "The Purloined Letter," 283.
26. Lacan, "Seminar on 'The Purloined Letter,'" 27, 28, 29, 26.
27. Poe, "The Purloined Letter," 281.
28. Poe, "The Purloined Letter," 297.
29. Lacan, "Seminar on 'The Purloined Letter,'" 16.
30. Weber, *Return to Freud*, 50.
31. Lacan, "Seminar on 'The Purloined Letter,'" 16, 17.
32. Lacan, "Seminar on 'The Purloined Letter,'" 17.
33. Poe, "The Purloined Letter," 288, 297.
34. Poe, "The Purloined Letter," 281.
35. Derrida, "Le Facteur de la vérité," 484.
36. Poe, "The Purloined Letter," 287.
37. Poe, "The Purloined Letter," 289.
38. Poe, "The Purloined Letter," 299.
39. Lacan, "Seminar on 'The Purloined Letter,'" 29–30.
40. Poe, "The Purloined Letter," 290.
41. Poe, "The Purloined Letter," 282.
42. Poe, "The Purloined Letter," 295–96.
43. Lacan, "Seminar on 'The Purloined Letter,'" 22–23.
44. Lacan, "Seminar on 'The Purloined Letter,'" 6.
45. Lacan, "Seminar on 'The Purloined Letter,'" 20–21.
46. Lacan, "Seminar on 'The Purloined Letter,'" 7, 11.
47. Jacques Lacan, "The Instance of the Letter in the Unconscious, or Reason since Freud" (1957), in *Ecrits*, 413.
48. Jacques Lacan, "Overture to This Collection" (1966), in *Ecrits*, 4.
49. [Derrida writes, "A 'literature,' then, can produce, can place onstage, and put forth something like the truth"; "Le Facteur de la vérité," 419).—Translator]
50. Jacques Lacan, *Le séminaire: Livre VI. Le Désir et son interprétation* (Paris: Edition de la Martinière, 2013).
51. Derrida, "Le Facteur de la vérité," 414.
52. Lacan, "Seminar on 'The Purloined Letter,'" 38.
53. "Is there a Lacanian *doctrine* of the truth? We might doubt this for two reasons. The first is a general one, and has to do with the terms of the question. That a purely homogeneous system is structurally impossible we have seen elsewhere" (Derrida, "Le Facteur de la vérité," 461–62).

54. Lacan, "Seminar on 'The Purloined Letter,'" 22.
55. Lacan, "Seminar on 'The Purloined Letter,'" 45.
56. Derrida, "Le Facteur de la vérité," 436–37, 438, 464.
57. Derrida, "Le Facteur de la vérité," 441, 444, 489, 492.
58. Lacan, "Seminar on 'The Purloined Letter,'" 27, 17, 21. [An alternative reading of this last line, based on the homophonic *sa ronde* and *ça rende*, would translate this last phrase as "the letter does not annul either the itinerary or the intersubjective effects that it renders [*que* '*sa ronde*']."—Translator]

Chapter 8

# The Other Synesthesia

Susan Bernstein

Walter Benjamin has remarked upon the strangeness of Valéry's remark: "'Das Problem mußte sich für Baudelaire folgendermaßen stellen—ein großer Dichter, doch weder Lamartine, noch Hugo, noch Musset zu werden.' [Baudelaire's problem . . . might have—indeed must have—posed itself in these terms: 'How to be a great poet, but neither Lamartine, nor Hugo nor Musset.'] This problem, Valéry says, 'war eigentlich Baudelaire. Er war seine Staatsraison [was essentially Baudelaire. It was his raison d'État].'"[1] But Baudelaire's "reason of state," or effort to establish himself as a name, does not work to preserve a subjective condition; instead it moves alogically through the materiality of language to fragment, serialize, expand, and realign. He operates with a peculiar kind of reason that I would associate with the continued flowering, or *floraison*, of his monumental *Fleurs du Mal*. The *raison* of this *floraison* is a random and specious connection turning on the duplicity of language that allows for such literal and asemic, and certainly asemantic, connections. "Reason of flower," which I pose here as an alternative to "reason of state," directs Baudelaire's imperative to make a name for himself, to singularize his self-articulation within and outside of a tradition. The simple stating and exposure of proper names takes up the space through which a sort of community spreads itself. But Flower Power does not gather together presences in a bouquet or aggregate individuals through presence into a whole. Rather, through resonance and dislocation, to use Jean-Luc Nancy's language, each singular plural—the many singulars—are exposed, set out, and brought into play. The delineation of a community of artistic friends in Baudelaire parallels, though in an inexact and skewed manner, the working of the parallel of the senses (synesthesia) and the aligning and translation among the arts (especially in Baudelaire's criticism). In what follows I begin to explore what might be an other synesthesia—that is, one that does not fuse the senses and transcend their differences but rather disarticulates final unity and opens up differences.

Both Nancy and Giorgio Agamben have worked on the remodeling of community as the exposure of singularities in an existential process that presupposes neither individuals who are then somehow joined (that is, any model of intersubjectivity) nor a model of language as an instrument of connecting preexistent speakers through a communicated content. The critique is ultimately aimed at the model of community as an organism or an organic totality. For Nancy the organic model of community culminates of course in fascism as an "incarnated communion."[2] Both Nancy and Agamben characterize community as an ecstatic movement that takes place through the exposure and exposition of singularities. Both describe community as a borderline experience, an experience of the limit that redefines the spatial model of inside and outside. In *The Coming Community*, Agamben writes, "The *outside* is not another space that resides beyond a determinate space, but rather, it is the passage, the exteriority that gives it access. . . . The threshold is not, in this sense, another thing with respect to the limit; it is, so to speak, the experience of the limit itself, the experience of being-*within* and *outside*. The *ek-stasis* is the gift that singularity gathers from the empty hands of humanity." This experience of ek-stasis, exposure or exposition is always singular, thus as it is in its articulated extension—what Agamben calls "whatever," "quodlibet": "The Whatever in question here relates to singularity not in its indifference with respect to a common property . . . but only in its being *such as it is*."[3]

In *The Literary Absolute* (1978), Nancy and Philippe Lacoue-Labarthe analyze and critique the incipient organicism of the Romantic model of collaborative community evident, for example, in the collective project of the Athenaeum. Despite the avant-gardism of the collective project, for them Jena Romanticism ultimately falls into the dream of a future presence that would overcome its constitutive fragmentation. In an article entitled "Friendship," Agamben develops a countermodel of friendship that allows for the common perception of collectivity yet does not build on identities. Working this out through a reading of Aristotle's *Nicomachean Ethics*, Agamben picks up on the verb *synaisthanesthai*, the concurrent perception or synesthesia of existence—one's own alongside of one's friends'—that he argues is constitutive of friendship. Following up on Nancy's work and on his own previous work on *The Coming Community*, Agamben specifies, "Friendship is the instance of this concurrent perception of the friend's existence in the awareness of one's own existence. But this means that friendship also has an ontological and, at the same time, a political dimension. The perception of existing is, in fact, always already divided up and shared or con-divided. Friendship names this sharing or con-division."[4]

Samuel Weber parts ways with Agamben in his discussion of friendship in an article titled "'And When Is Now?' (On Some Limits of Perfect Intelligibility)." The discussion first moves around the phrase from *Nicomachean Ethics*, which Derrida highlights in his book *Politiques de l'amitié*: "O friends, there are no friends."[5] Agamben traces out an etymological history of this phrase, which he claims Derrida ignores, and opts for a sixteenth-century correction that renders the phrase, "He who has many friends has no friends." The issue is the aspiration of the omega versus a subscript iota in the opening word. Agamben states that with the correction to the iota subscript (which changes the apostrophic *O!* to the dative *'oi*), the manuscript "became perfectly intelligible" ("Friendship," 3). As Weber's title makes clear, he particularly parts ways with this notion that friendship could be rendered "perfectly intelligible," arguing instead that the very force Derrida draws from the apostrophic sentence is a contradictory force or ambivalence that itself intervenes in the definition of friendship. Weber writes:

> What I . . . have designated as "ambivalent," and what Agamben for his part characterizes as a mixture of "affirmation" and "distrustful revocation," stretches the limits of intelligibility by splitting the object it intends. If friendship is something that can and must at the same time be "affirmed" and yet also "distrustfully revoked," then this fractures the "one and the same" of that "time" by removing it from itself. A certain irreducible spatiality, as the medium of non-identity and of alterity, is thus introduced into the self identity of "friendship," dislocating its meaning so that it no longer reflects a homogeneous and coherent internal structure or series of properties but rather appears as the resultant of a conflictual relation of forces. To be perfectly intelligible, then, would be to exclude or reduce the internal dissonance and distance that prevents the object it invests from supporting and sustaining a unified and univocal meaning.[6]

Weber allies this reduction of tension with the reduction or elimination of space. Agamben is guilty of this reduction a second time, when he invokes another instance of perfection. He reads a painting by Giovanni Serodine, *The Meeting of Saints Peter and Paul on the Way to Martyrdom*, as a "perfect allegory of friendship" (Agamben, "Friendship," 4; Weber, "'And When Is Now?,'" 5). What Weber objects to in both of these examples is the notion of *perfect legibility*; both examples imply a unified coherence without remnant. This would suggest a smooth continuum from sense perception to signification to a signified, which would all join in a perfect *correspondence*. The moment of perfect correspondence would take place in a moment of shared perception of the existence of the other. This phrase too is taken from Aristotle, the key terms being "concurrent perception," or *synaisthanomenoi* (the present participle of *synaisthanesthai*). As Weber makes clear, Agamben's interpretation has a double valence. On the one hand, Weber shows, Agamben shares with certain of his "friends" (Nancy, Derrida) the notion that friendship is differentially constituted and not an intersubjective relationship between previously existing entities: "*Friendship is the instance of this concurrent perception of the friend's existence in the awareness of one's own existence.* But this means that friendship also has an ontological and, at the same time, a political dimension. The perception of existing is, in fact, always already divided up and shared or con-divided. Friendship names this sharing or condivision. There is no trace here of any inter-subjectivity . . . existing itself is divided, it is non-identical to itself: the I and the friend are the two faces—or the two poles—of this condivision" (Agamben, "Friendship," 6). On the other hand, Weber argues, Agamben seems to reinstall an originary moment from which difference would distance itself, thus privileging the origin as presence or proximity over a subsequent deviation. Agamben writes, "The friend is not another I, but an otherness immanent in self-ness, a becoming other of the self. At the point at which I perceive my existence as pleasant, my perception is traversed by a concurrent perception that dislocates it and deports it towards the friend, towards the other self. Friendship is this de-subjectivization at the very heart of the most intimate perception of self" (6).

Thus Agamben's interpretation of friendship as a self-consistent rather than paradoxical thing allows this smooth becoming that is actually a fall or falling away from a self or an origin. Parallel to this the "original political synesthesia" read in Aristotle falls off or declines into the "consensus to which democracies entrust their fates in this latest extreme and exhausted phase of their evolution" (Agamben, 7). In Weber's view Agamben continues to privilege a primordial and pure origin that makes possible an exhausted decline and falling away into alterity. This movement is a continuous becoming that connects the proximity of bodies (Peter and Paul) to some kind of "meaning": in this case recognition and friendship somehow superseding the impossibility of recognizing what is too close. What Weber is parting with is really the smooth continuity of this becoming. He develops this by way of Derrida as follows:

> Both [Agamben and Derrida] deploy a notion of friendship that is determined by an irreducible alterity or heterogeneity. But whereas Agamben construes this alterity or heterogeneity in terms of a simultaneity of perception in which the self is "deported" by and toward the perception of another, Derrida develops his notion of friendship as the effect of a simultaneity in which there is no "becoming" but rather a discontinuous jump or leap or cut in the unity of the moment. . . . This temporality—or temporization, as his notion of différance would suggest—is performed not through a co-perception but rather through a co-reading and "co-signing" of texts, which retraces and reinscribes the trajectory of citations and re-citations of an original appeal that cannot be located as such. ("'And When Is Now?,'" 9)

Agamben's becoming suggests a continuous movement from sense perception to intelligibility. Weber intervenes and argues that there is no such continuity, but that every perception is already mediated through a semiotic context; every mark is already marked out by its iterability. Neither painting nor address can be "perfectly intelligible" without remainder or difference within it. I would like to bear this discussion in mind in turning, or re-turning, to the old question, or perhaps the new old question, of synesthesia in Baudelaire.

The proper names punctuating Baudelaire's writing set up a communicative network drawing together singulars into a common project. The unity of art famously emerges as an immense correspondence. I'll take just a moment to recall the communicative reciprocity of the sonnet of that name. Nature and art speak together the symbolic language that animates architectural elements and mirrors man back to himself:

> La Nature est un temple où de vivants piliers
> Laissent parfois sortir de confuses paroles;
> L'homme y passe à travers des forêts de symbols
> Qui l'oberservent avec des regards familiers.[7]

> Nature is a temple whose columns are alive and sometimes issue disjointed messages. We thread our way through a forest of symbols that peer out, as if recognizing us.[8]

While origin recedes, emanating resonances join and fuse, "dans une ténébreuse et profonde unité [into a deep dark unity]." These Pythagorean overtones resonate and overlap, bringing into vibration a cosmic unity of sympathetic ratios. This—what Claude Pichois and others call the "vertical" axis of correspondence—forms a simile for the joining of senses in the famous figure of synesthesia that follows: "Les parfums, les couleurs, et les sons se respondent [smells and colors and sounds concur]." (Baudelaire, *Œuvres Complètes*, 1: 11; *The Flowers of Evil*, 14). As Paul de Man has argued, the double valence of the term *comme* confuses this unifying simile with the uncontrolled numerical expansion of terms in the final stanza. The latter *comme* opens up a potentially infinite series of singularities that cannot be gathered together and begins to enact the "expansion des choses infinies [expansiveness of infinite things]" opened up in the poem.[9]

First, *comme*, in the sense of "like" or "as," works to join the disaggregated senses: "doux comme les hautbois, verts comme les prairies [sweet as oboes, green like the prairie]" (Baudelaire, *Oeuvres Completes*, 1:11; *The Flowers of Evil*, 14). Yet even here the comparisons are not quite symmetrical; the scent of the child's flesh is sweet, or soft, like oboes, and green like prairies. The first figure crosses smell, touch, and sound; the second connects smell and color. Sweet or soft must refer indirectly to the sound of the oboe—not the oboe itself—while green is an attribute of the prairies. Reason of flower suggests another reading here: *verts*, but without a "t": *vers*. Baudelaire's green poetry itself opens up as the prairie, the verdant ground on which flowers and correspondences grow. Green verse turns over (*verser*) the property of color into the space of writing (*vers*). Green, of course, forms the basis or ground in the essay "De la Couleur." *Vers* (toward) enacts the movement upward that elevates synesthesia into correspondence, "qui transportent l'esprit et des sens [singing ecstasy to the mind and to the senses]" (Baudelaire, *Œuvres Complètes*, 1: 11). These three senses of *vers* adjoin in the poem "Le Soleil" :

> Ce père nourricier, ennemi des chloroses,
> Éveille dans les champs les vers comme les roses;
> Il fait s'évaporer les soucis vers le ciel . . .
> Et commande aux moissons de croître et de mûrir
> Dans le Coeur immortel qui toujours veut fleurir! (*Œuvres Complètes*, 1: 83)

> This foster father, enemy of greensickness, makes verse spring like roses from the fields; makes care evaporate into air . . . and commands the harvest to increase and ripen, within the immortal spirit willing always to flower. (*The Flowers of Evil*, 112)

Verse arises like roses thanks to the enemy of chlorosis: both a fading of green and a becoming green. According to Webster's, *chlorosis* is both "an iron-deficiency anemia . . . that may impart a greenish tint to the skin—called also *greensickness*" and "a diseased condition in green plants marked by yellowing or blanching." As the sun descends, cares evaporate into the sky, "vers le ciel," green, toward or verse the sky (a senseless syntax). This working of *vers* is what Nancy or Lacoue-Labarthe might call an "unworking, "a *désœuvrement*, that dismembers the text just as rejuvenation and transcendence are invoked thematically. Cares and flowers rise up as the sun comes down into the cities. The immortal heart replaces the field (*champs*) of flowers as the place forever flowering, or at least forever wanting to flower.

The heart flowers in its exposure to the sun; it must be stimulated by something other than itself. Even in its solitude poetic voice is incited by the address of another, the stimulation of a figure. Like the rays of the sun, the gaze of—shall we call it the beautiful woman?—incites the flowering of verse, as in the poem "Que diras-tu ce soir, pauvre âme solitaire," which continues:

> Que diras-tu, mon coeur, coeur autrefois flétri,
> A la très belle, à la très bonne, à la très chère,
> Dont le regard divin t'a soudain refleuri? (*Œuvres Complètes*, 1: 43)

> What will you say this evening, poor solitary soul, what will you say, my long-ago withered heart, to the most-beautiful, the most-good, the most-cherished, from whose divine glance you have suddenly flowered again? (*The Flowers of Evil*, 57)

The self-address of poetic voice sets up a conversation among the speaker, the soul, and the heart, dispersing and multiplying what we infer is an "I," though no "I" is ever enunciated in the poem. The foregrounding of the heart in the second line syncopates the articulation of voice: the even alexandrine of the first line is disrupted, stumbles and stutters over the direct address, commas, and repetition of the word *coeur*. But the evenness resumes, gathering together the spiritual flesh, the perfume, the eye, the clarity, in a loose synesthesia. The rhythm of the poem gathers force and accelerates as the syntax detaches from the indicative and rises in the repeated subjunctives joining and reversing singularity and plurality:

> Que ce soit dans la nuit et dans la solitude,
> Que ce soit dans la rue et dans la multitude,
> Son fantôme dans l'air danse comme un flambeau. (*Œuvres Complètes*, 1: 43)

> Whether in night and solitary, whether in the street among a multitude, her apparition dances in the air like a torch. (*The Flowers of Evil*, 57)

This rising up breaks off in the appearance of a figure, "son fantôme," which then speaks as the voice of the Muse, the ultimate figure of inspiration and incitation through and by another.

The preceding poem, "Tout Entière," enacts a similar dialogue. A demon, or "the Demon," comes to the speaker, enunciated only indirectly as "me," and asks which compositional element of enchantment, of "her body," is most pleasing. The voice exclaims, "O mon âme! / Tu repondis à l'Abhorré" ("O my soul! you replied to the Shunned One"), and then quotes the soul's speech proffered over the next three and a half stanzas. This personified fragment of the self, the soul who is speaking, articulates the unity of the figure asked about through synesthesia:

> Ô métamorphose mystique
> De tous mes sens fondues en un!
> Son haleine fait la musique,
> Comme sa voix fait le parfum! (*Œuvres Complètes*, 1: 42)

> Oh mystic metamorphosis, melding all my senses into one! Her breath makes music, as her voice gives off perfume! (*The Flowers of Evil*, 56)

The speaker claims to be seduced by this figure and resounds in unison with it, a unison beyond analysis or decomposition. Synesthesia, though, keeps the senses apart syntactically even as it thematizes their fusion. The speaking soul becomes a painter, framing the figure it presents; likewise it remains distinct from the "me" and the Demon with whom it converses. (Here I'll just gesture at the similar structure of the neighboring poem, "Un Fantôme." In that poem the speaker says explicitly, "Je suis comme un peintre." The sections are titled "Les Ténèbres," "Le Parfum," "Le Cadre," and "Le Portrait.")

Synesthesia opens up the dispersion of the senses that makes fusion, combination, organization, and community possible. These poetic dialogues present the exposure of one speaker position to another; they do not present a realistic or psychological representation of intersubjectivity. Artistic community, for Baudelaire, consists in this syncopation of self that distends identity at the same time that it allows for resonance, concord, and discord. Baudelaire's singular identity—recall Valéry and Baudelaire's reason of state—emerges as a point in a multiplex network of names joined and dissociated by the rhythms and syncopations of synesthesia. The "I" falls out of the harmony of the spheres, as in "L'Heauton timoroumenos," in which the speaker asks:

> Ne suis-je pas un faux accord
> Dans le divin symphonie,
> Grâce à la vorace Ironie
> Qui me secoue et qui me mord? (*Œuvres Complètes*, 1: 78)[10]
>
> Am I not a discord in the divine symphony, thanks to voracious Irony who shakes me and bites? (*The Flowers of Evil*, 105)

The harmonious vibrations of correspondence draw back into bodily spasms and percussions heralding violence and battle:

> Tes chers sanglots retentiront
> Comme un tambour qui bat la charge!
>
> Your precious sobs will pound out like the drumbeat for a charge!

The eternal laughter invoked in the final stanza echoes the quaking of the shaken body, the battered tambourine, and the resounding sobs. The sense of spirit or identity is punctured and punctuated in intermittence with the body, extending in a non-self-identical relation of self-affection:

> Je suis la plaie et le couteau!
> Je suis le soufflet et la joue!
> Je suis les membres et la roue
> Et la victime et le bourreau!
>
> I am the wound and the knife! I am the slap and the face! I am the rack and the stretched, victim and hangman!

These lines specify and take apart the two parts of the Greek work forming the title: *heauton timoroumenos*, "the tormentor of oneself." The term is borrowed from a comedy by Terence. According to the Pléiade edition, it was used by De Quincey and in a letter from Charles Augustin Sainte-Beuve that Baudelaire would not have known. The intertextual resonance thus enacts the identification and differentiation that the term puts into place.

Baudelaire's writing is peopled by correspondences, letters addressed to and from mouthpieces whose lips break into the laughter of the unity of the arts—a unity unsubstantial, never present, constituted in the crossing over of senses. The poetics of synesthesia and correspondence distinguish Victor Hugo as the universal artist whose verse combines the arts of poetry, music, sculpture, and painting:

> La musique des vers de Victor Hugo s'adapte aux profondes harmonies de la nature; sculpteur, il découpe dans ses strophes la forme inoubliable des choses; peintre, il les illumine de leur couleur proper. (*Œuvres Complètes*, 2: 132)

> The music of Victor Hugo's *vers* adapts to nature's most profound harmonies; a sculptor, he carves out in his strophes the unforgettable form of things; a painter, he illuminates them with their own color. (my translation)

The grafting of the particular arts onto each other marks out the limits and planes of exposure between the various media, just as the line "les parfums, les couleurs et les sons se repondent" holds apart the singular terms it puts into communication. Correspondence takes place as this mutual exposure, not as a synthesizing transcendent unity. The persistence of proper names—concrete singularities that cannot be subsumed into a concept or whole—parallels the resilience of the senses in language.

"Les Phares," two poems away from "Correspondances" in *Les Fleurs du Mal*, presents a string of artists marking out relay points on a vast network across time and space. Each of the first eight stanzas is punctuated by a proper name: Rubens, Leonardo da Vinci, Rembrandt, Michelangelo, Puget, Watteau, Goya, and Delacroix. The stanzas present series of images only loosely connected to the proper name with which they are grouped; thus each artist or artist's name gives rise to a set of associations but remains syntactically free. For example:

> Rubens, fleuve d'oubli, jardin de la paresses . . .
> Léonard de Vinci, miroir profound . . .
> Goya, cauchemar plein de choses inconnues . . .
> Delacroix, lac de sang hanté des mauvais anges (*Œuvres Complètes*, 1: 13–14)

> Rubens, garden of oblivion, garden of laziness . . . da Vinci: deep dark mirror . . . Goya: bald nightmare of things unknown . . . Delacroix: lake of blood, haunted by evil angels. (*The Flowers of Evil*, 16)

The names hang suspended, as if they were apostrophes, but end up being instead the first term in an apposition. The duality of this function is marked in the difference between the original text and the translation, which replaces the ambiguous comma with a colon. Their placement, followed by a comma, installs a syncopated scansion. No system organizes this list. The names tend to open up spaces, as just quoted, but most notably perhaps "Michel-Ange, lieu vague ou l'on voit des Hercules / Se mêler à des Christs" ("Michelangelo: vague area where various Hercules are seen along with Jesus Christs"). A name is a *stanza*—a "room" in Italian—a garden, a vague place. This is strange, to call an artist a "vague place." Similarly the Delacroix stanza opens up a tableau-like scenario: "lac de sang hanté des mauvais anges." We know that a special relationship obtains between Delacroix and Baudelaire, marked here perhaps by the intrusion of poetry, *vers*, in the scene "un bois de sapins vert." But the green poetry is strange, picked up in the following line by "des fanfares étranges" ("strange fanfares") and rhyming vaguely with another proper name, "comme un soupir étouffé de Weber" ("like a stifled sigh from [Carl Maria von] Weber") (*Œuvres Complètes*, 1: 13–14; *The Flowers of Evil*, 16).

The ninth stanza presents another list, this time of expressive gestures, with the demonstrative pronoun that suggests a reference still only intimated: "ces malédictions, ces blasphèmes, ces plaintes, / ces extases, ces cris, ces pleurs, ces *Te Deum* ("these curses, these blasphemies, groans, ecstasies, cries, these tears, these *Te Deums*") (17). This repetitive enumeration gathers together the various artistic enunciations in a resounding sound wave, the "écho redit par mille labyrinths" ("echo rehearsed in a thousand labyrinths") (17). Community is established through repetition and echo, resaying and resounding: *redit, répété, renvoyé, Mille sentinelles, mille porte-voix, mille citadelles*—voices resounding, trying to find one another, "Un appel de chasseurs perdus dans les grands bois." We are reminded of the inverse correspondence of "Obsession" (also analyzed by Paul de Man), which might be read as one such *cri*. It begins, "Grands bois, vous m'effrayez comme des cathédrals" ("Forests, you frighten me, as do cathedrals") (*Œuvres Complètes*, 1: 75; *The Flowers of Evil*, 17, 101). Here the speaker is haunted rather than comforted by the returning echoes of the plaints of others (in particular De Quincey: "les échos de vos de Profundis"). The hypersignificance of an already made nature, an already populated exterior, threatens the originality of the poetic voice, itself now only an echo of an other:

> Je te hais, Océan! Tes bonds et tes tumults,
> Mon esprit les retrouve en lui; ce rire amer
> De l'homme vaincu, plein de sanglots et d'insultes,
> Je l'entends dans le rire énorme de la mer.

> You I hate, Ocean! Your bounding and your tumult I find again in my mind; that bitter laugh of the beaten man, full of sobs and insults, I hear it in the sea's enormous laughter.

The personified universe—the monoverse, the single poem—draws the speaker into an overly mediated linguistic context:

> Comme tu me plairais, ô nuit! Sans ces étoiles
> Dont la lumière parle un langage connu!
> Car je cherche le vide, et le noir, et le nu!

> How you would please me, O night! But for those stars whose light speaks a known language! For I seek the void, the dark, the naked!

The speaker finds comfort in the decomposition of its terms: the *nu* rather than the *connu*, the *toile* rather than the *étoile*. Refigured as painting, the darkness is populated instead by the lost sparks of the speaker's own perceptions. The celestial dissemination of these *milliers*, linked with the cast of thousands of "Les Phares," both connects and renders strange the stars and the eyes of the "I." The familiarity of the language of others is muffled; the life of these disappeared beings is syncopated: they live, having disappeared; perhaps they live on. The line is suggestive of the strange syncopations of the speed of light that allows for the possibility that we see a star already burned out or that the message emitted is received only by the one who has forgotten its code.

If correspondence sets up a kind of community here, it is not articulated by any sort of full presence or coming together of individual entities but by the syncopated exposure of rhythms to each other. We do not have the calm mirroring of the self in itself—in the first line of "Les Phares," "Comme l'air dans le ciel et la mer dans la mer" ("Like air in the atmosphere and sea in the sea")—but instead the self-differentiating rending of the ocean and its antagonistic relation to the speaker. In the quatrain quoted earlier, man and sea are linked by the quaking of laughter, "rire amer, rire de la mer," and the heaving of sobs. Similarly in the final stanza of "Les Phares" the sob connects artists through the ages, heaving up the spasm of finitude as it breaks against its own limit:

> Que cet ardent sanglot qui roule d'âge en âge
> Et vient mourir au bord de votre éternité. (*Œuvres Complètes*, 1: 14)

> Sob that rolls from age to age, to die at the brink of your eternity! (*The Flowers of Evil*, 17)

Let me return for a moment to the question of Delacroix, whose place in "Les Phares" is characterized by a play of red and green, the blood-lake and the green pines, which gives rise to the strange fanfares of Weber. (There is an editorial suggestion, by the way, that this quatrain was composed later than the others and added.) Baudelaire traces out a similar generation in his essay "De la Couleur," published in the 1846 *Salon*. The text lays out a space in which colors and elements extend and interact to emit energy and sound: "Supposons un bel espace de nature où tout verdoie, rougeoie, poudroie en pleine liberté, où toutes choses, diversement colorées suivant leur constitution . . . se trouvent en perpétuelle vibration, laquelle fait trembler les lignes et complète la loi du movement éternal et universel" (*Œuvres Complètes*, 2: 422). "Let us suppose a beautiful natural space where everything turns green, red, dusty or iridescent as it wishes . . . where everything is in a state of perpetual vibration which causes lines to tremble and fulfils the law of eternal and universal movement."[11]

Next an alternation between blue and green extends: "C'est la mer." Objects are then articulated in green resonance with the greening of the opening sentence ("tout verdoie"): "Les arbres sont verts, les gazons verts, les mousses vertes; le vert serpente dans les troncs, les tiges non mûres sont vertes; le vert est le fond de la nature, parce que le vert se marie facilement à tous les autres tons" ("The trees are green, the grass and the moss are green; the tree-trunks are snaked with green, and the unripe stalks are green; green in nature's ground-bass, because green marries easily with all the other colours"). The speaker emerges in the accusative as green continues to be glorified; at this point too color and prose break into song: "Ce qui me frappe d'abord, c'est que partout . . . le rouge chante la gloire du vert" ("What strikes me first of all is that everywhere . . . red sings the glory of green") (*Œuvres Complètes*, 2: 422; *Art in Paris*, 48).

The text continues to describe a sort of chiaroscuro of reflecting and correspondent images prefiguring the poetic technique of the symbol that will later also be confirmed in the Wagnerian leitmotif:

> Les arbres, les rocher, les granits se mirent . . . et déposent leurs *reflets* . . . . Ceux-ci se renvoient leur reflets. . . . De rouges fanfares s'élancent de tous côtés; une sanglante harmonie éclate à l'horizon, et le vert s'empourpre richement. (*Œuvres Complètes*, 2: 422–23)

> The sap rises and there is a flowering [*s'épanouir*] of *mixed tones*; trees, rocks and granite boulders gaze at themselves in the water and cast their reflections upon them. . . . Some colours cast back their reflections upon one another. . . . Fanfares of red surge forth on all sides; a harmony of blood flares up at the horizon, and green turns richly crimson. (*Art in Paris*, 49)

The green of verse asserts itself in this image prefiguring the Delacroix strophe of "Les Phares," laying itself down, *supposons*, as the common place of synesthetic articulation, moving through the irreducible interactions of color masses to resound in the red and bloody fanfare. In the same short essay Baudelaire famously quotes E. T. A. Hoffmann to spell out what is usually referred to as the doctrine of correspondence:

> Ce n'est pas seulement en rêve, et dans le léger délire qui précède le sommeil, c'est encore éveillé, lorsque j'entends de la musique, que je trouve une analogie et une réunion intime entre les couleurs, les sons et les parfums. Il me semble que toutes ces choses ont été engendrées par un même rayon de lumière, et qu'elles doivent se réunir dans un merveilleux concert. L'odeur des soucis bruns et rouges produit surtout un effet magique sur ma personne. Elle me fait tomber dans une profonde rêverie, et j'entends alors comme dans le lointain les sons graves et profonds du hautbois. (*Œuvres Complètes*, 2: 425–26)

> It is not only in dreams, or in that mild delirium which precedes sleep, but it is even awakened when I hear music—that perception of an analogy and an intimate connexion between colours, sounds and perfumes. . . . The smell of red and brown marigolds above all produces a magical effect of my being. It makes me fall into a deep reverie, in which I seem to hear the solemn, deep tones of the oboe in the distance. (*Art in Paris*, 51)

> Nicht sowohl im Traume als im Zustande des Delirierens, der dem Einschlafen vorhergeht, vorzüglich wenn ich viel Musik gehört habe, finde ich eine Übereinkunft der Farben, Töne und Düfte. Es kommt mir vor, als wenn alle auf die gleiche geheimnisvolle Weise durch den Lichtstrahl erzeugt würden und dann sich zu einem wundervollen Konzerte vereinigen müßten.—Der Duft der dunkelroten Nelken wirkt mit sonderbarer magischer Gewalt auf mich; unwillkürlich versinke ich in einen träumerischen Zustand und höre dann wie aus weiter Ferne die anschwellenden und wieder verfließenden Tiefen Töne des Bassetthorns.[12]

Baudelaire's quotation here prefigures its own later echo in "Correspondances." In the next essay in the 1846 *Salon*, Delacroix, like Hugo, crosses the arts. The two are set up in a transmedial chiasmus: "M. Victor Hugo est devenu un peintre en poésie; Delacroix . . . est souvent . . . un poète en peinture" (*Œuvres Complètes*, 2: 432; *Art in Paris*, 57)("M. Victor Hugo has become a painter in poetry; Delacroix . . . is often . . . a poet in painting"). Like Hugo, Delacroix has an exceptional relationship to the dictionary: "Pour E. Delacroix . . . la nature est un vaste dictionnaire" ("For E. Delacroix . . . nature is a vast dictionary") (*Œuvres Complètes*, 2: 433; *Art in Paris*, 58). In another essay the same figure is used to describe Hugo's ability to dip into the bottomless well of universal analogy, or correspondence (in the essay on Hugo in "Sur quelques uns de mes contemporains"). What joins and also distinguishes Hugo and Delacroix here is their ability to deploy available elements in original or new ways; their excellence resides precisely in the syntactical singularity of concrete utterances or usages, in the placed exposure of elements to one another. Like green and red Hugo and Delacroix are exposed to each other in the exterior of their extension, as signifiers spread out on a page, not as conscious or psychological subjects in communion. Subjects, that is, proper names, are joined in lines, *vers*, just as colors and sounds are juxtaposed in their reverse, that is, *rêves*, dreams, extended into reveries, the medium of synesthesia in Baudelaire's quote from Hoffmann (*Œuvres Complètes*, 2: 425–26).

In the waking dream of green *vers* or verse, waves break on the exposed edge of singularities. These encounters take place in the vague places, the "lieux vagues" of others, in the murmuring fanfare of repeated speech and commingling voices. "Edgar Poe dit, je ne sais plus où," writes Baudelaire (*Œuvres Complètes*, 2: 596), of the expansive nature of opium. Baudelaire mingles, shares, or divides his own voice with Poe's as well as Hoffmann's in articulating synesthesia, asking:

> Qui n'a pas connu ces admirables heures . . . où les sens plus attentifs perçoivent des sensations plus retentissantes . . . où le son tintent musicalement, où les couleurs parlent, où les parfums racontent des mondes d'idées? (*Œuvres Complètes*, 2: 596)
>
> Who has not known those miraculous moments . . . when the senses are keenest . . . when sounds chime like music [*tinter*], when colours speak, and scents tell of whole worlds of ideas? (*Art in Paris*, 143)

In the *Salon* of 1859, Baudelaire writes of an encounter with an unnamed sage whose dialogue draws them into a common place: "Nous causâmes tout d'abord de lieux communs, c'est-à-dire des questions les plus vastes et les plus profondes" ("We talked from the very beginning of *commonplaces* [not italicized in the French]—that is to say, of the vastest and most profound questions") (*Œuvres Complètes*, 2: 624; *Art in Paris*, 159).

The Pléiade edition glosses this as a reference to Delacroix. But as we saw in the *Salon* of 1846, it is actually Baudelaire who says this about him, just as he uses the same figure to describe Hugo. Baudelaire's own voice becomes syncopated in this self-citation. Similarly his own voice resounds in the association of Delacroix and Weber first articulated in 1846, taken up again in "Beacon Lights," "Les Phares"; the "fanfare" repeats the title of the poem as it weaves repeated terms across the years.

Baudelaire makes another anonymous appearance in the essay on Delacroix in the *Exposition Universelle* of 1855. Here (and I have argued this already elsewhere, so I engage in the same kind of syncopation I am describing)[13] he describes the material resilience of color while drawing attention to the hidden power of rhetoric: "Il semble que cetter couleur, qu'on me pardonne ces subterfuges de langage pour exprimer des idées fort delicates, pense par elle-même, indépendamment des objets qu'elle habille" ("If the reader will pardon me a stratagem of language in order to express an idea of some subtlety, it seems to me that M. Delacroix's colour *thinks on its own*, independently of the objects which it clothes") (*Œuvres Complètes*, 2: 595; *Art in Paris*, 141).

The singularity of Baudelaire's own quatrain is then invoked to expand further on the qualities of Delacroix's painting: "Un poète a essayé d'exprimer ces sensations subtiles dans des vers dont la sincérité peut faire passer la bizarrerie" ("A poet has attempted to express these subtle sensations in some lines whose sincerity must excuse their singularity") (*Œuvres Complètes*, 2: 595; *Art in Paris*, 141). Then follows the quatrain on Delacroix later included in "Les Phares." (The same technique, but with a signature, is used in Baudelaire's essay on Wagner, where he cites "Correspondances.") The community of artists, then, like the synesthesia of the senses, emerges through the murmuring repetition of letters and holds open the common place—the green ground or verse base, the inverted dream—the reverse, or *rêve-vers* (dream verse).

Repetitions, citations, syncopations, sobs, waves, tremors, quaking, laughter: these all structure the spasmodic dislocation of the other synesthesia—or of any synesthesia, or what Agamben might call "whatever" synesthesia. A network expands through Baudelaire's writing that sets the senses, the arts, and singular names into an interplay and circulation that can be understood as a common place, or a kind of community, not bound but connected by reason of flower: the nonreason that sees *raison* in *floraison* and thus deactivates the organic force of etymologism. Reason of flower, to repeat, is a random play on letters, a *Witz*. It is not reading, *lire*, but de-reading, *délire*. This *floraison* continues to expand and open up the flowers it locates, the singular spots of language put into place that expand the *Fleurs du Mal* into an ever-expanding network. The differences of senses, of media, and of singular names persist in multiple rhythms and interrelations that at times collide or coincide but do not fall into a harmony. The syncopated rhythm of a line of verse, the harmonious or bloody interactions of red and green, the evanescent fanfare of the interweaving of the arts: these crisscross and intersect one another but do not fall into a unifying beat. Beat itself, whether poetic or musical, remains one element among many.

The de-organizing of the senses through this inverse reading of synesthesia comes into view in Gilles Deleuze's notion of the body without organs. In *Logique de la sensation*, Deleuze suggests a community of arts that cuts across their difference: "La question de la séparation des arts, de leur autonomie resepective, de leur hiérachie éventuelle, perd toute importance. Car il y a une communauté des arts, un problème commun. En art, et en peinture comme en musique, il ne s'agit pas de reproduire où inventer des formes, mais de capter des forces" ("The question concerning the separation of the arts, their respective autonomy, and their possible hierarchy loses all importance. For there is a community of the arts, a common problem. In art, and in painting as in music, it is not a matter of reproducing or inventing forms, but of capturing forces). He thus suggests a unity of Rhythm, which he goes so far as to write with a capital letter, as the unity that manifests itself in any individual art: "Il apppartiendrait donc au peintre de *faire voir* une sorte d'unité originelle des sens. . . . Cette puissance, c'est le Rythme, plus profond que la vision, l'audition, etc." ("The painter would thus *make visible* a kind of original unity of the senses . . . This power is Rhythm, which is more profound than vision, hearing, et cetera" [37]). At the same time, rhythm cannot really have an identity of its own, since its very definition is to exceed the limits of the body as a unifying figure: "L'unité du rythme, en effet, nous ne pouvons la chercher que là où le rythme lui-même plonge dans le chaos, dans la nuit, et où les différences de niveau sont perpétuellement brassées avec violence" ("We can seek the unity of rhythm only at the point where rhythm itself plunges into chaos, into the night, at the point where the differences of level are perpetually and violently mixed").[14] Nancy, in contrast, stresses the heterogeneity of elements that prevents their gathering into a single sense. This heterogeneity culminates in the sense of touch:

> Mais à ce compte, que fait donc l'art, si ce n'est en somme toucher à, et toucher par l'hétérogénéité principielle du "sentir"? dans cette hétérogénéité de principe qui se résout elle-même en une hétérogénéité *du* principe, il touche au toucher lui-même: autrement dit, il touche à la fois au "*se* toucher" inhérent au toucher et à l' "interruption" qui lui est non moins inhérente.
>
> But what does art do if not finally touch upon and touch by means of the principal heterogeneity of "sensing"? In this heterogeneity in principle that resolves itself into a heterogeneity *of the* principle, art touches on the sense of touch itself: in other words, it touches at once on the "self-touching" inherent in touch and on the "interruption" that is no less inherent in it.[15]

Baudelaire too endorses this persistence of differences that form a synesthetic chain in the prose world of criticism, a prose forest that brings together the many arts and works in their singularity. All the arts, Baudelaire writes, "sont toujours le beau exprimé par le sentiment, la passion et la reverie de chacun, c'est-à-dire la variété dans l'unité, ou les faces diverses de l'absolu,—la critique touche à chaque instant à la métaphysique" ("the expression of the beautiful through the feeling, the passion and the dreams of each one—that is to say a variety within a unity, or the various faces of the absolute—so criticism touches at every moment upon metaphysics") (*Œuvres Complètes*, 2: 419; *Art in Paris*, 45, translation altered).

## Notes

1. Walter Benjamin, *Gesammelte Schriften* (Frankfurt am Main: Suhrkamp, 1991), 1: 615. For my understanding of Baudelaire's "reason of state" I am indebted to Kevin McLaughlin, *Poetic Force—Poetry after Kant* (Stanford: Stanford University Press, 2014), 55–77.
2. Jean-Luc Nancy, *La communauté désoeuvrée* (Paris: Christian Bourgois, 1984), 87.
3. Giorgio Agamben, *The Coming Community*, trans. Michael Hardt (Minneapolis: University of Minnesota Press, 1993), 68, 1.
4. Giorgio Agamben, "Friendship," *Contretemps* 5 (December 2004): 6.
5. Jacques Derrida discusses this phrase from Aristotle at length throughout his *Politiques de L'Amitié* (Paris: Editions Galilée, 1994).
6. Samuel Weber, "'And When Is Now?' (On Some Limits of Intelligibility)," *MLN* 122.5 (2007): 1028–50. JSTOR pagination: 4.
7. Charles Baudelaire, *Œuvres Complètes*, 2 vols. (Paris: Gallimard, 1975), 1: 11.
8. Charles Baudelaire, *The Flowers of Evil*, trans. Keith Waldrop (Middletown, Conn.: Wesleyan University Press, 2006), 14.
9. See Paul de Man, "Anthropomorphism and Trope in the Lyric," in *The Rhetoric of Romanticism* (New York: Columbia University Press, 1984), 239–62.
10. One might read this "Irony" in accord with de Man in "The Concept of Irony" in *Aesthetic Ideology*, ed. Andrzej Warminski (Minneapolis: University of Minnesota Press, 1996), in which de Man reads irony precisely as a moment of "parabasis" that interrupts a smoothly operating system of tropes.
11. Charles Baudelaire, *Art in Paris 1845–1862*, trans. Jonathan Mayne (Oxford: Phaidon Press, 1965), 48.
12. E. T. A. Hoffmann, *Kreisleriana* (Stuttgart: Reclam, 1983), 39–40.
13. See my *Virtuosity of the Nineteenth Century: Performing Music and Language in Heine, Liszt, and Baudelaire* (Stanford, Calif.: Stanford University Press, 1998).
14. Gilles Deleuze, *Francis Bacon—Logique de la Sensation*, 2 vols. (Paris: Éditions de la difference, 1984), 1: 39, 31, 33; *Francis Bacon: The Logic of Sensation*, trans. Daniel W. Smith (Minneapolis: University of Minnesota Press, 2005), 39.
15. Jean-Luc Nancy, *Les Muses* (Paris: Galilée, 1994), 36; Jean-Luc Nancy, *The Muses*, trans. Peggy Kamuf (Stanford: Stanford University Press, 1994), 18.

Chapter 9

# Parting with the Self

## Weber, Benjamin, Hölderlin

Kevin McLaughlin

Although the relation of Friedrich Hölderlin to German Romanticism is a key to the sphere in which poetry and philosophy interact in Walter Benjamin's *The Concept of Art Criticism in German Romanticism*, the critical and philosophical reception of this work has tended either to set this question aside or to neglect it altogether.[1] A recent essay by Samuel Weber offers a corrective to this tendency. In "From Reflection to Repetition: Medium, Reflexivity and the Economy of the Self" Weber offers a lucid reassessment of Hölderlin's significance in Benjamin's dissertation and thus brings to light a dimension of his interpretation of the German Romantics that, as Weber correctly points out, "has been almost entirely ignored" in the scholarship of the past few decades." In this way Weber illuminates a crucial point in the renewal of Kantian thinking to which Benjamin alludes in his 1917 letter and thus allows us to arrive at a better appreciation of the innovative view of the impact of Kant's aesthetic theory to which Benjamin had come during this time. Weber focuses on Benjamin's use of the term *medium* to describe Schlegel's theory of absolute reflection and emphasizes the "ambiguity (*Doppelsinn*)" surrounding this concept in the dissertation. Medium designates, on the one hand, "a dynamic of transformation and alteration" and, on the other hand, "a movement of the self coming full circle." Or, as Weber formulates it, medium is characterized as at once a self-consistent state of connectedness and an inconsistent, discontinuous "process of linkage."[2] The mediality that Benjamin attributes to Schlegel's theory of the literary work is marked, in other words, by the ambiguity between developmental reflection and transformative repetition. In a manner that is faithful to Benjamin's own critical procedure Weber follows up on an allusion to Hölderlin's commentary on his translations of Pindar's poetry. The point is to indicate, and at the same time to demonstrate, that the exact "connectedness" of the mediality concerning Hölderlin and Benjamin (and Weber, not to mention Pindar) depends upon a thirdness like the third-level reflection that Benjamin attributes to Hölderlin.

Weber's explication of Benjamin's allusion shows how the circulation of the "I" of Pindar's poem in and out of writing—a movement that itself does not come full circle—illustrates how the singular connectedness of thirdness in Hölderlin is differentiated from the concept of the medium of the work of art attributed to Schlegel:

> For Schlegel the work qua original is defined by its "criticizability," through which it is lifted above its limited singularity and into the medium of reflection as the unfolding of a unified Self. For Hölderlin, and for Benjamin, the process of reflection is supplanted by a process of writing—as ascription, circumscription, translation and commentary, in which reflection reveals itself to be a transformative process of repetition as reinscription. In this process the Self does not come full circle and thereby makes way for an "I" defined as singularity—which is to say, not as individual, simply, but as relational and differential.[3]

In the course of his essay Weber points out the significance of the "ambiguity" of the medium—as reflection, on the one hand, and repetition, on the other—for aesthetic theory, for the critical analysis of newer broadcast media, and for contemporary art. As suggested at the end of the passage just quoted, Weber also analyzes the consequences of this "ambiguity" for the concept of the "Self" and in particular for the emergence of an "I" that "does not come full circle" as a Self on the basis of an act of self-conscious reflection. This insight about the relation of a self to a discontinuous mediacy, to which Weber has returned in a remarkably wide range of contexts throughout his career, is of fundamental importance to Hölderlin's "philosophical relation to the Romantics" in the dissertation and thus to the reception of Kantian thinking that Benjamin sees spreading throughout the nineteenth century and beyond.[4]

The importance of Weber's insight into what he calls "an 'I' defined as singularity" comes to light by way of contrast with a dominant tendency in a school of Hölderlin scholarship that has emerged in Germany in recent decades. This point can be made clear by considering a fragment by Hölderlin that has been made into the cornerstone of this school of criticism. Affiliated with the work of Dieter Henrich, in particular his work leading up to the 1992 study *Der Grund im Bewußtsein*, this group of scholars has been engaged in the reconstruction of what it calls the German Romantic "constellation" of the 1790s—the connections and communication that passed by way not only of published writings but also of correspondence, lectures, and other channels.[5] On the basis of new philological and archival research these scholars seek to establish the philosophical validity of German Romanticism as the earliest critique of idealism and in particular of the supremacy accorded to the principle of self-consciousness in influential works of idealist philosophy of the mid-1790s, most prominently the first edition of Fichte's *Wissenschaftslehre* (1794–95). Up to a point this claim about Romantic theory and the importance of the critique of self-consciousness in Fichte's work follows the approach Benjamin takes in his dissertation. But when it comes to the question of Hölderlin's significance in this context, the new scholarship departs silently but decisively with the dissertation.[6] Crucial to the interpretation the "constellation" scholarship proposes is a key document not available to Benjamin, a manuscript by Hölderlin that was probably composed in early 1795 but was not published until 1961 under the title of "Judgment and Being" ("Urtheil und Seyn").[7] In the highly condensed set of propositions advanced in this text, Hölderlin levels a powerful critique at the concept of the "absolute I" in the first edition of Fichte's *Wissenschaftslehre*. Drawing on the probably false etymological connection of the German word for "judgment," *Ur-theil* as primal division, Hölderlin demonstrates how the unifying capacity of subjective self-consciousness is ultimately subordinate to what he calls "being" (*Seyn*).[8] Manfred Frank sums up the import of Hölderlin's manuscript for the German Romantic "constellation" as follows: "Here, even before idealism spread its wings, the self-sufficiency of self-consciousness is contested. . . . Self-consciousness stands in a relation of dependency to Being, understood as preidentical existence."[9] Frank and his colleagues contend that this critique of the principle of self-consciousness, and of philosophical first principles in general, came to be adopted collectively by the entire Jena group from the spring of 1795 to the fall of 1796. The insistence on the thoroughly corporate manner in which the movement came to embrace this thesis extends from Frank's claim that Schelling deserves to share credit with Hölderlin for the original conception of its critique of Fichte to Jürgen Stolzenberg's contention that Fichte himself had already become critical of his own concept of the "absolute I" by the time Hölderlin took aim at it in his note.[10]

But the force at issue in Hölderlin's writing, according to Benjamin, questions this critical position itself. This thesis, which is advanced in the first part of *The Concept of Art Criticism in German Romanticism*, is screened out by the new "constellation" research as it assimilates Hölderlin to the interpretation of the medium associated primarily with Schlegel in the dissertation. Nevertheless Benjamin is quite explicit on this point: the reflective force emerging in Hölderlin's writing is greater than the one animating the movement away from self-consciousness in Romanticism. While overpowering the self-conscious subject in Fichte, the German Romantic concept of the work of art as a "medium" of reflection is itself overpowered by the higher critical intensity of Hölderlin's writing. This superior force—in Kant's terms "violence" (*Gewalt*)—prevails over self-conscious subjectivity and also the self-consistency and sameness of the Schlegelian concept of the work of art as "medium," giving rise to what Benjamin calls a "higher stage of reflection."[11] It is here that we discover the thirdness analyzed by Weber in his essay on the "ambiguous" structure of the medium in the dissertation: "Nevertheless, on the third and every succeeding higher level of reflection, a disintegration (*Zersetzung*) in this original form takes place (*vor sich geht*) that announces itself in a peculiar ambiguity (*Doppeldeutigkeit*). . . . The rigorous original form of second-level reflection [formulated by Schlegel] is assailed and shaken (*erschüttert und angegriffen*) by the ambiguity (*Doppeldeutigkeit*) in third-level reflection."[12] The "ambiguity in third-level reflection" of Hölderlin's writing breaks out of the Romantic constellation and discloses the discontinuous space of the "philosophical relation" of the "wider Romantic circle." In this expanded sphere the work of art comes apart as a self-consistent medium, turning instead into a medium of what Weber describes as transformative singularity. The Schlegelian-Romantic concept of the work of art as an infinitely progressive medium submits to the more dynamic force of this sphere. The Romantic medium is, as Benjamin says, "assailed and shaken" by a disintegrating force that takes place by dividing itself and "preceding itself" (*vor sich gehen*)—taking a place that is occupied by and singularly transformed into a space where the very property of self-consistency no longer holds. Here this dynamic force issues out of what Benjamin calls "a peculiar ambiguity" ("eine eigentümliche Doppeldeutigkeit").

It is precisely this power struggle that is at issue in the fragment on which the new research on the Romantic "constellation" has sought to base its reading of Hölderlin, the manuscript of "Judgment and Being" recovered in 1961. It becomes especially clear in the last paragraph of this dense text, which focuses on the act of a speaking subject under the dynamic conditions analyzed by Kant in his critique of aesthetic judgment of the dynamic sublime. Hölderlin's main assumption throughout the text—that being in language is exemplary for "being as such" ("Seyn schlechthin")[13]—may be understood to take up the fundamental link in Kant between free speaking and freedom going back to "What Is Enlightenment?" (1784), which emphasizes the importance of the faculty of speech and the implicit obligation to exercise one's voice or to become vocal (*mündlich*).[14] The question of such a vocal capacity and the specific conditions under which its free exercise becomes possible are the subject of the final reflections in "Judgment and Being" on the act of saying "I." The capacity to say "I" is not eliminated in the space opened up by Hölderlin's fragment. The "I" remains, but it is divided, marked by "ambiguity." When I say "I am I," Hölderlin says repetitively, the unifying power of the verb *to be* is not powerful enough to eliminate all separation between the subject and the object; on the contrary it is the separation of "I" from "I" that makes it possible for me to say "I am I" as an expression of self-consciousness. Yet this separation necessarily presupposes some one (unified) thing that was divided. In other words, a higher order of "being as such" is implied by the separation that allows me to employ the grammatical formulation "I am I." Saying "I am I" and expressing self-consciousness depends, therefore, upon a unified state that as such goes beyond my capacity to be conscious of it, since consciousness requires separation. To say "I am I," in other words, I must be and I must not be self-conscious.[15] The extent to which Hölderlin insists on asserting the existence of the "I" in the tense space of this impossible position is indicated by the crucial sentences that come at the end the paragraph: "How can I say: I! without self-consciousness? Yet how is self-consciousness possible? In that I oppose me to myself, separate me from myself, yet notwithstanding this separation recognize me in the opposed [object] as the same (*dasselbe*). Yet to what extent as the same (*dasselbe*)? I can, I must ask in this manner; for in another respect it is opposed to itself. Therefore the identity is no unification of object and subject that as such takes place, and therefore the identity is not = absolute being."[16] Breaking down in this passage is not merely self-consciousness, as the constellation research argues, but sameness or what Weber calls "the Self."[17] The critique is not of self-consciousness but of Selfness (ipseity), *dasselbe*. The two "I"'s part with one another as an inconsistent medium—as a space that is not one in the classical Kantian sense of the first part of the *Critique of Pure Reason*. The disintegration of the sameness that would unify the "I" as subject and object thus lays out the nonspatial space where the saying of "I! without consciousness" becomes possible. Yet the space in question is not that of the Romantic "reflection medium" because it is not the same (*dasselbe*). Significantly Hölderlin had first written, "How may I say" ("Wie darf ich sagen"), but he revised the text and shifted the question from asking permission to asserting a power or ability to exclaim "I."[18] With this adjustment the question becomes as much the declaration of an unconditional capacity to exist in language as an assertion of the conditional limitation of self-consciousness. In this double sense the sentence demonstrates the tension between being (without consciousness) and judging (consciously) that makes it impossible for the "I" in question to be one and the same under these conditions.[19] The halting, and irreducible, leaps of linguistic being, which resists being developed into a "reflection medium," are emphasized by the punctuation in this passage that underscores the *feeling* of this dynamic existence, not reflective self-feeling (*Selbstgefühl*) but the discontinuous yet repetitive slipping away of the sameness of the Self: from the colon ("How can I say:"), to the exclamation point ("I!"), to the question mark ("without self-consciousness?").[20] The last section of "Judgment and Being" thus poses two interpenetrating questions: (1) "How can I say: I! without self-consciousness?" and (2) "Yet to what extent [are the I that exclaims and the I that is self-conscious] the same?"[21] The second question responds to an imperative that seems also to command the first and that is made explicit in the phrase: "I can, I must ask in this manner [about self-sameness]." As in Kant, the existence of the capacity to exclaim and to be in language implies the obligation to exercise this faculty freely.[22] But the questioning of sameness, which is presented as the exemplary form of existential expression in this passage, can be only a partial and self-parting engagement in the freedom of linguistic being because it becomes possible only in a sphere where the capacity for self-consciousness is overpowered by the faculty for a freedom of speech that liberates the speaker from awareness of itself as the same object—from a continuous context in which the exclaiming "I" and the self-conscious "I" occupy the same space. In the sphere described by Hölderlin the "I" is divided between a genuine but partial exclamation of being in language as such and an entirely artificial part of speech. The genuineness of this experience—which is, once again, not one in the classic Kantian sense criticized by Benjamin from the point of view of the "coming philosophy"—is made possible by the ambiguous poetic force to be found in Hölderlin. By elucidating Benjamin's critique of the Romantic medium Weber sheds light on this overlooked aspect of the reading of Hölderlin that is buried in *The Concept of Criticism in German Romanticism*.

In the remainder of this essay I will seek to demonstrate how Weber's comments on the singularizing force Benjamin encountered in Hölderlin—the force that disrupts or parts with the self—illuminate the approach taken to the question of the poetic medium in Hölderlin's poem "Celebration of Peace."[23]

✦

The ambiguity to which Benjamin points in his remarks on Hölderlin is also the point of departure for the 1921 essay "Toward the Critique of Violence." From the perspective of Kantian philosophy, Benjamin observes, words such as *life* and *man* disclose a fundamental ambiguity (*Doppelsinn*) deriving from their relation to two "spheres": one of mere existence (as in "mere life"), another consisting of an "irreducible, total condition" (as in "the irreducible, total condition that is *man*"). The difference between the mere existence of man and what is described as "the not-yet-existence of the just man" constitutes the fundamental ambiguity (*Zweideutigkeit*) of terms such as *life* and *man*: "Man does not coincide, at any price, with the mere life of the man, any more than with the mere life in the man or with any other of his conditions or qualities, indeed not even with the uniqueness of his bodily person." Benjamin takes an example of this "ambiguity" from Kant's "Toward Eternal Peace" (1795), noting at one point that the doubleness of words like *life* and *man*, which "is to be unlocked" with reference to the two spheres, is "analogous to that of the word *peace*."[24] Conventionally and erroneously used to describe what is always also the imposition of a new legal order through war, Benjamin notes, the word *peace* is employed otherwise by Kant, so that it signifies not merely the enforcement of a new worldly order but also the irreducible, total end of all such orders. This is the dual sense "in which Kant speaks of 'Eternal Peace.'"[25] In addition to being metaphorical and standing for political conditions brought about, for example, by agreements calling for the cessation of worldly conflict, the word *peace* in "Toward Eternal Peace" also contains an unmetaphorical dimension that stands for no worldly condition and that is in this sense unconditional and philosophical. In a phrase that draws on the chiasmus formed by this ambiguity in "Toward Eternal Peace" Benjamin describes the peace of which Kant writes as "equally unmetaphorical and political": unmetaphorical in the philosophical sense that peace refers to nothing in this world and political in the metaphorical sense that peace can stand for many things in this world, including another means of war.

By displaying an ambiguity associated with poetic language, critical philosophy defends its right to declare itself publicly on matters of revolution, war, and peace in "Toward Eternal Peace" along the lines of traditional defenses of poetry. Like the poets, Kant's philosophers concern themselves with a world of pure possibility that is hypothetical and therefore supposedly harmless in the real world of practical politics. Yet the ambiguity of peace in Kant's essay opens up a more complex relation of political philosophy to the worldly power from which it seeks the right to speak freely. In this sense the ambiguous power of philosophy is perhaps more deeply related to that of poetry, the political force of which was recognized—if not deployed—by its self-styled philosophical opponents from the start. When reflecting on a hypothetical peace treaty or even indirectly on an actual pact to which a fictional document may implicitly refer, such as the peace concluded between Prussia and the French revolutionary government on April 5, 1795 (four months before "Toward Eternal Peace" was sent to the publisher), philosophy is presented by Kant as posing no threat to state power on the basis of its exclusive responsibility to an other-worldly sovereign, namely reason. As a matter of fact the possession of political power interferes with this responsibility, according to Kant, and "corrupts" the freedom of the judgment that philosophers bring to political questions: "That kings should philosophize or philosophers become kings is not to be expected, but it is also not to be wished for, since possession of power unavoidably corrupts (*verdirbt*) the free judgment of reason. But that kings or royal peoples . . . should not let the class of philosophers disappear or be silent but should let it speak publicly is indispensable to both, so that light may be thrown on their business; and, because this class is by its nature incapable of forming seditious factions or clubs, it cannot be suspected of spreading *propaganda*."[26] Political power—specifically state power, the power of kings—corrupts philosophy because free judgment submits only to the higher moral law transcending the imperatives of individual self-preservation and collective well-being. From the perspective of critical philosophy these demands issue from the inclination to evil that is rooted in man. By making themselves responsible for subordinating these demands to the higher law of reason, Kant argues, philosophers belong to a "class" that is by its very "nature" incapable of "forming seditious factions." Yet the mode of rebellion to which this last phrase alludes raises a possibility that provides another instance of the ambiguity Benjamin finds in the political philosophical style of "Toward Eternal Peace." The phrase "forming seditious factions" translates the German "Rottierung: diese Klasse ihrer Natur nach der Rottierung . . . unfähig ist." *Rottierung* stems from *Rotte*, meaning faction, which is the word Luther chose to characterize the followers of Korah who rose up against Moses and were swallowed by the earth as divine punishment in the biblical account. (In the King James version this is translated as "Korah and his company.")[27] As a class defined by its responsibility to the higher moral law the philosophers, Kant suggests, are essentially incapable of belonging to the *Rotte*. But the sedition in question in this passage from "Toward Eternal Peace" refers specifically to rebellion against worldly power—the power of kings. The word *Rottierung*, deriving from a source that seems to allude to factionalism with regard to the higher law (the divinely ordained order against which Korah and his company rise up), is used to refer to a rebellion in the practical sphere of politics. Thus the ambiguity of the word *Rotte* in "Toward Eternal Peace" opens the possibility that the incapacity for revolt in the transcendental sphere might reveal an incapacity not to revolt against the state in the world of politics. In Kant's satirical essay this remains ambiguous.

Kant resolves the ambiguity two years later in his defense of the legitimacy of the state's right to use coercive force in the first part of the *Metaphysics of Morals*. The state is ultimately authorized to exercise force on the basis of its justified claim to control a finite portion of the earth's surface as a unified sphere. Human beings have a right individually to occupy the space and time where they happen to be (as distinct from the places where they choose to reside) and collectively to possess parts of the surface of the earth that extend beyond the spatiotemporal limits of their own bodily existence. The right to such collective nonphysical possession is legitimate only in a civil society that results from the "coercion (*Zwang*) which is necessary if people are to leave the state of nature."[28] The foundation for this right lies in the postulate that there is no usable thing in this world that is "without a lord" (*herrenlos*).[29] More precisely the ultimate legitimacy of the state's right to employ coercive force is based on a mythic personification of the land as a vassal who offers the use of his body in exchange for the protection of a lord. It is "as if the land were to say, 'if you cannot protect me you cannot command me.'"[30] As Peter Fenves has compellingly demonstrated, it is precisely this mythic source of state power in the first part of Kant's *Metaphysics of Morals* that served as the starting point for Benjamin's critique of violence.[31] For Benjamin justice emerges when the coercive power enshrined in the state's mythic right to use force is reduced to an absolute minimum. At these moments the inversely proportional strength of what Benjamin calls pure "revolutionary" force (*Gewalt*) is at its highest level. Tellingly Benjamin also returns to the story of Korah's faction to which Kant alludes. But Benjamin does so in order to resolve the ambiguity of the peace of "Toward Eternal Peace" in precisely the opposite direction of Kant's deduction of the state's right to use force in the *Metaphysics of Morals*. The coercive force of state power in Benjamin's telling is cast in the role of *die Rotte* and becomes subject to the "divine" or "revolutionary" violence exemplified by "God's judgment on the company of Korah."[32] The tables are turned, in other words, and the legal power of the state, which was ambiguously affirmed in Kant's "Toward Eternal Peace," is annihilated by revolutionary *Gewalt* along the lines of the divine punishment of Korah and his faction. According to Benjamin's reworking of the biblical tale, it is as if practical politicians of "Toward Eternal Peace" were swallowed up by the land they looked upon as lords regarding a feudal subject. Instead of offering itself up in exchange for protection—like a vassal to a lord—the land rises up and closes over those who assumed a right to possess it.[33] From the perspective developed by Benjamin everyone who claims possession of a portion of the earth's surface treads on the shaky ground of Korah's faction. For factionalism begins with the fall into the state of possessability in which the world expresses itself empirically, which is to say, in the transitory mode of finite space and time.[34] Pure *Gewalt* collapses the possessable dimension of the world (its existence in space and time) to which human beings unjustly cling. Pure *Gewalt* is in this sense an "expiatory force" that interrupts the history of guilt that begins with the possession of nature on the basis of myth (its personification as a vassal under the protection of a lord) and also the mythic conception of "empirical consciousness" to which such possession corresponds (what Husserl called the "natural attitude").[35] Like aesthetic judgment in Kant, and in particular like the aesthetic judgment of the "dynamic sublime," *Gewalt* resists materialization as an empirical event that belongs to cognitive experience. Or, as Benjamin puts it, "the expiatory force of *Gewalt* does not come to light for human beings."[36] But for Benjamin the source of this understanding of nonempirical force is detectable in the Hölderlinian cadences of the key sentence in which it is set forth at the end of "Toward the Critique of Violence": "Not equally possible and not equally urgent is, however, for human beings the decision when pure *Gewalt* in a specific case was real" ("Nicht gleich möglich noch auch gleich dringend ist aber für Menschen die Entscheidung, wann reine Gewalt in einem bestimmten Falle wirklich war").[37]

The starting point for my paper is that Benjamin develops his theory of "divine revolutionary force" both as a critique of Kant's defense in the *Metaphysics of Morals* of the right of the state to use force and as a reinterpretation of the aesthetic judgment of the dynamic sublime in the *Critique of Judgment* as refracted through the reading of Hölderlin. The thesis I pursue here is that the theory of "divine revolutionary force" developed in Benjamin's essay on violence comes into conflict with the force he encountered in Hölderlin—what I call poetic force. Significantly this conflict arises around the question of peace.

✦

Kant's "Toward Eternal Peace" is in part a reflection on the Peace of Basel, which was concluded in 1795. But this essay should be understood as part of the philosopher's complex response to the French Revolution—the revolution that declared war on Europe and in a sense on the world (the revolution that became what nineteenth-century German historians called *Revolutionskrieg*). For Kant, as Hannah Arendt points out, the world-historical sign of the French Revolution was a matter of aesthetic judgment, and as such it revealed to the philosophical observer the progressive purposiveness at work in human history. There is plenty of evidence that the poet Friedrich Hölderlin shared this view of the Revolution. Nevertheless precisely around the time of Kant's essay on peace (around the middle of the 1790s) Hölderlin also began reflecting on the special intensification of force that emerges in what Kant called the "dynamic sublime," a capacity for what Hölderlin comes to regard as a poetic mode of "being" interrupting the vision of purposiveness communicated by the philosophical experience of the French Revolution according to Kant. This decade was a time of ongoing conflict in Europe and thus, as Kant predicts, of peace treaties. One such agreement, the Peace of Lunéville concluded in 1801 between Napoleon and the Holy Roman emperor Francis II, provided the occasion for Hölderlin's "Celebration of Peace." This poem lays out a positive poetic vision of peace under the conditions of a force that explicitly removes the terms of Kant's defense of the state's right to use physical force, specifically the personification of the state as a lord and the land as a vassal (that is, the mythic source of state power, according to Benjamin). In this sense "Celebration of Peace," which Benjamin never read, can be read along the lines of "Toward the Critique of Violence"—up to a point.

The peace of Hölderlin's poetic response to Lunéville celebrates less the end of the war between Napoleon and the emperor of Austria than the end of war as such, which is to say, the end of world history and time. The exposition of this end in "Celebration of Peace" takes the form of four triads. It begins with the Greek historical-philosophical dimension, represented by the figure of Jupiter and the "thousand-year weather" of the "thunderer's echo" to which the opening triad builds (l. 32). This leads to the Christian dimension of the end in the second three-strophe section with the historical fate of Christ, the "youth" cut down "in the middle of his words," darkly overshadowed by a "deadly doom" ("ein tödlich Verhängnis") (ll. 48–50). As this application of this Homeric topos of the black cloud of death to the Christian God already suggests, the third triad is concerned with the reconciliation not just of the Greek and Christian gods but of all of the gods and men. The poem's final section reaches back to the first in the image of the mother and child who "look upon peace" hopefully and thus in the future on "ground still resounding with thunder" (ll. 121–25).[38] Peter Szondi underlines the "freedom" that Hölderlin takes in substituting concrete descriptions for the proper names (*antonomasias*) of both Greek and Christian gods. "No single figure of the hymn," Szondi observes, "is called by its own, traditional name. In place of the proper name a multiplicity of characterizations appears. Why this multiplicity, and how is it distributed (*wie verteilt sie sich*) to the two main characters of the account that is called 'Celebration of Peace'?"[39] By dividing up the names—according to what Szondi calls "the principle of name-giving" ("das Prinzip der Namengebung") in the poem—Hölderlin disseminates them in the medium of its language. The divisibility of the names allows them to be distributed (*Teilbarkeit* making possible *Verteilung*). The dividing up of the names of Jupiter and Christ in "Celebration of Peace" participates or takes part in the naming of the gods; the *Namengebung* could also be characterized as a *Namennehmen*.[40] In this sense the give-and-take of the *Namengebung* is the very mode of celebration taken by the poem.

The priority of the linguistic medium over the proper names of the gods—the supremacy of distribution over attribution—is in keeping with Hölderlin's insistence on the supreme sovereignty of mediacy in one of his famous Pindar commentaries: the "strict mediacy" ("die strenge Mittelbarkeit") that is the law for "mortals" and "immortals" alike.[41] The force of this law is nowhere more evident than at the very middle of "Celebration of Peace," in the transition from the sixth to the seventh of the poem's twelve strophes (between the second and third of the four triads). The sixth strophe moves through this transition in a way that turns on the status of the day of celebration as a middle space shared by god and man. Or, more precisely, a day of celebration to which both are subject, for there is a suggestion in the last lines of the strophe that such days are observed not just by mortals but also by immortals. The gods incline toward men, we are told, not primarily for the sake of mankind but "to hold days of celebration": "And to hold days of celebration / The high, the spirit / Of the world has inclined towards men" (ll. 76–78). The more conventional logic according to which the days of celebration would be understood as the means for the divine inclination toward humanity is reversed: the inclination of the gods is determined by the obligation to hold days of celebration. A god (Jupiter, for example) can also, however, *choose* days of work and thus with this choice enter into the sphere of history and time—resulting in "the thousand-year weather" of the poem's first triad. In this case the god takes part or shares in man's fate: "For once, however, even a god may choose day-work (*Tagewerk*) / Like mortals and share (*theilen*) all manner of fate" (ll. 81–82). But now the god appears as a lord, "the lord of time" ("der Herr der Zeit"):

> Denn längst war der zum *Herrn der Zeit* zu groß
> Und weit aus reichte sein Feld, wan hats ihn aber erschöpft?
> Einmal mag aber ein Gott auch Tagewerk erwählen,
> Gleich Sterblichen und theilen alles Schicksaal.
> Schicksaalgesez ist diß, daß Alle sich erfahren,
> Daß, wenn die Stille kehrt, auch eine Sprache sei.
> Wo aber wirkt der Geist, sind wir auch mit, und streiten,

Was wohl das Beste sei. So dünkt mir jetz das Beste,
Wenn nun vollendet sein Bild und fertig ist der Meister,
Und selbst verklärt davon aus seiner Werkstatt tritt,
*Der stille Gott der Zeit* und nur der Liebe Gesez,
Das schönausgleichende gilt von hier an bis zum Himmel.

For long now he had been too great to rule
As *Lord of Time*, and wide his field extended, but when did it
exhaust him?
For once, however, even a God may choose
Day work, like mortals, and share all manner of fate.
This is the law of fate, that all shall experience themselves,
That when the silence returns there shall be a language too.
Yet where the spirit is active, we too will stir and contest
What course might be the best. So now it seems best to me
If now the master completes his image and, finished,
Himself transfigured by it, steps out of his workshop,
*The quiet God of time*, and only the law of love,
That gently resolves all difference, prevails from here up to heaven.[42]

In this passage—at the very middle of Hölderlin's poem—the movement from the days of celebration to the days of work corresponds to the shift from the "spirit of the world" in strophe 6 to "the lord of time" in strophe 7. The spirit that is now, however, "too large" to remain the lord of time comes out of what had been his field and becomes the "god of time." This time is not the empirical temporality of history—not the time of thunder and war, not the medium of sounds sensuously affecting the ear—but the time of what Hölderlin calls "the quiet god" (l. 89). The time of this god is, Benjamin would say, "not temporal but image-like" (*bildlich*), and indeed Hölderlin describes it as a "time-image" (*Zeitbild*) in the next strophe (l. 111).[43] The image that emerges at this point in Hölderlin's poem in the rapid movement from "spirit" to "lord" to "god" is of a time when even the gods cease to be lords and thus of a time that is "without a lord" (*herrenlos*) (in other words, in direct contradiction to Kant's assertion in the *Metaphysics of Morals* that there is no usable thing in this world that is without a lord).[44] The correlate of this lordless time for Hölderlin is peace: a moment in which, as the third strophe of the poem states, "*Herrschaft* [dominion or domination but also lordship] is nowhere to be seen among spirits or mankind" (l. 28). Only then—when human *and* divine *Herrschaft* are not to be seen—does the sovereignty of peace appear. This occurs in the second strophe at the point where the god ceases his "day-labor" in the field of time and "disavows" or "disclaims" his "outland," a term that was more commonly understood in Hölderlin's day to signify the outer lands belonging to an estate but lying beyond its boundaries.[45] (The *Oxford English Dictionary* defines the cognate *outland* as a feudal term for a "portion of a manor or estate not retained by the lord but granted to the tenants.") The sovereignty of peace appears, in other words, only when the god ceases to be the *lord* of time ("der Herr der Zeit"). The lord of time is at this point affected by the force of a medium that resists subjection to the will of men and gods alike. Appropriately, therefore, the poet of "Celebration of Peace" does not so much deploy as communicate this force by imparting it as a medium. In keeping with the logic of the poem's *Namengebung*, which gives priority to the linguistic medium over the individual name (to the naming process over the name), the poet does not properly name the god and assert what Nietzsche calls this "lordly right" (*Herrenrecht*).[46] The source of this naming is the medium of the poem, not the "I" of the poet. In place of an "I" claiming the sovereign right to name there is the poem testifying to the figuring force of a medium affecting men and gods alike.[47] This poetic force, however, does not announce the coming of a millennium of peace—an announcement that would have been contradicted immediately by the historical record that Napoleon and others have left in the more than two centuries since "Celebration of Peace" was composed. But it also does not point to a peaceful purposiveness shaping human affairs gradually over time, as the French Revolution does from Kant's perspective. The poem is instead a piece of language celebrating its capacity to resist the effort to designate things and to make it into an instrument of mastery—a peace of language disowning and parting with an illusory power to appropriate the world. This peace is revolutionary exclusively in that, as the "lord of time" turns into the "god of time," the divine is turned out of power by the strict law of the poetic medium. Instead of overturning the worldly order along the lines of the biblical legend of Korah and his faction, the revolutionary force to which the "lord of time" becomes subject removes the divine from the sphere of revolutionary politics.

## Notes

1. Philippe Lacoue-Labarthe and Jean-Luc Nancy's pathbreaking study, *L'absolu littéraire: Théorie de la littérature du romantisme allemande* (Paris: Seuil, 1978), leaves the question of Hölderlin to the side, relegating it to a footnote (41n1). Lacoue-Labarthe returns to this question later in his work, but, as I demonstrate below, his interpretation does not offer a rigorous analysis of the "philosophical relation of Hölderlin to the Romantics." The new German *Konstellationsforschung*, to which I will return, entirely neglects Benjamin's thesis about Hölderlin.

2. Samuel Weber, "From Reflection to Repetition: Medium, Reflexivity and the Economy of the Self," the Spring 2009 Rodig Lecture, in *Rutgers German Studies Occasional Papers 10* (New Brunswick, N.J.: Rutgers German Studies, 2010), 9, 5, 7–8.

3. Weber, "From Reflection to Repetition," 11–12.

4. Hölderlin's "philosophical relation to the Romantics," Benjamin proposes, "determines the whole Romantic philosophy of art. And it is this determination that has made the Romantic philosophy of art so historically rich in consequences. Not only did it spread with the spirit of modern criticism, without being 'agnosticized' in its presuppositions or essence, but it also entered, in more or less clearly marked form, into the philosophical foundations of later schools of art, such as French Romanticism (which succeeded it) and German Neo-Romanticism." Walter Benjamin, *Gesammelte Schriften*, 7 vols. (Frankfurt am Main: Suhrkamp, 1972–89), 1: 1, 103 (hereafter *GS*); Walter Benjamin, *Selected Writings*, 4 vols. (Cambridge, Mass.: Harvard University Press, 1996–2003), 1: 175 (hereafter *SW*).

5. For an informed account of *Konstellationsforschung*, see Karl Ameriks, *Kant and the Historical Turn: Philosophy as Critical Interpretation* (Oxford: Oxford University Press, 2006), 289–306. Some of the key works by Henrich are *Konstellationen* (1991), *Der Grund im Bewußtsein* (1992), and *Hölderlins Denken in Jena 1794–95*. An English translation of some relevant essays by Henrich has been published under the title *The Course of Remembrance*. Among the most prominent of the philosophers who have been pursuing the approach taken by Henrich are Manfred Frank in Germany, Karl Ameriks in the United States, and Andrew Bowie in England.

6. I am aware of no refutation or even acknowledgment of Benjamin's interpretation of Hölderlin on the part of Henrich, Frank, and their colleagues. Indeed the extent to which the recent archival research on the Romantic constellation differs from or supports Benjamin's approach to German Romanticism as a critique of self-consciousness is also never addressed, as far as I know. The single allusion to Benjamin in Frank's *The Philosophical Foundations of Early German Romanticism* credits him merely with inventing the term *medium of reflection* in connection with Schlegel's work. Manfred Frank, *The Philosophical Foundations of Early German Romanticism* (Albany: State University of New York Press, 2004), 202.

7. Friedrich Hölderlin, "Urtheil und Seyn," in *Sämtliche Werke*, 8 vols. (Stuttgart: Cottanachfolger, 1943–85), 4: 216–17. For a description of Hölderlin's "Urtheil und Sein" and an account of its recovery, see Dieter Henrich, *Der Grund im Bewußtsein: Untersuchungen zu Hölderlins Denken (1794–1795)* (Stuttgart: Klett-Cotta, 1992), 682–707; Frank, *The Philosophical Foundations of Early German Romanticism*, 102. D. E. Sattler, editor of the Kritische Textausgabe of Hölderlin's *Sämtliche Werke* (1982), has argued that, by placing judgment before being, the title "Judgment and Being" leads to a "general misunderstanding." Sattler proposes the title "Seyn—, drükt die Verbindung des Subjects und Objects aus" (Being—, expresses the connection between subject and object). Sattler's explanation for this can be found in Hölderlin, *Sämtliche Werke, Briefe und Dokumente in zeitlicher Folge*, 12 vols. (Munich: Luchterhand, 2004), 4: 163.

8. Hölderlin may have encountered the pseudo-etymology of *Urteil* in Karl Leonhard Reinhold, *Versuch einer neuen Theorie der menschlichen Vorstellungsvermögen* (Prague: Widtmann and Mauke, 1789), 435–40, or in Johann Gottlieb Fichte, *Unpublished Writings on "Platner's Aphorisms 1794–1812,"* in *Gesamtausgabe der Bayerischen Akademie der Wissenschaften*, 4 vols. (Stuttgart-Bad Canstadt: Fromann, 1962), 2.4: 182. See Violetta L. Waibel, *Hölderlin und Fichte 1794–1800* (Paderborn: Schöningh, 2000), 140–45.

9. Frank, *The Philosophical Foundations of Early German Romanticism*, 107.

10. Jürgen Stolzenberg, "Selbstbewußtsein: ein Problem der Philosophie nach Kant: Zum Verhältnis Reinhold-Hölderlin-Fichte," *Revue Internationale de Philosophie*, 50 (197) (1996): 461–82.

11. Benjamin, *GS* 1.1: 30; *SW* 1: 129.

12. Benjamin, *GS* 1.1: 30–31; *SW* 1: 129, translation slightly modified.

13. Hölderlin, *Sämtliche Werke*, 4: 216.

14. Immanuel Kant, *Gesammelte Schriften*, Akademie der Wissenschaften, 29 vols. to date (Berlin: Reimer, De Gruyter, 1900–), 8: 35, 41.

15. Stolzenberg glosses this passage by tracing its connections to Reinhold's *Versuch einer neuen Theorie des menschlichen Vorstellungsvermögen* (1789). See Jürgen Stolzenberg, "Selbstbewußtsein: Ein Problem der Philosophie nach Kant: Reinhold-Hölderlin-Fichte," *Revue internationale de philosophie* 3 (1996): 474–78.

16. Hölderlin, "Urtheil und Seyn," 217 (my translation).

17. See Henrich, *Der Grund im Bewußtsein*, 92–113; Frank, *The Philosophical Foundations of Early German Romanticism*, 105–8.

18. Hölderlin, *Sämtliche Werke*, 4: 738.

19. Stolzenberg reduces the import of this sentence to a "rhetorical" question that has the "single meaning" of "an assertion about the specific epistemic status of the concept of the I: this status is determined by the concept of consciousness" ("Selbstbewußtsein," 472). Stolzenberg neglects the capacity of the first "I" by focusing on the second "I" of the sentence: "How can I say: I without self-consciousness."

20. Like "participation" in Kant, "being" in Hölderlin is a matter of a feeling "that borders closely on enthusiasm." A number of scholars have argued that the approach to "being" taken in "Urtheil und Seyn" resembles contemporary critiques of self-consciousness based on the category of feeling, in particular Jacobi's theory of "self-feeling" (*Selbstgefühl*) (Henrich, *Der Grund im Bewußtsein*, 60–113; Frank, *The Philosophical Foundations of Early German Romanticism*, 70–96; Ameriks, *Kant and the Historical Turn*, 269–88). But feeling in Hölderlin's text is precisely not that of a self. The punctuation stresses the importance of the peculiar feeling of being in a sphere that resists self-consciousness and self-sameness. The sentence—"How can I say: I! without self-consciousness?"—is to be read alongside Adorno's remarks on punctuation: "Gleicht nicht das Ausrufungszeichen dem drohend gehobenen Ziegefinger? Sind nicht die Fragezeichen wie Blinklichter oder ein Augenaufschlag? Doppelpunkte sperren, Karl Kraus zufolge, den Mund auf." Theodor Adorno, "Satzzeichen," in *Noten zur Literatur: Gesammelte Schriften*, vol. 2 (Frankfurt: Suhrkamp, 1974), 106.

21. It is an expression of the lack of development in the logic of this fragment that we cannot assert with certainty that this paragraph is the last one. It has been argued that the order of the paragraphs should be reversed because Hölderlin copied them on a piece of folded paper. In any case the paragraphs can be reversed even if we cannot be sure that they must be.

22. Given that the response to this imperative is a peculiar form of questioning, Hölderlin may be suggesting that the faculty involved resembles that of reason, which makes a similar imposition. On the way the freedom of reason in Kant requires the questioning of sameness (ipseity), see Jacques Derrida, *Voyous: Deux essays sur la raison* (Paris: Galilée, 2003), 195–217.

23. A version of this interpretation appears in my *Poetic Force: Poetry after Kant* (Stanford: Stanford University Press, 2014), 29–54.

24. Benjamin, *GS* 2.1: 201; *SW* 1: 251.

25. Benjamin, *GS* 2.1: 185–86; *SW* 1: 240. In her famous essay "L'Illiad ou le poème de la force," in *Œuvres* (Paris: Gallimard, 1999), Simone Weil writes of force manifested in relation to only one dimension of the ambiguous meaning of words like *life* to which Benjamin alludes. Force for Weil is the physical, empirical power "to transform a man into a thing" (529). In this way she overlooks the force of the poem to resist through the application of its own power of memorialization the reduction of man to bodily existence. By leaving the force of the poem out of her account of the "poem of force" Weil neglects the crucial tension and interplay in the *Iliad* between two kinds of force. Of course her objective in discussing the *Iliad* is not to assess the function of poetry and its force but rather to analyze the structure of what Étienne Balibar has recently called "extreme violence" (Weil, "L'Illiad," 386–401).

26. Kant, *Gesammelte Schriften*, 8: 369; Immanuel Kant, *Practical Philosophy* (Cambridge, U.K.: Cambridge University Press, 1996), 338.

27. Numbers 16:1.

28. Kant, *Gesammelte Schriften*, 6: 264; *Practical Philosophy*, 416.

29. Kant, *Gesammelte Schriften*, 6: 246; *Practical Philosophy*, 405.

30. Kant, *Gesammelte Schriften*, 6: 265; *Practical Philosophy*, 416.

31. Peter Fenves, *The Messianic Reduction: Walter Benjamin and the Shape of Time* (Stanford: Stanford University Press, 2010), 190–226.

32. Benjamin, *GS* 2.1: 199; *SW* 1: 250.

33. The biblical legend emphasizes that not just Korah and his men but all of their possessions are swallowed into the earth: "Nowhere upon earth remained a trace of them or of their possessions, and even their names disappeared from the documents upon which they were written." Louis Ginzberg, *Legends of the Jews* (Baltimore: Johns Hopkins University Press, 1998), 3: 298.

34. Benjamin writes in the early set of notes published in Scholem's diaries that Fenves explicates as providing the basis of his critique of *Gewalt*, "To every good, limited as it is by the spatio-temporal order, there accrues a possession-character that expresses its transitoriness" ("Besitzcharakter als Ausdruck seiner Vergänglichkeit"). Gershom Scholem, *Tagebücher nebst Aufsätzen und Entwürfen bis 1923*, 2 vols. (Frankfurt am Main: Jüdischer Verlag, 1995–2000), 1: 401; Fenves, *The Messianic Reduction*, 257.

35. Benjamin, *GS* 2.1: 162; *SW* 1: 103. Husserl's critique of the "natural attitude" ("natürliche Einstellung") is initiated in his *Ideas Pertaining to a Pure Phenomenology and to a Phenomenological Philosophy* published in 1913. For example, "*We put out of action the general positing, which belongs to the essence of the natural attitude*; we parenthesize anything and everything that this thesis encompasses with respect to being." Edmund Husserl, *Ideen zu einer reinen Phänomenologie und phänomenologischen Philosophie*, vol. 3 of *Husserliana* (The Hague: Nijhoff, 1976), 65; *Ideas Pertaining to a Pure Phenomenology and to a Phenomenological Philosophy: Third Book, Phenomenology and the Foundation of Sciences*, vol. 2 of *Collected Works* (Dordrecht: Kluwer Academic, 1998), 61. On the connection between Husserl and Benjamin on the "natural attitude" and on Benjamin's departure from Husserl's insistence that it can be "put out of

action" or "turned off" (*ausgeschaltet*) on the strength of the philosopher's force of will, see Fenves, *The Messianic Reduction*, especially 2–3.

36. Benjamin, *GS* 2.1: 203; *SW* 1: 252.

37. Benjamin, *GS* 2.1: 202–3; *SW* 1: 252.

38. Examples of the "deadly doom" ("tödliches Verhängnis"), the black cloud, that looms over those fallen in battle included *Iliad* 20: 417 (in Voss's translation: "Und Gewölk des Todes umhüllt ihn") and *Odyssey* 4: 180 (which Voss translates as "Bis uns die Schwarze Wolke des Todes endlich umhüllte"). See Jochen Schmidt, *Hölderlins geschichtsphilosophische Hymne "Friedensfeier," "Der Einziger," "Patmos"* (Darmstadt: Wissenschaftliche Buchgesellschaft, 1990), 31.

39. Peter Szondi, *Hölderlin-Studien: Mit einem Traktat über philologische Erkenntnis* (Frankfurt am Main: Suhrkamp, 1970), 71, 79 (my translation).

40. Indeed as Schestag points out, the central lines in Hölderlin's "The Rhein"—"in der Götter Nahmen / Theilnehmend"—draw on the common root of *nehmen* and *teilen* in the Greek *nemein* signifying "to allot, to distribute, etc." Thomas Schestag, "The Highest," in *The Solid Letter: Readings of Friedrich Hölderlin*, ed. Aris Fioretos (Stanford: Stanford University Press, 1999), 405–10.

41. Hölderlin, *Sämtliche Werk*, 5: 285.

42. Hölderlin, "Friedensfeier," in *Friedrich Hölderlin: Poems and Fragments*, translated by Michael Hamburger (London: Anvil Press Poetry, 1994), translation modified and with my emphasis.

43. "Celebration of Peace" begins with such a time-image. It is felt in the hearing of celebratory "tones" that open the poem and that perhaps allude to the Hölderlinian poetic doctrine of the "alternation of tones" informing these lines. Such "tones" are "heavenly"—too big for the medium of time in the classic sense—and thus they are said to be "echoing quietly" (l. 1).

44. Kant, *Gesammelte Schriften*, 6: 246; *Practical Philosophy*, 405. Hölderlin's poem "Wie wenn am Feiertage" sets up this same problematic in the ambiguity of its opening lines, what de Man calls the "ambiguity of metaphorical reference." Paul de Man, *Romanticism and Contemporary Criticism: The Gauss Seminar and Other Papers* (Baltimore: Johns Hopkins University Press, 1996), 62. The "they" that alludes to the poets are like either the property owners who go out to look at their land after a storm or the trees that experience the storm. For some illuminating remarks on de Man's critique of Heidegger's reading (more precisely, failure to read) this poem, see Andrej Warminski, "Discontinuous Shifts: History Reading History," *Romantic Circles: Praxis Series*, April 2011, www.rc.umd.edu/praxis/deman/warminski/warminski_notes.htm.

45. Szondi, *Hölderlin-Studien*, 89.

46. Friedrich Nietzsche, *Genealogie der Moral*, in *Kritische Gesamtausgabe* (Berlin: Walter de Gruyter, 1968), 6.2: 260.

47. The force of the poetic medium is a manifestation of what Hamacher calls "philological affect." See especially Werner Hamacher, *Für—Die Philologie* (Weil am Rhein: Urs Engeler, 2009), 33–37.

Chapter 10

# The "Cultured Nazi" and the Cut of the Shibboleth

## *Les Bienveillantes*, *Inglourious Basterds*, and the Globalization of English

Marc Redfield

In the early 1980s Saul Friedländer identified and criticized what he called a "new discourse" on Nazism. He had in mind a number of films and books that had appeared during the 1970s: among others, Luchino Visconti's *La caduta degli dei* (*The Damned*; 1969), Hans-Jürgen Syberberg's *Hitler: Ein Film aus Deutschland* (1977), Liliana Cavani's *Il portiere di notte* (*The Night Porter*; 1974), Michel Tournier's *Le roi des aulnes* (*The Ogre*; 1970), and George Steiner's *The Portage to San Cristóbal of A.H.* (1979). These various works, in Friedländer's view, offer a "comprehension of Nazism" that "passes through the mystical." Although the principal thrust of his study is critical—he accuses these works of neutralizing "the criminal side of Nazism" through "artifices of language, displacements of meaning, aestheticization, inversion of symbols"—Friedländer credits this "new discourse" with having foregrounded a mélange of "kitsch and death" that defines the "debased romantic inspiration" of the Nazi aesthetic. An analysis of this aesthetic helps bring into focus, as economic and sociopolitical analyses do not, the peculiar National Socialist blend of reaction (kitsch: an appeal to harmony, to things as they are) and apocalyptic fervor ("until now, organized societies or stable power structures were never attracted to apocalypse"). Friedländer hints at the threat of a certain mimetic contagion: the "new discourse" draws attention to these components of Nazi aestheticism because at some level it uncritically repeats and indulges in them. And it does so because this "debased romanticism" is tempting: Friedländer goes so far as to claim, at the end of his book, that the kitsch-death amalgam relays, in mystifying fashion, "the profound conflict of man facing modernity. . . . Neither liberalism nor Marxism responds to man's archaic fear of the transgression of some limits of knowledge and power . . . thus hiding what remains the fundamental temptation: the aspiration for total power, which, by definition, is the supreme transgression, the ultimate challenge, the superhuman combat that can be settled only by death."[1]

In the years since Friedländer sought to analyze these "reflets du nazisme," the rate of production of fictional and nonfictional works either about or in some way evocative of Nazism, the Third Reich, the European theater of World War II, or the Shoah has if anything increased. The reasons for this ongoing desire to represent, reconfront, or reanalyze the Nazi disaster are manifold, and some are easy enough to identify: the massive traumatic shock of the Holocaust; the dramatic mobility and savagery of the war; the fact that a good portion of this war occurred on culturally prestigious Western European terrain; the narrative and ideological appeal (which is also to say the commercial entertainment value) of a conflict readily figurable as a "good war." But commentary like Friedländer's responds to a persistent question. Neither the ethical imperative to remember Nazism's victims nor the narrative satisfactions to be had in typecasting Nazism as the ne plus ultra of evil in themselves fully explain the fascination that this regime, its crimes, its spectacles and symbols continue to command, particularly in First World contexts. The title of Susan Sontag's well-known essay on this topic, "Fascinating Fascism" (1974), to some degree sacrifices accuracy for alliteration, for Sontag is not so much concerned with the general phenomenon of fascism as with the cultural aftershocks of Nazism—its specific iconography and idiom. This fascination, it may be added, displays itself across a wide range of forms, genres, and tonalities. A dimension of inadvertent, ugly comedy, for instance, has limned the Nazi phenomenon since its mass propagation and reception in the 1930s. The national-aestheticist spectacle epitomized by Leni Riefenstahl's *Triumph des Willens* (1935) from the start lent itself to parody; in Anglo-American contexts (particularly in the wake of Charlie Chaplin's *The Great Dictator* [1940]), a few of the most recognizable elements of this spectacle—above all the Hitler mustache but also the goose-stepping troops, the stiff-arm salute, the screaming dictator—rapidly became irretrievably cartoonish, signifying self-parodic idiocy and providing popular culture with a source of endless, if sometimes ambivalent comic entertainment.[2] But the same cannot be said of the swastika. When routed through this master symbol, the historical and fetishistic thrust of Nazism has survived its comic demystifications.[3] Together with the most famous elements of SS paraphernalia (sig runes, black-and-silver dress uniforms), the swastika—the unframed display of which has been a criminal offense in Germany and some other European countries since the end of the war—continues to function as the closest thing to a magical or diabolical-sacred sign that secular Western culture possesses, generating energy across a variety of semiotic contexts (political, social, pornographic).[4]

As a political event National Socialism is an increasingly distant phenomenon, the product of long-vanished contexts, many specific to Weimar

Germany: the lost war; the failed 1919 revolution; relatively strong working-class movements in violent conflict with very strong reactionary forces; the hyperinflation ordeal; the punitive reparations that, by the end of the decade, contributed to the severity of Germany's suffering during the global crash of 1929—all of this, of course, combined with historically specific forms of racism and anti-Semitism. But as a politico-aesthetic event bound up with the Holocaust, National Socialism remains, for whatever we wish to call "the West," a hypercathected patch of history.[5] Friedländer is thus surely right to stress the importance of analyzing the Nazi aesthetic, and right to be intrigued by the ways authors utterly opposed to Nazism nonetheless seem tempted by forms of mimetic doubling when seeking to represent in some nonsuperficial way the Nazi phenomenon.[6] His identification of a mythic and mimetic temptation at work in the reception of Nazism deserves further consideration—not least since the explanation he finally offers us, "man's archaic fear of the transgression of some limits of knowledge and power," itself has a slightly mythic feel.

Let me therefore dwell with this theme a little longer. Writing in a different idiom than Friedländer and without referring to his text, but sharing some of his concerns, Philippe Lacoue-Labarthe and Jean-Luc Nancy offer an illuminating meditation on mimesis, myth, and aesthetic politics in their essay "The Nazi Myth."[7] Seeking to emphasize both the specificity of Nazism as a historical event and the broader Western ideological formations on which this event drew, Lacoue-Labarthe and Nancy diagnose a Nazi "myth *of* myth," with *myth* defined not as narrative or representation but as formative power: "the power to bring together the fundamental forces and directions of an individual or a people, the power of a subterranean, invisible, nonempirical identity . . . the power of the dream, of the projection of an image with which one identifies" (305). Myth is will-to-myth, a power of belief that wills itself into existence by incarnating itself in a figure or type: "For the type is the realization of the singular identity conveyed by the dream. It is both the model of identity *and* its present, effective, *formed* reality" (306). For reasons that Lacoue-Labarthe and Nancy trace back to the specific history of German nationalism, *race* names the locus, the dreamed type of this mythical power.[8] The Aryan race typifies the solar myth (and it is no accident that the swastika is a solar symbol): "The myth of the sun is nothing less than the myth of that which causes forms to come forth as such in their visibility, in the contour of their gestalt. . . . The solar myth is the myth of the formative force itself, of the original power of the *type*" (309). The "Jew" is not an opposite type but "the very absence of type"—the bastard or parasite shadowing the solar myth as the Aryan.

This analysis allows Lacoue-Labarthe and Nancy to elaborate on Walter Benjamin's famous description of fascism as the aestheticization of politics. The National Socialist spectacle represents "a fusion of politics and art, the production of the political as work of art," and more specifically "the construction, the formation, and the production of the German people in, through, and as a work of art" (303). Under the terms of such a biopolitics, animated by "the understanding of life as art, the understanding of the body, of the people, of the state as works of art" (310), spectacle achieves a certain density or intensity because it has to some degree become an end in itself: "The manipulation of the masses is not only a technique: it is also an end, because in the last instance it is the myth itself that manipulates the masses and realizes itself in them" (312). Or again: "The symbols of a mythical order, uniforms, gestures, parades, the enthusiasm of the ceremonial, as well as youth movements and all sorts of other associations, are not only techniques but ends in themselves: the finality of a total *Erlebnis* of the 'type'" (308).

The burden of Lacoue-Labarthe and Nancy's demonstration is to emphasize both the abyssal differences and a crucial point of overlap between the National Socialist dream of self-presence and embodiment-as-spectacle, on the one hand, and mainstream Western metaphysics, on the other. The Nazi myth of self-engenderment "is finally nothing more than the absolute, self-creating Subject, a subject whose essential property is not solely cognitive (like the subject of Descartes), nor solely spiritual (Eckehart), nor solely speculative (Hegel), but which somehow groups together and transcends all these determinations in an immediate and absolutely 'natural' essence: that of blood and race" (310). The argument is not that Nazism was in any meaningful way an "intellectual" movement. (The "somehow" in the sentence I just quoted registers the programmatic incoherence of the texts by Hitler and Rosenberg that Lacoue-Labarthe and Nancy have been examining.) Nor certainly are Lacoue-Labarthe and Nancy suggesting that the politicomythical Nazi spectacle had anything other than an obfuscating relationship to the brutal realities of life in post-1933 Germany. They insist, however, that there is a certain "logic," as well as a good deal of ideological power, to this spectacle: "We wish only to underline just how much this logic, with its double trait of the mimetic will-to-identity and the self-fulfillment of form, belongs profoundly to the mood or character of the West in general, and more precisely, to the fundamental tendency of the subject, in the metaphysical sense of the word" (312).

One way, therefore, to understand Western culture's lingering fascination with Nazism is as a half-disavowed negotiation of instabilities built into the modern subject—the subject of aesthetics, technics, self-formation. We might hypothesize that the Nazi spectacle—precisely *because* of its excess, its kitsch, its inadvertent comedy, its hidden-in-full-view monstrous criminality—provides late capitalist global culture with a safely distant mirror in which to contemplate its own autoimmune disorder, its own addiction to mediatized spectacle, even perhaps its own lethal geopolitics. Capitalism sets in motion a thoroughgoing commodification of the world and requires for its full development the elaboration of global communication and media systems.

Famously, under the impact of capitalism, all that is solid melts into air; the lure of an ever more profitable future devours the historical and traditional past; the standardizing yet also derealizing and deterritorializing effects of media become part of the fabric of quotidian life. (Such soulless modernity was precisely what the Nazis—who nonetheless early on made peace with big industry—propagandized as the threat from "America": a threat second only to the communist menace—and of course, equally ascribable to the machinations of international Jewry.) And yet, as Samuel Weber notes, capitalist culture finds it necessary ceaselessly to cover over, or at least *partly* cover over, the deterritorializing movement of its own mediatic reproduction:

> The media today are largely, although not exclusively, dominated by what can be called the Economy of the Self, defined as an instance that seeks to stay the same over time and space, by absorbing and assimilating all difference and alterity into itself. . . . This contributes to the survival of what Benjamin was later to analyze as the aura, which seeks to manifest a distance in proximity that is ultimately grounded in the ostensible self-identity of what it surrounds. Benjamin pointed to the Hollywood "star" and the European "dictator" as two instances of the survival of the "aura"; but a less spectacular contemporary example would be what in American English is called the "anchor" of news broadcasts, who precisely serves to "anchor" a movement that otherwise might explode or at least crack the frame of the isolated images presented in the Evening News.[9]

We might therefore posit that one way to ward off the dis-placing and disseminating power of capitalist production and of media technology (which is to say of *mediation* in general, including, as I shall emphasize in a moment, linguistic mediation), would be via a prophylactic detour through the Nazi, who, as the fanatical representative of a Leader, takes the "economy of the self" to an extreme. That is, it might be that a certain ambivalent and temporary identification with this figure—this figure *of* the myth of self-fashioning through identification—enables the tacit acknowledgment and warding-off of the impossibility of that very myth. This impossibility would be the Nazi's problem, not ours. The Nazi performs an *excessive* reinstatement of the "aura," *over*incorporates the Subject as race, *Volk*, and *Führer*. His excess is at once ludicrous and bound up with absolute evil. *We* are not that. And yet to tarry with representations of the Nazi is to risk doubling, colluding with, collaborating with the Nazi—which is what gives the whole operation its piquancy. A sadistic or aggressive impulse is no doubt often involved at such moments, but if one credits the analyses of Lacoue-Labarthe and Nancy, such investments would be part and parcel of a structural temptation of identification built into our culture's processing of Nazism. The mystical tone Friedländer identifies and chastises would represent only one particularly obsessive and aestheticized version of a much broader habit within contemporary Western culture.[10] Don DeLillo's bleakly comic novel *White Noise*, narrated by a midwestern college professor who has founded a department of "Hitler Studies," offers what is perhaps our culture's sharpest parody to date of this hyperbolic recirculation of the Nazi as a deracinated signifier within the "white noise" of media-saturated neoliberal consumerism.[11]

In what follows I shall be glancing off and on at DeLillo's shrewd novel while examining two prominent recent works, Jonathan Littell's novel *Les Bienveillantes* (2006) and Quentin Tarantino's film *Inglourious Basterds* (2009), both of which flesh out versions of the cliché of the "cultured Nazi," while also generating and exploring a relationship of mimetic doubling between these figures and the text's or film's own representational energies. These works differ in the ways in which (and the degree to which) they tempt us to identify with their Nazis, but Littell's novel and Tarantino's film do have one striking thing in common: both grant their Nazis specifically *linguistic* and, even more specifically, *polyglot* cultural capital. I think this is interesting enough to give us pause. No doubt the stereotype of the cultured Nazi habitually invokes the linguistic competence of a *Bildungsbürgertum* (the classics; French, English, Italian), but what we have here is something more focused and extreme. The framing context of Littell's novel turns on its first-person Nazi narrator's ability to pass as French, while the antic power of Tarantino's film receives a kind of allegorical expression in the polyglot verbal performances of its main villain, SS colonel Hans Landa (played by Christoph Waltz, who received an Oscar for his performance). Without in the least wishing to suggest that these works represent a new "new discourse" about Nazism, I do intend to argue that they relay with particular sharpness the anxieties and pleasures of identity formation in an era of mass mediation, which is also to say (in today's context; a century from now this will probably no longer be true) in an era of ever-increasing dissemination of English as the privileged language of global mediation. (One of the comic subplots of DeLillo's *White Noise* involves the professor of Hitler studies belatedly and secretly trying to learn a little bit of German: "As the most prominent figure in Hitler studies in North America, I had long tried to conceal the fact that I did not know German" [31].) In other words, and as is so often the case, these representations are as much or more (much more, in Tarantino's case, as we shall see) about their own condition of production as about Nazism in any limited or strictly literal sense.

✦

Narrated by a *Sicherheitsdienst* (security service) officer who participates in the unfolding of the Final Solution (from a sequence of *Einsatzgruppen* massacres that culminate in Babi Yar, to the extermination camps Belzec and Auschwitz), divided into chapters that, like the parts of a Bach suite, bear the names of eighteenth-century dances ("Toccata," "Allemandes I et II," etc.), orchestrated around the myth of Orestes, and sporting an elaborate pattern of twins and doubles, Littell's *Les Bienveillantes* self-consciously exposes itself to the sort of criticism Friedländer directed at his list of novels and films from the 1970s. It is unnecessary to review in any detail here the controversy this text generated first in France (where it won both the Grand prix du roman de l'Académie française and the Prix Goncourt in 2006) and subsequently in Germany and the United States (when it appeared in translation some three years later). The controversy displayed some significantly different inflections in these different contexts, but certain issues were always front and center: Was it ethically defensible for a novel to inhabit the psyche of a Nazi perpetrator over nearly a thousand pages, without any clear distancing mechanism? Was this character, Maximilian Aue, a successful novelistic creation; was the style of his prose good or bad; was the novel realistic or fantastic?[12] All of which funneled back into the question driving the debate: Was the novel a work of art or a vehicle for quasi-pornographic representations of the Nazi extermination of the Jews? Which is really to say: Does the novel and, by extension, its author *identify* with the Nazi protagonist? Even though (as was always pointed out) Littell is Jewish?

Littell clearly intended his text to solicit precisely such questions as part of its overall aesthetic performance.[13] In the present context I shall neither be considering this issue in its ramifications nor providing a sustained reading of this long and complex novel. But I need to say a little more about the novel's reception in France, since if we are interested in the significance of Aue's bilingualism, it becomes relevant to consider the way the French media was interested in Littell's. *Les Bienveillantes* is narrated from the vantage of a perpetrator who fled to France in 1945, where he has lived undisturbed for decades, passing as French:

> Quand tout fut enfin fini j'ai réussi à venir en France, à me faire passer pour un Français; ce n'était pas trop dificile, vu le chaos à l'époque, je suis revenu avec les déportés, on ne posait pas beaucoup de questions. Vrai, je parlais un français impeccable; c'est que j'ai eu une mère française; j'ai passé dix ans de mon enfance en France, j'ai fait le collège, le lycée, les classes préparatoires, et même deux années d'études supérieures, à l'ELSP, et comme j'ai grandi dans le Sud je pouvais même pousser une pointe d'accent méridional, de toute façon personne ne faisait pas attention.

> When it was all over, I managed to slip into France, to pass myself off as a Frenchman; in all the chaos, it wasn't too difficult. I returned along with the deported, we weren't asked many questions. It must be said that I speak perfect French; that's because I had a French mother; I spent ten years of my childhood in France, I went through middle school there, then high school, preparatory classes, and even

> two years of university, at the ELSP, and since I grew up in the South I could even muster a Provençal drawl, but in any case no one was paying attention.[14]

Aue's educational trajectory differs from Littell's in numerous ways. (Littell has occasionally felt obliged to underscore in interviews, "I am not Max Aue.") But like his protagonist Littell grew up mainly in France and went through the French school system up through the *baccalauréat*. He is now a French citizen, but when *Les Bienveillantes* appeared in 2006 he held a U.S. passport. (Littell was born in New York and is the son of Robert Littell, a *Newsweek* reporter and best-selling spy novelist.)[15] Littell's Americanness, of course, played a substantial role in the media uproar in France, particularly after *Les Bienveillantes* won the Prix Goncourt. Reporters to whom the author accorded an interview (he did not grant many, and he refused to appear on television) felt it important to report that he spoke French "sans accent." Wild rumors circulated that an editor at Gallimard had ghostwritten the text, or at the very least had had to clean it of countless anglicisms. Articles and web pages appeared listing real or putative anglicisms, German-language mistakes, and factual historical errors to be found over the course of the novel's 903 large-format pages. Also much discussed was the novel's "lancement à l'américaine"—the fact that a young and unknown writer had employed a literary agent (presumably on his famous father's advice) and driven an American-style bargain with France's most prestigious publishing house, collecting a substantial advance and keeping the international publishing rights (which is not usual in France).[16]

I mention the media discussion of American-style bookselling because it forms part of the larger contours of what might otherwise look like a sheer linguistic debate. The affair, however, would have played out very differently if Littell had been Czech or Congolese or Canadian (or even, for that matter, German—though in that case there certainly would have been an affair of a different order). The ambiguous Americanness of this author was what provoked both excitement and resentment; willy-nilly Littell had as the backdrop to his spotlighted appearance on the Parisian stage the global-size shadow of American culture and English-language media (massively expanded in the era of the Internet). An in-depth analysis of this (quite interesting) moment in the ongoing history of Franco-American and Franco-Anglophone cultural relations cannot be attempted here. My hope, though, is to be able convincingly to suggest that Littell's production of a teasing double of himself as the narrator of *Les Bienveillants* registers the pressure of this international backdrop.

Having stressed the specific role Littell's Americanness plays in this scenario, let me step back for a moment to the more general, and very ancient, question of the linguistic-political border. A vivid figure for this descends to us as the biblical narrative of the shibboleth: "Gilead then cut Ephraim off from the fords of the Jordan, and whenever Ephraimite fugitives said, 'Let me cross,' the men of Gilead would ask, 'Are you an Ephraimite?' If he said, 'No,' they then said, 'Very well, say "Shibboleth" (תלוביש).' If anyone said, "Sibboleth" (תלובים), because he could not pronounce it, then they would seize him and kill him by the fords of the Jordan. Forty-two thousand Ephraimites fell on this occasion" (Judges 12:5–6, NJB). As Jacques Derrida notes, there is no semantic or cognitive depth to the secret of the shibboleth.[17] The slaughtered Ephraimites knew the difference between *shi* and *si*; they just could not pronounce *shi*: "Il ne suffit pas de savoir la différence, il faut la pouvoir, il faut pouvoir la faire, ou savoir la faire—et faire veut dire ici *marquer*."[18] Generalized out of its specifically biblical context, *shibboleth* can signify any detail of grammar, diction, intonation, accent, or for that matter, any hard-to-falsify sign: male circumcision, for instance, or some ingrained cultural habit that betrays a would-be infiltrator (as when, say—glancing ahead to *Inglourious Basterds*—an English spy trying to pass as a German soldier orders three drinks with three fingers raised rather than with the thumb and the index and middle fingers raised).

Yet it must also be stressed that *it belongs to the essence of the shibboleth to be falsifiable*. As a nonsemantic semiotic mark that cannot be reproduced through mere knowledge or simple willpower, the shibboleth has lethal force. (Not for nothing is its ur-story that of mass murder at a border.) But this force is enabled and traversed by iterability—an iterability that no political will can fully control. It is always a structural possibility, if not always an empirical one, that there exists an Ephraimite who is an exceptional mimic (or has gone through special training or as a boy had a Gileadic nanny) and who will pass unscathed through the linguistic guillotine. The Nazis, as Lacoue-Labarthe and Nancy note at one point in their essay, broke with the romantic quest for identity in language, stressing instead blood and soil: the dream of an embodied Germanic immediacy. The Nazis' demotion of linguistic criteria formed a crucial part of their exaggeration of the ancient Western dream of unscathed, unimpeachable Life (though of course the Third Reich's efforts to establish and verify claims of "racial purity" involved all sorts of fallible bureaucratic and archival procedures). Indeed it may be said that, for the Nazi, the Jew represents the "enemy within" above all when the Jew speaks the *Volk*'s language with native competence; this is the ultimate insult to *nativity* per se—to the "naturalness" of race. Languages are permeable, and the shibboleth, however brutally efficient, is structurally unreliable.

Looping back now to *Les Bienveillantes*: we have here a controversy about a text that to a provocative degree identifies itself (or—and this is the literary difference, always uncertain, always at stake—*pretends* to identify itself) with a narrating Nazi consciousness but at the same time generates uncertainties about linguistic borders and expectations in relation to a globalized, capitalized media network (for "Americanness" and "the English language," in such a context, mean precisely that). Max Aue doubles his Jewish American author's ability to "pass" as French; in the context of this novel's reception in France this means that the provocative doubling of Nazi and Jew (a doubling that Littell's novel repeatedly though never unambiguously stages) functions as a lurid underscoring of the uninsurability of any linguistic-cultural border.[19] Not just the *French* linguistic-cultural border. I think the final critical gesture performed by Littell's novel in this regard is its deconstruction of the illusion that any medium can be "anchored" (to reinvoke Weber's example), including the technically reproducible, globalizing medium that American English exemplifies. This radical loss of anchoring exceeds and undermines, yet also produces, the possibility of the shibboleth's cut. The author's ambivalent yet powerful identification with his narrator plays out against this background. Having chosen to write this text from the perpetrator's viewpoint, Littell at once reenacts and undermines the willfulness of that identification by choosing to have his Nazi narrator mirror his own unchosen bilingualism.

A brief consideration of the beginning of *Les Bienveillantes* may serve to demonstrate how the novel weaves these issues into a prominent figure of its own production: the figure of the loom. Aue has flourished in postwar France as the director of a lace factory. A few pages into the novel he describes the office in which he is writing. It is a clean, well-lighted place, infiltrated by the incessant clicking of the mechanical looms:

> Mon bureau est un endroit agreeable pour écrire, grand, sobre, tranquille. Des murs blancs, presque sans décoration, un meuble vitré pour les échantillons; et au fond une grande baie vitrée qui donne en hauteur sur la salle des machines. Malgré un double vitrage, le cliquètement incessant des métiers Leavers emplit la pièce. Quand je veux penser, je quitte ma table de travail et vais me tenir devant la vitre, je contemple les métiers alignés à mes pieds, les mouvements sûrs et précis des tullistes, je me laisse bercer. (16)

> My office is a pleasant place to write, airy, sober, peaceful. White, almost bare walls, a glass cabinet for samples; and across from my desk a long bay window that looks out onto the factory floor. Despite the double-glazed glass, the incessant clatter of the Leavers looms resonates through the room. When I want to think, I leave my work table and go stand in front of the window; I gaze down at the looms lined up below, at the sure, precise movements of the workers, and let myself be lulled. (8)

Writing, and the thinking that both interrupts and shadows writing ("quand je veux penser"), are aligned not just with weaving (a trope so traditional that the text barely has to gesture at it) but with mechanical text(ile) production: with weaving machines and the clicking and clacking they make. Aue dwells on the machines, fascinated yet repelled by them. Their figurative status as writing machines—and guilt and confession machines—is underscored by the fact that they require lubrication by graphite, a substance that enables the production of (ultimately snow-white) lace only by blackening everything in its vicinity:

> Les métiers m'impressionnent toujours. Ils sont en fonte, on les a peints en vert, et chacun pèse dix tonnes. . . . Je ne m'en approche pas, pour éviter de me salir: tant de pièces mobiles doivent être constamment lubrifiées, mais l'huile, évidemment, ruinerait la dentelle, aussi on se sert de graphite, une mine de plomb broyée dont le tulliste saupoudre les organes en mouvement à l'aide d'une chaussette, comme un encensoir. La dentelle en sort noire, et elle recouvre les murs, comme le plancher, les machines, et les hommes qui les surveillent. (16)
>
> The looms always impress me. They are made of cast iron, were once painted green, and each one weighs ten tons. . . . I never go near them, to keep from getting dirty: all these moving parts have to be constantly lubricated, but oil, of course, would ruin the lace, so we use graphite, a fine black powder dusted over the moving parts of the mechanism with an old sock, swung like a censer. The lace comes out black, and it [*elle*] coats the walls, as well as the floor, the machinery, and the men who supervise it. (9, translation modified)

The ambiguous *elle* in that last sentence, which logically refers to the crushed lead, "une mine de plomb broyée," but wants grammatically to refer to the more immediate antecedent, *la dentelle*, nicely reenacts the contaminating movement of the graphite. (The lace blends into the lubricant that blackens it; black lead and black lace are everywhere.) But something else besides the narrator's spreading guilt, and his quasi-mechanical need to both confess and deny this guilt, is also being suggested here. Aue goes on to identify these Leavers looms as English in origin:

> Même si je n'y mets pas souvent la main, je connais bien ces grands engins. Les premiers métiers à tulle anglais, secret jalousement gardé, sont passés en contrebande en France au lendemain des guerres napoléoniennes grâce à des ouvriers fuyant les taxes douanières; c'est un Lyonnais, Jacquard, qui les a modifiés pour produire la dentelle, en y introduisant une série de cartons perforés qui déterminent le patron. Des roulaux, en bas, alimentent l'ouvrage en fil; au coeur du métier, cinq mille bobines, l'*âme*, sont serrées dans un chariot; puis un *catch-bar* (nous gardons en français certains termes anglais) vient tenir et balancer ce chariot avec un grand clappement hypnotique, d'avant en arrière. Les fils, guidés latéralement, par des *combs* en cuivre scellés sur du plomb, selon une chorégraphie complexe encodée par cinq ou six cents cartons Jacquard, tissent des noeuds;

> un *col de cygne* remonte le peigne; enfin apparaît la dentelle, arachnéenne, troublante sous sa couche de graphite, et qui vient lentement s'enrouler sur un tambour, fixé au sommet du Leavers. (16–17)

> Even though I don't often get my hands dirty, I know these great machines well. The first looms were British and a jealously guarded secret; a few were smuggled into France just after the Napoleonic Wars by workers fleeing the excise duties. They were modified to produce lace by a man from Lyon, Jacquard, who added a series of perforated strips to them to determine the pattern. Cylinders down below feed the thread upward; in the heart of the loom, five thousand bobbins, the soul, are slotted into a carriage; then a catch-bar (the English term has been carried over into French) grips and sets this carriage swinging front to back, with a loud hypnotic clapping. The threads are guided laterally, according to a complex choreography encoded within some five or six hundred Jacquard strips, by copper combs sealed onto lead, and are then woven into knots; a swan's neck carries the rake up; finally the lace appears, gossamer-like, disturbingly beautiful under its coat of graphite, slowly rolled onto a drum, fixed at the top of the Leavers. (9)

One can imagine the pleasure Littell took in researching these details: that innocent-looking white lace is born, as it were, with a dirty history, since it emerges graphite-black from the loom; that the Leavers loom, like Aue, secretly crossed into France in the wake of a catastrophic pan-European war; that these looms have not only an *âme* but a Mallarmean *col de cygne*—and a *catch-bar*, and *combs*. These English loanwords, embedded like catachreses in the French language whenever the French language sets out to describe a Leavers loom, paradoxically mark Littell's text *as* French. (Which is to say they establish a little site of untranslatability *into* English; Charlotte Mandell has had no choice but partly to efface the interlinguistic commerce of these sentences.[20]) Yet at the same time they mark a radical breach in the integrity of French (or, for that matter, of any so-called natural language). A language, as Derrida reminds us, is a unity only insofar as it lies open to grafting, only insofar as it is also a palimpsest of languages, a tissue of borrowings, loanwords, and calques.[21] (One thinks again of DeLillo, whose monoglottal narrator suffers white noise partly as an exposure to linguistic otherness even within his own native contexts: "More and more I heard languages I could not identify much less understand, although the tall boys were American-born and the checkout woman as well" [40].)

Therefore, although it would be possible to take the English origins of the Leavers loom as a coy figure for Littell's "nativity" in the English language, I think the real point here is the radically mongrel, nonnatural nature of all "natural" languages and, by extension, the irreducibility of language to the self that inhabits language, which is to say the irreducibility of language to a subject's will to power. For it is in the wake of this scene that Aue discusses his ability to pass the test of the shibboleth, in the passage I quoted earlier ("Quand tout fut enfin fini j'ai réussi à venir en France, à me faire passer pour un Français"). His passing the test is not a triumph of the will but the result of an empirical contingency: the fact that his speaking body has been scored and shaped by two languages. The fact that, like a spy or an actor, one can train to pass shibboleth tests does not alter the priority of language over the speaking subject (though it does underscore yet again the permeability of language systems and the dependence of the shibboleth on iterability). One passes the test of the shibboleth when, through whatever set of contingencies, the weave of differences upon which the shibboleth draws has carved up and produced one's speaking body. And that weave of differences—the differences making up the unity or totality of a language—exposes itself at every point to the other: the unity of a language, its cutting power as shibboleth, *is* this exposure to alterity.

"J'aime me perdre un peu dans le claquètement monotone et syncopé qui domine l'espace, ce battement métallique à deux temps, obsédant," Aue tells us (16). ("I like to lose myself for a while in the monotonous, syncopated clanking that fills the space, a metallic, obsessive two-step beat" [9]). A few sentences earlier he had commented, "Malgré un double vitrage, le cliquètement incessant des métiers Leavers emplit la pièce" (16). ("Despite the double-glazed glass, the incessant clatter of the Leavers looms resonates through the room" [8].) Two slightly different onomatopoeic words—"le *cliquètement* incessant"; "le *claquètement* monotone et syncopé"—relay the minimal differentiation of an iterative process of marking: a machinal marking devoid of semantic depth, powerful enough to produce textual differences that can mean life or death, indifferent to the subjectivities they enable. This cliquing and claquing, nonsemantic though it is, speaks eloquently after its fashion as it passes through the "double vitrage" shielding the space of the novel's autobiographical writing subject. It speaks of shibboleth-effects cutting and crossing, of text production in the era of mechanical reproducibility, of differential networks that exceed the acts of identification they enable—an excess that a subject can process as giddiness, as a feeling of having been brushed lightly by the sublime ("j'aime me perdre un peu"). *Les Bienveillantes* figures its own production here in terms that offer a radical critique of the fantasy of the self-productive subject. These language-looms unweave the fabric of the "Nazi myth," as Lacoue-Labarthe and Nancy define it; they chastise "French" linguistic chauvinism; by extension they also deconstruct the illusory effacement of temporal, spatial, cultural, and linguistic difference—the illusory effacement, that is, of *mediation*—within an "American" media apparatus dedicated to the reproduction of auratic effects.

✦

Except for his bilingualism and his extremely complicated sex life, Aue may fairly be described as an extreme version of a conventional figure: the "cultured Nazi," who knows his wine and his art history, reads some philosophy, appreciates good literature, talks learnedly about classical music, and so on.[22] ("That's what I like about you, Hauptstürmführer," another intellectual Nazi remarks to Aue at one point. "A member of the *Sicherheitsdienst* who quotes Tertullian instead of Rosenberg or Hans Frank is always a pleasure" [237/252].) In Aue we are being supplied with yet one more figure to remind us, should we still need reminding, that neither doctoral degrees nor a broad aesthetic culture offer protection against evil (even if, as Adorno maintains, "[Auschwitz] was the barbarity that all education goes against").[23] Hans Landa, the scene-stealing villain of Tarantino's *Inglourious Basterds*, is in this one respect, at least, a more surprising creation. We hear nothing about Landa's wine cellar or his love of Beethoven. He may be a "cultured Nazi"—and indeed he represents in certain respects a comic apotheosis of this stereotype—but his "culture" has been entirely absorbed into the mannered, antic, polyglot linguistic performances with which he torments and manipulates his victims.

When we meet Landa at the beginning of the film, we are in occupied France, in 1941, on a dairy farm: Landa arrives to interrogate the farmer, Perrier LaPadite, whom he suspects of harboring Jews. Landa introduces himself in elaborate, ironically polite French; partway through the conversation he switches to English, knowing that the hidden Jews do not speak it, though LaPadite (rather improbably) does. After Landa has verbally tortured LaPadite into revealing the hiding place of the Jews he switches back to French, makes his goodbyes, and in his native German orders his soldiers to shoot through the floorboards at the points the farmer has indicated. One young Jewish woman, Shosanna Dreyfus (Mélanie Laurent), makes a run for it and escapes; Landa, though he has her in the sights of his gun, lets her go, mockingly calling out, "Au revoir, Shosanna!" She will reappear as Emmanuelle Mimieux, the owner of the movie theater Le Gamaar in Paris, where some of the most important subsequent action of the film will take place.

*Inglourious Basterds* may be characterized as a loving and sadistic act of cinematic homage to and revenge on the screen Nazis who have played such a formidable role in American (and European) war movies over the past sixty years. (Here is DeLillo again, hitting a perfect-pitch dark-comic note as two characters discuss the frequency with which Hitler shows up in television shows: "He was on again last night." "He's always on. We couldn't have television without him" [63].) In order to pursue the question of why and how the polyglot Landa functions against that backdrop, I need to provide a capsule summary of the film's plot, or at least of those strands of the plot that require our attention. The film has five "chapters"; in the first Landa torments the French farmer as described; in the second we meet Aldo Raine (Brad Pitt) and members of his Jewish American commando unit, the

"Basterds," who operate behind enemy lines, killing and scalping Germans. Raine orders his men to take scalps, explaining that he is part Native American; when he allows prisoners to live, he carves a swastika on their forehead with his bowie knife. He himself bears upon his body, as Tarantino's script specifies, "one defining characteristic, a ROPE BURN around his neck—as if, once upon a time, he survived a LYNCHING. The scar will never once be mentioned."[24] In the third chapter the scene shifts to Paris; it is now 1944, and Shosanna Dreyfus has become the proprietor of Le Gamaar. A young German war hero, Frederick Zoller (Daniel Brühl), about whom a propaganda film is being made, becomes smitten with her; Zoller persuades Goebbels to hold the premiere of the film, *Stolz der Nation*, in Paris at Shosanna's theater. Shosanna realizes that if she sabotaged her own theater she could kill off several high-ranking Nazis, and she begins making plans to burn down the theater during the premiere, using the stocks of highly flammable nitrate film in the theater's basement.

In the fourth chapter another plot to assassinate the viewers of *Stolz der Nation* gets under way: the British have learned of the premiere and send a British officer, Lt. Archie Hicox (Michael Fassbender), who speaks excellent German, to rendezvous with the Basterds and with a German double agent, the actress Bridget von Hammersmark (Diane Kruger), with the purpose of raiding the theater.[25] Hicox and two German-speaking Basterds (one an Austrian-born Jew, Cpl. Wilhelm Wicki [Gedeon Burkhard]; the other a borderline psychotic, renegade German soldier, Sgt. Hugo Stiglitz [Til Schweiger], who has joined the Basterds after killing some Gestapo officers) meet up with von Hammersmark in a French tavern, La Louisiane, where celebrating German soldiers engage them in conversation; one soldier notices Hicox's "ungewöhnlichen Akzent," as does a Gestapo agent at another table. Over the course of an extended, tense scene, Hicox does his best to sound like a native German speaker, but he reveals his identity when he orders three drinks with three fingers (the scene I mentioned earlier, when discussing the notion of the shibboleth); in the ensuing shootout everyone is killed except von Hammersmark, who suffers a wound in her leg, and the three Basterds who have been hiding in the basement—Raine, Omar Ulmer (Omar Doom), and Donny Donowitz (Eli Roth)—who emerge to take part in the gunfight. Raine and von Hammersmark agree that the mission must continue since they have just learned that Hitler himself will be at the premiere, and they concoct the desperate strategy of having Raine, Ulmer, and Donowitz pretend to be Italians:

> BRIDGET: I know this is a silly question before I ask it, but can you Americans speak *any* other language than English?
>
> SGT. DONOWITZ: We [*gesturing to Aldo*] both speak a little Italian.
>
> BRIDGET: With an atrocious accent, no doubt. But that doesn't exactly kill us in the crib. Germans don't have a good ear for Italian. So you mumble Italian and brazen through it, is that the plan?

LT. ALDO: That's about it.
BRIDGET: That sounds good.
LT. ALDO: It sounds like shit, but what else we gonna do, go home?
BRIDGET: No, that sounds good. If you don't blow it with that, I can get you in the building. So, who does what?
LT. ALDO: Well, I speak the most Italian, so I'll be your escort. Donowitz speaks the second most, so he'll be your Italian cameraman. And Omar third most, so he'll be Donny's assistant.
ULMER: I don't speak Italian.
LT. ALDO: Like I said, third best. Just keep your fuckin' mouth shut.[26]

Chapter 5 is the big night. With Hitler and the entire Nazi top brass in the theater to see *Stolz der Nation*, Colonel Landa, who knows that von Hammersmark is a spy, intercepts her and her entourage, Raine, Donowitz, and Ulmer, in the lobby. There ensues one of the funniest scenes in the movie, as von Hammersmark explains in German to Landa that her Italian escorts speak no German; Raine says "Buongiorno" in a thick Tennessee accent; Landa unleashes a torrent of elegant Italian, and asks Raine, Donowitz, and Ulmer to repeat their names for him again and again, like a language teacher doing pronunciation exercises with slow pupils: "Comè? . . . Ancora una volta!" This time there is an unexpected twist to Landa's cat-and-mouse game. He allows Donowitz and Ulmer to proceed on their mission (they are suicide bombers with explosives taped to their ankles); he takes von Hammersmark, whom he knows to be a spy, to a private room and, in a particularly violent scene, strangles her; and he has Raine and another Basterd, Pfc. Smithson Utivich (B.J. Novak), arrested and taken to a café outside Paris that he has commandeered and outfitted with a radio and a radio operator. There Landa offers Raine a proposition: the war is going badly, and Landa is willing to betray the Nazi regime in exchange for safe passage, a pension, and (of all things) a house on Nantucket. He and Raine get on the radio with Raine's superiors; the deal is approved. Meanwhile, back in the cinema, the climax arrives: a giant blowup of Shosanna's face replaces *Stolz der Nation* (she has doctored the movie); the haunting, smoke-blue face explains (in English—we will need to come back to that little detail), "This is the face of Jewish vengeance!" Donowitz and Ulmer machine-gun Hitler and his circle; the nitrate film catches fire ("FLAMES LIKE OUT OF A GIANT BLAST FURNACE BURST THROUGH SHOSANNA'S FACE," as Tarantino's excited screenplay directions have it [160]); bombs explode and the theater burns, killing everyone inside. Finally we cut to a forest, where Raine and Utivich are bringing Landa to Allied lines. But before turning him over, Raine carves a swastika on his forehead. "When you go to your little place on Nantucket island, I imagine you gonna take off that handsome SS uniform of yours, ain't ya?" (Tarantino's screenplay directions note, "For the first time in the movie, Col. Landa doesn't respond" [164].) "That's what I thought. Now that . . . I can't abide." In the last shots of the movie we see a grisly close-up of Raine's knife carving into Landa's forehead, while Landa screams and the camera offers brief close-ups of his feet drumming and his hands clutching grass. The film ends with a Landa point-of-view shot upward: Raine and Utivich are looking down into the camera; bloody knife in hand, Raine says, "I think this just might be my masterpiece."

Landa plays a larger role in the film than this bare-bones summary of its plot indicates. He is the only character to appear in all five chapters. (There is a scene in chapter 3, for instance, in which Landa, in his capacity as head of security for Goebbels's event, interrogates Shosanna in a café: he orders her a glass of milk, broadly hinting to her that he knows perfectly well who she is, since in chapter 1 he had asked for and drunk a glass of milk at LaPadite's dairy farm.) Any scene involving Landa, furthermore, almost instantly becomes dominated by him. His role as a high-ranking *Sicherheitsdienst* officer provides the initial dramatic leverage—wherever he goes, people are afraid of him—but his elegantly menacing, comic to the point of zany linguistic performances outstrip their conventional dramatic frames. These performances are, of course, thoroughly cinematic: they are animated by the superb mobility of Waltz's face and body and of Tarantino's camera, and they draw generously on visual comedy. (During his interrogation of LaPadite, for instance, Landa requests permission to smoke and pulls out an enormous Sherlock Holmes calabash.) But it is nonetheless fair to say that at their core Landa's are fundamentally linguistic, and more specifically *foreign-language*, performances. Now and then Landa has occasion to be silkily eloquent in his native German, but those moments are unemphatic. His big scenes have him dominating subjects in French and English (the opening scene with LaPadite); in French (scenes with Shosanna in Paris); in Italian (the famous comedic scene); and again in English (his interrogation of Raine, another over-the-top performance during which Landa even pauses to inquire after the exact use of an American idiom—"Bingo!").[27]

In other words, Landa does Tarantino in different languages. He is the only character in *Inglourious Basterds* who puts on the manic conversational shows we associate with aggressive male characters in Tarantino scripts. Furthermore, since at the beginning of the film he allows the plot to unfold by letting Shosanna escape and at the end of the film allows the destruction of Le Gamaar to go forward ("If I do nothing . . . it's as if I'm causing [Hitler's] death, even more than yourselves" [144]), Landa plays a quasi-directorial role within the plot. There is thus a sense in which he "is" Tarantino. (Appropriately, in the scene in which Landa strangles von Hammersmark, the hands we see in the close-up are in fact Tarantino's, according to the IMDb web page on the film.)[28] And Landa is more even than that: at the end of the film, when his languages are stripped away, he becomes identified with the film itself and with the experience of viewing it. Once Raine, having reduced Landa to a screaming, swastika-inscribed body, takes Landa's metaphorical place in the director's chair by saying "This just might be my masterpiece," the Landa point-of-view shot that closes *Inglourious Basterds* not only forces the film's viewers to inhabit the point of view of the muted and mutilated villain but also suggests that Landa "is" the film, insofar as the silencing and branding of Landa seems to have something to do with the film's own self-acclamation as a masterpiece.

For our purposes the question to ask and answer is: Why, in this film so lovingly saturated with references and allusions to other films—so cinephilic as to have cinema "itself" destroy Hitler and his minions, burning up the celluloid Nazi by sending its own archive, its own antiquated nitrate film base, on a suicide mission—why, in this brave new digitalized but celluloidophilic and -pyrrhic alternative universe, should the Nazi villain be a charismatic character who comes close to being an allegorical figure both of foreign-language expertise and of the film's own production and reception?[29] (I note parenthetically that one more way in which Tarantino sets up a teasing identification between Landa and the "film itself" is by shooting extended scenes in German or French, contrary to normative Hollywood practice: both the film and its villain speak, at least for a while—until the end—many languages.[30]) Not that Landa is the film's only polyglot. Von Hammersmark joins him in speaking fluently all four of the film's languages; Hicox, he of the *ungewöhnlichen Akzent*, speaks excellent German; the German war hero Zoller speaks excellent French;[31] most of the German soldiers who have more than bit roles are able to summon up some English or French. Perhaps the most prominent narrative and cultural difference set up in this film is that between its stereotypically monolingual Americans ("I know this is a silly question before I ask it, but can you Americans speak *any* other language than English?") and its stereotypically polylingual Europeans. The Basterds are American tourists, blundering along without even a phrasebook.[32] Certainly one way to understand the drift of the film is therefore to read its conclusion as, among other things, the violent triumph of global English. Landa, the dark epitome of Continental polylingualism, is silenced; meanwhile in the Le Gamaar theater Shosanna's gigantic cinematic image cries out vengeance upon Nazism in English, the language of ("Jewish") Hollywood.[33] (Tarantino's script comments, "The way this HUGE IMAGE OF SHOSANNA'S GIANT FACE stares down at the auditorium of Nazis brings to mind Orwell's '1984' Big Brother" [159], reinforcing the link between this image and a stock figure of totalitarianism within global English-language mass culture.[34]) Shosanna's unexplained acquisition of this language forms part of the magic of her empowerment and accompanies the film's magical leap out of history (including even its own history, for the film begins, we recall, with a scene in which Shosanna's family, knowing no English, is consigned to death). The price of Nazism's magical, cinematic defeat seems to be that only English be spoken.

Such a reading can indirectly help explain the degree to which *Inglourious Basterds* reaffirms—if with a certain constitutive ambivalence—the power of the shibboleth.[35] Hans Landa is the polar opposite of Max Aue in this respect: Landa has no need and no desire to pass as a native speaker of any language other than his own. His linguistic performances are pure displays of mastery. They presume and even underscore his foreignness. (For all his clinical interest in the turns of idiom he makes no attempt to speak "natural" or demotic French or English; his diction, particularly in French, is elaborately artificial.) Landa thus ironically shares with his foil, the monoglottal hillbilly Raine, a position of cultural privilege that allows him, as it were, imaginatively to subordinate the shibboleth to willpower. Raine, so deeply ensconced in his Tennessee accent that he cannot manage even a single word of half-convincing Italian, does not need even to half-convince; he is saved by America's impending triumph and Landa's apolitical scheming. Lieutenant Hicox, representative of a fading British imperium, is the film's one ambivalent exception to the rule: his mission requires him to try to pass, and he does indeed prove able to stave off the linguistic guillotine for a while, but with such straining effort that when the shibboleth blade falls (extralinguistically, as the performance of a wrong hand gesture), its cut comes as the resolution of an unsustainable situation. The fact that the essential uninsurability of the shibboleth enables and marks this scene orients it all the more irrevocably toward an explosion of law-sustaining violence.[36] On the one hand Tarantino's film pays homage to linguistic diversity and the complexity and difficulty of languages; on the other hand it funnels the problem of the shibboleth into a triumph of will, as Landa and Raine move through the film with the sovereign indifference toward linguistic otherness proper to subjects ensconced in their politico-culturally dominant master languages. Landa's performance of invulnerability takes the form of sportive mastery; Raine's no longer bothers with such detours. In this sense Landa may be said, paradoxically, to prefigure the rule of English. He becomes thereby all the more a figure standing in for the film itself—an American film by a major American director who has *chosen* to incorporate German and French into the film's unfolding, as it maps its story of the globalization of English onto its story of the cinematic defeat of Nazism.

Why Nazism? And what does *Nazism* mean in a movie so energetically indifferent to merely factual history? Very little in some ways. Tarantino's script directives, replete with descriptions such as "the two Nazi motorcyclists" and "the Nazi driver" (2), echo Raine's massive cinematic simplification of Nazism to mean little more than "enemy"—to be sure, a Jew-hating and racist enemy, but also (in the absence of other evidence, let us say) anyone wearing a German uniform. On this level the film has no interest in making the usual discriminations between Wehrmacht and SS, between soldiers and party members, and so on; in the second chapter we see Raine carving his swastika on a low-ranking enlisted man, emphasizing, as he does to Landa at the end of the film, that this swastika functions to supplement and make permanent the soldier's *uniform*. And indeed, apart from his "handsome looking

SS uniform" (163), Landa, the magnetic villain who channels Tarantino and his film, is not much of a Nazi in any substantive sense (as Waltz has noted in various interviews). Landa speaks some cheerfully vicious racist lines, but his anti-Semitism, like his speaking in foreign tongues, comes across mainly as a weapon for breaking his victims. He is a career professional and a pure opportunist—capitalism's *Homo economicus*, we could even say, exaggerating the point a little—who, being perfectly willing to "barbecue the whole high command," as Raine puts it (163), ends up playing a substantive role in the film's cinematic *defeat* of the Nazis.

In this film, therefore, *Nazism* flattens down to uniform and spectacle and becomes a mirror in which opponents see themselves. Tarantino's revenge fantasy again and again touches the stops of its basic theme: to destroy the enemy you must (almost) become the enemy.[37] This act of identification drives the film to the point that *Inglourious Basterds* can be accused of "turning Jews into Nazis," as Daniel Mendelsohn puts it: "In history, Jews were repeatedly herded into buildings and burned alive. . . . In *Inglourious Basterds*, it's the Jews who orchestrate this horror. In history, the Nazis and their local collaborators made sport of human suffering; here, it's the Jews who take whacks at Nazi skulls with baseball bats, complete with mock sports-announcer commentary, turning murder into a parodic 'game.' And in history, Nazis carved Stars of David into the chests of rabbis before killing them; here, the 'basterds' carve swastikas into the foreheads of those victims whom they leave alive."[38] In fairness it may be noted that the film peppers its fiercely specular exchanges with little signs that point toward grayer areas of ideological or human complexity (Shosanna's patronymic, Dreyfus, for instance, which cues memories of French anti-Semitism; a fleeting reference to Vichy; a sympathetic young German soldier celebrating—until he is killed in the La Louisiane shootout—the birth of his son).[39] Even Raine's carving of swastikas on foreheads—an act that routes the energies of revenge fantasy through the master fetish of Nazism itself—is more complexly contextualized than might at first appear. It is surely not by accident that Tarantino reserves swastika-carving for Raine, the markedly non-Jewish leader of the Basterds. To have a Jew play this role may have been too much even for this movie to bear, for Raine becomes the mirror image of a neo-Nazi as he carves his favored fetish on his Nazi victims, honing his technique ("You know, Lieutenant, you're getting pretty good at that," [Tarantino, 38]), working toward his "masterpiece." Raine's men meanwhile take scalps—as though, seeking to return Nazis to their own violence, the Basterds need to recall and identify with the victims of America's own genocidal history. It is here that Tarantino's insistence on Raine's "one defining physical characteristic, a ROPE BURN around his neck—as if, once upon a time, he survived a LYNCHING," finds its place in the film's phantasmagorics. The rope burn is asymmetrical to the swastika. The swastika is the German racist's sign of *identity*, whereas the rope burn records the suffering that the American racist inflicts on his *victim*. Thus while the Basterds pretend to be Native Americans, Raine, the white southerner (who claims to be part Apache), appropriates the iconography of the black victim of southern white racism. Symbolically situating themselves in the place of America's racialized others, Raine and his Basterds take revenge—not, however, on white America but on a surrogate: the Nazi as *über*-white supremacist. (And this, I stress again, is the limit of the film's presentation of Nazi ideology: a uniform, plus racism.[40])

Somewhat deviously, therefore, Tarantino's film suggests the surrogate character of the violence it wreaks on its Nazis. At the same time the mirroring relationships remain coercive. The swastika that Raine carves in human foreheads renders *Nazi* a slur only insofar as it both reiterates the Nazi fetish and reconfigures an array of Jewish signs. An updated mark of Cain, it is the upwardly displaced antithesis of circumcision, marking its bearer as outcast from the law; it carries the memory of concentration camp tattoos; more directly it repeats and avenges the Stars of David that were worn on clothing to identify victims or, in the wilder atrocities recollected by Mendelsohn, carved into flesh. All of these allusions can be returned to the cut of the shibboleth, the violent mark with which a community asserts its difference from its others. And of course, as uniform supplements inscribed directly on faces, Raine's swastikas promise deeper, more securely identifying cuts than those incised by language. *Inglourious Basterds* thus not only pays tribute to the law of the linguistic shibboleth but also reenacts the Nazi flight from language to "blood," erecting the fleshly swastika as a fetish against the potential uncertainty of linguistic borders and linguistic differences.

As I have noted, the marking of Landa signals a muting of all languages except English within the film. His marking must thus be read in the context of the postwar American culture industry's fetishization of the swastika as the luminous, auratic, mass-marketable sign of evil. It is the sign that remains when English has triumphed, and its inscription rhymes with the imposition of American military and cultural power. That, it seems to me, is why at the end of the film we are seeing through Landa's eyes. Far more overtly than *Les Bienveillants*, *Inglourious Basterds* suggests that a certain unacknowledged, ambivalent identification with an imagined (and indeed quite imaginary) Nazi can play a role in negotiating the fundamental insecurity of selves and identities in an era of mass reproducibility. Alluding at every point to a vast cinematic archive, Tarantino's film activates the major topoi of Western mass culture's processing of Nazism, from the comical desk-pounding dictator to the spectacle of ceremonial kitsch. ("The lobby of Shosanna's cinema, pimped out in Nazi iconography . . . [The auditorium] now resembles something out of one of Tinto Brass's Italian B-movie ripoffs of Visconti's 'The Damned'" [72].) Burning all that up, the film hints at a degree of symbiosis between cinema itself and the lush images of evil that are now being ecstatically destroyed. Yet, after all, not everything is burned up—the seductively sinister amoral pseudo-Nazi who helped destroy the Nazis remains. He remains in order to be reduced to the swastika itself as a mark of flesh-inscribed identity—an *excessive* mark of identity. The polyglot Landa mirrors this polyglot film because he relays the fantasy of a subject's will to power over and above language—the fantasy of a subject sublimely indifferent to the cut of the shibboleth or the drift of the signifier. Yet *we* are not (quite) *that*. Landa is a surrogate; his excessive identity fantasy, reiterated in and as the swastika to which he is reduced, becomes a silent scar marking a new and phantasmatically monolingual world order. Landa's defacement causes *Inglourious Basterds* to identify all the more sharply with its cinema Nazi, yet the ferocity of this repetition also hints at the vast mobility that underwrites and enables all marks, no matter how historically burdened or how violently inscribed.

## Notes

1. Saul Friedländer, *Reflets du nazisme* (Paris: Seuil, 1982). I cite from the somewhat expanded and revised translation, *Reflections of Nazism: An Essay on Kitsch and Death* (New York: Harper and Row, 1984), 127, 22, 30, 134, 136. This study predates but in some respects interestingly complements Friedländer's late-1980s debate with the German historian Martin Broszat over the "normalization" of the Third Reich as an object of study (by assimilating it into larger historical patterns, focusing on *Alltagsgeschichte*, etc.); in the mid-1980s Friedländer was also involved in the bitter *Historikerstreit* triggered by Ernst Nolte's provocations.

2. This is partly because (to anticipate one of the main themes of my essay) mass-mediatized popular culture has been dominated by the U.S. culture industry, which after the war had plenty of anti-Nazi material on which to build. Still the fact remains that comic mockery was able to devour only a portion of the Nazi spectacle. (I am about to discuss the swastika and SS paraphernalia, which have followed a different semiotic path.) The figure of Hitler is a complex case. Hitler obviously continues to excite fascination in Western culture, though the comic inoculation has had quite widespread effects. It has become impossible, I think, for viewers of *Triumph des Willens* to evade undergoing an alienation effect—one that Riefenstahl certainly did not intend—whenever Hitler is in the frame, not just because one knows of crimes committed and of horrors lying ahead but also, and more immediately and viscerally, because the mustache, the drooping forelock, and so on have become as always already self-parodic as the bolts and scars of a cinematic Frankenstein monster. The film remains capable of delivering a fascist thrill, but in large part *despite* its reverential attention to the too iconic dictator.

3. Comedic genius has done its best; one thinks of course of the irrepressible Mel Brooks, who dares all in *The Producers* (1968).

4. Sontag focuses particularly on the role of Nazi paraphernalia in sadomasochistic sexual culture; she explains this conjunction, no doubt somewhat hastily, as "a response to an oppressive freedom of choice in sex (and other matters), to an unbearable degree of individuality." Susan Sontag, "Fascinating Fascism" (1974), in *Under the Sign of Saturn* (New York: Farrar, Straus and Giroux, 1980),

73–105, quote at 104. The deployment of Nazi signifiers goes far beyond specifically S/M contexts. For a conceptually thin but empirically helpful compendium of Nazi motifs in contemporary popular culture, see Marcus Stiglegger, *Nazi-Chic und Nazi-Trash: Fascistische Ästhetik in der populären Kultur* (Berlin: Bertz und Fischer, 2011). Focused mainly on music and film, Stiglegger's survey offers an overview of Nazi motifs in hard rock, heavy metal, punk, and goth movements and in films from the Italian Nazi-exploitation films of the 1970s to the recent zombie film *Dead Snow* (2009). (Stiglegger touches briefly on "brown scene" music and clothing in Germany, but he is mainly interested in the circulation of Nazi motifs in global popular culture.) Appearing after Stiglegger's book was published, the schlock-Nazi parody film *Iron Sky* (2012) from the Finnish director Timo Vuorensola makes an interesting addition to the list; the film comes with Wagner-inspired music by the Slovenian band Laibach, which is famous for its Žižekesque strategies of overidentification.

5. This includes historical studies. "Since its demise, the Third Reich has been examined in more detail than any other modern dictatorship," according to a recent study setting out on its own detailed examination: Nikolaus Wachsmann, *KL: A History of the Nazi Concentration Camps* (New York: Farrar, Straus and Giroux, 2015), 19.

6. Friedländer is particularly exercised by the example of George Steiner, whose novel *The Portage to San Cristóbal of A.H.* (1979) mystifies Hitler "as the false Messiah who could annihilate creation" (*Reflections of Nazism*, 127) by giving credence to the old canard of Hitler's secret Jewish identity and by allowing the eponymous A.H. the last word in the novel, in the form of a speech in which he claims to have derived his vision from the Jews. "The argument Hitler develops in this book and that no one answers is simple: Jewish fanaticism, which rests on the assurance of being the chosen people, a unique conception in antiquity, gave birth to a tide that finally led to another chosen race, the Nazis" (112). At issue for Friedländer is "the *apparent* identification of the author with some of A.H.'s arguments," arguments that set up a mythic doubling of Nazi and Jew (113).

7. Philippe Lacoue-Labarthe and Jean-Luc Nancy, "The Nazi Myth," trans. Brian Holmes, *Critical Inquiry* 16.2 (1990): 291–312. I refer to this text but have checked it against the French version that appeared in booklet form a year later: Philippe Lacoue-Labarthe and Jean-Luc Nancy, *Le mythe nazi* (Marseille: Éditions de l'aube, 1991). The authors explain that this essay developed out of "a relatively brief exposé delivered on 7 May 1980," so its original drafts were composed about the same time that Friedländer was writing *Reflets du nazisme*. Lacoue-Labarthe and Nancy developed some of their thoughts as Lacoue-Labarthe, *La fiction du politique* (1987), and Nancy, *La communauté désoeuvrée* (1986).

8. Lacoue-Labarthe and Nancy derive the main terms under analysis from Adolf Hitler, *Mein Kampf* (1925), and Alfred Rosenberg, *Der Mythus des 20. Jahrhunderts* (1930). The first part of Lacoue-Labarthe and Nancy's essay traces a specifically German context for Nazism, arguing, "It is because the German problem is fundamentally a problem of *identity* that the German figure of totalitarianism is racism," and "It is because myth can be defined as an *identificatory mechanism* that racist ideology became bound up in the construction of a myth [of the Aryan]" (296). Since Plato myth has been understood as "a fiction, in

the strong, active sense of 'fashioning,'" providing models or types "in imitation of which an individual, or a city, or an entire people, can grasp themselves and identify themselves" (297). Within this broader Western mimetic tradition, Lacoue-Labarthe and Nancy argue, the postbaroque German effort to appropriate a means of national and cultural identification came to stress myth, symbol, and aesthetic spectacle in ways that created the specific historical possibility of Nazism.

9. Samuel Weber, "From Reflection to Repetition: Medium, Reflexivity and the Economy of Self," the Spring 2009 Rodig Lecture, in *Rutgers German Studies Occasional Papers 10* (New Brunswick, N.J.: Rutgers German Studies, 2010), 18. Among Weber's many texts devoted to versions of this theme, see also the essay "Mass Mediauras, or: Art, Aura, and Media in the Work of Walter Benjamin," in *Mass Mediauras: Form, Technics, Media* (Stanford: Stanford University Press, 1996), 76–107, for a masterful account of the decay and reinvigoration of the aura in the era of technical reproducibility. It would be interesting to explore the ways Nazi vitalism might both resemble and be distinguished from the "system of guilt and debt" that Weber diagnoses within capitalism: "For what is at stake in the system of guilt and death is the redeemability of life as pure immanence, as essentially immune from death and destruction" ("Guilt, Debt," unpublished ms., 20).

10. Sontag's broad explanation of the fascination of fascism is perhaps in the end not broad enough: "National Socialism . . . stands for an ideal or rather ideals that are persistent today under the other banners: the ideal of life as art, the cult of beauty, the fetishism of courage, the dissolution of alienation in ecstatic feelings of community; the repudiation of the intellect; the family of man (under the parenthood of leaders)" ("Fascinating Fascism," 96). Such impulses, which Sontag assimilates to a "romantic ideal," no doubt inform Riefenstahl's photography and film (which is Sontag's immediate target here), but the advantage of Lacoue-Labarthe and Nancy's critique is that it identifies a structural lure that does not have to take the form of explicit "fascist longings in our midst" in this sense (97). It must be added that of course any number of political, social, cultural, and psychological contexts will always be in play in contemporary evocations or deployment of Nazi codes. The motives that drive, say, an unemployed teenager in the former East Germany to identify with Nazism will obviously be different from those motivating an Italian director to make a film that strikes critics as overaestheticizing in its portrayal of Nazis.

11. Don DeLillo, *White Noise* (New York: Penguin, 1985). The narrator, Jack Gladney, expresses little knowledge of or interest in the historical context of Nazism; he teaches his course with a focus on "the continuing mass appeal of fascist tyranny, with special emphasis on parades, rallies and uniforms" (25). Both he and other characters are drowning in media technology (the "white noise" of the title) and obsessed with "aura": "We can't get outside the aura. We're part of the aura" (13).

12. Put more expansively: Is the novel's fine-grained historical realism compatible either with Aue's improbable ability to pop up, like a Nazi Zelig, everywhere from Babi Yar to Hitler's bunker, or with Aue's fantastic personal eccentricities? (He takes pleasure in being sodomized as a way of imagining himself as his sister, Una, for whom he has an incestuous passion; he seems, like Orestes, to have

murdered his mother and stepfather; parts of the novel involve highly elaborate erotic hallucinations.) I cannot engage these issues in the present context. Let me simply note that *Les Bienveillantes* has garnered some genuinely thoughtful reviews in various contexts: in the United States, see in particular Daniel Mendelsohn in the *New York Review of Books*, March 26, 2009, and Samuel Moyn in the *Nation*, March 23, 2009; in Germany, see, e.g., the site dedicated to the novel by the *Frankfurter Allgemeine Zeitung* (available at http://www.faz.net/). The contribution from Klaus Theweleit on the *FAZ* site is of interest, since Littell drew on Theweleit's work in constructing Aue's inner life. We know this from the author himself: Littell's "Theweleitian" study of Léon Degrelle, *Le sec et l'humide: Une brève incursion en territoire fasciste* (Paris: Gallimard, 2008), carries a postface by Theweleit. On the back cover Littell explains, "Ce texte a été écrit en 2002, alors que je menais des recherches en vue d'un autre livre, depuis publié. Il est né de la rencontre entre les thèses d'un chercheur allemand brillant et insaisissable—Theweleit—et un text d'un fasciste belge où celui-ci, par le jeu des images et de la langue, laisse lire la structure même de sa pensée."

13. Littell gave Aue his own birth date, for instance, and in interviews he has commented more than once that, although of course he "is not" Aue, his novel intends to negotiate why and how relatively ordinary human beings in certain contexts do terrible deeds.

14. Jonathan Littell, *Les Bienveillantes* (Paris: Gallimard, 2006), 17–18; Jonathan Littell, *The Kindly Ones*, trans. Charlotte Mandell (New York: HarperCollins, 2009), 10. Subsequent references, first French, then English, are cited in the text.

15. Littell tried repeatedly to obtain French citizenship in 2006 but was refused; after the stunning success of his novel the French government, embarrassed, offered him amends. As *Le Figaro* reported on March 9, 2007, "Les fonctionnaires . . . avaient exhumé les textes du Code de la nationalité et trouvé un article 'sur mesure' pour le cas Littell: le '*21–21*.' Ce dernier considère en effet que '*la nationalité française peut être conférée par naturalisation sur proposition du ministre des Affaires étrangères à tout étranger francophone qui en fait la demande et qui contribue par son action émérite au rayonnement de la France et à la prospérité de ses relations économiques internationals*' [The functionaries . . . had exhumed the texts of the National Code and found an article 'tailored' to the Littell case: the '21/21,' which in fact states that '*French nationality may be conferred by naturalization on the recommendation of the minister of foreign affairs to any francophone foreigner who makes the request and who contributes through his meritorious action to the glory of France and the prosperity of French international economic relations*']." Perhaps a capsule biography would be helpful. Born in New York in 1967, Littell moved to France at the age of three and attended French schools mainly in France but at some points in New York; he took the *baccalauréat* from the Lycée Fénelon, and then went to Yale University, where he majored in French. He worked for humanitarian NGOs in Bosnia, Chechnya, Sierra Leone, and other countries before quitting to research *Les Bienveillantes* in 2001. Littell now lives in Barcelona.

16. It was also learned that the manuscript was submitted to Gallimard under a (thin) pseudonym, "Jean Petit." Some documentation for these and other details may be found conveniently packaged in Paul-Éric Blanrue's otherwise

extraordinarily pointless and empty-headed *Les Malveillantes—Enquête sur le cas Jonathan Littell* (Paris: Scali, 2006), which the author rushed into print while these controversies were fresh.

17. The word *shibboleth* means either "flowing stream" (as in Isaiah 27:12 and Psalms 69:2) or "ear of corn" (as in Ruth 2:2 and Isaiah 17:5). Since it seems odd that the Ephraimites would be unable to pronounce the *shin* phoneme (common as it is across Semitic dialects), scholars have speculated that the author of Judges is making the *shin* stand in for a more difficult phoneme, such as ṯ (which, lacking a grapheme, could not be represented directly): see Ian Young, *Diversity in Pre-Exilic Hebrew* (Tübingen: J. C. B. Mohr, 1993), 188. If this is true, then the word *shibboleth* itself points toward an unwritable word, a word that has to be misinscribed so that a word signifying the test of its own pronunciation can enter scripture.

18. Jacques Derrida, *Schibboleth, pour Paul Celan* (Paris: Galilée, 1986), 50–51. "Le schibboleth ne résiste pas à la traduction en raison de quelque inaccessibilité de son sens au transfert, en raison de quelque secret sémantique mais par ce qui en lui forme l'entaille d'une différence non signifiante dans le corps de la marque—écrite ou orale, écrite dans la parole comme peut l'être une marque dans la marque, une incision marquante à même la marque" (55–56). A potentially lethal technology of identification, the shibboleth can also carve out the space of resistance to power (hence "la terrifiante ambiguïté du *schibboleth*, signe d'appartenance et menace de discrimination, discernement indiscernable entre l'alliance et la guerre" [88]).

19. Examples of this doubling are legion and deserve extensive and patient analysis. Late in the novel, for instance, Aue's twin sister, Una, tell him, "'En tuant les Juifs nous avons voulu nous tuer nous-mêmes, tuer le Juif en nous, tuer ce qui en nous ressemble à l'idée que nous nous faisions du Juif'" (801–2). "'By killing the Jews,' she said, 'we wanted to kill ourselves, kill the Jew within us, kill that which in us resembles the idea we have of the Jew'" (874). Elsewhere in the novel fictive and historical Nazis stress the doubling they imagine exists between Jew and Nazi. For instance, a fictional Nazi character possessed of "a Jewish-sounding name" ("[un] nom en consonance juive" [414/448]), Mandelbrod, tells Aue, "All our great ideas come from the Jews" (420/455), and the historically real *Einsatzgruppe* commander Otto Ohlendorf offers Aue an extensive disquisition on this theme:

> Le Führervernichtungsbefehl est une chose terrible. Paradoxalement, c'est presque comme un ordre du Dieu de la Bible des Juifs, n'est-ce pas? Maintenant, va frappe Amalek! Voue-le à l'anathème avec tout ce qu'il possède, sois sans pitié pour lui, tue hommes et femmes, enfants et nourissons, boeufs et brebis, chameaux et ânes. Vous connaissez ça, c'est dans le premier livre de Samuel. Lorsque j'ai reçu l'ordre, c'est à ça que j'ai songé. . . . Nous devons accepter notre devoir de la même manière qu'Abraham accepte le sacrifice inimaginable de son fils Isaac exigé par Dieu. Vous avez lu Kierkegaard? Il appelle Abraham le chevalier de la foi, qui doit sacrifier non seulement son fils, mais aussi et surtout ses idées éthiques. Pour nous c'est pareil, n'est-ce pas? Nous devons consommer la sacrifice d'Abraham. (211)

> The Vernichtungsbefehl is a terrible thing. Paradoxically, it's almost like an order from the God of the Jews' Bible, isn't it? Now go and strike Amalek, and utterly destroy all that they have, and spare them not; but slay both man and woman, infant and suckling, ox and sheep, camel and ass. You know that, it's in the first Book of Samuel. When I received the order, that's what I thought about. . . . We have to accept our duty in the same way that Abraham accepts the unimaginable sacrifice of his son Isaac demanded by God. You've read Kierkegaard? He calls Abraham the knight of faith, who must sacrifice not only his son, but also and especially his ethical principles. For us it's the same, isn't that so? We have to accomplish Abraham's sacrifice. (223–24)

20. This passage in Littell's text also self-consciously sets a translator the unenviable task of choosing between faithfulness and skill, for, were a translator to translate literally "nous gardons en français certains termes anglais," she would retrace the text's *appellation d'origine*, like a finger running over a scar. Mandell's skillful solution is to drop the pronoun and substitute a passive formulation.

21. While we are at it: *les Bienveillantes* is a calque or literal translation of Εὐμενίδες, "the kindly ones." *Shibboleth* (in French, *schibboleth*) is a loanword (as is *calque*, in English).

22. Though an extensive consideration of this character would involve various qualifications. Aue comes across as so French that at times it is a little hard to imagine him as a German (as several critics of the novel have complained). He is a frustrated *littérateur* who has been compelled by circumstances to study law, in which he holds a doctorate; he reads Blanchot, Stendhal, and Flaubert and hangs out with such figures as Brasillach on his trips to Paris.

23. Theodor Adorno, "Erziehung nach Auschwitz," *Gesammelte Schriften* 10.2 (1966): 674–90, quote at 674: "[Auschwitz] war die Barbarei, gegen die alle Erziehung geht."

24. Quentin Tarantino, *Inglourious Basterds: A Screenplay* (New York: Little, Brown and Weinstein Books, 2009), 19.

25 Here and elsewhere I am following the screenplay's use of the Anglicized forms *Bridget* and *Frederick*.

26. I am not quoting directly from the screenplay, but for the ur-version of the scene, see 122–23. Tarantino's original screenplay differs considerably from the film as shot (and of course as released), and I have modified the quotation to match what we hear in the film. In the screenplay Omar is named Hirschberg, and Tarantino provides two extra lines after Bridget's question about whether they speak any languages besides English: HIRSCHBERG: "Other than Yiddish?" BRIDGET: "Preferably."

27. In this scene Landa, speaking in English, stresses to Raine that from the point of view of a state, the Basterds are "terrorists." (Indeed at this point in the film some of them are suicide bombers.) As it happens the real-life Nazi regime did in fact make great use of the term *terrorist* to describe partisan resistance and air war attacks, but historical accuracy is not this film's concern, and the fact that Landa is speaking *English* and that the Basterds are blowing themselves up along with their target sets up another intriguing layer of reference and cross-identification that invokes the attacks of September 11, 2001 (as well as twenty-first-century violence

in the Middle East, as filtered through dominant Western media channels). I have written about the charged terms *terror* and *terrorist* in *The Rhetoric of Terror: Reflections on 9/11 and the War on Terror* (New York: Fordham University Press, 2009), but must leave to another occasion or another critic an analysis of how these coy allusions function in this scene in *Inglorious Basterds*. At the very least Tarantino is providing another reminder of the global projection of American power, the English-language filter accompanying that projection, and the fluid reversals whereby state violence justifies its terror through a quasi-identification with the "terrorist" (who "declared war on us," according to George Bush; see my *Rhetoric of Terror* for an analysis of this speech act in the context of the phantasmagorics of the American "war on terror").

28. This wordless scene of sexualized violence marks an intriguing interruption in Landa's (and I do mean Landa's) theatrical performance (Walz is playing a character who is himself constantly playing himself as a character). Landa's linguistic flights are always backed up by violence—framed by speech-acts that command lethal force—but this is the only moment in the film in which Landa personally kills someone, in sharp contrast to the scene at the end of the film's first chapter, in which Landa spares Shoshana (if only for future cat-and-mouse games) while his soldiers shoot her family. In its wordlessness and corporeal excess the strangling scene to some extent looks forward to Landa's loss of language at the end of the film, and may also be said to be foreshadowed by the spasm of laughter with which Landa greets von Hammersmark's explanation of why she has a cast on her foot ("Bergsteigen!?")—though his body-twisting fit of laughter forms part of the psychological torture he is inflicting, and is literally wiped off his face as he returns to von Hammersmark and the Basterds to embark on the Italian-lesson scene. The strangling scene also ends with Landa collecting himself and moving on, but in the wake of an act of violence that is essentially a rape and leaves him flushed and perspiring. Since the hands here are Tarantino's, the film may be read both as self-consciously complicit in the silencing of its *other* truly polyglot character, and as registering the sexualized violence that militarized violence between men stands ready to unleash on women.

29. Since this essay was written—in 2010, for a symposium in honor of Samuel Weber held at the Château de la Bretesche in Missillac, France—scholarship on the texts I discuss has continued to accumulate. I have to leave for a later date a proper engagement with the evolving archive of work on Littell's novel and Tarantino's film, but it is worth mentioning a collection of essays on the latter: Robert von Dassanowsky, ed., *Quentin Tarantino's* Inglorious Basterds: *A Manipulation of Metacinema* (New York: Continuum, 2012). The collection documents Tarantino's cinematic allusions far beyond my ability to do so, while inevitably engaging some of the same prominent themes (especially the doubling-cum-reversal of perpetrator and victim and of "Nazi" and "us") that I am exploring.

30. Tarantino has emphasized in interviews the importance he put on having characters actually speak the languages they should be speaking in the story and on having these characters played by native speakers, thereby differentiating *Inglourious Basterds* from the hoary Hollywood tradition of imagining away linguistic difference. It may be noted in passing that some of the vast number of films to which *Inglourious Basterds* alludes grant substantial importance to the theme of foreign language expertise, perhaps above all the film to which

Tarantino's misspelled title pays homage, *Quel maledetto treno blindato* directed by Enzo Castellari (translated as *Inglorious Bastards*; 1978). I will say a little more about that in a moment.

31. Zoller also says some words in English in the film within the film, *Stolz der Nation.* As a trivial note: Daniel Brühl, who plays Zoller, is bilingual in German and Spanish, having been raised as a child in both languages.

32. The two members of the Basterds who speak German are native speakers (and are played by native German speakers): the German soldier (Stiglitz) and a very recent émigré to the United States from Austria (Wicki); both die in the shootout at the French tavern. (Landa identifies their bodies during his inspection of the carnage.) Raine and his two Jewish henchmen, Donny Donowitz (aka "the Bear Jew," known for beating German soldiers to death with a baseball bat) and Omar Ulmer, loom large as monoglots in the scenes I have quoted or alluded to. Tarantino's original script exaggerates and has extra fun with Donowitz's and Ulmer's monolingualism: in a scene cut from the final film the two try to communicate with each other in vaudeville-fake Italian while in the cinema waiting to set off their bombs: "They speak in ITALIAN-ISH SUBTITLED IN ENGLISH: SGT. DONOWITZ (ITALIAN-ISH): I-a-go-a toilet-a, set-a Boom-a (I go to the toilet and set the bomb)" (149). The near-slapstick humor ironizes the monolingualism of its American characters, but also inevitably conveys a touch of a dominant culture's contempt for foreign language skills.

33. This was a decision made after Tarantino wrote the script, which has Shosanna speaking her lines "in FRENCH" (159). On the other hand, the script offers its own signal—if a considerably less dramatic one—that Shosanna has magically acquired the language of Hollywood; she pauses in a conversation with Marcel to make a rather elaborate English-language pun on Frank Capra and corniness (this in relation to Goebbels's propaganda film *Lucky Kids*, which she has just been required to screen): "Well, when I was watching that Boche (said in English) Capra-corn abomination, (back to French) I got an idea" (74).

34. It would also be relevant here to think of Weber's unpacking of Walter Benjamin's account of the aura's survival under fascism. "Fascism," Weber writes, paraphrasing and elaborating Benjamin, "allows the mass to look itself in the face and thereby to find a gaze that ostensibly looks back. Fascism thus reinstates the aura of the world-picture by means of the very media that undermine it" ("Mass Mediauras," 102). ("World picture" refers to Heidegger's "Die Zeit des Weltbildes," a text Weber analyzes earlier in his essay; the Heideggerian critique of technics looms massively behind Lacoue-Labarthe and Nancy's reading of the "Nazi myth" as well.)

35. Ironically in Castellari's *Inglorious Bastards* the shibboleth test *is* passed: the lead hero, Lt. Robert Yeager, played by Bo Svenson (who was born in Sweden to a Russian mother and Swedish father and emigrated to the United States as a teenager), is an American fighter pilot who speaks German well enough to pass as German. (The character explains at one point to an incredulous American companion that he had had a "German nanny" as a child in Minnesota.) Svenson has a small role in Tarantino's film as an unnamed American colonel, and Castellari himself has a cameo as a German general in the final movie theater scene.

36. The one other sustained effort to "pass" in the film is Shosanna's disguising herself as Emmanuelle Mimieux, but this is not a *linguistic* passing

(and furthermore it is hinted that Landa knows perfectly well who she is). The question of who can pass as what spills over into Tarantino's casting. Michael Fassbender, who plays Lt. Archie Hicox, is a German Irish actor who grew up in Ireland and as an actor has essentially the same difficulty trying to pass as German as his fictional character has. (Fassbender worked with a German voice coach, Lena Lessing, and also had to train his middle-class British accent.) Meanwhile, according to the IMDb trivia site for the film, Diane Kruger showed that the test of the shibboleth can be passed. Her English is so good that "Quentin Tarantino thought she was an American, and doubted whether she could master the German dialogue and accent. Upon audition, she quickly proved to him that she was a native speaking German." See http://www.imdb.com/title/tt0361748/trivia.

37. Some scenes in Tarantino's original screenplay that did not make it into the finished film accentuate this theme. Shosanna tells her lover Marcel, "If we're going to obliterate the Nazis we have to use their tactics" (84); she and Marcel then torture the French owner of a processing lab until he agrees to develop their film: "GASPAR, the fatherly figure of all the experimental French filmmakers in the decade before German rule, takes a SAVAGE BEATING at the hands of his friend Marcel. Shosanna watches, pitiless" (85).

38. Daniel Mendelsohn, "Inglourious Basterds: When Jews Attack," *Newsweek*, August 13, 2009, http://www.newsweek.com/2009/08/13/inglourious-basterds-when-jews-attack.html.

39. We hear very little about collaboration in the film beyond some short scenes featuring Goebbels's French mistress. It should perhaps be stressed that *Inglourious Basterds* presents a deliberately stripped-down alternative universe from its opening shots onward. In May 1941, the date the film gives for its opening scene at the LaPadite farm, organized roundups of (mainly non-French) Jews were just beginning in occupied France. (The notorious Vel' d'Hiv *rafle* was still more than a year away.) Because the German authorities had an interest in preserving, even in the occupied zone, the façade of Vichy self-policing, *razzias* were conducted not by the SS but by the regular French police. The IMDb entry on bloopers in *Inglourious Basterds* comments, "Colonel Landa and his minions would have had nothing much to do in occupied France." They certainly would not have been tasked with extermination missions; Tarantino is projecting onto France, one could say, a stylized version of the murderous German policies being pursued in the East. But this is not, I think, a "blooper"; in the celluloid-imaginary world of this film Jews are pursued and murdered by the SS, period. These stark simplifications permit the specular pattern that Mendelsohn criticizes, according to which the film's Jews take revenge on a totalizable enemy by imitating the enemy's atrocities and, in that sense, "becoming" the enemy.

40. Thus when we meet Goebbels in the film's third chapter he is ranting about blacks: "It's only the offspring of slaves that allows America to be competitive athletically" (55). In addition to comparing Jews to rats during his interrogation of LaPadite, Landa compares "Negroes" to "gorillas" ("Negroes—gorillas—brain—lips—smell—physical strength—penis size" [12]), and when he finds out that Shosanna has a "negro in her employ," he offers a subtler sneer (69). (These lines are spoken in German, English, and French, respectively, but I am simply quoting here from Tarantino's English-language screenplay.)

Chapter 11

# Loose Words, or Arche-Reading

Peter Szendy

> *Glas* also proposes, in its fashion, a program, a problematic ensemble, a system, if you like, of anticipation as concerns these "reading effects," and its reception or non-reception. . . . What type of effect (of reading or non-reading) is absolutely *unanticipable*, out of sight, structurally out of sight . . . for the . . . logic of the scenes where *Glas foresees*, advances at every turn as the foresight, the foreseeing organism of its reading and its non-reading (on occasion they can be the same thing), where *Glas* reads or over-reads itself in itself and outside of itself?
>
> —Jacques Derrida, *Ja, or the faux-bond*

Among the many things I owe Samuel Weber (he who has so often raised the question of the debt),[1] there is one question in particular that I would like to pose to him, a question that he does not explicitly ask himself in the way I imprudently venture to but that everything in his writing, it seems to me, calls for: Does not coming after Derrida also entail interrogating reading differently, giving reading a place, a role that would be derived not only from writing?

Evidently I am not the first to notice the important place occupied by reading, both as a practice and as a question, in Weber's work.[2] Not only is reading one of his main concerns, but it is also one of his most constant and most regular resources. Few thinkers have known how to develop, like him, a true art of reading (besides, *the art of reading* is a phrase that he insisted on countersigning, borrowing it from Adorno),[3] while never ceasing to interrogate, to question all the theoretical arraignments (*arraisonnements*) that attempt to *catch* the reader in her activity or act.

*Caught in the act of reading*: such is the title of the essay that Weber devoted to Wolfgang Iser's theory of reading. Iser finds himself caught, so to speak, in the act of reading that he attempted to catch; he finds himself caught by surprise (*pris ou surpris*) while reading, thus betraying his phenomenology-inspired theoretical premises: on the one hand, "notwithstanding his use of the term *text*, Iser conceives reading as essentially a process of visualization (or image construction)"; on the other hand, at stake for Iser is the "power of the text to control the reader's response." That is to say, the "wandering viewpoint" of the reader should not "go too far astray and get lost"; it should not wander outside the frame programmed or foreseen (*prévu*) by the text.[4] *Fore-seen*, yes, literally previsualized for the reader, even if the unreachable overview, the totalization of perspectives, is continually pushed back to the horizon.

It is thus by a controlled visualization, according to Iser, that the reader brings the text back to life, restoring its lost presence: "Reading could be called upon to function dialectically, as the negation of a negation, the re-presentation of an irremediably extraneous representation—in short, as the vivifying actualization of a dead letter. This is, mutatis mutandis, the position adopted by certain contemporary 'phenomenological' theorists of reading, such as Wolfgang Iser. But it is also a position masterfully analyzed, in the first publications of Derrida, as a writing that refuses to know its own name."[5]

If, for Derrida, reading is evidently not inscribed in the ideal horizon of a visibility that would regulate the multiplicity of viewpoints, it remains nonetheless determined, as Weber suggests, by the textual or scriptural paradigm. This is not to say that reading would be, for Derrida as for Iser, ultimately controlled by the text; indeed the text in the Derridean sense probably means the impossibility of any control in the face of a dissemination that nothing, no ultimate authority could stop or catch. But it *remains* that reading does not seem to have, for Derrida, an autonomous role, that it is submitted, if not to a text that it repeats at least to a general textuality that absorbs and includes it in advance. Reading would thus be, for Derrida, but a scriptural form among others: it would be confused with or in writing as arche-writing, thereby losing its singularity.

Indeed in a certain *scene* of deconstruction reading is nothing but writing or rewriting. Or, more precisely, since reading is for the most part absorbed or dissolved in (arche-)writing, it undifferentiates itself in writing like one gets lost in the crowd: "'Reading and writing,' although obviously inseparable and complementary, are assigned quite distinct places in what might be called the tragicomic drama of deconstruction. . . . 'Writing' occupies a prominent position, plays the leading role, whereas 'reading,' although never absent, is more difficult to situate. Anticipating, I will suggest—retaining, for a while, the theatrical code—that its place is that of an 'extra' (in French: *figurant*), an actor who has no lines to speak and whose main function is usually to get lost in the crowd."[6] Notice the theatrical lexicon affecting the vocabulary of reading, which prepares and ushers in its scenography; when it comes to reading, in Weber theater—I will return to this—is never far.

Reading thus seems to have no room of its own, no "proper place," no autonomy "in the deconstruction of metaphysics."[7] Which is to say that it does not have any proper role *in the deconstruction of the proper*. Here is the difficulty, here is what, as Weber himself appears to suggest, seems to condemn him to act with a certain precipitation or anticipation. Because when he invokes the stage (*scène*) of a theater, when he *stages* reading, he does so, admittedly, in anticipation, "anticipating." He turns toward what is *ahead*, further, after: namely, the question of reading, posed *over there*, before us, waiting for us. And he does so by risking *necessarily* going too fast—we will see why—*necessarily* exposing himself to cut corners, rushing hastily toward this "theatrical code" that, though still pending, must also be kept, "retain[ed] for a while." In short, this theatricality, which promises to be the very stage of the interrogation to come on what reading means, is simultaneously what will come after and what was already there before.

✦

Before-after Derrida, there is Benjamin.

It is probably Benjamin, among the extras of the crowd, advancing, surreptitiously coming on stage in the strange movement of a precipitation that retains, of an anticipation that preserves.

For, on the one hand, Benjamin will have *anticipated* Derrida; he will have come before him, as Weber suggests in *Benjamin's -abilities*, in advance "allow[ing] the notion of textuality to be 'generalized.'" And to be generalized precisely *from the theater stage*—that of the *Trauerspiel*—as if the concept of allegory developed in *The Origin of German Tragic Drama* was a sort of arche-writing avant la lettre: marked by "the stamp of writing," the Benjaminian allegory would *already* be, for Weber, an architext whose theatrical code *still ought to be retained*, by *returning* to it.[8]

This is why, on the other hand, Benjamin is also this *after*, this future (*cet à-venir*) promised like a scene of reading or readability rather than of writing. After the scene of writing, yes, instead of it, that is also *before* it (*plutôt qu'elle, c'est-à-dire aussi* plus tôt), there would be *another scene* that ought to be played *against* it, *right up against* it. An archi-scene doubling or redoubling the other one, in the call and raise (*relance et surenchère*) expressed in this sentence by Benjamin often quoted by Weber: "Was nie geschrieben wurde, lesen."[9]

"To read what was never written": How are we to hear this? When this sentence appeared for the first time in his short essay "On the Mimetic Faculty," Benjamin continued, "Such reading is the most ancient: reading before all languages, from the entrails, the stars, or dances. Later the mediating link of a new kind of reading, of runes and hieroglyphs, came into use." A reading therefore that would come prior to any historically attested form of writing (rune or hieroglyph), or even, as Weber suggests, a reading that would come prior "to all writing."[10]

What would it be, this arche-reading,[11] this absolutely antescriptural reading that consequently would demand to find its place, to be situated in or articulated with the Derridean notions of arche-writing and architext?

✦

Let me begin again.

What I call arche-reading is evidently for Benjamin a prophetic reading ("from the entrails, the stars"). But in what sense?

After his short 1933 essay "On the Mimetic Faculty" (which was only posthumously published in 1955), it was in the paralipomena and variants to "On the Concept of History" that Benjamin cited again the sentence that Hofmannsthal had put in Death's mouth at the close of his 1894 lyrical drama, *Der Tor und der Tod*. As the protagonist, Claudio, has just fallen dead at her feet, Death says, slowly retreating:

> Wie wundervoll sind diese Wesen,
> Die, was nicht deutbar, dennoch deuten,
> Was nie geschrieben wurde, lesen.
>
> How wonderful these beings are,
> Who do interpret the uninterpretable,
> And what was never writ, they read.[12]

Reading therefore seems to be a synonym for interpretation. Reading (*lesen*) rhymes with interpreting (*deuten*) in Hofmannsthal's lines, to which Benjamin alludes in those terms:

> If one looks upon history as a text, then one can say of it what a recent author has said of literary texts—namely, that the past has left in them images comparable to those registered by a light-sensitive plate. "The future alone possesses developers strong enough to reveal the image in all details. Many pages in Marivaux or Rousseau contain a mysterious meaning which the first readers of these texts could not fully have deciphered" (Monglond . . .). The historical method is a philological method based on the book of life. "Read what was never written," runs a line in Hofmannsthal. The reader one should think of here is the true historian.[13]

In this context evidence suggests that Hofmannsthal's line, prepared as it is by the quotation by a "recent author,"[14] should not be understood literally: "read what was never written" here means *read what has not yet been deciphered*, read what remains to be read. Read what was written in a writing surely as yet never decoded but undoubtedly *inscribed*.

So that, here as elsewhere, a reading that corresponds to such a writing is condemned to be but the repetition (of the repetition) of the text, according to the inexorable paradigm thus formalized by Weber:

> Reading could thus be determined as the effort to reduce difference and repetition to a minimum, the effort of a representation to efface itself before that which it represents, in this case, the text, but without impinging upon or usurping the originality of its model. This interpretation of reading, however, would add nothing new to the general scenario of supplementarity or of *différance* . . . . If writing is presented, within the closure of metaphysics, as the representation of a representation, as the signifier of a signifier, the repetition of a repetition, then reading appears only to reiterate all that once again, adding hardly a wrinkle.[15]

It is this wrinkle, or this fold, that must hold our attention.

What would be a reading that, without being doomed to repeat the text by representing it, would not in turn become writing, would not be dissolved in the general paradigm of the architext, of which it would then be, repeatedly, the repetition?

A reading in no way repeating the text, and therefore escaping all submission to the textual authority, would probably no longer be a reading. Let us say that it would be an impossible reading. A prophetic reading, doubtless, since what it would attempt to read would not have taken place yet, would not have been there, in the text. Yet we should not understand such a prophetic character in the same sense as the "recent author" quoted by Benjamin who refers to a future allowing us to delve into the imprinted past by developing it (*en le révélant*) but rather in a sense that gestures toward the essay "On the Mimetic Faculty," that is, toward this reading prior to all writing that perhaps Benjamin tried to indicate. A reading that one should be able to declare *purely prophetic*, driven by a pure movement of anticipation announcing no encrypted content destined to be deciphered one day, nothing that is in some way already written and waits to be repeated in reading: just *a pure reading to come*.

If reading thus is certainly no longer reading, every reading worthy of the name invents itself with reference to this impossible pure reading, each time measuring itself against it, as it is *in spite of all* inscribed in the text.

For such would be the paradox of reading, such its constitutive aporia: it dreams its sovereign autonomy with regard to the text, an absolute freedom that would make it purely and strictly a reading rather than a repetition. But it dreams it—seeks it, constructs it—*in the text*, where it must confine itself lest it no longer be reading.

Hence the question that awaits us: How could a pure reading, the pure prophecy or prediction of a reading, predicting or prophesying nothing, no decipherable content, be inscribed in a text, when such a reading—aporetic, impossible—precisely dreams to be emancipated from any repetition or representation that would bind and subject it to the text?

✦

That there be, as Weber writes, a reader "inscribed in" the text, or several,[16] that there be readings that are *prescribed* within the text is what we experience, in a more or less explicit way, every time we read.

Let us open, for example, a book that has been read and commented upon on many occasions: let us read—and this is not one example among others, because at stake in this text is the very sovereignty of the reader[17]—let us reread Hobbes's *Leviathan*. Let us lend an ear to the textual inscription of two ostensibly antagonistic reading regimes: a ratiocinating or logocentric regime and a prophetic regime.

Between the second and third part of *Leviathan*, at the beginning of chapter 32 (§1), one comes across one of these words or phrases that seem trivial and yet fold the text upon itself in order to inscribe in it a cumulative or capitalizing movement. Hobbes writes, "I have derived the Rights of Soveraigne Power, and the duty of Subjects hitherto, from the Principles of Nature onely."[18] What, unostentatiously, this "hitherto" prescribes, whether we like it or not, is a reading that hoards and adds what it reads as it reads. A reading that binds as it reads (*qui lie en lisant*), that gathers what is read in a discourse (*logos*), given this binding property proper to reading that Heidegger praises in a very short text entitled "Was heisst lesen?": "What is [*calls forth*] reading? That which is sustained and directive in reading is gatheredness. To what is it gathered? To what is written, to what is said in writing." ("Was heisst lesen? Das Tragende und Leitende im Lesen ist die Sammlung. Worauf sammelt sie? Auf das Geschriebene, auf das in der Schrift Gesagte.")[19]

Such a reading can be called, must be called *logocentric*, of course.[20] But then one must show that the gathering focused on what writing says (*concentré sur le dit de l'écrit*) is inscribed in or prescribed by the text—by every text, doubtless—in that it determines in advance the act of its reading. Here in the passage from *Leviathan* the agent of this gathering is this "hitherto" that, much like its other counterparts ("in sum" and many other homologous locutions), is a representative of the text in the text: acting as a substitute for what is written earlier, the "hitherto" is not unlike a delegate or a deputy of the text sending itself ahead of itself in order to construct itself through cumulative representations, through *mandates*.

Now, after having thus been folded upon itself thanks to the cumulative recapitulation allowed by its mandataries, Hobbes's text predicts and anticipates what will come next: "in that I am next to handle" the subject will be "prophetical" words. Prophecy and prophets will be at stake, then; they will be the object, the theme of the text. But it is also another regime of reading that they will inscribe, as a watermark or between the lines.

Why? And what is a prophet, for Hobbes?

Let us read the triple definition of the prophet given in chapter 36 of *Leviathan*, entitled "Of the Word of God and of Prophets" (§7): "The name of PROPHET, signifieth in Scripture sometimes *Prolocutor*; that is, he that speaketh from God to Man, or from man to God: And sometimes *Praedictor*, or a foreteller of things to come: And sometimes one that speaketh incoherently, as men that are distracted."[21]

Depending on the meaning we want to give to the prefix *pro-*, the prophet (from *pro-* and *phêmi*, "I say") is the one who speaks *instead of* or the one who says *in advance*. Either, therefore, he gives his voice to speak in place of somebody else, or he says in advance what is yet to be. Or, Hobbes adds, as if there were a third possibility unrelated to the other two, the prophet is merely someone who happens to be crazy, that is, more literally, "distracted." From the first to the second meaning the value and authenticity of the prophecy diminishes and the prophetic word turns into an imposture, more and more deprived of consistency or coherence as it disengages itself from its anchorage in the divine word, in the *logos*, but also as it loses its specificity: "When by Prophecy is meant Praediction, or foretelling of future Contingents; *not only* they were Prophets, who were Gods Spokesmen, and foretold those things to others, which God had foretold to them; *but also* all those Impostors, that pretend by the helpe of familiar spirits, or by superstitious divination of events past, from false causes, to foretell the like events in time to come."[22]

*Not only* the spokespersons *but also* the diviners of all sorts: there are more and more prophets, leaving no stones unturned, using all the means at hand, breaking all links between ("false") causes and effects. Impossible to be *accounted for*, unbound from any authoritative word, the prophecy then abandons its legitimate and legitimized province; it somehow loses its conduct or its content to become a simple way to relate to language in general; contentless, thereby apt to welcome any future event, the prophecy is nothing other than the pure principle of the looseness of words (*déliaison des mots*): "And for Incoherent Speech, it was amongst the Gentiles taken for one sort of Prophecy, because the Prophets of their Oracles, intoxicated with a spirit, or vapor from the cave of the Pythian Oracle at Delphi, were for the time really mad, and spake like mad-men; of whose loose words a sense might be made to fit any event."[23]

Thus losing its specificity to become a mere modality of the commerce with signs, the prophecy starts to talk, allegorically, about the reader. And, rereading this passage, going another time through the three meanings of the word *prophet*, we come to realize that it is our own reading that is at stake: (1) The reader indeed lends her voice and speaks for another, that is, for the text for which she acts as the *prolocutor* (in the same way the actor is the character's spokesperson); (2) in so doing she continually anticipates, rushes toward what she has not yet been able to read, toward what has not been written yet; (3) so much so that she is structurally dis-tracted, sundered from the *tractus* of textual linearity, finding herself dealing with "loose words" that nothing, no *logos*, can gather in an absolute guarantee of meaning.

✦

*Loose words* could be a synonym for the "disjunctive, atomizing principle of the allegorical vision" Benjamin refers to when, alluding to the establishment of the capital letter in German orthography, he conceives it as an agent of the ruin and fragmentation of language in isolated words.[24] That is, unbound, loose or loosened, or *detailed*.

This detailing logic of allegory is caught, for Benjamin, in what he calls "antinomies": on the one hand, the detail is not important, since "any person, any object, any relationship can mean absolutely anything else"; but on the other hand, details are infinitely important; they acquire a "power" that makes them appear "incommensurable" precisely because of their capacity to point to something else, by virtue of their status as "props of signification."[25] It is this allegorical significance (*signifiance*), entirely constituted by differential relationships, that predicts or anticipates what Derrida calls "architext."

Yet it is in an eminently theatrical fashion that the Benjaminian allegory thus anticipates or prophesies arche-writing. Weber forcefully insists that it is from a certain *theatrical code* that Benjamin anticipates Derrida.[26] But why insist? Why flag this theatricality? If, for a philosophy of architextuality, this is probably but a detail, precisely, we should recall, in the perspective that concerns us here, this remark by Benjamin: "Basically, then, the *Trauerspiel*, too, which grew up in the sphere of the allegorical, is, in its form, *a drama for the reader*. Although this says nothing about the value or the possibility of its stage-performance. But it does make it clear that the chosen spectator of such examples of the *Trauerspiel* concentrated on them with at least the same thought and attentiveness as the reader; that the situations did not change very frequently, but that when they did, they did so in a flash, like the appearance of the print when a page is turned."[27] Along with Benjamin, on the stage of a drama that addresses the act of reading, that is dedicated to it, we are trying to think what may well be also *the mourning-play of reading*, its *Trauerspiel*, within what Weber has called "the tragicomic drama of deconstruction."

It is this *Trauerspiel* of reading that I believe we can hear very distinctly in this page of "Sauf le nom," where Derrida reads—does he read? does he write?—the conclusion (*Beschluss*) of Angelus Silesius's *The Cherubic Wanderer*: "Friend, let this be enough; if you wish to read beyond, / Go and become yourself the writ and yourself the essence." ("Freund es ist auch genug. Jm fall du mehr wilt lesen / So geh und werde selbst die Schrifft und selbst das Wesen.") Having quoted these two closing lines, Derrida continues, "The friend . . . is asked, recommended, enjoined, *prescribed* to render himself, by reading, beyond reading: beyond at least the legibility of what is currently readable, beyond the final signature—and for that reason to *write*."[28]

Beyond reading, in the hyperbole of arche-reading, when we move toward what is not yet readable, toward the unreadable that attracts reading and sets it in motion like a magnet, there would be, Derrida says, countersigning someone else's text, writing (*l'écriture*).

And yet.

Without dreaming at all of escaping the architext—indeed with the allegory we are *already* there—without yearning for any "outside the text" (*hors-texte*), what we question by rereading Benjamin alongside Weber is the *inscription* of something beyond reading announcing itself as arche-reading. That is to say, as this impossible possibility: *read what has never been written*.

In other words, my question aims toward a reading that, in the text, would absolutely precede the text.[29]

Why? To what end?

Because arche-reading, in that it rushes ahead of any form of writing, *prior to all writing*, would be the opening and the clearing of the path; it would be the heading or the "reading head" (*tête de lecture*), the tip where reading gets carried away, is set loose and rushes ahead of itself in pursuit of itself. Where it attempts to capture itself properly, binding itself to itself in the promise or prophesy of itself: reading *itself*.

Let us say, let us risk saying therefore, repeating Derrida's words, that the prophetic arche-reading is what *opens* all reading.[30] Not on an outside—not on an outside of the text, which there is not—but, within the text that never ceases to be read, on what carries reading before the text as well as before itself.

**Translated by Antoine Traisnel**

## Notes

1. See Samuel Weber, "The Debt of Criticism: Notes on Stanley Fish's *Is There a Text in This Class?*" and "The Debts of Deconstruction and Other, Related Assumptions," in *Institution and Interpretation: Expanded Edition* (Stanford: Stanford University Press, 2001). See also Samuel Weber, "Closing the Net: 'Capitalism as Religion' (Benjamin)," in *Benjamin's -abilities* (Cambridge, Mass.: Harvard University Press, 2008), 257ff. My own debts to Weber are legible here and there, especially in *Hits: Philosophy in the Jukebox*, trans. Will Bishop (New York: Fordham University Press, 2012), 162, 176, 178.

2. See Simon Morgan Wortham, *Samuel Weber: Acts of Reading* (Surrey, U.K.: Ashgate, 2003).

3. "The Art of Reading" is the title of the first part of an essay first published in 2000 and then in Samuel Weber, *Theatricality as Medium* (New York: Fordham University Press, 2004), 229ff: "After the End: Adorno." Weber comments on the last of Adorno's *Hegel: Three Studies*: "Skoteinos or How to Read Hegel," trans.

Shierry Weber Nicholsen (Cambridge, Mass.: MIT Press, 1994). Among other things Adorno affirms that Hegel "requires repeated readings, and requires them objectively and not merely to familiarize oneself with his subject matter" (92). It is important to note that the phrase taken up by Weber, "the art of reading," occurs just prior to a passage on Hegel's *politics*: "Hegel's logic is not only his metaphysics; it is also his politics. The art of reading him should take note of where something new begins, some content, and where a machine that was not intended to be a machine is simply running and ought not to keep on doing so. At every moment one needs to keep two seemingly incompatible maxims in mind: painstaking immersion in detail, and free detachment" (94–95).

4. Samuel Weber, "Caught in the Act of Reading" (1986), in *Institution and Interpretation: Expanded Edition* (Stanford: Stanford University Press, 2001), 183, 188. See Wolfgang Iser, *The Act of Reading: A Theory of Aesthetic Response* (Baltimore: Johns Hopkins University Press, 1980).

5. Samuel Weber, "Reading and Writing *chez* Derrida" (1983), in *Institution and Interpretation*, 93.

6. Weber, "Reading and Writing *chez* Derrida," 92.

7. Weber, "Reading and Writing *chez* Derrida," 93.

8. Weber, *Benjamin's -abilities*, 228, 307.

9. See Weber, *Benjamin's -abilities*, especially 207, 308. This sentence by Benjamin (that he himself borrows from Hofmannsthal) appears in a draft of *Über den Begriff der Geschichte* and in *Über das mimetische Vermögen*. See Walter Benjamin, "Paralipomena to 'On the Concept of History,'" in *Selected Writings*, vol. 4: *1938–1940* (Cambridge, Mass.: Harvard University Press, 2006), 405; Walter Benjamin, "On the Mimetic Faculty," in *One-Way Street and Other Writings*, trans. Edmund Jephcott and Kingsley Shorter (New York: Harcourt Brace, 1978), 162–63.

10. Weber, *Benjamin's -abilities*, 308.

11. Obviously this has nothing to do with the notion of *archi-reader* once proposed by Michel Riffaterre in *Essais de stylistique structurale* (Paris: Flammarion, 1971), which he defined as "sum of readings" (46). If Michel Lisse similarly deals with *archilecture*, it is in a very different sense from the one I am interested in here. See *L'Expérience de la lecture, 2: Le glissement* (Paris: Galilée, 2001), 15, 18, 189. At stake for Lisse in the "case" of reading seems to be the repetition, validation, or prolongation of the deconstruction of logocentrism initiated by Derrida. That is, Lisse proposes to "emancipate reading from the sway of listening," from its subjection to "what is heard" (13), in order to "no longer reduce reading to listening *or* looking" (18, emphasis mine) but to envision it as "divided between listening and looking" (15). In sum, reading "must combine listening and looking" (189) in what Lisse calls the "eareye [*orœil*]" (18). It is for this reason that Lisse believes arche-writing and arche-reading complement and continue each other ("to arche-writing *corresponds* an arche-reading" [189, emphasis mine]), whereas it is precisely their tension, or even their incompossibility, that this essay wishes to bring out: the locus—I will get there—of the impossibility of reading as its most proper possibility.

12. Hugo von Hofmannsthal, *Death and the Fool*, trans. Elisabeth Walter (Boston: Gorham Press, 1914), 45, translation modified.

13. Benjamin, "Paralipomena to 'On the Concept of History,'" 405.

14. André Monglond, *Le Préromantisme français* (Grenoble: Arthaud, 1930), 1:13.

15. Weber, "Reading and Writing *chez* Derrida," 92–93.

16. See Samuel Weber, "Reading: 'To the Very End of the World,'" in *Modern Language Notes* 111.5 (1996), 827: "The reader, as inscribed in *Tristram Shandy* . . ."

17. As I tried to show in "L'image du pouvoir et le pouvoir de la lecture (le *Léviathan*, en somme)," *Geste*, no. 4 (November 2007). Weber also devoted some remarkable pages to *Leviathan*: see "Toward a Politics of Singularity: Protection and Projection," in *Religion: Beyond a Concept*, ed. Hent de Vries (New York: Fordham University Press, 2008), 626ff.

18. Thomas Hobbes, *Leviathan*, edited by Richard Tuck (Cambridge, U.K.: Cambridge University Press, 2013), 255.

19. Martin Heidegger, "Was heisst lesen?" (1954), in *Aus der Erfahrung des Denkens: 1910–1976* (Frankfurt am Main: Klostermann, 1983), 111. I quote the translation by J. Sallis in *Hermeneutics and Deconstruction,* ed. Hugh J. Silverman and Don Ihde (Albany: State University of New York Press, 1985). Heidegger continues, "Authentic reading is a gatheredness to that which, unbeknown to us, has hardly claimed our essence, regardless of whether we comply with it or withhold from it. Without authentic reading, we are also not able to see what has us in sight nor to gaze upon any appearance or semblance." ("Das eigentliche Lesen ist die Sammlung auf das, was ohne unser Wissen einst schon unser Wesen in den Anspruch genommen hat, mögen wir dabei ihm entsprechen oder versagen. Ohne das eigentliche Lesen vermögen wir auch nicht das uns Anblickende zu sehen und das Erscheinende und Scheinende zu schauen.")

20. Following Derrida, Michel Lisse speaks of the "logocentric weight" ("poids logocentrique") of Heidegger's "definition of reading" (*L'Expérience de la lecture*, 48).

21. Hobbes, *Leviathan*, 290.

22. Hobbes, *Leviathan*, §8, 291, emphasis mine.

23. Hobbes, *Leviathan*, 292.

24. Walter Benjamin, *Origin of German Tragic Drama*, trans. John Osborne (London: Verso, 1998), 208.

25. Benjamin, *Origin of German Tragic Drama*, 175, translation modified. Benjamin writes:

> Jede Person, jedwedes Ding, jedes Verhältnis kann ein beliebiges anderes bedeuten. Diese Möglichkeit spricht der profanen Welt ein vernichtendes doch gerechtes Urteil: sie wird gekennzeichnet als eine Welt, in der es aufs Detail so streng nicht ankommt. Doch wird, und dem zumal, dem allegorische Schriftexegese gegenwärtig ist, ganz unverkennbar, das jene Requisiten des Bedeutens alle mit eben ihrem Weisen auf ein anderes eine Mächtigkeit gewinnen, die den profanen Dingen inkommensurabel sie erst erscheinen last und sie in eine höhere Ebene hebt, ja heiligen kann. Demnach wird die profane Welt in allegorischer Betrachtung sowohl im Rang erhoben wie entwertet.

26. Cf. Weber, "God and the Devil—in Detail," in *Benjamin's -abilities*, 242: "Details . . . are *required* by baroque allegory, but as *Requisiten des Bedeutens*,

indispensable theatrical props of signification. . . . What distinguishes Benjamin's interpretation of the baroque detail is that its spatial dimension becomes distinctively theatrical."

27. Weber, "God and the Devil—in Detail," 185, emphasis mine.

28. Jacques Derrida, "Sauf le nom," trans. John P. Leavy Jr., in *On the Name*, edited by Thomas Dutoit (Stanford: Stanford University Press), 41.

29. Which does not amount to presupposing a preexisting and already constituted reader. See Jacques Derrida, "This Strange Institution Called Literature," in *Acts of Literature*, ed. Derek Attridge (London: Routledge, 1992):

> By definition the reader does not exist. Not before the work and as its straightforward "receiver." The dream we were talking about concerns what it is in the work which produces its reader, a reader who doesn't yet exist, whose competence cannot be identified, a reader who would be "formed," "trained," instructed, constructed, even engendered, let's say *invented* by the work. Invented, which is to say both found by chance and produced by research. The work, then, becomes an institution forming its own readers, giving them a competence which they did not possess before. . . . If we trusted the current distinction between competence and performance, we would say that the work's performance produces or institutes, forms or invents, a new competence for the reader or the addressee who thereby becomes a countersignatory. It teaches him or her, *if s/he is willing*, to countersign. What is interesting here is thus the invention of the addressee capable of countersigning and saying "yes" in a committed and lucid way. But this "yes" is also an inaugural performance. (74)

Or: "A reader is not a consumer, a spectator, a visitor, not even a 'receiver'" (51).

30. See Jacques Derrida, *Of Grammatology*, trans. Gayatri Chakravorty Spivak (Baltimore: Johns Hopkins University Press, 1997), 158. Derrida, initiating a "justification" of what he calls his "principles of reading," speaking of "a task of reading," admits that "this moment of doubling commentary should no doubt have its place in a critical reading." That is, even though it is expected to "produce" something, it must also *reproduce* the text, otherwise "critical production would risk developing in any direction and authorize itself to say almost anything." *But*, Derrida adds, "this indispensible guard-rail has always only *protected*, never *opened* a reading."

# *Toward a Conclusion*

Chapter 12

# Vous voulez rire!

## Interview with a Passing Journalist

Jacques Derrida

As we shall see, this was, and is, no laughing matter.
And that, I repeat, is no laughing matter.[1]

Q. Thank you for having granted me this interview on the subject of Sam Weber—well on Sam Weber or about him, as you will.[2]

A. Vous voulez rire, you must be joking, aren't you? On his *subject*, *on* him, or *about* him? Let me ask you this first question, with your permission. If this first preliminary question does count, it is above all because it touches on the *place*. Where are we? Where are we located? Around him, near or far from him, confronting him as an object, behind him, alongside him? Where is *he*?

Now you know that nothing is taken more *seriously* by Sam Weber, in a more constant, acute, lucid manner than the location, the place, the situation, the position, the locality of the apparatus, the scene of the *montage*. Fortunately, you have the same technical term to say something of a certain technique, in English—"montage." It will help you, because Weber is always very attentive to *montage*. In all the arts, from painting or photography to cinema, through literature, a process consists in putting into place a *dispositif* (you would doubtless say an *apparatus*), in situating it artificially, in the agreed upon or convened, that is, conventional or institutional unity of a place, by adjusting some pieces, by assembling them in an *assemblage*—you have this word in English as well—or still, as one says in French, "mounting" a theatrical play. When, literally or figuratively, such a montage links the machinic to the theatrical, it will always have situated something like the foyer of Weberian thought. In the first place, precisely, whenever the focus is on the *subject*, this highly ambiguous word, and above all when one wants to speak of *the subject of the subject*. To say that he takes it seriously is never to exclude on his part a playful verve, an amused thinking of the playful, the comic, the *Witz* ("joke" or *mot d'esprit*),[3] laughter, so many things that we will, I insist, have to distinguish. They all have a different relation, a differential proximity to art, to *tekhné* and to technics, so many things that themselves entertain a different commerce with, a differential proximity to the singular and unheard-of deconstruction engaged by Weber. This commerce is also an economy, for the economic dimension, an economy of saving, notably, remains essential to the interpretation of the joke. Freud explicitly recalls it in an appendix on humor published in *Imago* in 1928—he avows one limit there: "In my volume on *Jokes and Their Relation to the Unconscious* (1905), I in fact considered humour only from the economic point of view. My object was to discover the source of the pleasure obtained from humour, and I think I was able to show that the yield of humorous pleasure arises from an economy in expenditure upon feeling."[4]

From the very first pages of his last book, to which I refer you without delay, Weber thus retraces the organizing move of his problematic, the major *topos*, in sum, of his book, and I would almost be tempted to say of all his books, namely the topology or topography, the thinking of location or of place. About the passage I am about to quote, he refers, and I believe that he has good reasons for doing so, to the place as *chora* (a reference to Plato's *Timaeus*) rather than as *topos* (a theme that is doubtless more Aristotelian). He immediately insists on a motif to which I am also sensitive, which we should all be, you and I, very sensitive to, when speaking *on the subject of*, *on*, or *about* "someone." It is not only the motif of the *unity* but, more radically, at the outset in any case, that of the *indivisibility* of the "subject": "This is a book about *place* and *positioning* rather than about human beings. . . . The essays here collected retrace how the development of aesthetic theory can be understood as a (perhaps ultimate) effort to defend the notion of the indivisibility of place as a condition of the individuality of the subject. . . . For without the unity of place, the unity of the subject becomes difficult to conceive."[5]

I would be tempted to underscore or privilege even further this value of indivisibility. It is the very "condition," Weber literally says so, the first chance of place, of localizing determination, of emplacement. There is not a place *first* given and that would *then* be divisible or indivisible. On the contrary, it is the postulate of indivisibility that makes place or emplacement possible (exemplarily that of the subject). It is indeed a postulate, a request, a demand, that I believe is necessarily (it is necessity itself) bound to fail. *As desire and for life.* It is at once irresistible and destined to fail. Inevitable, this failure moreover gives life and movement their chance: the other of death itself. Chance is intimately allied to failure, as possibility is to impotence. (Bataille is right to note this on the subject of laughter; I would like to say a word about this later.) Indivisibility, on the other hand, is both death and absolute sovereignty. All these predicates can be transferred to the concept of "subject." They occupy the place of the subject. It is through indivisibility that sovereignty has always been characterized as ipseity of the subject, its sovereign decision, its absolute responsibility as irresponsibility—I have tried to demonstrate it elsewhere—and in the form of an undeniable aporia: if a subject *acts*, if it *decides*, if it *is* what is possible for it, what is *in its power*, if it deploys its possibilities as its predicates, then it decides nothing, it makes explicit what it is, what it is capable of, what is within its range and in its nature, and it becomes then irresponsible. This is indeed the place of the sovereign: the latter is, moreover, in its ipseity, the indivisible subject which, being responsible to no one, authorizing itself at the same time to make and suspend the law, deciding on exceptions to the law, becomes *at once* absolutely responsible and absolutely irresponsible, etc. What I would like to attempt to think or to name, by wending my way in the wake of Weber, would perhaps be this indecisive experience between classic sovereignty—marked by the indivisibility of the place—and a certain laughter. Sovereignty is a terrifying thing, but as allegation, it always makes me laugh a little, irresistibly. The so-called sovereign makes one laugh, to be sure, but spontaneously it doesn't know how to. In spite of the claim of Bataille, who will have wanted to change the meaning of the traditional concept of sovereignty while piously keeping the old word, which is also a bit ridiculous, ineffectual and hypocritical. Perhaps it's because the sovereign cannot laugh spontaneously, at himself above all, that he often needs fools around him.

Not just any sovereignty, to be sure, and not just any laughter. What do we mean by "laughing like mad" (*fou rire*) for instance, and "itching to laugh"? They do not necessarily stem from "jokes." Does laughter interrupt, threaten, or on the contrary reassure? Does it ruin or confirm the sovereignty of the subject, its economy, or its ipseity? And if it does a little of that all at once, what new distinctions would we need? I have the still obscure feeling that deconstruction, in particular there where it converges with the question of technics, will have had to treat this in sum quasi-political or hyperpolitical question of the relations between laughter and sovereignty. You know that for Bataille . . .[6]

Q. Let's not multiply preambles, if you please. We agree it will be an improvised exchange of *Q and A*.[7] You will be able to reread everything *après coup*, once the interview is translated. But allow me to insist, in the name of what I believe to be the ethics and deontology of journalism, that is to say, my duty toward my readers. They ask you to be more concise and clearer, more spontaneous, more direct than usual, at least as much as possible. Do not multiply protocols as you have just started doing. Above all don't transform, as I hear you like to do, our exchange into a critical or "deconstructive" reflection on the genre of the interview and on the press in general. Our subject is not newspapers, nor even the media . . .

A. *Vous voulez rire*, you must be joking, I'll wind up believing so. I wonder whether there isn't a *quid pro quo* between us. You know, life is full of *quiproquos* as it's sometimes written, in one word. One mistakes this one for that one, one for the other. Generally, it's good for a laugh, whether one likes it or not. Why is that? I'll tell you later the story of my meeting with Sam Weber.[8] There was (we're still laughing about it, and everyone with us, but why?) an original and theatrical *quiproquo* and we're still trying to figure out which *deus ex machina* providentially staged it when I got off the plane thirty-five years ago in Berlin. Sam Weber first mistook someone else for me, *qui pro quo*. Can that ever be straightened out? And yet, through this *quiproquo* I like to think that we recognized each other, so to speak. Even though Diderot speaks profoundly of "*quiproquos* of friendship," there may be *quiproquos* without misunderstanding, and even marvelous "*quiproquos* of friendship" that are not flaws or breaches of truth, only basic experiences that consist in taking the other for what he is, that is to say *yet another*, other than himself, a "divisible" other, precisely, other than his persona, other than what he thinks he is, other than himself, etc. But *quiproquo* is often the technique or the resource of a certain theater, at times tragic, more often comic: a character takes one for another.

I make on purpose this reference to theater in homage to Weber, who is both a philosopher-dramaturge, a thinker and an author of the stage, of *mise*-en-scène, a theoretician of all technical apparatuses consisting in "posing," "disposing," "setting," and "staging," *mettre en scène*. In theater, opera, cinema, in all the media: written newspapers, radio, cinema, and television.

Q. You're starting again to multiply digressions. I told you that our subject was not newspapers nor even the media . . .

A. You must be kidding; it's a joke. How dare you ask me not to think about the very genre that we practice here and now, interviews, or about the press and the media? Where are we after all? You really want us to avoid talking about the place where we are? About the element in which we are discussing? About the supposed addressees to whom you alluded as though you knew them in advance? I was told that you came to talk with me about Sam Weber. Now I repeat the question of *place* (you do say "place" in English)—in which something *takes place* (you do say "takes place") always remains for him the first and the most necessary question, no matter what. We will by the way have thousands of problems of translation, for if in French *lieu* and *place* are near synonyms, the subtle difference that separates them is lost in the English "place." In any case place is definitely for Weber the condition of the subject, of the indivisible individual and of the event, of what "takes place."[9] It can be read or deciphered on each page of all his texts . . .

Q. But what then is the link of all those themes to the subject with which I have been entrusted? You know very well what a "subject" means for the press. I was asked to ask you about "deconstruction and technics." More precisely about the "techniques of deconstruction" in Sam Weber. As a journalist, even though I went to college for a while, I don't understand very well myself what this means. Could you start by explaining to my readers, in as pedagogical a manner as possible, "in a nutshell," as we say in English, how "deconstruction" should be understood? We'll see about "technics" later.

A. Later? But you're making fun of me! Deconstruction and technics have always been fused together in one and the same question!

Q. Above all, before anything else, could you talk to us of all that in (*chez*) Sam Weber *himself*, in your meeting with him, for example, in his life and his works? Above all from the political standpoint, that goes without saying, given the interest of our readers, and particularly after the major event that, everyone agrees, was September 11?

A. How do you want me to answer such questions without laughing, seriously? You say "*in* Sam Weber." Now without ever managing to do so, above all not "in a nutshell"[10] (what a word, don't you think? I believe it to be dangerously comical, as any *quiproquo*), I would like to be able to say what the name of Sam Weber has strangely inscribed within me, in me, at the heart of my life and of my work for decades. And you must know in the first place that Weber is the one who wrote on the French word *chez* immortal pages that I will neither try to mimic nor to summarize. Once again I refer you and your readers to them.[11] There you would find, among other things, and always through the elegance of an inimitable irony, a cartography of ongoing path-breaking, all the most original and the most typical trajectories of Weberianism: the logic of *ambivalence* (which is always relayed by that of unstable, antithetical, undecidable significations of the uncanny[12] or the *unheimlich*, starting from but also beyond what Freud says about it), the taking into account of *place*—both the place of the actor and that of the spectator—the meditation on the event as that which "takes place,"[13] takes the place, takes up, thus repeats the place-of (thus re-places and replaces, too, substitutes, supplants and supplements), in short on "place" as placing in general. *Chez*, isn't that so, the word always announces the place, the location, the locality, the habitation, the cabin [=*case*], the *casa*, the domicile, proximity, property, emplacement—with, taking the place of place, the prosthetic and repetitive replacement, which is thus also never far removed from the technical–the *topos*, spacing, point of view, the relation to, etc. Hence the incessant meditation on theatricality and on the paradoxical logic of the repetition that is played out there, on the stage in general, in the media (Weber has extremely well analyzed their decisive role in this "September 11" which you, like everyone else—like all journalists—want to place at the beginning of our conversation). This immense treatise on *chez* (an untranslatable word) is found in *Institution and Interpretation*.[14]

*Institution and Interpretation*, moreover, be it said too quickly, parenthetically as it were . . .

Q. More parentheses! When will you start tackling our subject frontally? You want to ridicule us, my readers and myself.

A. No, this is no laughing matter. I am dealing with the subject. *Institution and Interpretation*, that could be the title or the subtitle of all that Weber will have problematized, that is to say, deconstructed through all his books. It is always for him a matter of submitting the interpretation *of* interpretation to the preliminary analysis of its institutionalization, of its institutional setting in place and its staging. Here one must understand *interpretation* in all the senses of the term: the hermeneutical sense (Schleiermachian or Gadamerian), the "Nietzschean" sense, the "Freudian" sense, the "Heideggerian" sense, but also the instrumental sense, be it the work of interpretation of musicians, opera singers or theater or cinema actors. There is no interpretation that is not as though in advance taken and determined by its institutionalization, by the position or disposition of its institutional—and thus technical—apparatus. For there is no *institution*, *nomos*, or *thèsis*, there is nothing thetic or thematic, thus *positional*, without *tekhnè*, there is no "natural," physical interpretation, at least in the arrived at, and historically belated sense of *physis*. This is the whole question of deconstruction as far as technics is concerned, Weber has done so much to guide us and help us explore this problematic. That irreducible link between interpretation and institution is exemplarily valid, I repeat, for psychoanalytic interpretation, for interpretation as the reading of philosophical or literary texts, in the university or elsewhere, for theatrical, cinematographic or musical interpretation, for the interpretation of facts and historical events by historiographical machines or, there we are, by apparatuses in the media.

Since you are interested in the question of technics, institution is precisely the place or the moment, the advent of the becoming-technical of invention, a certain repetitive instrumentalization of intention or of the supposed origin. Does it come *after* the origin? Does it repeat it? Is this institutional technologization second or secondary, as it is often believed? Does it come to repeat and double what has already taken place without it? Or is it, as I would be tempted to believe, like Sam Weber doubtless, the co-originary double, the very condition, the strange ("uncanny," *unheimlich*) setting to work of the instituting event? Here is perhaps what must be debated. Here is what is constantly and luminously in debate in Weber's entire oeuvre, everywhere where he speaks of repetition, iterability, of the strangeness of the "*uncanny*" or the *Unheimliche*,[15] that is to say, almost everywhere. If deconstruction always comprises an interpretive strategy, if it is also a tireless interpretation of interpretation, by the same token it lets itself be marked by a certain technicity, right *from the origin*. It is technical and coextensive to any question of technics, even though it is not merely *one* simple technique, a knowhow, in the sense of a teachable method or transmittable rules of procedures; and even if it is also an attempt to reinterpret the great question of technics. In that sense, deconstruction is never wild or natural, foreign to any institution, even though it is as well and most of the time a counter-institution; Weber has thought it extremely well, he has formulated and set it to work in thousands of ways. We will have to return to it.

Q. Couldn't you spare us all these "we will have to return to it"? There is not much time and space left. Say what you want to say without delay and without detour. My readers, and even my editor . . .

A. No, *vous voulez rire*, you must be joking, mustn't you, you want me to answer without detour while you ask me impossible questions on the subject of someone who counts among those, quite rare on the whole, who almost throughout adult life have helped me, as Kant would put it, to "orientate" myself "in thinking"—and in the world. You know, I have always felt alone, isolated, painfully but jealously solitary. In "life" and in "thinking." Like everybody, you would say laughingly. Yes, but I am I and I alone can bear witness to it. The more one suffers thus, the more one sharpens this suffering, the more one needs, in order to *orient oneself*, exceptional friends who testify to this testimony and whose vigilance watches over your vagaries, sometimes to avoid them, sometimes to cultivate them. For this isolation blinds one at times, and it is always very risky. Sam Weber is for me one of those rare friends. In *Was heisst sich im Denken orientieren*—I don't know if your readers know this—Kant rightly asks himself: "But how much and how correctly (*mit welcher Richtigkeit*) would we think if we did not think, so to speak, in community with others (*gleichsam im Gemeinschaft mit andern*) to whom we communicate our thoughts and who communicate their thoughts to us!"[16]

For someone as spontaneously allergic as I am to any "community," I find the trust and gratitude that have right away and so enduringly tied me, in so many areas, countries, languages, to the thought and to the person of Sam Weber, to be incommensurable, absolutely incomparable. You know, one always writes a little under surveillance, that is to say, for the few who observe you within yourself, in you, where they are lodged, where they have their own place, from which they are ready to unmask you, to point out your weaknesses, to encourage you or discourage you. Whether one wants it or not, one writes for them, one works with them, one speaks and one thinks *in their place* (*chez eux*), in order to fulfill their expectations, doubtless, but also at times so as to try to deceive their scrutiny and surprise them. They are more than spectators-readers; they are the actors, and even the true signatories of what we risk in writing. One watches while the other sleeps or dreams, and in the end one no longer knows who does what. One no longer knows who signs. Sam Weber has been for me, for decades, one of these very rare guardians. (I wonder how you are going to translate the word *bienveilleur*, which says both "benevolent goodness" and "impeccable vigilance.") I say "watch" and watch well, *veiller* and *bien veiller*, but one should not here trust the authority of the vigilant consciousness of the *ego cogito* over what we call "thinking." The secret economy of a friendship in thinking, like the one I speak of here, passes, I believe, by way of the day and the night dream. By way of the unconscious, if you prefer. Whatever watches in an uncanny, *unheimlich* way over my work,[17] as well as over whatever I might think (of the world, of philosophy, of politics, etc.), what surveys me with an intransigent benevolence, is not only the vigilance of certain friends such as Sam Weber. It is not only their dream; it is also, first and foremost, what they think of and do with *the dream*.

Thus, to mention only that example and orient myself toward what for Weber, from the very start, connects the motifs of the dream, of deconstruction (of sense, meaning),[18] and of technics, I refer you to the beginning of the magnificent chapter titled "The Meaning of the Thallus" in a book to which one must always return, *The Legend of Freud* (which was, I recall once again, published in German in 1979, which is always highly significant for understanding Weber's singular path between languages, cultures, and traditions). From the start Weber recalls that *Die Traumdeutung*, *The Interpretation of Dreams*, as it is translated, is for Freud a "technique" (*Technik*) to get at a "meaningful structure" (*ein sinnvolles Gebilde*; the word *Gebilde*, just as *Gestalt*, could also serve as a guiding thread throughout Weber's oeuvre). Now if it resembles a "method of interpretation," this "technique" guides us toward phenomena full of meaning ("meaningful"), to be sure, but in which what constitutes their essence is not their "meaning" or their "semantic content" but the "particular form" that the dream-work impresses on those dream-thoughts.[19] For dreams, Freud says, are a particular "form" of thinking. Hence a technique of interpretation that does not essentially concern the presentation or representation (*Darstellung* or *Vorstellung*) of meaning any more, but rather what Weber calls a certain way of de-presenting, of dis-figuring or dis-locating, of changing place, of dis-placing placement (*Ent-stellen*).[20] Here is where technics and deconstruction are allied so as to displace the question of the presence, of the presentation or the representation of meaning by carrying them, from placement to placement, from setting in place to putting in place (*Stellen*, *Darstellung*, *Vorstellung*) toward a dislocation (*Ent-stellung*). This simple and brief indication suffices to explain the interest that Weber evinces, through all this German lexis on which he has written a lot, for the question of technics that Heidegger will organize around the *Gestell*. If you reread closely "The Meaning of the Thallus" (we can't do it here), you will see why, according to Weber, "Freud's dream here is of a sphere beyond—*jenseits*—interpretation . . ."[21] Not that one must "transcend hermeneutic questions as such." It is only a matter of "widening and transforming their scope."[22] Now this is made necessary, once again, by a "place" (*eine Stelle*, Freud says) that must be left in the night. It is the canonical and obscure *place* of the dream-navel (*der Nabel des Traums*). We have all turned around that place. As far as I am concerned, I do not want to come back to it here. In the text that I once dedicated to that passage and which I take the liberty of pointing out to you,[23] I already referred at length to *The Legend of Freud*, which I would like here, without retracing my steps, to approach from another point of view, that of place, precisely, and what links place to technics, in order to follow, at least along the dots (for a continuous and saturating reading would require two hundred pages) the original movement of Weber's demonstration, of Weber's writing (of his deconstructive technique, if you will). It leads him first through a path of rare complexity and exceptional refinement toward putting into question an *interpretive technique* and its presuppositions, those of Freud but also those of Lacan. This technique keeps as ultimate destinations (1) the hermeneutic determination of a *meaning*; (2) the topological determination of a *central place*; (3) the substantive determination, the nomination of this semantic center, which it is a matter, then, by naming, by substantivizing it, to begin to substantialize and even to subjectivize. It is easier to move from substantive to substance and to subject. At issue, then, are the place and the center, meaning and the name. Clarifying what he said about it in the first German version, Weber recalls that for Lacan the whole interpretation of "everything in the unconscious that unfolds" "is diffused like a mycelium—as Freud says in regard to the dream—*around a central point*." It is always a question of "the subject qua indeterminate."[24] Weber notes with a smile that if for Freud and Lacan what counted was to see the meaning of the dream *erecting itself*, "*rising* majestically,"[25] surging forth out of its mycelium, the meaning of the phallus—then "Lacan's Baedeker might suffice." The ironic allusion to the Baedeker hides a quotation of Freud. He had declared he scorned being satisfied with Baedekers. In the present instance, it is against both Freud and Lacan that Weber mocks the Baedeker, for nothing permits us to conclude that the navel of dreams is either "central" or "empty." On the contrary, it seems "curiously full, oversaturated, and if it presents difficulties to our understanding, it is because it contains too much rather than too little. In short, whatever else it may be, a *Knäuel* [*navel*] is not simply a béance (or an *Abgrund*). And, above all, nothing permits us to assert that the chains and trains, strands and snares that compose the meshwork of the 'navel' are neatly 'diffused' *around* a center."

If I draw your attention to that passage, it is not merely because of the importance, in effect considerable, of the theoretical stake, of the content of interpretations, of the meaning of the dream and of the techniques of interpretation that it calls for. Not only because, at this point, Weber opposes in an interesting and convincing way Freud to Lacan: "If Freud's description of this navel differs from Lacan's, it is precisely because it brings into movement just what Lacan seeks to arrest: the very notion and place of a *center*."[26] No, it is at least for *two other reasons*.

A.[27] The first is that we have here one of the brilliant examples (there would be others, but we must choose) of the Weberian technique, of his inimitable signature, of his deconstructive style as much as his argumentative writing style. The operation puts to work an extreme attention to the letter of several languages, through a passage that translates but also invents in the very transfer. This transfer generates an idiom between German, French, and English (just as at this passage of borders that keeps the memory of our first meeting in *quiproquo* at the Berlin airport in 1968 remind me that I need to tell it to you at some point). Thus the English verb "straddle" will be invested with a unique theoretico-poetical mission. At first glance, Weber advances it as the mere translation of *aufsetzen*. Freud's navel neither includes nor comprises nor again contains any center. It straddles the unknown, "dem Unerkannten aufsitzt." Once he has translated, in an irreproachable manner, *aufsetzen* by "straddle," Weber marvelously explores and exploits all the resources of the English word, its history, its polysemy, the different registers of its rich tropology. In the two pages, the reading of which I recommend to you (one should quote everything; I cannot do so here), he analyzes the seven meanings given by the *OED*, then recalls that the verb derives from "stride." Then he emphasizes, in an incontestable manner, both the notion of progressive movement and the apparently opposed notion of arrested movement,[28] namely, of the "position" that matters so much to him. But equally and above all, guided by the conclusion of the *OED* entry, the notion of "divaricate" which will both confirm and relaunch the contradiction or the disseminal and uncanny divergence between movement and immobility.[29] It moves and it does not move; it moves in place. Weber quotes again the *OED*: "*Divaricate*: (fr. Dis- +*varicare*, f. *various*, straddling). 1. *intr*. To stretch or spread apart; to branch off or diverge; in *Bot*. and *Zool*. to diverge widely. 2. trans. To stretch or open wide apart or asunder. 3. To cause or spread out in different directions."

Q. Doesn't that way of reading by translating, by traveling, by transferring, by analyzing contradictory, diverging, uncanny meanings,[30] by displacing things in place, from digression to digression, from divergence to divergence, describe above all, mirror-like, what you were calling the Weberian operation? And yourself, at this moment . . .

A. *Vous voulez rire*, you must be joking, no? But it is true that I am interested, following Weber's footsteps, in the proximity of *laughing* to *reading*, *rire* and *lire*. I would like to go as far as possible in this direction but I don't know whether your newspaper will give us the time and the space. In French the difference between *lire* and *rire* amounts to the mere replacement of one letter and that will remain untranslatable to you. Here I am reading, I am trying to read with you and to help your readers share my admiration. I would like to lead them patiently toward the moment when they are able, if they so wish, to think of laughing. And think, according to Weber, the place and the overflowing of laughter, of what is called in French the *fou rire*, laughing like mad (beyond the sense and the will, perhaps beyond economy and the very economy of expenditure) or splitting one's sides with laughter. Why "split"? What of this splitting of the body?

But if you interrupt me all the time, we won't get anywhere; your newspaper won't give us the necessary space. So from this strange straddling of meanings (*straddling*[31] is also, is first what happens between, above, and beyond all those meanings clustered around the same word), Weber is going to extirpate in an apparently magical but impeccably rational way a whole ramified series of significations (I let you read: the body, the legs that bestride and straddle with a wholly other signification and with a wholly other function than those with which I had played in French between English legs and *legs*, the French legacy in *The Postcard*, around *Beyond the Pleasure Principle*), the position ("equivocal position"), investment ("occupation," *Besetzung*), imposition and imposture. "Does not such a compromise . . . have to up the ante to stay in the game?" The outbidding scene, and the logic of "upping the ante" is everywhere in Weber. Freud's legs stand thus on both sides of an "untenable alternative," and "straddle" straddles all of the meanings of the *OED*, the so-called primal scene of which would be in sum but a graphic figuration. It is then a matter of interpreting a language of Freud, whose *Bildersprache* does not so much present and represent meaning as dis-place and de-present it (*entstellt*). The verb *ent-stellt* disorients any hermeneutics that would consist in making meaning present, and on the other hand, in the movement or the belonging of the lexis of the (notoriously Heideggerian) question of the technique of *Gestell* (*Vorstellung*, *Darstellung*, *Gestell*), etc., it refers first of all to the place (*Stelle*), to what is put or held in place. And indeed, Weber explains to us, Freud is not content with designating the dream-navel as the "place" (*Stelle*) where the dream straddles the unknown. He describes that unknown, or rather what emerges from it, the dream-wish surging forth "as the mushroom out of its mycelium." It is then, I refer you to it again, that the thallus replaces the phallus (one letter to be substituted suffices again) to displace and replace the Lacanian logic of the phallus and what the Lacanian reading "would like to forget: that the dream-navel cannot be reduced to a question of the phallus, of the *béance,* split or absent center of a subject, for one simple reason: the thallus."[32]

Once more, the main stake is topo- or khoragraphic; the question is that of the place: "The dream-navel, as it is inscribed and described in Freud's text, points us in another direction, less visible, but not invisible either. The question raised here concerns the *site* of the navel, the place on which the dream-wish rises. The question, in short, is that of the *signification of the thallus*." Having recourse one last time to the *OED*, Weber insists that the definition of the thallus consists only of negations (it is like an apophantic theology) and underscores the absence of root ("true roots are absent"). No wonder, then, that it is so difficult to "see more radically," as Lacan promises.

Of all that, that I must once more let you reread closely, Weber draws two conclusions that matter to us. For they must indeed speak to the concern in your question regarding deconstruction and technics. One is that we touch here the *limits of interpretation*. We have to change the very concept of meaning that commands hermeneutics. The question is not to renounce interpretation but to reinterpret the limits of interpretation and, in order to do so, to stand upon them on the two sides of the limit and to straddle them somehow (moreover the place is a system of limits and delimitations). By so doing, the point is to affect *the very concept of meaning* with a transformation that dis-places it, that is to say, that changes its relation to place and thus to what *imposes* a place on it and displaces it. This is where the deconstructive technique of interpretation concerns precisely the articulation between technics and spacing, technics and *taking place*,[33] between *tekhnè* and place. We are dealing with a topo- or rather a khora-technology. "For, if at the limits of interpretation we discover, not the abyss of an absent center, but a navel and a thallus, the very notion of *meaning* has begun to change before our eyes—particularly if our eyes are directed at Freud's text."[34]

At that point, second conclusion, a dramatic turn, a coup de théâtre happens, or the operation of the properly Weberian opus or opera. It will orchestrate at the same time the concert of the transferential multiplicity of linguistic idioms (at least three languages, as always, which capitalize on their respective plays on words), the power of denomination, and, if you want to have a laugh, *si vous voulez rire*, the essential experience of laughter (good or bad joke).[35] The word translated as "straddle" has another meaning in German: *Jemanden* or *etwas aufsitzen* can signify "to be duped or deluded by someone or something. By the unknown (*das Unerkannte: dem Unerkannten aufsitzt*), for instance," Weber notes, adding without transition, "Or by the terms introduced by Lacan: for instance, that of the *Nom du Père* (Name-of-the-Father), which, he suggested, must also be read as: *Les non-dupes errent* (the non dupes err). Yet if this error must be understood as constitutive of the very gesture of denomination itself, then this cannot be without consequences for every form of discourse that seeks to articulate truth by means of naming: be it that of Freud, of Lacan, or of this text itself."

Weber does not exonerate his own text; he does not except his own denomination; he does not put it outside the game. For at stake are play and joke,[36] deception and imposition in assigning the name, in the replacement, for example, of phallus by thallus. This is where Weber's laughter breaks out. Discreetly, as in a Jewish joke, in making fun of himself he tells the truth about all. But the play that makes one laugh, a bad joke traps all effort to articulate meaning. Any interpretation has as origin and end the violence of a thesis, that is, of a position which, setting itself up, imposes itself upon you and dupes you. Imposition is an imposture; such is the technique of interpretation that must be deconstructed (by laughing at laughter, at the bad joke).[37] It deconstructs not a revelation of meaning but through the counterimposition of a countertechnique.[38] Note the lexis chosen by Weber; it is a variation on thesis (*Setzung*) (and as soon as there is *thesis*, there is *tekhnè*), on the thetic position, which, as one says in French, imposes, makes an impression, and on whatever in itself places or places itself: posture, imposture, imposition. The word "play" signals here both toward the play (*le jeu*), the joke, even the bad joke that deludes,—and toward theater. When you've read these lines, you will have understood why the question of laughter shakes Sam Weber's body and corpus, particularly when he wonders about laughter in Freud, about its economy and its aneconomy:

> From this vantage point, the meaning of the thallus begins to appear to be—or rather to play—a very bad joke on all attempts to articulate meaning. For the ramifications of Freud's description of the dream-navel suggest that interpretation originates and ends in a kind of calculated deception: in a posture necessarily, and structurally, an imposture, and perhaps also an imposition.
>
> In any case, it is beyond doubt that such questions were what impelled Freud to move—walking, striding, straddling—from his interpretation of dreams, the royal road to the unconscious, to the less regal realm of jokes. As we shall see, this was, and is, no laughing matter.[39]

A magnificent formulation. It returns at the end of the following chapter, precisely titled "The Joke: Child's Play." There again (in a superb chapter that I will let you read), we find again twice the same gesture, whether about the play or about Lacan:

1. The field of "play" or of wit or the "joke," the passage or the derivation from one to the other is not circumscribable, it encompasses and overflows theory, it is a metatheory that teaches us that there is no metatheory that is not laughable. The theory of "play" and of "joke" is still an *effect* of play and an *effort*, always ineffectual, to master the play and the play on words.[40] The latter always gets the better of theory (and then I tell myself: it is that shared conviction that perhaps makes us always laugh together, Sam and I). Listen to him: "For such play is designed to provide the ground and kernel not merely of the joke alone, but also of the theory that seeks to comprehend and to master the joke. This theory, we recall, seeks to succeed where others—Freud's predecessors—have failed: to organize the 'disjecta membra' of the joke into an organic whole. But the psychogenetic derivation of the joke from play is still lacking what is perhaps the most characteristic aspect of the joke. And that, we repeat, is no laughing matter."[41] The repetition of this formulation in the English version well indicates that the problem is serious.[42] It

does not lend itself to laughter. But its seriousness is not exterior or superior to laughter. It concerns the passage from play to *Witz* and the failure of a psychogenetic derivation between one and the other. It is possible to follow throughout Weber's oeuvre the direct or indirect attempt to account, without laughing and while laughing, for that failure.

2. We find here again, at this end of the chapter, a new reservation on the subject of the couple of concepts on which Lacan has for so long founded his discourse as well as his technique, namely the oppositional distinction between the Symbolic and the Imaginary. It is about the *fort! Da*: "Indeed, if this other seems destined to replace the absent mother and to revenge the child, it would provide us with yet another reason for regarding the Symbolic as a lure of the Imaginary, as the discursive continuation of the ambivalent strategy of narcissism."[43]

Q. I have some trouble following you, I admit. On two occasions, you have insisted on these reservations as far as Lacan is concerned, but I was asked, in my newspaper, to interrogate you on certain reservations—prudent, it is true, but insistent—from Weber on the subject of your own reservations on the subject of Lacan. For instance, I am told, in *Mass Mediauras*,[44] on two occasions, in a discourse that is indeed nuanced and complicated, Weber seems not to exclude that your reading of the "Seminar on 'The Purloined Letter'" may be contested, and even refuted. He even insists, from one page to the next, in spite of "perhapses" that leave much to think about, "Derrida 'reads' Lacan's text, even if one may well contest that reading." And further: "Derrida 'frames' Lacan (in all senses) by demonstrating—and it is a demonstration that *can* be discussed, contested, perhaps even refuted—*how* and *where* Lacan's 'Seminar on the *Purloined Letter*' ignores or avoids the question of the frame, and above all, of its own frame, the enabling condition of its own authority."

A. He is quite right and all the *perhapses* wonderfully complicate the deal. This is not the place to discuss those texts that are too difficult for an interview. Not only do I believe that Weber is right, but do not forget that I admitted myself, within the play of that reading, that Lacan was right, on more than one occasion, and recalled that he was on the side of reason itself. "Reason will always be right [aura raison]. By itself."[45] Which means both spontaneously, by itself, and by overcoming itself, by vanquishing itself, by being stronger than itself, which "avoir raison de," getting the better of, means in French. All that is therefore a chessboard too complicated for an interview. From the point of view of deconstruction, at first glance, the first wrong, the first naivety, is to pretend to "be right," "avoir raison." I recall that the book itself, *The Postcard*, which is also, through and through, from its pseudo *Envois*, the play of an abyssal fiction, starts with these words: "Yes you were right." What happens when one admits that the other is right? The answer to that question is anything but simple and rational. But let's leave it at that, I am not here to discuss my texts. It is Sam Weber that we need to talk about. Singularly. But before coming back to it, I would like to say a word about the terrible question of the debt; of the insolvable question of the insolvent debt. Not from the point of view of this powerful text titled "The Debts of Deconstruction and Other, Related Assumptions,"[46] but of a more recent passage, in *Mass Mediauras*, precisely the one in which he does not exclude that my reading of Lacan might be contestable—a friendly, polite way of saying that clearly gives to understand that that reading may and must indeed be contested ("Derrida 'reads' Lacan's text; even if one may well contest that reading"). What interests me most in this very equivocal passage is the reminder, in the form of an avowal so to speak, that any text is indebted, and even to the one it criticizes and contests. I would not be any less indebted to Lacan when I contest him than Sam Weber when he contests my contestation; and I will not even mention Lacan's debts, not only to thinkers of earlier generations, from Plato to Freud and Heidegger, but with regard to young people, much younger than he . . . Let's leave it at that (and even, Weber will insist in an irresistible crescendo, my contestation that may itself be "discussed, contested, even refuted"). In this passage that I will quote at length, Weber explains why, rightly so, and how not to admit that he is right, psychoanalysis cannot not become an institution, whereas deconstruction neither can nor must become an institution: ". . . I am not certain that it is either possible, necessary or desirable that deconstruction become an institution. There is enormous pressure to move deconstruction in this direction, if only because it is, to a large extent, situated within areas–such as that of the university—where legitimacy is often measured in terms of institutional standing. The best way to resist such pressure is to keep transforming what is called deconstruction, never allowing it, nor its practitioners to rest on their accumulated laurels (real or not). . . . Deconstruction 'is' the movement of this undoing, which is why it cannot and should never hope to become an institution, as psychoanalysis has tried–with differing success—to be."

> **Go from there to debt in mediauras p. 227, then**
> **then come back to debt and to Mass . . . 63–64**
> **debt impossible to repay I and I. p. 58[47]**

Therefore this singularity paralyzes me when faced with the curious questions you ask me. This is why I cannot take them seriously and ask you if "you're joking." A first temptation would be to respond by orienting myself toward what *orients*, precisely, Sam Weber's thought as well as his body, toward his privileged care for topography, toward his constantly renewed interest for the site, the *orientation* of the body and the gaze, between the left and the right (of which Kant speaks so well and of which he recalls that they *situate* my so-called body proper, in an irreducibly sensible and preconceptual fashion), toward topo*logy*, the discourse on location and the location of discourse, toward the place, more precisely the taking-place as event, toward the emplacement, the site of the analytic situation, the site of the dramatico-theatrical situation, of the position facing the stage, the cinema, or the television screen. The original setting to work of deconstruction by Weber has chosen its proper place in these places. For instance, watch what he teaches us about the "age of the media," in his idiom. He does it moreover by signing a new idiomatic lexicality. But, another remarkable trait, Weber precisely invents *his* idiom by traversing several languages at once; he *plays* (for he always plays) between several languages. He travels from one language to the other, not in order to discover there blissful, virgin, intact islands between continents but in order to call forth from the abyss still unknown linguistic landscapes, *unheimlich* archipelagoes, semantic straits and isthmuses propitious to explorations but also to the most unheard-of contaminations.

I will take one example, but it could be multiplied. It is a matter of both Weber's "technique," his *way of doing things*, and of telecommunicational technics, of TV, of TV *set*,[48] of event, taking-place, of deconstruction, and, above all, of place. Thus see what happens, what occurs, what "comes to pass," as he says in such an untranslatable fashion, on pages 6 and 7 of his introduction to *Mass Mediauras*, especially around the lexis of "set, setting," the wealth and superabundant ambiguity of which as well as the resistance to translation Weber sets to work, in place, on the stage. The subtitle of that book indissociably juxtaposes three concepts that form the most specific and the most "consistent" network of Weberian deconstruction: *Form, Technics, Media*. Technics (technology, techniques, these two different concepts being combined in an interesting fashion in the English "technics") is also what combines media and the concept of "form," indeed of a "form" in a paradoxically Kantian sense. For it is precisely this concept of "form" that installs, sets the stage of the whole book, but a book precisely dedicated to the setting in which the media unfold.[49] Now Weber recalls the Kantian tradition of this concept of form: not in the place where Kant succeeds in his effort to elaborate its problematic but where he fails and in the end relinquishes it to its own defeat, to its irresistible deconstruction, there where thinking presses around what remains precisely in construction, "undone."

For a deconstruction is neither decided nor calculated through and through, starting from a willed technical project. It is ongoing, it occurs, it takes place, it is done there where it gets undone or remains incomplete. It entails technique, to be sure, but this technique does not master, it is not totally mastered; it is situated, affected, as much as situating and active. Here then is the promised example of Weberian argumentation: an abyssal procedure, a powerfully formalizing stylistic and rhetorical turn, a play, too, a laughter of thinking that I find typical of deconstructive writing, of Weber's "technique." I say abyssal *there where*, in that *place* where the *setting in place*, the *emplacement*, the *localization* of the *taking-place* is both staged and "en abyme," begins ( "sets") to install ("setting") its machinic and local apparatus ("set, 'setting"): "For without the unity of place, the unity of the subject becomes difficult to conceive. It is the function of esthetic theory, as it is developed by Kant, to help secure this ever more problematical unity of place by introducing the no less problematical notion of form. That Kant's effort, in the *Third Critique*, is more significant in coming undone than in succeeding 'sets' the scene for the following essays, which explore the unraveling of form as the 'setting' for the rise of the media."[50] Weber cites and poses the absolute question of place, that of orientation itself: not "What is orientation in thinking?" but this time "Where in the World are We?" A quotation from a title read in the media, thus, in the *L.A. Times* at the time of an earthquake. This title in the form of a question quoted from a media announces then developments to come on "Television: Set and Screen." The word "set" seems already difficult to translate in the wealth of its overdeterminations. In that sense and to that extent, one could say that its "deconstructive" force resists any translating machine, thus any technique that would only be a technique. Weber starts from the GPS (Global Positioning System). The GPS is a technical apparatus allowing all movement on earth to be localized with a precision unequalled up to now. **I read quote at length p. 6/7.**

"Vous voulez rire": a strange expression, don't you think? Do you understand it well? Let's dwell a moment on these three words. "Vous voulez rire,"—an expression quite idiomatic in French, I believe. Not just a verbal expression but a gesture that is quite idiomatic. That gesture, then, is part of a "pragmatics" that would take into account a "sociolinguistic gesture" that is quite difficult to translate. With this we are already in "deconstruction" as the experience of impossible translation and of "more than one language." (What is unique and precious for me, among other things, in all that I owe Sam Weber, is to live in more than one linguistic culture at once, the German, English, and French; he is "chez lui—at home" everywhere, and *I* am learning to follow him . . .). "You're kidding" or "Who are you kidding?" is very close to "vous voulez rire" as a social gesture (which is to say, from a pragmatic point of view).[51] But it is not exactly the same thing. The explicit reference to *laughter* and above all to the "will" is missing. In German, *dass ich nicht lache*, the will of the other is not named either. "Vous voulez rire," in some very determined situations, is a retort used to denounce and refuse a proposition that one does not *want* to take seriously. One declares thus by the same token that one neither *can* nor *must* take it seriously (come on, I neither want nor can take seriously the cascade of questions and answers you pose to me). One has even the duty of denouncing and even of rejecting with irony a proposition that is excessive and out of place. Thus it is—you see the paradox already—an ironic, a somewhat derisive way of refusing to answer on the pretext that the very question, the demand or the proposition is too comical. Intentionally or not (another difficulty!). By laughing coldly, by pretending to be serious, but drily, *tongue in cheek*, one asks the other if he is serious and if he is not laughing or joking; if all this is not "a joke." (I note quickly in passing, already, but we will have the opportunity of coming back to it, that "joke," *Witz*, etc., could be the title of an immense question, the network of which invades in depth but also as a spin, a rhizome, an irresistible parasite [laughter is also irresistible], in all its dimensions [political, historical, theatrical, literary, and above all psychoanalytical], with an imperturbable but also ironic constancy, Sam Weber's entire oeuvre and thinking, leaving nothing intact there and forcing us to shake everything up from top to bottom). What is laughter, "joke," wit, etc.?[52] Where does it come from? Why and how does it come to pass? What is this strange event? Is laughter proper to man? Can one do without the unconscious in order to account for it? What does it signify as far as social ties and intersubjectivity are concerned, etc.? Here are questions that Sam Weber will have developed better than anyone. He will have inaugurated a new elaboration of them. And he **has showed us that this question strangely deranged, defamiliarized everything (*unheimlich*). I would like to show, if you have the patience to listen to me, the way in which this question of the event of laughter is inseparable from those that** interest your readers, as you tell me, for example between "deconstruction and technics." But some detours will be necessary. By telling you "vous voulez rire," I suspect you, I feign to suspect you, for instance, of not being serious and of posing me one or several impossible questions "to have a laugh" or to "caricature" a serious interview, to laugh at me, at your colleagues, or your public, or whomever. Aren't you having a laugh at everyone's expense? And, perhaps, hence my own irony, without knowing it, without having the faintest idea.

For you see, the one who, for a laugh or by pretending to laugh, tells the other, as I've just done, "vous voulez rire," knows full well that the other is not laughing. And that's the whole problem. One laughingly accuses, but one accuses the other of not being serious, of laughing therefore, but without knowing how to laugh or without knowing that he laughs. It is diabolically complicated, don't you think? How are we going to continue? This is why the expression is interesting (you see, I'm beginning to go on too long, I'm drifting, I'm going to make you waste your time, and I'm misleading your readers, taking them down remote paths). How could one *want or will to laugh, vouloir rire*? Decide to laugh? What is the relation between the voluntary decision (consciousness and intention, etc.) and laughter, explosive laughter, laughing like mad? The philosophical friendship that binds me to Sam Weber, our friendship *tout court*: I will dare say that it belongs to the experience of that question and first of all to the shared experience of that very laughter, of that breaking out in mad laughter. Involuntary, undecided, even unconscious. Hence its strength and its intensity, hence its fidelity. Fidelity can only be unconscious.

Q. Precisely, I wanted to ask you when and in what circumstances you met Sam Weber. Couldn't you answer me with facts or short quotations rather than with digressions? Especially by orienting things toward "deconstruction and technics," toward things political and above all toward September 11, which was, I believe, a major event. You know, my readers would like above all to know how you met Sam Weber. Rumors abound on that subject . . .

A. All right, I'll try, I'll tell you. But first, since you want quotations, I'll give you one. But once again an argued detour is required. Saying that laughter is not decided does not mean that there is on the one hand laughter, and, on the other, decision, but perhaps that decision itself cannot be decided. That's serious. Do you have any idea what *decision* means? And the essence of laughter? In any case, if there's one thing I will not endorse from Bataille, it's the idea that laughter is sovereign, if that word keeps a tie with its traditional sense. And if the word is no longer attached in this way, why then still keep it?

Q. These are questions that are not dealt with in journalism school; at least not in the one to which, as soon as I had to leave university . . .

A. Me neither, I don't deal with them, but I do believe I know what others think they know when they use those words (decision, laughter), and I cling to that in order to pose questions. This after all is perhaps what deconstruction is, and it can become a technique: doing as if one believed one knew what others believe they know on such and such a subject, and not believing in what one believes to know about what others believe they know. At first, it is not a technique, but it can become a technique. For that one must know how to laugh. But what does knowing how to laugh mean? Can laughter be learned? Is it taught like a technique? Like a knowledge or a science? No, isn't it? Laughter is perhaps the only thing that is not taught; and that remains fundamentally foreign to teaching as such. Laughter only takes place a single time each time, every time one time, unpredictably, like an event that one doesn't see coming. So how could it become a technique, here's the problem. Do you follow me?

Q. Yes, now yes. At least I believe so.

A. Then what would happen if a decision was no more decided than laughter—or tears or laughing till crying, and you would need to link these two questions. And to tie them to the great question of calculation, and therefore technics; for what is not decided is what is not calculated. What is not calculated seems to exceed, in a single instant, technics itself, do you follow, for we are indeed speaking of "deconstruction and technics," as you seem to wish. Let's make then this hypothesis: *a decision is not decided* (another difficulty of the idiom that you'll have trouble translating: a decision is decided or is not decided, means two things: (1) that *one* decides [or not], that decision decides, or yet again, (2) something that can only be said in French, as far as I know, that the decision decides *itself*, reflexively, that it decides *itself* by itself or not, that it decides to decide, to decide *itself*, through a sort of will to will, etc. Therefore if a decision is no more decided than laughter [or tears or laughing till crying], what remains of the most powerful concept of the most powerful tradition in Western thought, one which, with the connected and indissociable concepts of will, ego, consciousness, intention, responsibility, etc., seems to found ethics, politics, law, and even philosophy[53]) . . . Perhaps one is surprised by it, passively, as by an event that arrives to you. The decision arrives to you. Here is a paradoxical and revolutionary proposition. A little comical, even. If someone came and told you: I was surprised by my decision, you would be tempted to burst into laughter, and your readers as well. Well then, if you follow Weber when he analyzes laughter or laughing like mad——since the very beginning but particularly in *Mass Mediauras*, I bet that you will have one of the best guiding threads of his thinking. For instance, to start with, your readers should turn to **the following passage from "Catching Up with the Past,"**

Thank you. Let's try, but I sense that it will be difficult for me to improvise. You want us, then, to speak of Sam Weber, of deconstruction, of technics, all that, right. If I try to control in public the admiring effusion of my gratitude to Sam Weber, I'm immediately possessed by a double question. It could have the following form: *Who* is Sam Weber, and *what* is the essence of the political? Obviously these are two distinct and even highly heterogeneous questions. One concerns someone; the other, the essence of something. Now I would like not only to link them together, as those of two equally singular figures, one singular, the other general; one rather private, if not secret, the other public and commonly shared. But both *for me*. Who is Sam Weber for me, as that "who," "the one who" tells me something of the essence of the political. I would like above all to open a place for the history, for the very historicity of this double question. What relation does it entertain with "deconstruction," "technics," all that, all those things that you want to talk about? That question, the historicity of the question of the essence of the political, inasmuch as it is tied to the singular history of a singularity, I do not ask it concerning *the subject of* Sam Weber, but I tell myself that I would like to pose it to him, one day, for him to answer it, himself, in his name. I do say "in his name." I cannot speak in his name, of course; and yet it is what I am about to do, just as every time one does it, one takes the risk, and laughing and by laughing at one's own denial, one allows oneself to say what someone else thinks of something. When I say, "Plato thinks that . . ." or "Plato says that . . . ," I begin ridiculing myself by allowing myself to speak in his name while denying it, by alleging some impossible knowledge about that subject. It is comical, and I am sure that I say something stupid when saying, "Plato thinks that . . ." . . . Since I know well that he will have said better in his name all that I could attempt to say and interpret in his name, let's say that I would speak above all of his name, his proper name, his own and so singular given name, and above all of his signature.

Q. I have difficulty understanding what you're saying, and I'm sure that my readers, not all of whom have spent time at university, as I did, will not understand anything. Couldn't you explain yourself in a little more concrete, pedagogical, intelligible way? A little more communicative?

A. No, do not ever ask me that. Rather, ask your readers to read Plato.

Q. I will pass the message on to them. For the time being, I address myself to you, for they say, Jacques Derrida, that you know Sam Weber well. You have been his friend for a long time. How did you meet him? What do you think of his life and of his works? Finally is there a link between the two? Politically, above all, since you have just alluded to what you strangely call "the essence of the political," particularly since September 11?

A. *Vous voulez rire*, you must be joking. Note that if one wanted to laugh together, and know why one laughs, one would still or already need to appeal to Weber. I take him to be a great thinker of laughter, here is what I would like to talk about with you. If you insist on the questions you've just asked, it would be better to stop right away. How can you expect me to reply in that form at a moment's notice? All that you say is true or "makes sense," of course. Sam is an old friend, a very dear friend. Exceptional. I admire his life and his works, there is indeed a link between the two. But one would need centuries to talk about them and as for our meeting in Berlin in 1968, a ten-hour interview would be indispensable. For September 11, a ten-month interview. The preliminary question, that *I* would like to ask *you*, is that of the profession that *you* exercise. For I believe it is time that all the journalists in the world answer questions and answer on their own, answer first the questions they believe they must ask. How did you prepare for this interview? What are you expecting from it? How did you prepare yourself? Did you read all the books by Sam Weber? Which are all provocations to thinking journalism through. Above all modern journalism, written and audiovisual media. And mine? What is your technique? How do you deal with the problem of the relations between your technique, the economic-political constraints of your newspaper and your professional duties? For you do have, don't you, duties and responsibilities, in particular to the subject that you're supposed to tackle, to begin with, Sam Weber himself. Me, too, by the way.

Q. Precisely, that is the question I'm asking myself. How does one become a good journalist? Could you advise me on that subject? I address myself to you because somebody told me that he had heard you talk one day about something like the profession or, I don't know any more, the profession of faith of the journalist. It appears that this question has always obsessed you and that you never miss an opportunity to return to it. You apparently even defined God, in front of Weber himself, as someone who is said to have said to Abraham, on Mount Moriah, "Above all, no journalists!"[54]

When asking you at which date one spoke of this thing, the "journalist," as a profession with a recognized status in a private or public institution, you would have, I am told, declared something like this: a journalist, who, tomorrow, would want to honor his profession, think of his new responsibilities in a public space transformed by new sociopolitical structures and, indissociably, by new technologies of "communication"; someone who would also want to wonder whether the word "communication" is still appropriate; someone who would want as well to re-elaborate appropriately the deontological, ethical, juridico-political, philosophical, as well as the technical and professional questions of his "profession"; someone who would want to take into account what the responsibility of a public speech implies as far as his image, his theatricality, and even his cinema are concerned, as to the philosophy and the psychoanalysis of such responsibility, he would do well to read and meditate Sam Weber's great oeuvre. What do you mean by that? I am asking you because I find myself in the situation that you would have, I am told, described in this way. For a long time I, too, have felt that hope or that anguish. It started as soon as I had to give up my studies at the university and became a journalist. It did not work out very well at the university, but I thought that journalism was what is the closest, in spite of everything. It seems that all the questions I'm asking myself would require such an approach, as they say, or a deconstructive technique. Could you tell me briefly what must be understood here by "technique" (I believe I understand that), but above all by "deconstruction"? And the link between the two? And what is Weber's relation or contribution, in his life and in his works, to "deconstruction," since you've known him? And above all since September 11. You've already told me something very important, earlier, already, without seeming to suspect it, and I'm sure that it will interest our readers in the entire world: so you met him in Berlin in 1968! Thus more than thirty years before September 11! More than twenty years before the fall of the Berlin Wall! That's very impressive, it's very important, politically speaking above all. Was it before or after the "events" of May '68?

A. Just after. But forgive me, I believe it would be better to stop here, I feel very tired all of a sudden. It's age, doubtless, or emotion, and your questions are too difficult. Really beyond measure. And in a style, with a rhythm that for me are untreatable. I must leave you, I feel all of a sudden very tired. The first question one should answer in order for your questions and my answers to make sense would be, "Who is, singularly, irreplaceably, Sam Weber?" In himself, for himself, for others—and for me as well, of course? This is what matters to me first, and this is the question to which I am far from having one single, ready answer.

Q. Forgive me, I feel that I've been very awkward. It's a mistake, a strange misunderstanding. But I beg you, let's try again. If I miss this interview, my newspaper will make me pay dearly for it, I risk losing my job and having to return to the university, where I'm not sure I will be taken back. And furthermore you, too, have duties, as a public and politically committed intellectual: you must communicate in an intelligible fashion and make yourself accessible in the public space. If you turn down this interview, you will confirm a rumor that's already quite old: that you are haughty, elitist, and hermetic; that you refuse to talk to people, to explain to them, to fight obscurantism. Now one must fight ignorance and obscurantism, mustn't one, it's very important, and even more so since September 11?

A. Really? What *happened* on September 11? September 11 of which year? There you have a good question.

Q. September 11, 2001, the twin towers,[55] all that, don't you think like everyone else that it was a major, unprecedented event?

A. No. Let's put an end, if you will, to what you have yourself just called a strange misunderstanding. You're tireless and I'm more and more tired. Can *you* tell me what an event is, a major, unprecedented event? And what happened on September 11, 2001? Those are good "deconstructive" questions and, since that seems to interest you, those are questions that are posed between deconstruction and technics. Sam Weber has articulated them better than anybody.

Q. You see, we're getting closer to our subject. Let's continue. I'm sure that together and with a little good will, we will manage to overcome what I've awkwardly called, in part for a laugh, our strange misunderstanding. My readers will be very interested in what Sam Weber said about September 11 and the relations between deconstruction and technics. Where, in the first place?

A. All right, let's try. Indeed we have common responsibilities in the public space, duties toward your readers, and I would not want you to have to go back to the university where things, in the last instance, do not always work better than in written or radio-televisual news, even in journalism schools. But don't interrupt me unless it's really indispensable, and remind me of saying a word about what you have "called," you say, "in part for a laugh, our strange misunderstanding."

About "deconstruction and technics," about deconstruction as a technique and as a question of technics, about the rigorous delimitations of that problematic, all the texts by Weber without exception are of a rare and indispensable pertinence. I would like to come back to that a bit later. On September 11 (2001, right?), Weber has, in the weeks that followed (December 15, 2001), admirably put to work a concept of theatricalization that he had not ceased to elaborate for decades in the most diverse contexts and corpuses. He shows well that this theatricalization—wait, regarding theatricalization, I would like to take a big step backward in our exchange, if you will allow me, and start over from the beginning. Do not interrupt me before I interrogate you myself, if you would. As I was saying, *my* preliminary question is "Who is Sam Weber?" Himself? Singularly? Who is he, and what does he do? What does he sign?

As for the one who bears that proper name (though a little common all the same, isn't it?), as for that thinker, that writer, that philosopher, that dramaturge, that professor, that absolutely singular friend, that figure unique for me, the irreplaceable chance that encountering him will have granted me, a theatrical first scene, a first paradigm comes to my memory as obvious: "Politikos," Plato's *Statesman*. I say theatrical scene because it is one and because Weber is a man of theater; he thinks theatricality, and not only from the point of view of the spectator; he thinks the being-spectator in general and he does theater. And then I say "paradigm" because in *The Statesman*, it is not only a matter of such and such a paradigm (*paradeigma*) but of thinking the paradigm in general. What is a paradigm in general, the Stranger asks himself when facing Younger Socrates (278e ff.). After which comes the immense and famous discussion around the paradigm of the weaver (υφαντης, *Weber*, if you prefer) and the art of weaving. I will not recall all that work of analysis but merely the moment when the Stranger defines the art of weaving as the art of συμπλοκη, of stitching together. The weaver possesses the art of stitching together the warp and the woof, **and this paradigm?**

I would like to describe SW not only as an artist weaver (royal politics, etc.), who knows how to stitch together, analyze, etc., but *I* would like to unravel the way in which SW is absolutely singular in that paradigm . . .

UNCANNY Misunderstanding[56]

insist at the beginning on translation (in *Mass Mediauras* p. 61)

laughter and theater 12ff.

I replaced someone who had taken my place at SW's place, in his car.

**Translated by Brigitte Weltman-Aron and Dragan Kujundžić**

## Notes

["Vous voulez rire!" is an unfinished text about Samuel Weber by Jacques Derrida, and one of the last he worked on. The essay is published here for the first time in French, and its English translation was specifically undertaken for this book. The text consists of thirty-three manuscript pages, single spaced; the minimal changes to the original version of the text in the English translation and in the French transcription include punctuation and formatting to comply with the standards of the press. We are grateful to Marguerite Derrida for making this essay available for publication. The translators also wish to thank Samuel Weber for his invaluable suggestions and comments on the translation.

Derrida's title is followed by an asterisk and a footnote that reads: "*(leave the title in French, do not translate it)."—Translators]

1. Samuel Weber, *The Legend of Freud* (Minneapolis: University of Minnesota Press, 1982), 83, 99. A first version of that work was published in German with the title *Freud-Legend, Drei Studien zum Psychoanalytischen Denken* (Olten: Walter-Verlag, 1979). A minute comparison between the two works would be of great interest. It would bring into relief numerous alterations, *displacements* above all, changes of place, then, and new developments. The two chapter conclusions quoted in the epigraph stage again, in a playful manner but otherwise, and this time redoubled, a sentence that closes a subchapter of the first German version: "Und darüber gibt es für die Freudsche Theorie des Witzes nichts zum lachen" (126). So many things we are forewarned not to hasten to confuse: *le rire*, *le mot d'esprit* (laughter, joke, *Lachen, Witz*, etc.). [The epigraph is in English in the original. Samuel Weber's works are quoted in English in the original throughout.—Translators]

2. [The initials "**Q.**" and "**A.**" throughout are in English in the original. —Translators]

3. [In the original: "du *Witz* (*joke* ou mot d'esprit)."—Translators]

4. [Sigmund Freud, "Humour," in vol. 21 of *The Standard Edition of the Complete Psychological Works of Sigmund Freud*, trans. James Strachey (London: The Hogarth Press, 1961), 161.—Translators]

5. Samuel Weber, *Mass Mediauras: Form, Technics, Media* (Southwood, Australia: Power Publications, 1996), 4.

6. Interrupted by the journalist, I clarify here, after rereading, in which direction I would have liked to explore Bataille's texts on the subject of what links sovereignty to laughter. Let's clarify at the risk of repeating ourselves: sovereignty, at least as Bataille understands it, is very close to holiness, at times also to health, between *holy* and *healthy*, an impotent sovereignty, and therefore almost opposed, in its ungraspable concept, to the classic concept of sovereignty (dominion, mastery, superiority higher than height and greater than greatness, absolute power over self and others, decisory will, etc.). One wonders at times for what reasons, in my eyes highly problematic, Bataille still maintains its name just as he claims to make a clean slate of the concept.

One would in particular need to reread and analyze here, in *Guilty* [trans. Stuart Kendall (Albany: State University of New York Press, 2011); *Le coupable, Somme athéologique II* (Paris: Gallimard, 1961)] the whole chapter titled "The Divinity of Laughter." The experience of laughter (always ecstatic, as that of sovereignty) is described there either as that of sovereign ipseity at its height, or as the very opposite of the master's sovereignty, par excellence of the master in the Hegelian sense. Most of the time, the border between the two laughters remains undecided or permeable. That passage from one laughter to the other is thought-provoking. It is often, particularly in Bataille, a passage from laughter to tears and from tears to laughter. But this passage is also a *leap*—a quasi-intemporal instant that neither can nor must maintain itself, other than suspended between the possible and the impossible. Thus:

> As deadline, man marks the expiration of an interrogation, becoming a being subjectively (tending toward autonomy in nature, thus conceiving himself in laughter). (79/122)
>
> I've always recoiled before deadlines: I've been afraid of being *what I was*—LAUGHTER ITSELF! ("Itching to Laugh," 80/123)
>
> God *was*, more gently than myself. God or his absence were no less *laughable*, one or the other: laughable appearances. (83/129)
>
> After a long rest, the *absence* of the starry sky makes me laugh. (84/130)
>
> Elaborating a philosophy of work (the *Knecht*, the emancipated slave, the worker, who becomes God in the *Phenomenology*), Hegel suppressed chance—and laughter.
> (Laughing *in my way*, I felt in the contraction of laughter something painful, agonizing. It was terrible and delicious. It was *healthy*.) (86/133)
>
> But who could die laughing? . . . Uncontrolled laughter escapes the sphere accessible to language; it is a leap that cannot be defined by its conditions. Laughter is suspended, it leaves the one who laughs in suspense. . . . It affirms nothing; appeases nothing. Laughter is the leap from the possible to the impossible—and from the impossible into the possible. But it is only a leap: maintaining it would reduce the impossible to the possible *or the inverse*. ("Laughter and Trembling," 90/139)
>
> In laughter, ecstasy is delivered, immanent. Ecstatic laughter does not *laugh*, but it opens me infinitely. Its transparency is crossed by an arrow of laughter, sent from a mortal absence. . . . By laughing I celebrate the marriage of power and loss. . . . The *interrogation* still wants failure, it wants *failure to succeed* (that it should be loss that succeeds). . . . Whatever it is that is gaping and mortally wounded in laughter is the violent suspension that nature does to itself. (92/142–43)
>
> Strange that real wealth has a blind allure, that divinity should cleave to impotence. Hegel's constrained position, or Goethe's funereal beauty. Only "infinite laughter" enlightens me. (95–96/149 [translation modified])

7. [Italicized and in English in the original.—Translators]
8. [For a description of the first meeting between Derrida and Weber, see chapter 13, note 4 of this volume.—Editors]
9. ["ce qui a lieu, ou '*takes place*'" in the original.—Translators]

10. [In English and italics in the original.—Translators]
11. "Reading and Writing——*chez* Derrida," in Samuel Weber, *Institution and Interpretation* (Minneapolis: University of Minnesota Press, 1987), 85ff.
12. [In English and italics in the original.—Translators]
13. ["ce qui a lieu, *takes place*" in the original.—Translators]
14. See *Institution and Interpretation*, especially chapters 7 and 8. On the obsessive recurrence of the lexis of ambivalence or ambiguity, see, among hundreds of examples, 91; on *theatrical* or *spectacular* space (opera, cinema, television, photography, etc.), the "tragicomic drama of deconstruction," the "theatrical code," on what "dramatically . . . alters the dramatic scene as such," see, for example, 93, 115, and *passim*, in pages where the "perhaps" and Nietzsche's "dangerous perhapses" were thematized (I have just noticed it, I had forgotten it), well before I myself, indebting myself once more to him, made a guiding motif of them in *Politiques de l'amitié* (Galilée, 1995) [*Politics of Friendship*, translated by George Collins (London: Verso, 1997)], cf. 115.

That is found precisely in a chapter entitled "The Debts of Deconstruction," which not only profoundly deals with the question of debt since the Nietzsche of *The Genealogy of Morals*, but indebts me thus myself in advance. Once more. And by inscribing any deconstruction in a "scene of debt," if not in a filiation of credit, Weber removes from it any chance of being a sovereign and sovereignly productive originality, which is to say, more originary than any "technical" operation. The space of technics is always that of borrowing, credit, of debt and genealogical filiation. Wherever there is technique, there is debt. The simplicity of the origin is altered. Even though, as we shall see, following Weber, it is immediately linked to the delay of some indebtedness, *that* delay does not wait, it is quasi-originary: technical spacing opens up from and at the origin, its delay is without delay.

But this does not simply mean, for all that, that deconstruction is a technique among others; we will have to complicate that later. The meditation on what is not only ambivalent, but *unheimlich*, "uncanny," is explicitly deployed, in the same article, for instance on p. 117. But so often elsewhere as well!

15. ["Uncanny" is italicized and in English, "unheimlich" and "Unheimliche" are italicized and in German in the original.—Translators]
16. [Immanuel Kant, "What Is Orientation in Thinking?," trans. H. B. Nisbet, in Kant, *Political Writings*, ed. H. S. Reiss (Cambridge, U.K.: Cambridge University Press, 1991), 247, translation slightly modified.—Translators]
17. ["Uncanny" is in English and italics and "unheimlich" is in German and italics in the original.—Translators]
18. [In English and italics in the original.—Translators]
19. See Weber, *The Legend of Freud*, 65–66.
20. Weber, *The Legend of Freud*, 67.
21. Weber, *The Legend of Freud*, 72.
22. Weber, *The Legend of Freud*, 74.
23. Jacques Derrida, "Résistances," in *Résistances—de la psychanalyse* (Paris: Galilée, 1996), 23ff.; Jacques Derrida, *Resistances of Psychoanalysis*, trans. P. Kamuf, P. A. Brault, and M. Naas (Paris: Stanford University Press, 1998), 10ff.
24. Jacques Lacan, *Les quatre concepts fondamentaux de la psychanalyse* (Paris: Seuil, 1973), 28; Jacques Lacan, *The Four Fundamental Concepts*

*of Psychoanalysis*, trans. Alan Sheridan (New York: Norton, 1998), quoted in Weber, *The Legend of Freud*, 79.

25. Weber underscores "rising" because, at the end of the sentence, the question will be about the phallus, about the meaning that would thus rise theatrically right in the middle of the stage, as a phallus.

But on my part I would underscore "majestically" as well: majesty is also height and greatness (superlative of *magnus*: what is higher than height and greater than greatness) and, in the whole lexical tradition of semantics or of political theory, *majestas*—Bodin will have underscored it at the beginning of his book, *Les six livres de la République* [*On Sovereignty: Six Books of the Commonwealth*]—is the fundamental Latin word for *sovereignty*. A crime of lese-majesty is a crime against the sovereign. What returns to the stage here indeed concerns, as a single and self-same erection, the central and heightened place of the phallus inasmuch as it signifies the very signifier of the sovereign—the sovereign signifying or the sovereign signifier.

26. Weber, *The Legend of Freud*, 80. Elsewhere, later, Weber seems at least to complicate that "centrism," and even that phallocentrism of Lacan. He always does it in the theatrological code that he ceaselessly privileges as if in the last instance everything was a coup de théâtre. In *Return to Freud: Jacques Lacan's Dislocation of Psychoanalysis* (Cambridge, U.K.: Cambridge University Press, 1991; German edition, Vienna: Passagen Verlag, 1990), he insists on the contrary that for Lacan, Freud's phallocentrism tends to "deconstruct" all "centrism," "insofar as the phallus stages the drama of the signifier. The signified is the signifier *struck down*. . . . Reading in this sense—and it is the sense of the Return to Freud announced by Lacan—means relearning how to be *struck* by the signifier. And by its stage. In the theater of the unconscious, one never gets over being stage-struck" (151).

27. ["A." does not designate the answer here, but the first of the two reasons mentioned by Derrida in the preceding paragraph. However, no "B." follows in the original.—Translators]

28. On this contraction of movement and immobility, see the very beautiful pages dedicated to the Heideggerian *Gestell* (*Gestell: stell: emplacement*) in *Mass Mediauras*. Nothing surprising in finding there the always inevitable motif of the *uncanny*, and always in a thinking experience of the stakes of translation. Thus:

> In the English translation, the word (*Gestell*) is rendered as "enframing." Although this takes the collecting function of the *Gestell* into account, it effaces the tension between verb and noun that resounds in the German and that points to the strange, indeed uncanny, mixture of movement and stasis that distinguishes the goings-on of modern technics and upon which Heidegger places considerable emphasis.
>
> This tension resounds in the word proposed by Lacoue-Labarthe to render *Gestell*: *installation*. I would like to suggest another possibility, one that has the virtue of pointing to the lexical "root" of *Gestell: stell: emplacement*. (*Mass Mediauras*, 71)

29. ["Uncanny" is in English and italics in the original.—Translators]

30. ["Uncanny" is in English and italics in the original.—Translators]

31. ["Straddling" is in English and italics in the original.—Translators]

32. Weber, *The Legend of Freud*, 81.
33. [In English and in italics in the original.—Translators]
34. Weber, *The Legend of Freud*, 82.
35. ["Good or bad joke" is in English in the original.—Translators]
36. ["Joke" is in English and in italics in the original.—Translators]
37. ["Bad joke" is in English and in italics in the original.—Translators]
38. [In the original, Derrida wrote: "Elle déconstruit non pas une révélation du sens mais par la contre-imposition d'une contre-technique." "Pas" might be a typo for "par." In which case, the sentence should read: "It deconstructs not through a revelation of meaning but through the counterimposition of a counter-technique."—Translators]
39. Weber, *The Legend of Freud*, 82–83.
40. [In the first sentence of this paragraph, "play" and "joke" are given by Derrida in English and in italics after the original *jeu* and *plaisanterie* in French; and in the second sentence, they are used in English in the original.—Translators]
41. Weber, *The Legend of Freud*, 99.
42. The formulation appears only once, if I am not mistaken, and in a slightly different form in the preceding German version: "Und darüber gibt es für die Freudsche Theorie des Witzes nichts zu lachen" (126).
43. Weber, *The Legend of Freud*, 98.
44. Weber, *Mass Mediauras*, 226–27.
45. Jacques Derrida, *La Carte postale, de Socrate à Freud et au-delà* (Paris: Aubier-Flammarion, 1979); *The Post-Card: From Socrates to Freud and Beyond*, trans. Alan Bass (Chicago: University of Chicago Press, 1987), 483. [Derrida quotes *La Carte postale* and provides the translation in a footnote.—Translators]
46. Weber, *Institution and Interpretation*, 102ff.
47. [These three lines, along with all other passages in boldface in this chapter, are also in boldface in Derrida's original.—Translators]
48. ["Set" is in English and in italics in the original.—Translators]
49. [In the original, Derrida alternates between the English "form" and the French "forme"; "sets" and "setting" are in English and in italics in the original. —Translators]
50. Weber, *Mass Mediauras*, 4.
51. ["You're kidding" and "Who are you kidding" are in italics and in English in the original.—Translators]
52. ["La plaisanterie, la 'joke' . . ." in the original.—Translators]
53. (Heidegger himself, even, . . . awakening/consciousness, in a note on 99ff.).
54. Reference. [Jacques Derrida, "Above All, No Journalists!," trans. Samuel Weber, in *Religion and Media*, ed. Hent de Vries and Samuel Weber (Stanford: Stanford University Press, 2002).—Translators]
55. [In English in the original.—Translators]
56. ["Uncanny" is in English in the original.—Translators]

# Vous voulez rire!

## Entretien avec un journaliste de passage

As we shall see, this was, and is, no laughing matter.
And that, I repeat, is no laughing matter.[1]

Q. Merci de m'avoir accordé cet entretien au sujet de Sam Weber—enfin sur Sam Weber ou autour de lui, comme vous voudrez.

A. Vous voulez rire, non? A son *sujet, sur* lui ou *autour* de lui? A moi de vous poser cette première question, si vous le permettez. Si elle compte, cette première question préalable, c'est d'abord qu'elle touche au *lieu*. Où sommes-nous? Où nous tiendrons-nous? Autour de lui, près ou loin de lui, en face de lui comme d'un objet, derrière lui, à ses côtés? Où est-il, lui?

Or vous savez que rien n'est pris plus *au sérieux* par Sam Weber, de façon plus constante, aiguë, lucide, que le lieu, la place, la situation, la position, la localité du dispositif, la scène du *montage*. Heureusement, vous avez le même mot technique pour dire quelque chose d'une certaine technique, en anglais, le "montage." Cela vous aidera, car Weber est toujours très attentif au *montage*. Dans tous les arts, de la peinture ou de la photographie au cinéma, en passant par la littérature, un processus consiste à mettre en place un dispositif (vous diriez sans doute un *apparatus*), à le situer artificiellement, dans l'unité convenue, et donc conventionnelle ou institutionnelle d'un lieu, en ajustant des pièces, en les assemblant dans un "assemblage"—vous avez aussi ce mot en anglais—; ou encore, comme on dit en français à "monter" une pièce de théâtre. Quand, littéralement ou par figure, un tel montage lie le machinique au théâtral, il aura toujours situé quelque chose comme le foyer de la pensée weberienne. En premier lieu, justement, quand il s'agit du *sujet*, ce mot si équivoque, et surtout quand on veut parler *au sujet du sujet*. Dire qu'il la prend au sérieux, cela n'exclut jamais de sa part une verve ludique, une pensée amusée du ludique, du comique, du *Witz* (*joke* ou mot d'esprit), du rire, autant de choses qu'il nous faudra, j'y insiste, distinguer. Elles ont toutes un rapport différent, une proximité différentielle à l'art, à la *tekhnè* et à la technique, autant de choses qui entretiennent elles-mêmes un commerce différent, une proximité différentielle à la déconstruction singulière et inédite engagée par Weber. Ce commerce est aussi une économie, car la dimension économique, celle de l'épargne, notamment, reste essentielle à l'interprétation du mot d'esprit. Freud le rappelle explicitement dans un appendice publié dans *Imago* en 1928 sur l'humour—il y avoue une limite: "Dans mon livre *Le mot d'esprit et ses rapports avec l'inconscient* paru en 1905, je n'ai en réalité traité l'humour que du point de vue économique. Je cherchais à découvrir la source de plaisir que procure l'humour, et je pense avoir montré que le bénéfice de plaisir dû à l'humour dérive de l'épargne d'une dépense affective."

Dès les premières pages de son dernier livre, je vous y renvoie sans tarder, Weber retrace ainsi le mouvement organisateur de sa problématique, le *topos* majeur, en somme, de son livre, et je serais presque tenté de dire de tous ses livres, à savoir la topologie ou la topographie, la pensée du lieu ou la place. Autour du passage que je m'apprête à citer, il se réfère plutôt, et je crois qu'il a de bonnes raisons de le faire, au lieu comme *chora* (référence au *Timée* de Platon) plutôt que comme *topos* (thème sans doute plus aristotélicien). Il insiste aussitôt sur un motif auquel, comme lui, je suis sensible, auquel nous devrions être très sensibles, vous et moi, au moment de parler *au sujet de, sur* ou *autour de* "quelqu'un." C'est non seulement le motif de *l'unité* mais, plus radicalement, de façon préalable en tout cas, celui de l'*indivisibilité* du "sujet":

"This is a book about *place* and *positioning* rather than about human beings. . . . The essays here collected retrace how the development of aesthetic theory can be understood as a (perhaps ultimate) effort to defend the notion of the indivisibility of place as a condition of the individuality of the subject. . . . For without the unity of place, the unity of the subject becomes difficult to conceive."[2]

Je serais tenté de souligner ou de privilégier encore davantage cette valeur d'indivisibilité. Elle est la "condition" même, Weber le dit littéralement, la première chance de la place, de la détermination localisante, de l'emplacement. Il n'y a pas une place *d'abord* donnée et qui serait *ensuite* divisible ou indivisible. C'est la postulation d'indivisibilité qui au contraire rend possible le lieu ou l'emplacement (exemplairement celui du sujet). Il s'agit bien d'une postulation, d'une requête, d'une demande dont je crois qu'elle reste nécessairement (c'est la nécessité même) vouée à l'échec. *Comme désir et pour la vie.* Elle est à la fois irrésistible et promise à l'échec. Inévitable, cet échec donne d'ailleurs la chance même de la vie et du mouvement, l'autre de la mort même. La chance s'allie intimement à l'échec, comme la possibilité à l'impuissance (Bataille a raison de le noter au sujet du rire, je voudrais en dire un mot tout à l'heure). L'indivisibilité, au contraire, c'est à la fois la mort et la souveraineté absolue. Tous ces prédicats sont transférables sur le concept de "sujet." Ils occupent la place du sujet. C'est par l'indivisibilité qu'on caractérise depuis toujours la souveraineté comme ipséité du sujet, sa décision souveraine, son absolue responsabilité comme irresponsabilité; j'avais essayé de le démontrer ailleurs, et en forme d'indéniable aporie: si un sujet *fait*, s'il *décide*, s'il *est* ce qui lui est possible, ce qui est *en son pouvoir*, s'il déploie ses possibles comme ses prédicats, alors il ne décide de rien, il explicite ce qu'il est, ce dont il est capable, ce qui est à sa portée et dans sa nature, et il devient alors irresponsable. C'est bien la place du souverain: celui-ci d'ailleurs est, dans son ipséité, le sujet indivisible qui, n'étant responsable devant personne, s'autorisant lui-même à la fois à faire et à suspendre la loi, décidant de l'exception à la loi, devient *à la fois* absolument responsable et absolument irresponsable, etc. Ce que je voudrais tenter de penser ou de nommer, en frayant mon chemin dans le sillage de Weber, ce serait peut-être cette expérience indécise entre la souveraineté classique—marquée par l'indivisibilité de la place—et un certain rire. La souveraineté est une chose terrifiante, mais elle me fait toujours, en tant qu'allégation, un peu rire, irrépressiblement. Le soi-disant souverain fait rire, certes, mais spontanément, il ne sait pas rire. Contrairement à ce que prétend Bataille qui aura voulu changer le sens du concept traditionnel de souveraineté tout en gardant pieusement le vieux mot, ce qui est aussi un peu ridicule, vain et hypocrite. C'est peut-être parce que le souverain ne sait pas rire spontanément, surtout pas de lui-même qu'il a souvent besoin de bouffons autour de lui.

Point n'importe quelle souveraineté, certes, et point n'importe quel rire. Qu'appelle-t-on un "fou rire," par exemple, et une "envie de rire"? Ils ne naissent pas nécessairement de "mots d'esprit." Est-ce que le rire interrompt, menace ou rassure au contraire? Est-ce qu'il ruine ou confirme la souveraineté du sujet, son économie ou son ipséité? Et s'il fait un peu tout cela à la fois, de quelles nouvelles distinctions aurions-nous besoin? J'ai le sentiment encore obscur que la déconstruction, en particulier là où elle se confond avec la question de la technique, aura dû traiter de cette question en somme quasi politique ou hyperpolitique des rapports entre le rire et la souveraineté. Vous savez que pour Bataille . . .[3]

**Q.** Ne multiplions pas les préambules, s'il vous plaît. Nous sommes d'accord, ce sera un échange improvisé de *Q and A*. Vous pourrez tout relire après coup, l'entretien une fois traduit. Mais permettez-moi d'y insister, au nom de ce que je crois être l'éthique et la déontologie du journalisme, c'est-à-dire de mon devoir envers mes lecteurs. Ceux-ci vous demandent d'être plus bref et plus clair, plus spontané, plus direct que d'habitude, enfin autant que possible. Ne multipliez pas les protocoles comme vous venez de commencer à le faire. Ne transformez surtout pas, on me dit que c'est votre inclination, notre échange en réflexion critique ou "déconstructive" sur le genre de l'entretien et sur la presse en général. Notre sujet, ce n'est pas le journal ni même les medias . . .

**A.** Vous voulez rire, je vais finir par le croire. Je me demande s'il n'y a pas là entre nous un *qui pro quo*. Vous savez, le *quiproquo*, comme on l'écrit parfois en un seul mot, il y en a toujours dans la vie. On prend celui-ci pour celui-là, l'un pour l'autre. En général ça fait rire, qu'on le veuille ou non. Pourquoi donc? Je vous raconterai plus tard ma rencontre avec Sam Weber. Il y eut là (nous en rions encore, et tout le monde avec nous, mais pourquoi?) un *quiproquo* originel et théâtral dont on se demande encore quel *deus ex machina* l'a providentiellement mis en scène à ma descente d'avion, il y a trente cinq ans à Berlin. Sam Weber a d'abord pris quelqu'un d'autre pour moi, *qui pro quo*. Cela se répare-t-il jamais? Et pourtant, à travers ce *quiproquo*, j'aime à penser que nous nous sommes, pour ainsi dire, reconnus. Bien que Diderot parle profondément des "*quiproquo* d'amitié," il peut y avoir du *quiproquo* sans méprise, et même de merveilleux "*quiproquo* d'amitié" qui ne sont pas des fautes ou des manquements à la vérité, seulement de ces expériences fondamentales qui consistent à prendre l'autre pour ce qu'il est, c'est-à-dire *encore un autre*, un autre que lui-même, un autre "divisible," justement, un autre que son personnage, un autre que ce qu'il croit être, un autre que soi, etc. Mais le *quiproquo*, c'est souvent la technique ou le ressort d'un certain théâtre, parfois tragique, plus souvent comique: un personnage prend l'un pour l'autre.

Je fais à dessein cette référence au théâtre en hommage à Weber qui est à la fois un philosophe-dramaturge, un penseur et un auteur de la scène, de la *mise* en scène, un théoricien de tous les dispositifs techniques qui consistent à "poser," "'disposer," à "mettre" et à "mettre en scène." Au théâtre, à l'opéra, au cinéma, dans tous les media: journaux écrits, radio, cinéma et télévision.

Q. Vous recommencez à multiplier les excursions. Je vous ai dit que notre sujet, ce n'est pas le journal ni même les medias . . .

**A.** Vous plaisantez, c'est une blague. Comment osez-vous me demander de ne pas réfléchir sur le genre même que nous pratiquons ici même, l'entretien, ou sur la presse et les media? Où sommes-nous donc? Vous voulez vraiment que nous évitions de parler du lieu où nous sommes? de l'élément à travers lequel nous nous entretenons? des supposés destinataires auxquels vous faisiez allusion comme si vous les connaissiez d'avance? On m'avait dit que vous veniez pour parler avec moi de Sam Weber. Or je le répète, la question du *lieu* (vous dites *place* en anglais), dans lequel quelque chose *a lieu* (vous dites *takes place*) reste toujours pour lui la première et la plus nécessaire des questions, quoi qu'il arrive. Nous aurons d'ailleurs mille problèmes de traduction, car si en français "lieu" et "place" sont à peu près synonymes, la subtile différence qui les sépare se perd dans l'anglais "*place*." En tout cas la place est bien pour Weber la condition du sujet, de l'individu indivisible et de l'événement, de ce qui a lieu ou "*takes place*." Cela se lit ou se déchiffre à chaque page de tous ses textes . . .

Q. Mais alors quel est le lien de tous ces thèmes avec le sujet dont on m'a chargé? Vous savez bien ce qu'on appelle un "sujet" dans la presse. On m'a demandé de vous interroger sur "déconstruction et technique." Plus précisément sur les "techniques de la déconstruction" chez Sam Weber. En tant que journaliste, bien que j'aie fait quelques études, je ne comprends pas bien moi-même ce que ça veut dire. Pourriez-vous commencer par expliquer à mes lecteurs, de façon aussi pédagogique que possible, *in a nut shell*, comme nous disons en anglais, ce qu'il faut entendre par "déconstruction"? Nous verrons pour la "technique" ensuite.

**A.** Ensuite? Mais vous vous moquez de moi! Déconstruction et technique sont soudées, depuis toujours, en une seule et même question!

Q. Surtout, avant tout, pourriez-vous nous parler de tout ça chez Sam Weber *lui-même*, de votre rencontre avec lui, par exemple, de sa vie et de son œuvre? Surtout du point de vue politique, cela va de soi, compte tenu de l'intérêt de nos lecteurs, et en particulier après cet événement majeur que fut, tout le monde s'accorde à le dire, le 11 septembre?

A. Comment voulez-vous que je réponde sans rire, sérieusement, à de telles questions? Vous dites "*chez* Sam Weber." Or sans en être jamais capable, surtout pas *in a nutshell* (quel mot, vous ne trouvez pas? je le crois dangereusement comique, comme tout *quiproquo*), j'aimerais arriver à dire ce que le nom de Sam Weber inscrit étrangement en moi, chez moi, au cœur de ma vie et de mon travail depuis des décennies. Et vous devez savoir en premier lieu que Weber est celui qui a écrit sur le mot français "chez" des pages immortelles que je ne tenterai ni de mimer ni de résumer. Je vous y renvoie encore, vous-même et vos lecteurs.[4] Vous y trouveriez, entre autres choses, et toujours à travers l'élégance d'une ironie inimitable, une cartographie des frayages en cours, toutes les trajectoires les plus originales et les plus typiques du weberianisme: la logique de l'*ambivalence* (qui est toujours relayée par celle des significations instables, antithétiques, indécidables de l'*uncanny* ou de *unheimlich*, à partir, mais aussi au-delà de ce qu'en dit Freud), la prise en compte de la *place*—et la place de l'acteur et celle du spectateur–, la méditation sur l'événement comme ce qui a lieu, *takes place*, prend la place, reprend, donc répète la place-de (donc re-place et remplace aussi, substitue, supplée), bref sur la "place" comme placement en général. "Chez," n'est-ce pas, le mot annonce toujours le lieu, la location, la localité, l'habitation, la case, la *casa*, le domicile, la proximité, la propriété, l'emplacement–avec, prenant la place de la place, le remplacement prothétique et répétitif, donc technique, qui n'en est jamais loin—, le *topos*, l'espacement, le point de vue, le rapport à, etc. D'où la méditation incessante sur la théâtralité et sur la logique paradoxale de la répétition qui s'y joue, sur la scène en général, sur les media (Weber a fort bien analysé leur rôle décisif dans ce "11 septembre" dont vous voulez, comme tout le monde, comme tous les journalistes, que nous commencions par parler). Cet immense traité du "chez" (mot intraduisible) se trouve dans *Institution and Interpretation*.[5]

*Institution and Interpretation*, d'ailleurs, soit dit trop vite comme entre parenthèses . . .

Q. Encore des parenthèses! Quand commencerez-vous à aborder de front notre sujet? Vous voulez nous ridiculiser, mes lecteurs et moi-même.

A. Non, il n'y a pas de quoi rire. Je traite le sujet. *Institution and Interpretation*, cela pourrait être le sur-titre ou le sous-titre de tout ce que Weber aura problématisé, c'est-à-dire déconstruit à travers tous ses livres. Il s'agit toujours pour lui de soumettre l'interprétation *de* l'interprétation à l'analyse préalable de son institutionnalisation, de sa mise en place et de sa mise en scène institutionnelle. Il faut ici entendre l'*interprétation* à tous les sens de ce terme: le sens herméneutique (schleiermachien ou gadamerien), le sens "nietzschéen," le sens "freudien," le sens "heideggerien," mais aussi le sens instrumental, qu'il s'agisse du travail d'interprétation des musiciens, des chanteurs d'opéra ou des acteurs de théâtre ou de cinéma. Il n'y a pas d'interprétation qui ne soit comme d'avance prise et déterminée par son institutionnalisation, par la position ou la disposition de son dispositif institutionnel—et donc technique. Car il n'y a pas *d'institution*, de *nomos*, ou de *thèsis*, il n'y a rien de thétique ou de thématique, donc de *positionnel* sans *tekhnè*, il n'y a pas d'interprétation "naturelle," physique, du moins au sens survenu et historiquement tardif de la *physis*. C'est toute la question de la déconstruction quant à la technique, voilà ce que Weber a tant fait pour nous guider et pour nous aider à explorer cette problématique. Ce lien irréductible entre interprétation et institution, il vaut exemplairement, je le répète, pour l'interprétation psychanalytique, pour l'interprétation comme lecture de textes philosophiques ou littéraires, dans l'université ou ailleurs, pour l'interprétation théâtrale, cinématographique ou musicale, pour l'interprétation des faits et événements historiques par les machines historiographiques ou, nous y sommes, par les dispositifs médiatiques.

Puisque la question de la technique vous intéresse, l'institution, c'est justement le lieu ou le moment, l'avènement du devenir-technique de l'invention, une certaine instrumentalisation répétitive de l'intention ou de l'origine supposée. Vient-elle *après* l'origine? la répète-t-elle? Cette technologisation institutionnelle est-elle seconde ou secondaire, comme on le croit souvent? Vient-elle répéter et doubler ce qui a déjà eu lieu sans elle? Ou bien est-elle, comme je serais tenté de le croire, sans doute comme Sam Weber, le double co-originaire, la condition même, l'étrange (*uncanny, unheimlich*) mise en œuvre de l'événement instituant? Voilà peut-être ce dont il faut débattre. Voilà ce qui est en débat de façon constante et lumineuse dans tout l'œuvre de Weber, partout où il parle de répétition, d'itérabilité, de l'étrangeté de l'*uncanny* ou de l'*Unheimliche*, c'est-à-dire à peu près partout. Si la déconstruction comporte toujours une stratégie interprétative, si elle est aussi une inlassable interprétation de l'interprétation, elle se laisse marquer du même coup par une certaine technicité, et cela *dès l'origine*. Elle est technique et coextensive à toute question de la technique, même si elle n'est pas seulement *une* simple technique, une façon de faire, au sens de la méthode enseignable et des règles de procédures transmissibles; et même si elle est aussi une tentative pour réinterpréter la grande question de la technique. En ce sens, la déconstruction n'est jamais sauvage et naturelle, étrangère à toute institution, même si elle est aussi et le plus souvent une contre-institution: Weber l'a fort bien pensé, il l'a de mille façons formulé et mis en œuvre. Nous devrons y revenir.

Q. Ne pourriez vous pas faire l'économie de tous ces "nous devrons y revenir"? Il ne nous reste plus beaucoup de temps et de place. Dites ce que vous voulez dire sans attendre et sans détour. Mes lecteurs, et même mon éditeur . . .

A. Non, vous voulez rire, n'est-ce pas, vous voulez que je réponde sans détour alors que vous me posez des questions impossibles au sujet de quelqu'un qui compte parmi ceux, assez rares en somme, qui, durant presque toute une vie d'adulte, m'ont aidé, comme dirait Kant, à m'"orienter dans la pensée"—et dans le monde. Vous savez, je me suis toujours senti seul, isolé, douloureusement mais jalousement solitaire. Dans la "vie" et dans la "pensée." Comme tout le monde, diriez-vous en riant. Oui, mais moi c'est moi et je suis seul à pouvoir en témoigner. Plus on souffre ainsi, plus on aiguise cette souffrance, plus on a besoin, pour *s'orienter*, d'amis exceptionnels qui témoignent de ce témoignage et dont la vigilance veille sur vos égarements, ici pour les éviter, là pour les cultiver. Car cet isolement aveugle parfois, il est toujours très risqué. Sam Weber est pour moi l'un de ces rares amis. Dans *Was heisst sich im Denken orientieren*, je ne sais pas si vos lecteurs le savent, Kant a raison de s'interroger: "Mais penserions-nous beaucoup et penserions-nous bien *(mit welcher Richtigkeit)*, si nous ne pensions pas pour ainsi dire en commun avec d'autres *(gleichsam im Gemeinschaft mit andern)*, qui nous font part de leur pensée et auxquels nous communiquons les nôtres?"

Pour quelqu'un d'aussi spontanément allergique que moi à toute "communauté," je trouve incommensurables, absolument incomparables la confiance et la reconnaissance qui m'ont tout de suite lié, et de façon si durable, dans tant de domaines, de pays, de langues, à la pensée et à la personne de Sam Weber. Vous savez, on écrit toujours un peu sous surveillance, c'est-à-dire pour quelques-uns qui vous observent au-dedans de vous mêmes, chez vous, où ils se sont logés, où ils ont leur propre place, depuis laquelle ils sont prêts à vous démasquer, à relever vos faiblesses, à vous encourager ou à vous décourager. Qu'on le veuille ou non, on écrit pour eux, on travaille avec eux, on parle et on pense *chez eux* pour répondre à leur attente, sans doute, mais aussi parfois pour tenter de tromper leur inspection et les surprendre. Ce sont plus que des spectateurs-lecteurs, ce sont les acteurs, voire les vrais signataires de ce que nous risquons en écrivant. L'un veille pendant que l'autre dort ou rêve, et à la fin on ne sait plus qui fait quoi. On ne sait plus qui signe. Sam Weber est pour moi, depuis des décennies, l'un de ces très rares bienveilleurs (je me demande comment vous allez traduire ce mot, "bienveilleur," qui dit à la fois la bonté bienveillante et la vigilance impeccable). Je dis "veiller" et bien veiller, mais il ne faut pas se fier ici à l'autorité de la conscience vigilante de *l'ego cogito* sur ce que nous appelons la "pensée." L'économie secrète d'une amitié de pensée, comme celle dont je parle, je crois qu'elle passe par le rêve, diurne et nocturne. Par l'inconscient, si vous préférez. Ce qui veille de façon *uncanny, unheimlich*, sur mon travail, comme sur ce que je pense de quoi que ce soit (du monde, de la philosophie, de la politique, etc.), ce qui me surveille avec une bienveillance intransigeante, ce n'est pas seulement la vigilance de certains amis comme Sam Weber. Ce n'est pas seulement leur rêve, c'est aussi, c'est d'abord ce qu'ils pensent et font *du rêve*.

Ainsi, pour ne prendre que cet exemple et m'orienter vers ce qui, dès le départ, lie pour Weber les motifs du rêve, de la déconstruction (du sens, *meaning*) et de la technique, je vous renvoie au début de ce magnifique chapitre intitulé "The Meaning of the Thallus" dans ce livre auquel il faut toujours revenir, *The Legend of Freud* (qui fut, je le rappelle encore, publié en allemand en 1979, ce qui est toujours fort significatif pour comprendre le singulier chemin de Weber entre les langues, les cultures et les traditions). Dès le départ, Weber rappelle que *Die Traumdeutung, L'interprétation des rêves*, comme on traduit, est pour Freud une "technique" (*Technik*) pour accéder à une "meaningful structure" (*ein sinnvolles Gebilde*: le mot "*Gebilde*," comme celui de "*Gestalt*" pourrait aussi servir de fil conducteur dans tout l'œuvre de Weber). Or, si elle ressemble à une "méthode d'interprétation," cette "technique" nous guide vers des phénomènes pleins de sens ("meaningful"), certes, mais dans lesquels ce qui constitue leur essence ce n'est pas leur "meaning" ou leur "semantic content" mais la "particular form" que le travail du rêve imprime à ces pensées du rêve.[6] Car les rêves, dit Freud sont une "forme" particulière de pensée. D'où une technique d'interprétation qui ne concerne plus essentiellement la présentation ou la représentation (*Darstellung* ou *Vorstellung*) du sens mais ce que Weber appelle une certaine façon de dé-présenter (*de-presenting*), de dé-figurer ou de dis-loquer, de changer de place, de dé-placer le placement (*Ent-stellen*).[7] Voilà où technique et déconstruction s'allient pour déplacer la question de la présence, de la présentation ou de la représentation du sens en les entraînant, de placement en placement, de mises en place en remises en place (*Stellen, Darstellung, Vorstellung*) vers une dis-location (*Ent-stellung*). Cette simple et brève indication suffit pour expliquer l'intérêt que Weber porte, à travers tout ce lexique allemand, sur lequel il a beaucoup écrit, à la question de la technique que Heidegger organisera autour du *Gestell.* Si vous voulez bien relire de près "The Meaning of the Thallus" (nous ne pouvons le faire ici), vous verrez pourquoi, selon Weber, "Freud's dream here is of a sphere beyond—*jenseits*—interpretation."[8] Non qu'il faille "transcend hermeneutic questions as such." Il s'agit seulement de "widening and transforming their scope."[9] Or cela est rendu nécessaire, une fois encore, par une "place" (*eine Stelle*, dit Freud) qui doit être laissée dans la nuit. C'est la canonique et obscure *place* de l'ombilic du rêve (*der Nabel des Traums*). Nous avons tous tourné autour de ce lieu. Je ne veux pas y revenir ici pour mon compte. Dans le texte[10] que j'avais jadis consacré à ce passage et auquel je me permets de vous renvoyer, je m'étais déjà longuement référé à *The Legend of Freud* que je voudrais ici, sans revenir sur mes pas, aborder d'un autre point de vue, celui de la place justement, et de ce qui lie la place à la technique, pour y suivre, au moins en pointillés (car une lecture continue et saturante demanderait deux cents pages) le mouvement original de la démonstration, de l'écriture (de la technique déconstructive, si vous voulez) de Weber. Elle le conduit d'abord à travers un chemin d'une rare complexité et d'un raffinement exceptionnel vers la remise en question d'une *technique interprétative* et de ses présupposés, ceux de Freud mais aussi ceux de Lacan. Cette technique garde pour ultimes destinations (1) la détermination herméneutique d'un *sens*, (2) la détermination topologique d'une *place centrale*, (3) la détermination substantive, la nomination de ce centre sémantique qu'il s'agit ainsi, en lui donnant un nom, en le substantivant, de commencer à substantialiser, voire à subjectiver. On passe plus facilement du substantif à la substance et au sujet. Il y va donc de la place et du centre, du sens et du nom. Précisant ce qu'il en disait dans la première version allemande, Weber rappelle que pour Lacan toute l'interprétation de ce qui "s'épanouit dans l'inconscient" et "se diffuse, tel le mycelium, comme dit Freud au sujet du rêve, autour d'un point central. C'est toujours du sujet en tant qu'indéterminé qu'il s'agit."[11] Or Weber note en souriant que s'il s'agissait, pour Freud et Lacan, de voir le sens du rêve *s'ériger* majestueusement ("*rising* majestically"),[12] en surgissant hors de son mycelium, la signification du phallus, "Lacan's Baedeker might suffice." L'allusion ironique au Baedeker cache une citation de Freud. Celui-ci avait déclaré ne pas aimer se satisfaire des Baedeker. Or dans le cas présent, c'est à la fois contre Freud et Lacan que Weber se moque du Baedeker, car rien ne permet de conclure que l'ombilic des rêves soit "central" et "vide." Au contraire, il semble "curiously full, oversaturated and if it presents difficulties to our understanding, it is because it contains too much rather than too little. In short, whatever else it may be, a *Knaël* [*navel*] is not simply a béance (or an *Abgrund*). And above all, nothing permits us to assert that the chain and trains, strands and snares that compose the meshwork of the 'navel' are neatly 'diffused' *around* a center."

Si j'attire votre attention sur ce passage, ce n'est pas seulement à cause de l'importance, en effet considérable, de l'enjeu théorique, du contenu des interprétations, du sens du rêve et des techniques d'interprétation qu'il appelle. Ni seulement parce que, à ce point, Weber oppose de façon intéressante et convaincante Freud à Lacan. ("If Freud's description of this navel differs from Lacan's, it is precisely because it brings into movement just what Lacan seeks to arrest: the very notion and place of a *center*.")[13] Non, c'est pour au moins *deux autres raisons*.

A. La première, c'est que nous avons ici un des exemples brillants (il y en aurait d'autres mais nous devons choisir) de la technique weberienne, de sa signature inimitable, de son style déconstructif comme de son style d'écriture argumentative. L'opération met en œuvre une extrême attention à la lettre de plusieurs langues, au cours d'un passage traducteur mais aussi inventif dans le transfert même. Ce transfert est générateur d'idiome, entre l'allemand, le français et l'anglais (comme à ce passage des frontières qui garde la mémoire de notre première rencontre en *quiproquo* à l'aéroport de Berlin en 1968, rappelez-moi que je dois vous la raconter à un moment ou à un autre). Ainsi le verbe anglais "straddle" va se trouver investi d'une mission théorico-poétique unique. Au premier abord, Weber l'avance comme la simple traduction de "aufsetzen." L'ombilic de Freud ne comporte, ne comprend ni ne contient aucun centre. Il chevauche l'inconnu, "dem Unerkannten aufsitzt." Une fois qu'il a traduit, de façon irréprochable, *aufsetzen* par *straddle*, Weber explore et exploite de façon merveilleuse toutes les ressources du mot anglais, son histoire, sa polysémie, les différents registres de sa riche tropologie. Dans les deux pages dont je vous recommande la lecture (il faudrait tout citer, je ne le puis ici), il analyse les sept sens donnés par l'*OED*, puis il rappelle que le verbe vient de "stride." Puis il y met en relief, de façon incontestable, et la valeur de mouvement progressif et la valeur apparemment opposée de l'arrêt,[14] à savoir de la "position" qui lui importe tant. Mais aussi, et surtout, guidé par la conclusion de l'article du *OED*, la valeur de "divaricate" qui va à la fois confirmer et relancer la contradiction ou la divergence disséminale et *uncanny* entre mouvement et immobilité. Ça bouge et ça ne bouge pas, ça bouge sur place. Weber cite encore le *OED*: "*Divaricate*: (fr. *Dis-+varicare*, f. *various*, straddling), 1. *intr*. To stretch or spread apart; to branch off or diverge; in *Bot*. and *Zool*. to diverge widely. 2. trans. To stretch or open wide apart or sunder. 3. To cause or spread out in different directions."

Q. Est-ce que cela ne décrit pas avant tout, comme en miroir, ce que vous appeliez l'opération weberienne, cette façon de lire en traduisant, en voyageant, en transférant, en analysant les significations contradictoires, divergentes, *uncanny*, en déplaçant les choses sur place, de digression en digression, de divergence en divergence? Et vous-même, en ce moment . . .

A. Vous voulez rire, non? Mais il est vrai que je m'intéresse, dans le sillage de Weber, à la proximité entre *rire* et *lire*. Je voudrais aller aussi loin que possible dans cette direction mais je ne sais pas si votre journal nous en donnera le temps et la place. En français la différence entre lire et rire tient au seul remplacement d'une lettre et cela vous restera intraduisible. Ici je lis, j'essaie de lire avec vous et d'aider vos lecteurs à partager mon admiration. Je voudrais les conduire patiemment vers le moment où ils pourront, s'ils le souhaitent, penser à rire. Et penser, selon Weber, la place et le débordement du rire, de ce qu'on appelle en français le "fou rire" (au-delà du sens et du vouloir, peut-être de l'économie et de l'épargne même) ou se tordre de rire. Pourquoi se tordre? Quoi de cette torsion du corps?

Mais si vous m'interrompez tout le temps, nous n'y arriverons pas, votre journal ne nous donnera pas la place voulue. Donc, à partir de cet étrange chevauchement des sens (le chevauchement, le *straddling*, c'est aussi, c'est d'abord ce qui se passe entre, au-dessus et par delà tous ces sens à même le même mot), Weber va extirper de façon apparemment magique mais d'une impeccable rationalité toute une série ramifiée de significations (je vous laisse lire: le corps, les jambes, les *legs* qui enjambent et chevauchent en une toute autre signification et avec une toute autre fonction que celles avec lesquelles, en français, j'avais joué entre les *legs* anglais et le legs, l'héritage français dans *La carte postale*, autour de *Au-delà du principe de plaisir*) la position ("equivocal position"), l'investissement ("occupation," *Besetzung*), l'imposition et l'imposture. "Does not such a compromise have to up the ante to stay in the game?" La scène de la surenchère, et la logique du "to up the ante" est partout chez Weber. Les jambes de Freud se tiennent ainsi des deux côtés d'une "untenable alternative" et "straddle" chevauche tous les sens du *OED* dont la dite scène primitive ne serait en somme qu'une figuration graphique. Il s'agit alors d'interpréter un langage de Freud dont la *Bildersprache* présente et représente moins le sens qu'elle ne le dé-place et dé-présente (*entstellt*). Ce verbe, *ent-stellt*, met en déroute toute herméneutique qui consisterait à rendre présent le sens et d'autre part, dans la mouvance ou l'appartenance du lexique de la question (notoirement heideggerienne) de la technique du *Gestell* (*Vorstellung, Darstellung, Gestell*), etc., il se réfère avant tout à la place (*Stelle*), à ce qui se met ou se tient en place. Et en effet, nous explique Weber, Freud ne se contente pas de désigner l'ombilic du rêve comme la "place" (*Stelle*) où le rêve chevauche l'inconnu. Il décrit cet inconnu ou plutôt ce qui émerge hors de lui, le désir du rêve qui surgit "comme le champignon hors de son mycelium." C'est alors, je vous y renvoie encore, que le thallus remplace le phallus (il y suffit encore d'une lettre à substituer) pour déplacer et remplacer la logique lacanienne du phallus et ce que la lecture lacanienne "would like to forget: that the dream-navel cannot be reduced to a question of the phallus, of the béance, split or absent center of a subject, for one simple reason: the thallus."[15]

Une fois de plus, l'enjeu principal est topo—ou khoragraphique; il s'agit de la place: "The dream-navel, as it is inscribed and described in Freud's text, points us in another direction, less visible but not invisible either. The question raised here concerns the *site* of the navel, the place on which the dream-wish rises. The question in short, is that of the 'signification du thallus.'" Recourant une dernière fois à l'*OED*, Weber insiste sur le fait que la définition du thallus consiste seulement en négations (c'est comme une théologie apophatique) et souligne l'absence de racine ("true roots are absent"). Rien d'étonnant dès lors qu'il soit si difficile de "see more radically," comme le promet Lacan.

De tout cela, que je dois encore une fois vous laisser relire de près, Weber tire deux conclusions qui nous importent. Elles doivent en effet répondre au souci de votre question sur la déconstruction et la technique. L'une c'est que nous touchons ici aux *limites de l'interprétation*. Il nous faut changer jusqu'au concept de sens qui commande l'herméneutique. Il ne s'agit pas d'abandonner l'interprétation mais de réinterpréter les limites de l'interprétation, et pour cela de se tenir sur elles, sur les deux bords de la limite et de les chevaucher en quelque sorte (*straddle*) (la place est d'ailleurs un système de limites et de délimitations). Ce faisant, il s'agit d'affecter le *concept même de sens* d'une transformation qui le dé-place, c'est-à-dire qui change son rapport à la place et donc à ce qui lui *impose* une place et le déplace. C'est là que la technique déconstructive de l'interprétation concerne justement l'articulation entre technique et espacement, technique et *taking place*, entre la *tekhnè* et le lieu. On a affaire à une topo—ou plutôt à une khora-technologie. "For, if at the limits of interpretation we discover, not the abyss of an absent center, but a navel and a thallus, the very notion of *meaning* has begun to change before our eyes—particularly if our eyes are directed at Freud's text."[16]

A ce moment-là, seconde conclusion, se produit le coup de théâtre, ou l'opération de l'opus ou de l'opéra proprement weberien. Il va orchestrer à la fois le concert de la multiplicité transférentielle des idiomes linguistiques (trois langues au moins, comme toujours, et qui capitalisent leurs jeux de mots respectifs), le pouvoir de la nomination et, si vous voulez rire, l'essentielle expérience du rire (good or bad joke). Le mot traduit par *straddle* a un autre sens en allemand: *Jemanden or etwas aufsitzen* peut vouloir dire "être trompé ou induit en erreur par quelqu'un ou par quelque chose. Par l'inconnu (*das Unerkannten: dem Unerkannte aufsitzt*) par exemple," note Weber qui ajoute sans transition: "Or by the terms introduced by Lacan: for instance, that of the *Nom du Père* (Name-of-the Father), which, he suggested, must also be read as: *Les non-dupes errent* (the non dupes err). Yet if this error must be understood as constitutive of the very gesture of denomination itself, then this cannot be without consequences for every form of discourse that seeks to articulate truth by means of naming: be it that of Freud, of Lacan, or of this text itself."

Weber n'exonère pas son propre texte, il n'excepte pas sa propre nomination, il ne la met pas hors jeu. Car il s'agit aussi de jeu et de *joke*, et de tromperie et d'imposition dans l'assignation du nom, dans le remplacement de phallus par thallus par exemple. C'est là que le rire de Weber éclate. Discrètement, comme dans une histoire juive, il se moque de lui-même en disant la vérité de tous. Mais le jeu qui fait rire, une mauvaise plaisanterie (*bad joke*) piège tout effort pour articuler le sens. Toute interprétation a pour origine et pour fin la violence d'une thèse, à savoir d'une position qui, se posant, s'impose à vous et vous trompe. L'imposition est une imposture, voilà la technique de l'interprétation qui doit être déconstruite (en riant du rire, de la *bad joke*). Elle déconstruit non pas une révélation du sens mais par la contre-imposition d'une contre-technique.[17] Remarquez le lexique choisi par Weber, c'est une variation sur la thésis (*Setzung*) (et dès qu'il y a *thesis*, il y a *tekhnè*), sur la position thétique qui, comme on dit en français, en impose, fait impression, et sur ce qui en elle place ou se place: posture, imposture, imposition. Le mot "play," ici, fait signe à la fois vers le jeu, la plaisanterie, voire la mauvaise plaisanterie qui induit en erreur—et vers le théâtre. Quand vous aurez lu ces lignes, vous aurez compris pourquoi la question du rire secoue le corps et le corpus de Sam Weber, en particulier quand il s'interroge sur le rire chez Freud, sur son économie et son anéconomie:

> From this vantage-point, the meaning of the thallus begins to appear to be—or rather to play a very bad joke on all attempts to articulate meaning. For the ramifications of Freud's description of the

> dream-navel suggest that interpretation originates and ends in a kind of calculated deception; in a posture necessarily, and structurally, an imposture, and perhaps also an imposition.
>
> In any case, it is beyond doubt that such questions were what impelled Freud to move (walking, striding, straddling) from his interpretation of dreams, the royal road to the unconscious, to the less regal realm of jokes. As we shall see, this was, and is no laughing matter.[18]

Magnifique formule. Elle revient à la fin du chapitre suivant, justement intitulé "The Joke: Child's Play." Là encore (dans un superbe chapitre que je vous laisse lire), nous retrouvons deux fois le même geste, qu'il s'agisse du jeu ou qu'il s'agisse de Lacan.

1. Le champ du "jeu" (play) ou du mot d'esprit, de la plaisanterie (*joke*), le passage ou la dérivation de l'un à l'autre n'est pas circonscriptible, il englobe et déborde la théorie, c'est une métathéorie qui nous enseigne qu'il n'y a pas de métathéorie qui ne soit risible. La théorie du "play" et de "joke" est encore un *effet* du jeu et un *effort*, toujours vain, pour maîtriser le jeu et le jeu de mot. Celui-ci a toujours raison de la théorie (et je me dis alors: c'est cette conviction partagée qui peut-être nous fait toujours rire ensemble, Sam et moi). Ecoutez-le: "For such a play is designed to provide the ground and kernel not merely of the joke alone, but also of the theory that seeks to comprehend and to master the joke. This theory, we recall, seeks to succeed where others—Freud's predecessors—have failed: to organize the 'disjecta membra' of the joke into an organic whole. But the psychogenetic derivation of the joke from play is still lacking what is perhaps the most characteristic aspect of the joke. And that, we repeat, is no laughing matter."[19] La répétition de cette formule dans la version anglaise[20] marque bien que le problème est sérieux. Il ne prête pas à rire. Mais son sérieux n'est pas extérieur ou supérieur au rire. Il concerne le passage du jeu au *Witz* et l'échec d'une dérivation psychogénétique entre l'un et l'autre. On peut suivre d'un bout à l'autre de l'œuvre de Weber la tentative, directe ou indirecte pour rendre compte, sans rire et en riant, de cet échec.

2. Nous retrouvons ici, en cette fin du chapitre, une nouvelle réserve au sujet du couple de concepts sur lequel Lacan, pendant si longtemps, a fondé et son discours et sa technique, à savoir la distinction oppositionnelle entre le symbolique et l'imaginaire. C'est à propos du *fort! Da*: "Indeed, if this other seems destined to replace the absent mother and to revenge the child, it would provide us with yet another reason for regarding the Symbolic as a lure of the Imaginary, as the discursive continuation of the ambivalent strategy of narcissism."[21]

Q. J'ai quelque mal à vous suivre, je l'avoue. A deux reprises vous insistez sur ces réserves quant à Lacan mais on m'a demandé, dans mon journal, de vous interroger sur certaines réserves (prudentes, il est vrai mais insistantes) de Weber au sujet de vos propres réserves au sujet de Lacan. Par exemple, me dit-on, dans *Mass Mediauras*,[22] à deux reprises, dans un discours en effet nuancé et compliqué, Weber semble ne pas exclure que votre lecture du "Séminaire sur *La lettre volée*" puisse être contestée, voire réfutée. Il insiste même, d'une page à l'autre, malgré des "peut-être" qui laissent beaucoup à penser: "Derrida 'reads' Lacan's text, even if one may well contest that reading." Et plus loin: "Derrida 'frames' Lacan (in all senses) by demonstrating—and it is a demonstration that *can* be discussed, contested, perhaps even refuted—*how* and *where* Lacan's Seminar on *The Purloined Letter* ignores or avoids the question of the frame, and above all, of its own frame, the enabling condition of its own authority."

A. Il a tout à fait raison et tous les *peut-être* compliquent à merveille la donne. Ce n'est pas ici le lieu de discuter ces textes trop difficiles pour une interview. Non seulement je crois que Weber a raison mais n'oubliez pas que j'ai moi-même, dans le jeu de cette lecture, donné raison à Lacan, à plus d'une reprise et rappelé qu'il était du côté de la raison même. "La raison aura toujours raison. D'elle-même."[23] Ce qui veut dire à la fois spontanément, d'elle-même et en se surmontant, en se vainquant elle-même, en étant plus forte qu'elle même, ce que veut dire "avoir raison de" en français. Tout cela est donc un échiquier trop compliqué pour un entretien. Du point de vue de la déconstruction, à première vue, le premier tort, la première naïveté, c'est de prétendre avoir "raison." Je rappelle que le livre lui-même, *La Carte postale*, qui est aussi, de part en part, depuis ses pseudo *Envois*, le jeu d'une fiction abyssale, commence par ces mots: "Oui tu avais raison," "*Yes you were right*." Qu'est-ce qui se passe quand on donne raison à l'autre? La réponse à cette question est tout sauf simple et rationnelle. Mais laissons cela, je ne suis pas ici pour discuter de mes textes. C'est de Sam Weber qu'il nous faut parler. Singulièrement. Mais avant d'y revenir, je voudrais dire un mot de la terrible question de la dette; de l'insoluble question de la dette insolvable. Non pas du point de vue de ce texte puissant intitulé "The Debts of Deconstruction and Other, Related Assumptions"[24] mais d'un passage plus récent, dans *Mass Mediauras*, celui précisément où il n'exclut pas que ma lecture de Lacan soit contestable—formule de politesse amicale qui laisse clairement entendre qu'en vérité cette lecture puisse et doive être contestée ("Derrida 'reads' Lacan's text; even if one may well contest that reading"). Ce qui m'intéresse le plus dans ce passage si équivoque, c'est le rappel, en forme d'aveu en somme, que tout texte est endetté, et même auprès de celui qu'il critique et conteste. Je ne serais pas moins endetté à l'égard de Lacan quand je le conteste que Sam Weber quand il conteste ma contestation; et je passe sous silence les dettes de Lacan, non seulement à l'égard de penseurs de générations antérieures, de Platon à Freud et à Heidegger mais à l'égard de jeunes gens beaucoup plus jeunes que lui . . . laissons (et même, insistera

Weber dans un irrésistible crescendo, ma contestation qui peut être elle même "discussed, contested even refuted"). Dans ce passage que je vais citer longuement, Weber explique pourquoi, justement, et comment ne pas lui donner raison, la psychanalyse ne peut pas ne pas devenir une institution, alors que la déconstruction, elle, ne peut ni ne doit devenir une institution: "I am not certain that it is either possible, necessary or desirable that deconstruction become an institution. There is enormous pressure to move deconstruction in this direction, if only because it is, to a large extent, situated within areas—such as that of the university—where legitimacy is often measured in terms of institutional standing. The best way to resist such pressure is to keep transforming what is called deconstruction, never allowing it, nor its practitioners to rest on their accumulated laurels (real or not) . . . Deconstruction 'is' the movement of this undoing, which is why it cannot and should never hope to become an institution, as psychoanalysis has tried—with differing success—to be."

> **De là passer à dette in mediauras p. 227, puis**
> **puis revenir à dette et à Mass . . . 63–64**
> **dette impayable I and I. p. 58**

Cette singularité me paralyse donc devant les drôles de questions que vous me posez. C'est pourquoi je n'arrive pas à les prendre au sérieux et vous demande si "vous voulez rire." Une première tentation serait de répondre en m'orientant vers ce qui *oriente*, justement, et la pensée et le corps de Sam Weber, vers son souci privilégié de la topographie, vers son intérêt constamment renouvelé pour le site, *l'orientation* du corps et du regard, entre la gauche et la droite (dont Kant parle si bien et dont il rappelle qu'elles *situent* mon corps dit propre, de façon irréductiblement sensible et pré-conceptuelle), vers la *topologie*, le discours sur la place et la place du discours, vers le lieu, plus précisément l'avoir-lieu comme événement, vers l'emplacement, le site de la situation analytique, le site de la situation dramatico-théâtrale, de la position face à la scène, l'écran de cinéma ou de télévision. La mise en œuvre originale de la déconstruction par Weber a élu son lieu propre en ces lieux. Regardez par exemple ce qu'il nous enseigne de "l'âge des media," dans son idiome. Il le fait d'ailleurs en signant une nouvelle lexicalité idiomatique. Mais, autre trait remarquable, Weber invente justement *son* idiome en traversant plusieurs langues à la fois, *il joue* (car il joue toujours) entre plusieurs langues. Il voyage d'une langue à l'autre, non pas pour y découvrir des îles bienheureuses, vierges, intactes entre les continents mais pour faire émerger de l'abîme des paysages linguistiques encore inconnus, des archipels *unheimlich*, des détroits et des isthmes sémantiques propices aux explorations mais aussi aux contaminations les plus inouïes.

Je vais en prendre un exemple, mais il pourrait être multiplié. Il y va bien à la fois de la "technique," de la *façon de faire* de Weber, et de technique télécommunicationnelle, de TV, de TV *set*, d'événement, d'avoir-lieu, de déconstruction et surtout de place. Voyez ainsi ce qui se passe, ce qui arrive, ce qui "comes to pass," comme il le dit de façon si intraduisible, dans les pages 6 et 7 de son Introduction à *Mass Mediauras*, notamment autour du lexique de "set, setting," dont Weber met en œuvre, en place, en scène, aussi bien la richesse, la surabondante équivoque que la résistance à la traduction. Le sous-titre de ce livre juxtapose de façon indissociable trois concepts qui forment le réseau le plus spécifique et le plus "consistant" de la déconstruction weberienne: *Form, Technics, Media*. La technique (la technologie, les techniques, ces deux concepts différents étant soudés de façon intéressante dans l'anglais *technics*) est aussi ce qui soude aux media le concept de "form," en vérité d'une "forme" en un sens paradoxalement kantien. Car c'est justement ce concept de "form" qui installe ("sets") la scène de tout le livre, mais un livre justement consacré au "setting" dans lequel se développent les media. Or ce concept de forme, Weber en rappelle la tradition kantienne: non pas en ce lieu où Kant réussit dans son effort pour en élaborer la problématique mais où il y échoue et finalement l'abandonne à sa propre défaite, à son irrésistible déconstruction, là où la pensée se presse autour de ce qui reste justement en chantier, "undone."

Car une déconstruction ne se décide ni ne se calcule de part en part, à partir d'un projet technique volontaire. Elle est en cours, elle arrive, elle a lieu, elle se fait là où ça se défait ou ça s'inachève. Elle comporte de la technique, certes, mais cette technique ne maîtrise pas, elle ne se maîtrise pas totalement, elle est située, affectée, autant que situante et active. Voici donc l'exemple promis de l'argumentation weberienne: une procédure abyssale, une tournure stylistique et rhétorique puissamment formalisatrice, un jeu aussi, un rire de la pensée que je trouve typiques de l'écriture déconstructive, de la "technique" de Weber. Je dis abyssale *là où*, en ce *lieu* où la *mise en place*, l'*emplacement*, la *localisation* de l'*avoir-lieu* se met à la fois en scène et "en abyme," commence (*sets*) à installer (*setting*) son dispositif machinique et local (*set, setting*):

"For without the unity of place, the unity of the subject becomes difficult to conceive. It is the function of esthetic theory, as it is developed by Kant, to help secure this ever more problematical unity of place by introducing the no less problematical notion of form. That Kant's effort, in the *Third Critique*, is more significant in coming undone than in succeeding 'sets' the scene for the following essays, which explore the unraveling of form as the 'setting' for the rise of the media."[25]

Weber cite et pose la question absolue du lieu, celle de l'orientation même: non pas "Comment s'orienter dans la pensée?" mais cette fois "Where in the World are We?" Citation d'un titre lu dans les media, donc, dans le *L.A. Times* au moment d'un tremblement de terre. Ce titre en forme de question citée depuis un media annonce alors des développements à venir sur "Television: Set and Screen." Le mot "set" paraît déjà difficile à traduire dans la richesse de ses surdéterminations. En ce sens et dans cette mesure, on pourrait dire que sa force "déconstructrice" résiste à toute machine à traduire, donc à toute technique qui ne serait que technique. Weber part du GPS (Global Positioning System). Le GPS est un dispositif technique permettant de localiser tout mouvement sur la terre avec une précision jusqu'ici inégalée GPS **Je lis citer longuement p. 6/7.**

"Vous voulez rire," étrange expression, vous ne trouvez pas? Est-ce que vous l'entendez bien? Arrêtons-nous un instant sur ces trois mots. "Vous voulez rire," voilà une expression assez idiomatique en français, je crois. Non seulement une expression verbale mais un geste assez idiomatique. Ce geste relève donc d'une "pragmatique" qui prendrait en compte un "geste socio-linguistique" assez difficile à traduire. Nous voilà déjà dans la "déconstruction" comme expérience de la traduction impossible et du "plus d'une langue." (Ce qu'il y a d'unique, et de précieux pour moi, entre autres choses, dans tout ce que je dois à Sam Weber, c'est de vivre dans plus d'une culture linguistique à la fois, l'allemande, l'anglaise et la française; il est "chez lui" partout, et moi, j'apprends à le suivre. . . .) "You're kidding" ou "Who are you kidding," c'est très proche de "vous voulez rire," en tant que geste social (du point de vue pragmatique, donc). Mais ce n'est pas exactement la même chose. Il y manque l'allusion explicite au rire (*laughter*) et surtout au "vouloir." En allemand "dass ich nicht lache," le vouloir de l'autre n'est pas davantage nommé. "Vous voulez rire," dans certaines situations fort déterminées, c'est une réplique dont on se sert pour dénoncer et refuser une proposition qu'on ne *veut* pas prendre au sérieux. On déclare ainsi, du même coup, qu'on ne *peut* ni ne *doit* la prendre au sérieux (je ne veux ni ne peux prendre au sérieux la cascade de questions et de demandes que vous m'adressez, voyons). On a même le devoir de dénoncer, voire de rejeter avec ironie une proposition excessive et déplacée. C'est donc, vous voyez déjà le paradoxe, une façon ironique, un peu rieuse, de refuser de répondre sous prétexte que la question même, la demande ou la proposition est trop comique. Intentionnellement ou non (autre difficulté!). En riant froidement, en faisant semblant d'être sérieux, mais en pince-sans-rire, *a tongue in the cheek*, on demande à l'autre s'il est sérieux et s'il n'est pas en train de rire, de plaisanter; si tout ceci n'est pas "a joke." (Je note vite en passant, déjà, mais aurons l'occasion d'y revenir, que *joke*, *Witz*, etc. cela pourrait être le titre d'une immense question dont le réseau envahit en profondeur, mais aussi en vrille, en rhizome, en parasite irrésistible [le rire est aussi irrésistible], dans toutes ses dimensions [politique, historique, théâtrale, littéraire, psychanalytique surtout], avec une constance imperturbable mais aussi ironique tout l'œuvre et toute la pensée de Sam Weber, n'y laissant rien intact et nous contraignant à tout remuer de fond en comble.) Qu'est-ce que le rire, la plaisanterie, la "joke," le mot d'esprit, etc.? D'où ça vient? Pourquoi et comment cela arrive-t-il? Qu'est-ce que cet étrange événement? Le rire est-il le propre de l'homme? Peut-on se passer de l'inconscient pour en rendre compte? Que signifie-t-il quant au lien social et à l'intersubjectivité, etc.? Voilà des questions que Sam Weber aura mieux développées que quiconque. Il en aura inauguré une nouvelle élaboration. Et il nous a montré que cette question dérangeait étrangement, dépaysait tout (unheimlich). Je voudrais montrer, si vous avez la patience de m'écouter, en quoi cette question de l'événement du rire est inséparable de celles qui intéressent, me dites-vous, vos lecteurs, par exemple entre "déconstruction et technique." Mais il y faudra quelques détours. En vous disant "vous voulez rire," je vous soupçonne, j'affecte de vous soupçonner, par exemple, de ne pas être sérieux et de me poser une ou plusieurs questions impossibles "pour rire" ou pour "caricaturer" un entretien sérieux, pour vous moquer de moi, de vos collègues ou de votre public ou de je ne sais qui. N'êtes vous pas en train de rire et de vous moquer du monde? Et peut-être, d'où mon ironie à moi, sans le savoir, sans en avoir la moindre idée.

Car voyez-vous, celui qui, pour rire, ou en feignant de rire, dit à l'autre, comme je viens de le faire "vous voulez rire," il sait bien que l'autre ne rit pas. Et c'est tout le problème. On accuse en riant, mais on accuse l'autre de ne pas être sérieux, de rire, donc, mais sans savoir rire ou sans savoir qu'il rit. C'est diablement compliqué, vous ne trouvez pas. Comment allons-nous continuer? L'expression est donc intéressante (vous voyez, je commence à être trop long, je dérive, je vais vous faire perdre du temps et j'égare vos lecteurs sur des sentiers écartés). Comment pourrait-on *vouloir rire*? Décider de rire? Quel est le rapport entre la décision volontaire (la conscience et l'intention, etc.) et le rire, l'éclat de rire, le fou rire? L'amitié philosophique qui me lie à Sam Weber, notre amitié tout court, j'oserai dire qu'elle appartient à l'expérience de cette question et d'abord à l'expérience partagée de ce rire même, de cet éclat de fou rire. Involontaire, indécidé, inconscient même. D'où sa force et son intensité, d'où sa fidélité. La fidélité ne peut être qu'inconsciente.

Q. Je voulais justement vous demander quand et dans quelles circonstances vous avez rencontré Sam Weber. Est-ce vous ne pourriez pas me répondre avec des faits ou des citations brèves, plutôt que par des digressions? Surtout en orientant les choses du côté de "déconstruction et technique," de la chose politique et surtout du 11 septembre qui fut, je crois, un événement majeur. Vous savez, mes lecteurs voudraient surtout savoir comment vous avez rencontré Sam Weber. Des rumeurs courent à ce sujet . . .

A. D'accord, je vais essayer, je vous raconterai ça. Mais d'abord, puisque vous voulez des citations, j'en introduis une. Mais il y faut encore un détour argumenté. Dire que le rire ne se décide pas, cela ne veut pas dire qu'il y a d'un côté le rire, de l'autre la décision, mais peut être que la décision elle-même ne se décide pas. Ça c'est grave. Vous savez, vous, ce que ça veut dire, *décision*? Et l'essence du rire? En tout cas, s'il y a une chose que je ne partagerai pas avec Bataille, c'est l'idée que le rire est souverain si ce mot garde une attache à son sens traditionnel. Et s'il ne garde à cet égard aucune attache, alors pourquoi le garder encore?

Q. Ce sont des questions dont on ne traite pas dans l'école de journalisme; du moins dans celle vers laquelle, dès que j'ai dû quitter l'université . . .

A. Moi non plus, je ne traite pas, mais je crois savoir ce que les autres croient savoir quand ils se servent de ces mots (la décision, le rire), et je me raccroche à ça pour poser des questions. C'est peut-être ça la déconstruction, et ça peut devenir une technique: faire comme si on croyait savoir ce que les autres croient savoir à tel ou tel sujet, et ne pas croire à ce qu'on croit savoir que les autres croient savoir. Au départ, ce n'est pas une technique, mais ça peut devenir une technique. Pour ça il faut savoir rire. Mais savoir rire, qu'est-ce que ça veut dire? Est-ce que ça s'apprend, le rire? Est-ce que ça s'enseigne, comme une technique? Comme un savoir ou une science? Non, n'est-ce pas? C'est peut-être la seule chose qui ne s'enseigne pas, le rire; et qui reste foncièrement étrangère à l'enseignement comme tel. Le rire n'a lieu qu'une seule fois à la fois, chaque fois une fois, imprévisiblement, comme un événement qu'on ne voit pas venir. Alors comment cela pourrait-il-devenir une technique, voilà le problème. Vous me suivez?

Q. Oui, là, oui. Enfin je crois.

A. Eh bien, que se passerait-il si une décision ne se décidait pas plus que le rire—ou les larmes ou le rire aux larmes, et il vous faudrait lier ces deux questions. Puis les lier à la grande question du calcul, et donc de la technique; car ce qui ne se décide pas, c'est ce qui ne se calcule pas. Ce qui ne se calcule pas semble excéder, en un seul instant, la technique même, vous me suivez, car c'est bien de "déconstruction et technique" que nous parlons, comme vous semblez le souhaiter. Faisons donc cette hypothèse: une *décision ne se décide pas* (encore une difficulté de l'idiome que vous aurez du mal à traduire: une décision se décide ou ne se décide pas, cela veut dire deux choses: 1. qu'*on* décide (ou non), que la décision décide ou encore, 2. chose qui ne peut se dire qu'en français, que je sache, que la décision *se* décide, réflexivement, qu'elle *se* décide elle-même ou non, qu'elle *se* décide à décider, à se décider, par une sorte de volonté de volonté, etc. Si donc une décision ne se décide pas plus que le rire (ou les larmes ou le rire aux larmes), qu'est-ce qui reste du concept le plus puissant de la tradition la plus puissante de la pensée occidentale, celle qui, avec les concepts connexes et indissociables de volonté, d'ego, de conscience, d'intention, de responsabilité, etc., semble fonder l'éthique, la politique, le droit, et même la philosophie?[26] . . . Peut-être est-on surpris par elle, passivement, comme par un événement qui vous arrive. La décision vous arrive. Voilà une proposition paradoxale et révolutionnaire. Un peu comique, même. Si quelqu'un venait vous dire: j'ai été surpris par ma décision, vous seriez tenté d'éclater de rire, avec vos lecteurs. Eh bien si vous suivez ce que Weber analyse du rire ou du fou rire—depuis toujours mais en particulier dans *Mass Mediauras*, je gage que vous aurez un des meilleurs fils conducteurs de sa pensée. Vos lecteurs devraient se reporter, par exemple, pour commencer, à **tel passage de "Catching Up with the Past."**

Merci. Essayons, mais je sens que j'aurai du mal à improviser. Vous voulez donc qu'on parle de Sam Weber, de la déconstruction, de la technique, tout ça, bon. Si j'essaie de dominer en public l'effusion admirative de ma reconnaissance pour Sam Weber, je me laisse aussitôt envahir par une double question. Elle pourrait avoir la forme suivante: *qui* est Sam Weber *et quelle* est l'essence du politique? Évidemment ce sont deux questions distinctes, voire fort hétérogènes. L'une porte sur quelqu'un, l'autre sur l'essence de quelque chose. Or je voudrais non seulement les lier entre elles, comme celles de deux figures également singulières, l'une singulière, l'autre générale, l'une plutôt privée, sinon secrète, l'autre publique et communément partagée. Mais toutes les deux *pour moi*. Qui est Sam Weber pour moi, en tant que ce "qui," "celui qui" me dit quelque chose de l'essence du politique. Je voudrais surtout ouvrir un lieu pour l'histoire, pour l'historicité même de cette double question. Quel rapport entretient-elle avec la "déconstruction," la "technique," tout ça, toutes ces choses dont vous voulez parler? Cette question, l'historicité de la question de l'essence du politique, en tant qu'elle se lie à l'histoire singulière d'une singularité, je ne me la pose pas *au sujet de* Sam Weber mais je me dis que j'aimerais la lui poser, un jour, pour qu'il y réponde, lui, en son nom. Je dis bien en son nom. Je ne peux pas parler en son nom, bien sûr; et pourtant c'est ce que je m'apprête à faire, comme chaque fois qu'à le faire, à en prendre le risque et riant et en riant de ma propre dénégation, on se permet de dire ce que quelqu'un pense de quelque chose. Quand je dis "Platon pense que . . ." ou "Platon dit que . . . ," je commence à me ridiculiser en me permettant de parler en son nom tout en le déniant, en alléguant quelque savoir impossible à ce sujet. C'est comique et je suis sûr que je dis une bêtise en disant "Platon pense que . . ." Comme je sais bien qu'il aura mieux dit en son nom tout ce que je pourrais tenter de dire et d'interpréter en son nom, disons que je parlerais surtout de son nom, de son nom propre, de son nom propre et si singulier d'état civil et surtout de sa signature.

Q. Je comprends mal ce que vous dites et je suis sûr que mes lecteurs, qui n'ont pas tous passé quelque temps à l'université, comme moi, n'y comprendront rien. Ne pourriez-vous pas vous expliquer de façon un peu plus concrète, pédagogique, intelligible? Un peu plus communicative?

A. Non, ne me demandez jamais ça. Demandez plutôt à vos lecteurs de lire Platon.

Q. Je leur passerai le message. Pour l'instant, je m'adresse à vous car on dit, Jacques Derrida, que vous connaissez bien Sam Weber. Vous êtes son ami depuis longtemps. Comment l'avez vous rencontré? Que pensez-vous de sa vie et de son œuvre? Enfin y a-t-il un lien entre les deux? Politiquement, surtout, puisque vous venez de faire allusion à ce que vous appelez étrangement "l'essence du politique," et en particulier depuis le 11 septembre?

A. Vous voulez rire. Remarquez que si on voulait rire ensemble, et savoir pourquoi on rit, il faudrait encore ou déjà en appeler à Weber. Je le tiens pour un grand penseur du rire, voilà de quoi j'aimerais parler avec vous. Si vous tenez aux questions que vous venez de poser, il vaut mieux s'arrêter tout de suite. Comment pouvez-vous espérer que je réponde sous cette forme au pied levé? Tout ce que vous dites est vrai ou "makes sense," bien sûr. Sam est un vieil ami, un ami très cher. Exceptionnel. J'admire et sa vie et son œuvre, il y a bien un lien entre les deux. Mais il faudrait des siècles pour en parler et quant à notre rencontre, à Berlin en 1968, un entretien de dix heures serait indispensable. Pour le 11 septembre, un entretien de dix mois. La question préalable, celle que je voudrais, moi, *vous* poser, c'est celle du métier que *vous* exercez, vous. Car je crois qu'il est temps que tous les journalistes du monde répondent à des questions et répondent d'eux-mêmes, répondent d'abord des questions qu'ils croient devoir poser. Comment avez-vous préparé cet entretien? Qu'en attendez-vous? Comment vous êtes-vous préparé vous-même? Avez-vous lu tous les livres de Sam Weber? qui tous sont des provocations à penser le journalisme. Surtout le journalisme moderne, les medias écrits et audio visuels. Et les miens? Quelle est votre technique? Comment traitez-vous le problème des rapports entre votre technique, les contraintes économico-politiques de votre journal et vos devoirs professionnels? Car vous avez, n'est-ce pas, des devoirs et des responsabilités, en particulier devant le sujet que vous êtes censé aborder, à commencer par Sam Weber lui-même. Moi aussi d'ailleurs.

Q. Justement, c'est bien la question que je me pose. Comment devient-on un bon journaliste? Pourriez-vous me conseiller à ce sujet? Je m'adresse à vous parce que quelqu'un m'a dit vous avoir entendu parler, un jour, de quelque chose comme la profession ou, je ne sais plus, la profession de foi du journaliste. Il paraît que cette question vous a toujours obsédé et que vous ne perdez pas une occasion d'y revenir. Vous auriez même défini Dieu, devant Weber lui-même, comme quelqu'un qui aurait dit à Abraham, sur le mont Moriah: "Surtout pas de journalistes!"[27]

En vous demandant à quelle date on a parlé de cette chose, le "journaliste," comme d'une profession à statut reconnu dans une institution privée ou publique, vous auriez, me dit-on, déclaré à peu près ceci: un journaliste qui, demain, voudrait honorer sa profession, réfléchir à ses nouvelles responsabilités dans un espace public transformé par de nouvelles structures socio-politiques et, indissociablement, par de nouvelles technologies de la "communication"; quelqu'un qui voudrait aussi se demander si le mot de "communication" convient encore; quelqu'un qui voudrait aussi réélaborer comme il convient les questions déontologiques, éthiques, juridico-politiques, philosophiques mais aussi techniques et professionnelles de sa "profession"; quelqu'un qui voudrait prendre en compte ce que la responsabilité d'une parole publique implique quant à son image, sa théâtralité, voire son cinéma, quant à la philosophie et à la psychanalyse d'une telle responsabilité, celui-là serait bien inspiré de lire et de méditer la grande œuvre de Sam Weber. Qu'entendez-vous par là? Je vous le demande parce que je me trouve dans la situation que vous auriez, me dit-on, décrite ainsi. Depuis longtemps, moi aussi, je ressens cette espérance ou cette angoisse. Ça a commencé dès que j'ai dû abandonner mes études universitaires et devenir journaliste. Ça ne marchait pas bien à l'université mais j'ai pensé que le journalisme, c'était ce qu'il y a de plus proche, malgré tout. Il paraît que toutes les questions que je me pose exigeraient une démarche, comme on dit, ou une technique déconstructive. Pourriez-vous me dire en deux mots ce qu'il faut entendre ici par "technique" (ça, je crois comprendre) mais surtout par "déconstruction"? Et le lien entre les deux? Et quel est le rapport ou l'apport de Weber, dans sa vie et son œuvre, à la "déconstruction," depuis que vous le connaissez? Et surtout depuis le 11 septembre. Vous m'avez déjà dit quelque chose de très important tout à l'heure, déjà, sans avoir l'air de vous en douter, et je suis sûr que cela intéressera nos lecteurs dans le monde entier: vous l'avez donc rencontré à Berlin en 1968! Donc plus de trente ans avant le 11 septembre! Plus de vingt ans avant la chute du Mur de Berlin! C'est très impressionnant, c'est très important, politiquement parlant surtout. Était-ce avant ou après les "événements" de mai 68?

A. Juste après. Mais pardonnez-moi, je crois qu'il vaut mieux s'arrêter ici, je me sens tout à coup très fatigué. C'est l'âge, sans doute, et l'émotion, et vos questions sont trop difficiles. Vraiment démesurées. Et dans un style, à un rythme intraitables pour moi. Je dois vous laisser, je me sens tout à coup très fatigué. La première question à laquelle il faudrait répondre pour donner un sens à vos questions et à mes réponses, ce serait "qui est, singulièrement, irremplaçablement Sam Weber?" En lui-même, pour lui, pour les autres—et pour moi aussi, bien sûr? Voilà ce qui m'importe d'abord et voilà la question à laquelle je suis loin d'avoir une seule réponse toute prête.

Q. Pardonnez-moi, je sens que j'ai été très maladroit. C'est une méprise, un étrange malentendu. Mais je vous en prie, essayons encore. Si je manque cet entretien, mon journal va me le faire payer cher, je risque de perdre mon job et d'être obligé de retourner à l'université où je ne suis pas sûr qu'on me reprendra. Et puis vous avez aussi des devoirs, en tant qu'intellectuel public et politiquement engagé: vous devez communiquer de façon intelligible et vous rendre accessible dans l'espace public. Si vous refusez cet entretien, vous confirmerez une rumeur déjà bien ancienne: vous seriez hautain, élitiste et hermétique, vous refuseriez de parler aux gens, de leur expliquer, de lutter contre l'obscurantisme. Or il faut lutter contre l'ignorance et l'obscurantisme, n'est-ce pas, c'est très important, et encore plus depuis le 11 septembre?

A. Ah bon? Que s'est-il donc passé le 11 septembre? Le 11 septembre de quelle année? Voilà une bonne question.

Q. Le 11 septembre 2001, les twin towers, tout ça, vous ne pensez pas, comme tout le monde que cela fut un événement majeur et sans précédent?

A. Non. Mettons fin, je vous en prie, à ce que vous venez vous-même d'appeler un étrange malentendu. Vous êtes infatigable et je suis de plus en plus fatigué. Pouvez-vous me dire, vous, ce qu'est un événement, un événement majeur et sans précédent? Et ce qui s'est passé le 11 septembre 2001? Voilà de bonnes questions "déconstructives" et, puisque cela semble vous intéresser, ce sont là des questions qui se posent entre déconstruction et technique. Sam Weber les a mieux articulées que quiconque.

Q. Vous voyez, nous approchons notre sujet. Continuons, je suis sûr que nous arriverons à dépasser ensemble, avec un peu de bonne volonté, ce que j'ai maladroitement appelé, un peu pour rire, notre étrange malentendu. Mes lecteurs seront très intéressés par ce que Weber a dit du 11 septembre et des rapports entre déconstruction et technique. Où ça, d'abord?

A. D'accord, essayons. Nous avons en effet des responsabilités communes dans l'espace public, des devoirs envers vos lecteurs, et je ne voudrais pas que vous soyez obligé de retourner dans l'université où les choses, au fond, ne se passent pas toujours mieux que dans les journaux écrits ou radiotélévisuels, même dans les écoles de journalisme. Mais ne m'interrompez que si c'est vraiment indispensable, et faites-moi penser à vous dire un mot de ce que vous avez "appelé," dites-vous, "un peu pour rire, notre étrange malentendu."

Sur "déconstruction et technique," sur la déconstruction comme technique et comme question de la technique, sur les délimitations rigoureuses de cette problématique, tous les textes de Weber, sans exception, sont d'une rare et indispensable pertinence, je voudrais y revenir un peu plus tard. Sur le 11 septembre (2001, n'est-ce pas?), Weber a, dans les semaines qui ont suivi (le 15 décembre 2001) admirablement mis en œuvre un concept de théâtralisation qu'il n'avait cessé d'élaborer depuis des décennies dans des contextes et à propos de corpus les plus divers. Il montre bien que cette théâtralisation—attendez, à propos de théâtralisation, je voudrais faire un grand pas en arrière dans notre échange, si vous le permettez, et tout reprendre au début. Ne m'interrompez pas avant que je ne vous interroge moi-même, si vous voulez bien. Comme je vous le disais, ma question préalable, à moi, c'est "qui est Sam Weber?," lui-même? Singulièrement? Qui est-il et que fait-il? Que signe-t-il?

Quant à celui qui porte ce nom propre (quoiqu'un peu commun tout de même, non?), quant à ce penseur, cet écrivain, ce philosophe, ce dramaturge, ce professeur, cet ami absolument singulier, cette figure pour moi unique, la chance irremplaçable que sa rencontre m'aura accordée, une première scène théâtrale, un premier paradigme me saute aux yeux de la mémoire: "Politikos," *Le politique* de Platon. Je dis scène de théâtre parce que c'en est un et que Weber est un homme du théâtre, il pense la théâtralité, et non seulement du point de vue du spectateur, il pense l'être spectateur en général et il fait du théâtre. Et puis je dis paradigme parce que dans *Le politique*, il y va non seulement de tel ou tel paradigme (*paradeigma*), mais de penser le paradigme en général. Qu'est-ce qu'un paradigme en général, se demande l'Etranger devant Socrate le jeune (278e ff.)? Après quoi vient l'immense et célèbre discussion autour du paradigme du tisserand (υφαντης, *Weber*, si vous préférez) et de l'art du tissage. Je ne rappellerai pas tout ce travail d'analyse mais seulement ce moment où l'Etranger définit l'art de tisser comme l'art de la συμπλοκη, de l'entrelacement. Le tisserand détient l'art d'entrelacer la chaîne et la trame, **et ce paradigme?**

Je voudrais non seulement décrire SW comme artiste tisserand (politique royale, etc.) qui sait entrelacer, analyser, etc. mais je voudrais, moi, démêler ce qu'a d'absolument singulier SW dans ce paradigme . . .

UNCANNY Malentendu

insister au début sur traduction (dans *Mass Mediauras* 61)

rire et théâtre 12ff.

j'ai remplacé quelqu'un qui avait pris ma place chez SW, dans sa voiture

## Notes

[Derrida's title "Vous voulez rire" is followed by an asterisk and a footnote that reads: "*(laisser le titre en français, ne pas le traduire).—Translators. For the disposition of this text, which Derrida did not have a chance to complete, see the first note to the English translation.—Editors]

1. Samuel Weber, *The Legend of Freud* (Minneapolis: University of Minnesota Press, 1982), 83, 99. Une première version de cet ouvrage fut publiée en allemand sous le titre *Freud-Legend, Drei Studien zum Psychoanalytischen Denken* (Olten: Walter-Verlag, 1979). Une comparaison minutieuse entre les deux ouvrages serait d'un grand intérêt. Elle relèverait de nombreux remaniements, des *déplacements,* surtout, des changements de place, donc, et des développements nouveaux. Les deux conclusions de chapitre cités en exergue remettent ainsi en scène, de façon joueuse, mais autrement, et cette fois redoublée, une phrase qui clôt un sous-chapitre de la première version allemande: "Und darüber gibt es für die Freudsche Theorie des Witzes nichts zum lachen" (126). Autant de choses, nous en sommes avertis, à ne pas se hâter de confondre: le rire, le mot d'esprit (*laughter, joke, Lachen, Witz,* etc.).

2. Samuel Weber, *Mass Mediauras: Form Technics Media* (Southwood, Australia: Power Publications, 1996), 4.

3. Interrompu par le journaliste, je précise ici, après relecture, dans quelle direction j'aurais aimé explorer les textes de Bataille au sujet de ce qui lie au rire la souveraineté. Précisons au risque de nous répéter: la souveraineté telle du moins que Bataille l'entend, toute proche de la sainteté, parfois aussi de la santé, entre *saint* et *sain,* souveraineté impuissante et donc presque opposée, dans son concept insaisissable, au concept classique de souveraineté (seigneurie, maîtrise, supériorité plus haute que la hauteur et plus grande que la grandeur, pouvoir absolu, sur soi et sur les autres, volonté décisoire, etc.). On se demande parfois pour quelles raisons, à mes yeux fort problématiques, Bataille en maintient encore le nom au moment où il prétend faire table rase du concept.

Il faudrait en particulier relire et analyser ici, dans *Le coupable, Somme athéologique II* (Paris: Gallimard, 1961), tout le chapitre intitulé "La divinité du rire." L'expérience du rire (toujours extatique, comme celle de la souveraineté) y est décrite tantôt comme celle de l'ipséité souveraine à son sommet, tantôt comme l'opposé même de la souveraineté du maître, par excellence du maître au sens hégélien. Le plus souvent la frontière demeure indécise ou perméable entre les deux rires. Ce passage d'un rire à l'autre donne à penser. C'est souvent, chez Bataille en particulier, un passage du rire aux larmes et des larmes au rire. Mais ce passage est aussi un *saut*—un instant quasi intemporel qui ne peut ni ne doit se maintenir, autrement que suspendu, entre le possible et l'impossible. "Noces du possible et de l'impossible, de la puissance et de l'impuissance." Ainsi:

> Comme échéance, l'homme est celle de la mise en question, devenant un être subjectivement (tendant à son autonomie dans la nature, ainsi se concevant elle-même dans le rire). (122)
>
> Toujours j'ai reculé devant l'échéance: j'avais peur de ce que j'étais: LE RIRE MÊME. ("L'envie de rire," 123)
>
> Dieu *était,* plus doucement que moi, Dieu ou son absence n'étions pas moins l'un que l'autre *risibles*: apparences risibles. (129)
>
> Après une longue détente, *l'absence* du ciel étoilé me fit rire. (130)
>
> Hegel élaborant la philosophie du travail (c'est le *Knecht*, l'esclave émancipé, le travailleur qui dans la *Phénoménologie* devient Dieu) a supprimé la chance—et le rire.
>
> (Riant à *ma façon*, j'ai senti dans la contraction du rire je ne sais quoi de douloureux, d'agonisant. C'était terrible et délicieux. C'était *sain.*) (133)
>
> "Mais qui rirait à mort? . . . Le rire éperdu sort de la sphère accessible au discours, c'est un saut qui ne peut se définir à partir de ses conditions. Le rire est suspendu, le rire laisse en suspens celui qui rit. . . . n'affirme rien, n'apaise rien. Le rire est le saut du possible dans l'impossible—et de l'impossible dans le possible. Mais ce n'est qu'un saut: le maintien serait la réduction de l'impossible au possible *ou l'inverse.* ("Rire et tremblement," 139)
>
> Dans le rire, l'extase est déliée, immanente. Le rire de l'extase ne *rit* pas, mais il m'ouvre infiniment. Sa transparence est traversée de la flèche du rire; issue d'une mortelle absence. . . . Je célèbre en riant les noces de

> l'échec et de la puissance. . . . La *mise en question* veut encore l'échec, elle veut la *réussite de l'échec* . . . . Je ne sais quoi de béant et de mortellement blessé, dans le rire, est la violente mise en suspens que la nature fait d'elle-même. (142–43)
>
> Etrange qu'une richesse véritable ait l'allure aveugle, que le divin tienne à l'impuissance: la position contrainte de Hegel ou, chez Goethe, une beauté de nécropole. Seul m'éclaire un "rire infini." (149)

4. "Reading and Writing—*chez* Derrida," in Samuel Weber, *Institution and Interpretation* (Minneapolis: University of Minnesota Press, 1987), 85ff.

5. Cf. Weber, *Institution and Interpretation*, ch. 7 et 8 notamment. Sur la récurrence obsédante du lexique de l'ambivalence ou de l'ambiguïté, cf. entre des centaines d'exemples, 91; sur l'espace *théâtral* ou *spectaculaire* (opéra, cinéma, télévision, photographie, etc.), le "tragicomic drama of deconstruction," le "theatrical code," sur ce qui "dramatically . . . alters the dramatic scene as such," cf. par exemple, 93, 115, et passim, au cours de pages où le "perhaps" et les "dangerous perhapses" de Nietzsche furent thématisés (je viens de m'en apercevoir, je l'avais oublié), bien avant que je n'en fasse moi-même, m'endettant une fois de plus auprès de lui, un motif directeur de *Politiques de l'amitié* (Paris: Galilée, 1995), cf. 115.

Cela se trouve justement dans un chapitre intitulé "The Debts of Deconstruction" qui non seulement traite avec profondeur la question de la dette depuis le Nietzsche de la *Généalogie de la morale,* mais m'endette ainsi moi-même par avance. Une fois de plus. Et en inscrivant toute déconstruction dans une "scène de la dette," sinon dans une filiation du crédit, Weber lui ôte toute chance d'être une originarité souveraine et souverainement productrice, c'est-à-dire plus originaire que toute mise en œuvre "technique." L'espace de la technique est toujours celui de l'emprunt, du crédit, de la dette et de la filiation généalogique. Là où il y de la technique, il y a de la dette. La simplicité de l'origine est altérée. Bien qu'il soit, nous le verrons à suivre Weber, immédiatement lié au retard de quelque endettement, ce retard, lui, n'attend pas, il est quasi originaire: L'espacement technique s'ouvre dès l'origine, son retard est sans retard.

Mais cela ne signifie pas simplement, pour autant, que la déconstruction soit une technique parmi d'autres; il nous faudra compliquer cela plus tard. La méditation sur ce qui est non seulement ambivalent, mais *unheimlich, uncanny* se trouve explicitement déployée, dans le même article, par exemple p. 117. Mais si souvent ailleurs aussi!

6. Cf. Weber, *The Legend of Freud*, 65–66.

7. Weber, *The Legend of Freud*, 67.

8. Weber, *The Legend of Freud*, 72.

9. Weber, *The Legend of Freud*, 74.

10. Jacques Derrida, "Résistances," in *Résistances—de la psychanalyse* (Paris: Galilée, 1996), 23ff.; Jacques Derrida, *Resistances of Psychoanalysis*, tr. P. Kamuf, P. A. Brault, et M. Naas (Stanford: Stanford University Press, 1998), 10ff.

11. Jacques Lacan, *Les quatre concepts fondamentaux de la psychanalyse* (Paris: Seuil, 1973), 28, cité par Weber, *The Legend of Freud*, 79.

12. Weber souligne "rising" car il va être question, à la fin de la phrase, du phallus, du sens qui se dresserait donc, théâtralement, au beau milieu de la scène, tel un phallus.

Mais je soulignerais pour ma part, aussi bien, "majestically": la majesté, c'est aussi la hauteur et la grandeur (superlatif de *magnus*: ce qui est plus haut que la hauteur et plus grand que la grandeur) et, dans toute la tradition lexicale de la sémantique ou de la théorie politique, la *majestas*, Bodin l'aura souligné au début de son livre, *Les six livres de la République*, c'est le mot latin fondamental pour dire la *souveraineté*. Un crime de lèse-majesté est un crime contre le souverain. Ce qui se remet ici en scène concerne bien, comme une seule et même érection, la place centrale et surélevée du phallus en tant qu'il signifie le signifiant même du souverain—le souverain signifiant ou le signifiant souverain.

13. Weber, *The Legend of Freud*, 80. Ailleurs, plus tard, Weber semble au moins compliquer ce "centrisme," voire ce phallocentrisme de Lacan. Il le fait toujours dans le code théâtrologique qu'il privilégie sans cesse comme si en dernière instance tout était coup de théâtre. Dans *Return to Freud: Jacques Lacan's Dislocation of Psychoanalysis* (Cambridge, U.K.: Cambridge, 1991) (édition allemande, Passagen Verlag, 1990), il insiste au contraire sur le fait que, pour Lacan, le phallocentrisme de Freud tend à "déconstruire (*deconstructing*)" tout "centrisme," "insofar as the phallus stages the drama of the signifier. The signified is the signifier *struck down* . . . . Reading in this sense—and if it is the sense of the Return to Freud announced by Lacan—means relearning how to be *struck* by the signifier. And by its stage. In the theater of the unconscious, one never gets over being stage-struck" (151).

14. Sur cette contraction du mouvement et de l'immobilité, voir les très belles pages consacrées au *Gestell* heideggerien (*Gestell, stell*: *emplacement*) dans *Mass Mediauras*. Rien d'étonnant à ce qu'on y retrouve le motif toujours inévitable de l'*uncanny*, et toujours dans une expérience pensante des enjeux de la traduction. Ainsi:

> In the English translation, the word [*Gestell*] is rendered as "enframing." Although this takes the collecting function of the *Gestell* into account, it effaces the tension between verb and noun that resounds in the German and that points to the strange, indeed uncanny, mixture of movement and stasis that distinguishes the goings-on of modern technics and upon which Heidegger places considerable emphasis.
>
> This tension resounds in the word proposed by Lacoue-Labarthe to render *Gestell*: *installation*. I would like to suggest another possibility, one that has the virtue of pointing to the lexical "root" of *Gestell: stell: emplacement*." (*Mass Mediauras*, 71)

15. Weber, *The Legend of Freud*, 81.
16. Weber, *The Legend of Freud*, 82.
17. ["Pas" might be a typo for "par."—Translators]
18. Weber, *The Legend of Freud*, 82–83.
19. Weber, *The Legend of Freud*, 99.
20. Elle n'apparaît qu'"une fois, si je ne me trompe, et sous une forme un peu différente, dans la version allemande antérieure": "Und darüber gibt es für die Freudsche Theorie des Witzes nichts zu lachen" (126).
21. Weber, *The Legend of Freud*, 98.
22. Weber, *Mass Mediauras*, 226–27.

23. Jacques Derrida, *La Carte postale, de Socrate à Freud et au-delà* (Paris: Aubier-Flammarion, 1979); *The Post-Card: From Socrates to Freud and Beyond*, trans. Alan Bass (Chicago: University of Chicago Press, 1987), 483. "Reason will always be right [*aura raison*]. By itself."

24. Weber, *Institution and Interpretation*, 102ff.

25. Weber, *Mass Mediauras*, 4.

26. (Heidegger lui-même, même, . . . éveil/conscience. en note 99ff.).

27. référence [Jacques Derrida, *Surtout, pas de journalistes!* (Paris: Galilée, 2016).—Translators]

Chapter 13

# Screen Memories

## Samuel Weber in Conversation with Irene Albers and Sima Reinisch

**Irene Albers:** When I contacted you, you told me that since you left the Freie Universität-Berlin (FU) in 1975 for Johns Hopkins University you never again had direct contact with the Institut für Allgemeine und Vergleichende Literaturwissenschaft [AVL].[1] You were, like the founding members of the CPSU, "made to disappear from history or rather from the account of history." You write that the role that you played in the years of the founding of the AVL is "barely legible anymore, at least in the official writing of history." Let us then make your role in the history of the institute legible once more! To begin with some facts: When were you at the institute? In which function?

**Samuel Weber:** Just to prevent misunderstandings, I hope it was clear that my comparison with the "founding members of the CPSU" was somewhat ironic! [Remark added.] I went to Berlin as a "wissenschaftlicher Assistent" in September 1967 and stayed at the AVL until 1975, actually only until 1974, since I then went to Johns Hopkins for a year for the first time. But only in 1975 did I officially cut ties with the FU.

**IA:** What did the prehistory look like? Had you been awarded your doctorate yet? How did it come about that you became an assistant at the institute? Did you know Szondi or his writings beforehand?

**SW:** The prehistory was as follows: Since 1963 I was pursuing my Ph.D. at Cornell University under Paul de Man and went to Frankfurt in 1965 to study with Adorno and to translate his *Prisms* into English. When I arrived in Berlin I had not yet received my doctorate—that happened relatively late, only in 1971, a few years after I had started working at Kiebitzweg [the name of the street where the AVL Institute is located]. Szondi had arranged for one of his assistants to be from abroad. I believe Robert Kimber, from Princeton, held this post before me. Szondi had asked Paul de Man and Adorno (perhaps others too) whether they by chance knew someone suitable for the assistant job. Both named me: Adorno because I studied with and translated him in Frankfurt at the time; de Man because I was pursuing my Ph.D. with him. As I remember, all that was needed then to decide the matter was a brief meeting at the Frankfurt airport, where Szondi was passing through. I was thus hired initially, like all visiting assistants, for two years. Later the contract was renewed with the same terms as the regular assistant jobs. I received my habilitation shortly after my doctorate in 1973 and became assistant professor for the rest of my time there. Of course I knew Szondi's writings (which were not that numerous: "An Essay on the Tragic," the short text about modern theater, and, most important, the Hölderlin studies, which I held in high esteem). Naturally I was quite happy to be able to work with him in Berlin. He was one of only a few literary scholars in Germany who knew both the "Frankfurt School" and Anglo-American literary criticism well.

**IA**: Do you remember your arrival in Berlin? Your first encounter with Szondi? Your first impressions of "Kiebitzweg"?

**SW**: I have to admit that my fragmentary memory has preserved more of the political situation at the time than of the first impressions of Kiebitzweg. I arrived in Berlin only a few months after the murder of Benno Ohnesorg at the anti-shah demonstrations in front of the Berlin Opera. In September 1967 I then heard with surprise and disappointment the inaugural address by the new governing mayor of Berlin, Pastor Heinrich Albertz, who—despite his previous affiliation with the Confessing Church and the left wing of the Social Democratic Party—defended and justified the police operation. That came as a shock to me, and in a way more or less screened out everything else. Kiebitzweg was of course an idyllic place with respect to the nascent student movements and the occupations of the universities that began soon after. The classes were all relatively small, except for the lectures of Szondi himself.

I don't remember my first encounter with Szondi. But I do remember this: shortly after I arrived, Szondi invited me to speak with him. I have only this one selective memory: he suddenly showed me the number tattooed on his arm. I was rather shocked! We scarcely knew each other, and I found this very personal. Why did he show me this? Perhaps because he guessed that I was of Jewish heritage, not a German. He must have felt very lonely at the time, shortly after his separation from Alexandra Kluge. I don't know what he was looking for. We never spoke about this afterwards; I would never have asked him about something so personal. From this point onward I thought that things would not go well between us. I only thought that I would never be able to do justice to such a claim, if this was his attitude toward me.

Another, somehow similar event that happened shortly after my arrival stands out in my memory. It was at a reception of some sort given by Jacob Taubes, who had taught at Columbia before coming to the FU as director of the Institute for Hermeneutics. I had known several of Taubes's former students at Columbia, and through them he had probably heard of me prior to our meeting. After greeting me warmly, he then said—I am recalling its sense, because I can't remember the original wording—"Sam, you should consider switching to the Hermeneutic Institute. You really are more of a philosopher than a literary person, no?" I can't remember what I responded exactly, but I was troubled and surprised at the attempt to lure me away from one of his colleagues with whom he had close and apparently friendly relations. Naturally I stayed in Kiebitzweg, and I could and should have told Taubes that despite my great interest in philosophy I still felt very much at home in a literature department. In any case, I felt that I had to recount the story to Szondi, who also was somewhat shocked, but perhaps less surprised than I was, or so I remember it, anyway.

**IA:** How did you perceive Szondi's conception of the subject as general *and* comparative literature, which at the time in Germany was unique? (We are under the impression that there existed in Szondi's founding ideas—which were programmatically developed against the comparative literature programs at other German universities [Mainz, Tübingen]—a latent conflict between the "general" and the "comparative." Would you agree?)

**SW:** At first I did not perceive such a tension in Berlin because comparative literature as I knew it from the USA never separated the two directions that you mention but rather always sought to combine the comparative with the general. But there were indeed soon other tensions that did not quite map onto this polarity but concerned rather the status of history with respect to language—and correspondingly were critical of traditional hermeneutics. At the time Szondi gave lectures on hermeneutics as well as seminars on structuralism, choices that reflected this tension but also Szondi's effort to synthesize the two approaches.

**Sima Reinisch:** Do you remember the seminars that you gave at the institute? The course listings announce seminars with titles as varied as "Fiction and Reality in the Novel (with special consideration of Sterne's *Tristram Shandy*)," "Joyce: *Ulysses* and His Import on the Novel in the 20th Century," "Translation as Interpretation: Shakespeare's Sonnets and Their Translations," "Theory of Metaphors," "Psychoanalytic and Literary Hermeneutics," "Jacques Lacan," and "The Uncanny as Literary Structure."

**SW:** To be honest, I unfortunately have, at least at the moment, no continuous recollection of those seminars. I know that in addition to the regular seminars I also convened weekend workshops that were attended not only by students of comparative literature but also by people from outside: Hanns Zischler, for instance, and Hans-Jörg Rheinberger, who together then translated Derrida's *Of Grammatology* into German. In this regard one should note that comparative literature in the States served as a haven for all those who in Europe would have probably studied philosophy but were instead repelled by the narrowness of Anglo-American analytic philosophy. Yet "comparative literature" remained tied to questions of language and languages in a way that largely distinguished it from "continental" philosophy as well and even today in part continues to do so.

But I can relate at least one anecdote from the first seminar—it must have been a pro-seminar—that I gave at the FU. It was the first time that I taught at all; in contrast to today, at the time most graduate students in the U.S. did not have to teach at all during their studies. It was thus my very first teaching experience, and in a foreign language at that. I had chosen Sterne's *Tristram Shandy* as the main text to secure a certain linguistic "advantage" over my German students, who at the time were not that much younger than I. These included, if I recall correctly, Werner Hamacher and Hans-Thies Lehmann. In any case, I gave a long introductory speech; I don't recall the content at all, but I am sure that I tried to present the overarching importance of this unique "novel," which has accompanied me throughout my life. Afterwards I asked those present if there were any questions. Embarrassed silence. Until finally, after a painfully long pause, a student raised her hand to ask whether there existed a "reserve shelf"! Today this might appear completely normal and legitimate—at least it does to me—but at that moment I despaired not only of myself but also of the whole profession of teaching. . . . Fortunately I soon learned how to prepare a pro-seminar better and a little more about teaching in general, but at the time I had no clue!

**IA:** A comment from the course listings on your seminar "Introduction to the Lyric in English, German, and French Romanticism" from the winter semester 1971–72 reads, "A critique of previous attempts to determine the concept of romanticism constitutes our starting point—from there, the specific problems and thematic constellations of the Wordsworthian text will be brought out by 'close readings,' and the exegetic relevance of social history will then be discussed. In this context, one must not overlook that social history, too, is only accessible to us through texts, and that its object cannot constitute itself without interpretation and reading. The question of the mediation of literature and society is thus also a question about the relationship between different kinds of texts. Escaping the danger of replacing an idealist dogmatism by a materialist dogmatism will be difficult if this relation is left to the side." This sounds, on the one hand, like an invitation to a conversation, on the other, like a very fundamental critique of the materialist and social-historical approaches that Szondi had established at the institute. Were there discussions in this regard?

**SW:** There certainly must have been discussions, but here too I am lacking concrete memories. In retrospect it seems that the critique of Szondi was rather directed against the vulgar-Marxist tendencies that were spreading throughout German studies at the time and that frequently presented a claim to exclusiveness—a claim I deemed at the time and still consider to be disastrous. But you are also right that the criticism was probably in part also directed against the "historicist" tendency in hermeneutics that was represented at Kiebitzweg, too. When Derrida gave a lecture on Mallarmé in 1969, a Ph.D. student of Szondi's asked him aggressively how his method dealt with the historical reality of the scaffold. (Or was it the guillotine?) This makes me think of an anecdote Herbert Marcuse once told. At the time of *One-Dimensional Man*, he was invited by the Cambridge (Massachusetts) Marxist Club to present the theses of this book that was very popular at the time. A member of the club stood up after Marcuse's speech and asked, "Herr Marcuse, have you never heard of the proletariat?" Marcuse briefly considered and responded, "No, I haven't!" I can only speculate why the atmosphere at Derrida's lecture was so aggressive. Derrida, by the way, was shocked by this aggressiveness! It was as though it was not permissible to question the concept of history. To do so was considered in some quarters to be completely immoral, politically reactionary, irresponsible. In the end, this criticism was directed not only at poststructuralism but at a whole tradition going back at least to Nietzsche (and indeed to Kant), a tradition that questions the cognitive status of a teleological perspective that knows from the beginning where everything is headed. The resulting tension certainly has to be put back into the politically polarized context of the time, but for me this explanation cannot serve to justify politically condemning everyone who questioned a dialectical understanding of history.

**IA:** In your seminars you took up the impulses of structuralist and poststructuralist textual studies as well as Jacques Lacan's psychoanalysis long before German universities started discussing them. The reception in Germany crucially began with your 1978 book *Return to Freud: Jacques Lacan's Dislocation of Psychoanalysis*. Is it true that your book stems from your seminars at Kiebitzweg? How were these theories discussed at the AVL Institute? Was there competition with the more social-historically oriented works?

**SW:** I can only answer generally, since, as I said, I don't have more exact memories of the courses that I taught. First, there was unfortunately more of a separation than a debate between those who, let's say, started from the more traditional hermeneutic conception of history—including social history—and the students, with whom I was mainly in contact, who were more interested in the directions of poststructuralism that at the time were still new. For instance, I don't recall any public discussions between the two groups—which doesn't mean that they didn't take place. But one had enough to do with working through the new movements and did not want to dedicate energy to discussions that wouldn't necessarily have been all that productive.

The book *Return to Freud* partly goes back to my seminars but also the workshops that took place outside of regular university activities.

**IA:** Who were your students, and what became of them?

**SW:** I never considered myself to have had "students" in the proper—that is, possessive—sense of the word; Szondi had students. Those who studied in Kiebitzweg came almost without exception to work with him. I was merely a mediator, because I had a certain head start with respect to my knowledge of French critical theory; through my teaching at the institute I tried to develop and transmit this knowledge. I have already mentioned some of the most renowned students who studied with me: Werner Hamacher, Hans-Thies Lehmann, Wolfgang Hagen, Hans-Jörg Rheinberger, and Hanns Zischler. Further Henriette Beese, who unfortunately died much too young and who, more than anyone else, worked to bring together the two main tendencies, the poststructuralist with the hermeneutic.

**SR:** In a letter to Derrida from May 26, 1969, you write, "Je suis d'ailleurs très content avec l'intérêt suscité chez les étudiants—à peu près dix—réunis dans notre groupe de travail. J'ai même l'impression que le climat ici est très favorable à la réception d'une pensée comme la vôtre, surtout chez les jeunes étudiants."[2]

**SW:** If I wrote about "young students," then I meant those with whom I was working. We formed a very enthusiastic and committed group, for we had the feeling that we were on to something entirely new and important—not only for literature but for all aspects of our existence. There were, of course, others who did not see it that way. Unfortunately there was very little communication between the two groups.

**IA:** How did you, as an American, perceive university politics in Berlin at the time? Was there a demand for political philology at the AVL Institute? Was Szondi a role model in this regard?

**SW:** As an American I have to answer this first in American English: I found the political debate at the university to be "like a breath of fresh air"! I had not experienced anything like that in the States—but I also spent most of the years that saw the emergence of a critical American student movement in Germany. However it seemed to me that the latter never had the historical—the socioeconomic—consciousness that existed in German student circles. Instead political involvement was driven mainly by moral considerations—and by fear of having to go and die or be mutilated in Vietnam, a war that few students believed in. Moralism of a somewhat different but no less dubious kind existed in the German student movement as well, but it was somewhat tempered through a historical consciousness, however skewed—a consciousness that easily succumbed to dogmatism, in part for just the reasons you quoted from my course description. Admittedly it was nevertheless easy for me, and the other "Kiebitzianer"—perhaps too easy—to sympathize with the student movements in the Massenfächer ("mass disciplines") since we were far enough from the Rostlaube to stay protected from the harshest conflicts.[3]

**SR:** Let us turn to Derrida. The course listings from 1968 onwards show that Derrida came to [the FU in] Dahlem multiple times for guest lectures. Do you know when Szondi began to engage with Derrida's works? What part did you play with regard to those invitations? One of your letters to Derrida, from February 28, 1968, suggests that you took the initiative with the first invitation of Derrida. How did this come about? Did you know Derrida already from your time in the U.S.?

**SW:** I cannot say anymore when exactly Szondi began to read Derrida—whether it was before I arrived in the fall of 1967 or only after that. Derrida was little known at the time. I therefore assume that I took the initiative for the first invitation of Derrida, but the invitation itself, of course, could only have taken place with Szondi's approval and support. The fact that Szondi asked me to pick up Derrida from the airport as well as the letter that you already mentioned seem to me to support this assumption.[4] I was made aware of Derrida relatively early by de Man and read the first part of *Of Grammatology* in 1965 or 1966 in the French journal *Critique* even before the publication of the book. Derrida, who always had a fine sense for protocol, nevertheless wrote that he had been invited by Szondi, which in any case is formally correct.

**SR:** You write in your first letter to Derrida, "J'espère que vous viendrez à Berlin et je suis convaincu que votre œuvre aura une influence extrêmement favorable sur la stagnation infortunée des sciences humaines en Allemagne."[5] Can you comment on this, and describe this "unfortunate stagnation"?

**SW:** Even though this may sound a little exaggerated, Szondi himself said similar things about German studies at the time. My model for literary scholarship was Paul de Man. Literary criticism in the States had already developed an agonistic tradition through the debates between New Critics and Chicago Critics. To me at least the intellectual atmosphere in Anglo-American literary studies seemed much livelier and indeed more sophisticated than in Germany at the time, when books by Hugo Friedrich (*The Structure of Modern Poetry*) and Wolfgang Kayser (*The Linguistic Work of Art*) set the tone! When I arrived in Frankfurt at Adorno's Institute for Social Research, I was quite shocked! I had expected the teaching of Frankfurt "critical theory" to have something of an anti-authoritarian stance, but what I experienced there seemed, in its form at least, no less authoritarian than what it purported to criticize: students who sometimes merely repeated what their teachers presented, teachers who went through texts separating what was progressive from what was regressive, et cetera. Of course this was not true of Adorno's lectures and seminars, and there were other notable exceptions. But it did mark much of the overall atmosphere against which the students rebelled. However, this rebellion was not always intellectually fruitful. Although the seminars in Frankfurt took place on a high level, I was disappointed by their homogeneity. I was fortunately in an exceptional position because I had come a long way as a sort of pilgrim to translate Adorno. I also did not depend on him—after all, I was pursuing my Ph.D. with de Man—so I was cut some slack, whereas most of his students were quite intimidated. During a café visit I dared to say to Adorno, "Herr Professor, you have read Heidegger and the other authors you criticize, but it seems to me that your students don't always find that to be necessary—they take over your criticism without having themselves seriously read the criticized authors."

**SR**: Derrida's first lecture in July 1968 was announced with the title "La Fin du Livre" ["The End of the Book"]. It took place within the framework of one of Szondi's seminars, "Problems of a Structuralist Literary Criticism," that read, among others, the founding documents of poststructuralism published the previous year in Paris: *De la grammatologie*, *L'Ecriture et la différance*, and *La Voix et le phénomène*. In one of your letters to Szondi, from March 1967, you write that you are planning a seminar on "structuralism and poetry." Why did Szondi end up giving this course?

**SW**: I believe that was because at the time it was not actually structuralism that interested me but rather poststructuralism. To this day I find the distinction between structuralism and poststructuralism very useful—in contrast to the notion of postmodernity, a term that has never made much sense to me. I experienced poststructuralism as a quite specific shift from a thinking of systems as self-contained totalities to one that construes the systematic as an ineluctable result of violence and violation. This strikes me as especially prominent in the writings of Derrida and Lacan. From this point of view, a violent-violating moment is constitutive of any system because the latter's constitution is delimited by exclusions. The question for me was always therefore *how* to deal with such conflicts without trying to merely deny or to harmonize them. In this respect I thus believed and still find the distinction between structuralism and poststructuralism to be useful. By contrast, what interested Szondi—at least this was my impression at the time—was mainly the question "What can we take from these movements that will be useful for reading literature?" A text such as "Les chats de Charles Baudelaire" by Jakobson and Lévi-Strauss was exemplary for him in this regard. For me, by contrast, their discussion was completely uninteresting. The question that concerned me and still does is rather: In what way does language—and languages—as a "mode of meaning" (Benjamin) question the concept of the system?

**SR:** You mentioned already Derrida's second lecture from July 1969, "On the Concept of Mimesis." At its center stood the interpretation of two passages from Plato's *Philebus* and Mallarmé's *Mimique* (later published under the title *La double séance*). Do you remember further details from this lecture?

**SW:** From the lecture I recall only the detail already mentioned. But the lecture was presumably well suited to present Derrida's deconstruction of "representation" philosophically as well as aesthetically. I therefore considered the text a very important one at the time. It concerns the idea of mimesis and a confrontation between Plato and Mallarmé. On the one hand, mimesis is understood Platonically, as the representation of a pregiven model, of a preexisting reality; on the other, mimesis is conceived of as a process that in a certain way brings forth as well as undermines the reality it mimes. Mallarmé's way of writing in *Le Livre*, the graphic arrangement of the writing, became a new model of a reality that does not rest on presence. It was a fantastic text . . . in contrast to "Les chats"!

**SR:** How would you describe Szondi's relationship to Derrida's understanding of deconstruction? His statements about Derrida testify to simultaneous admiration and criticism. For instance, on November 20, 1970, he reported a critical development at the institute to Herbert Dieckmann: "By contrast, an esotericism à la Derrida is spreading at our Institute (I dislike saying this since I like Derrida a lot); one fantasizes about texts like Liszt fantasized on themes from Bach. Philology, in the meantime, stands in the corner." And in a letter to Jean Bollack, whom he asks to edit his essay "Lecture de Strette" ["Reading 'Engführung': An Essay on the Poetry of Paul Celan"] about Celan's poem "Engführung," he writes, "Si je vois bien, il y a un certain 'style,' mi-Szondi, mi-Derrida (que je trouve de plus en plus intéressant et dangereux à la fois)."[6] Did Szondi attempt to integrate deconstructive "readings" into his hermeneutical philology?

**SW:** You have described Szondi's stance on deconstruction quite correctly; at least it corresponds to my memory. On the one hand, he held in high esteem Derrida's meticulous analysis of textual details coupled with his ability to intuit larger connections and implications in those details. On the other hand, he regarded the claim to radically question the concept of history and even the concept of truth as extremely dangerous, insofar as it at the same time did not leave the concept of objectivity unscathed. He therefore sought to find an alternative through recourse to the hermeneutical tradition. In this respect too he was influenced more by Foucault than by Derrida—although

Derrida's occupation with language and literature, as I already mentioned, pleased him quite a bit, whereas Foucault had less to offer in this regard. However, if you find a really innovative thinker—be it Derrida, Adorno, Heidegger, or Benjamin—then it is not easy for those who follow to avoid a certain epigonality. As a teacher Szondi felt obligated and legitimized to criticize this tendency.

An anecdote: As the one at the institute who worked a lot with Derrida and Lacan, I felt particularly affected by the criticism. When I had finally finished my dissertation on Balzac, I obviously showed it to Szondi. He then wanted to translate it for his publication series—Henriette Beese was supposed to provide the translation—and publish it. But when I asked him for his opinion on the work he refused to discuss it with me at all. At the time I found that, and I still find it now, quite extraordinary: one decides to translate and publish a work but refuses to tell the author what one thinks about it. Surely he would have had many critical things to say about it and wanted to spare himself and me this unpleasantness. But why publish it, then? Out of magnanimity to a young colleague? As a negative example of where "deconstruction" could lead? To this day I don't know. . . . Before the project could be realized, however, Szondi took his own life, and thus translation and publication came to nothing.

**SR:** In the winter semester of 1973–74 Derrida was a visiting professor at the institute and gave a biweekly seminar that was also reported on in *Der Spiegel*. The course listings announced it under the title "La question de la signature: L'exemple de Jean Genet" [The Question of the Signature: The Example of Jean Genet]. In addition you offered a seminar titled "Introduction to Textual Studies: *De la grammatologie*" (according to the course listings, together with Derrida). How did this invitation come about, and do you remember the content of those events?

**SW:** I am embarrassed to admit once again that I don't have any precise recollections of those events any more. That I gave a joint seminar with Derrida at Kiebitzweg is completely "new" to me . . . and yet apparently quite old! I can only assume—but this is only speculation, not recollection—that I organized the sessions between Derrida's biweekly visits. Derrida himself always read a fully formulated text—that in this case was later published under the title *Glas*.

**IA:** You began to engage with Lacan already before Szondi's death. What was Szondi's position in this regard? Was there competition between you and Szondi (for the best students? The most interesting topics?)?

**SW:** It is interesting that you link the question concerning my work on Lacan with Szondi's death as well as with a possible competition between him and me! Those surprising connections might merit a psychoanalytic interpretation that I of course cannot undertake here. Concerning my work on Lacan (and Freud), it is even older than that on Derrida. When I was still studying at Cornell, before I came to Frankfurt, I was lucky to encounter a teacher, Eugenio Donato, who worked intensely on Lacan very early on. I thus knew of Lacan long before I came to Berlin. (A parenthetical remark: the sad task of informing Szondi's father, who was not an analyst but all the same a very famous psychiatrist, of his son's suicide fell to me.) Although I don't have any recollections of Szondi working much on Freud or Lacan in his scholarship or teaching, he was surely confronted with them early on through his father's profession and writings. Perhaps it was precisely this paternal relationship to psychoanalysis that was an obstacle preventing him from engaging with Freud more closely. I also cannot imagine that Szondi would have found Lacan's "baroque" writing style attractive. His understanding of intellectual work and responsibility was in this case diametrically opposed to that of Lacan, or at least so it seems to me. I am also not sure that Szondi would have approved of the development in Derrida's writing towards an ever more pronounced theatricalization had he lived to witness it.

Concerning the question of whether there was competitiveness between me and Szondi, I can say that I never thought of or experienced the situation in this way. After all, Szondi was already a very renowned scholar, whereas I was still working on my dissertation. How could a competitive relationship arise there? The quoted passages from the letters show that Szondi had a distanced relationship to poststructuralism—appreciative but also critical—whereas I valued Derrida and Lacan (but also Benjamin) as thinkers who might usher in a new epoch. So there were divergences between us, but to speak of a competition seems completely inappropriate. As I've said, students came to the institute not to study with me but to study with Szondi; no competition was possible or conceivable in that regard. Perhaps I had the function of a "supplement" at the institute in those days.

**IA:** We found a "revised development plan" in the archives that Szondi still signed in July 1971 and that contains a description of a research project of yours on textual studies. Can you tell us anything about that?

**SW:** I was surprised myself when I read this "revised development plan" again; I had completely forgotten about it, and even today I barely remember the context in which the plan had been undertaken. I was able to realize the project to publish a journal with a focus on "textual studies" only after coming to Johns Hopkins—namely in the form of a yearbook, *Glyph* (1976–81). But what surprised me in the Berlin development plan was the way this project for expounding "textual studies" came first under the rubric "research." Nevertheless, in retrospect this research project does seem to me to be compatible with the other "work at the Institute" that was described in the rest of the development plan. That Henriette Beese as well as Szondi signed the document testifies to the attempt to organize Kiebitzweg as a place where diverging but not necessarily mutually exclusive conceptions of "comparative literature" could coexist.

**IA:** Your project concerning textual studies stands here next to topics of comparative literature ("Afterlife of Antiquity," historical topics, etc.) without mediation or transition. Did a "split" of the institute exist already before Szondi's death? Is it true that in 1971 Szondi, faced with the new theoretical direction that you represented, proposed a splitting of the institute into a historical-comparative and a theoretical literature department?

**SW:** Once again I don't remember anything involving a "splitting of the institute." There was surely a group that followed the newer French and partly American directions in textual and literary criticism with enthusiasm, and others who did not share this enthusiasm and even regarded it with a certain suspicion. That was the case at Kiebitzweg, but maybe even more so in the other literature departments. It seems quite plausible, even probable, to me that Szondi as a sole professor in the institute was himself "of two minds," but I don't believe that the divergence at Kiebitzweg played an essential role in that regard. It was rather the general development of the university as well as a certain alienation from German politics as a whole (including the radical leftist student movement) that contributed to this split. If I am informed correctly, however, Szondi had been planning his departure from Berlin and especially his return to Zurich for a long time. But I don't remember anything about Szondi's proposing to divide the institute into a historical-comparative and a theoretical literature department; after all, he was too involved with both directions to desire an institutionalization of their separation.

**IA:** Szondi pursued the development of the institute quite intensely. Why did he want to go to Zurich in 1971? How did you make sense of that at the time? How do you see it today?

**SW:** I have to respond cautiously here because I don't have an exact answer to this question. I believe that he had already applied earlier for the chair of comparative literature at the University of Zurich; Paul de Man was then given that position. If this is true—one can certainly find that out—then his wish to live and teach in Zurich antedated his coming to Berlin. But, as becomes clear in his published letters, he felt increasingly alienated and isolated by the development of university politics at the FU and by the general political climate in Germany. In those days there was much pressure to take a clear stand, for or against. And that was something that in many cases was impossible for Szondi. But his letters make clear that Szondi always maintained a certain distance from Germany, surely also a result of his earlier experiences in World War II.

**IA**: After Szondi's death you were part of the so-called (preliminary) board of directors of the AVL Institute. How did you conceive of your role back then? What (institutional and substantive) perspective did you develop for the institute "after" Szondi (in the double sense)? Whom would you have liked to see succeed Szondi?

**SW**: As I remember, I saw my role as one of helping with a difficult transition into a very uncertain future. But the unresolved tension between a hermeneutic-historical, "philological" approach to literary texts on the one hand, and a textual criticism for which the unity of meaning could not be the ultimate horizon—this divergence could hardly be bridged by a single scholar. Szondi, as a kind of "founding father," had achieved this to a certain degree, but I cannot remember or think of anyone else who could have continued this tightrope act productively. In addition the problem of the "professional perspective" already posed itself not just for individual students but for the institute as a whole. Since comparative literature, in contrast to the philologies, was not taught at the high school level, it became increasingly difficult to conduct a training in general and comparative literature other than as a very marginal activity, tailored to very few people and restricted to a very small number of jobs. The negotiation with Wolfgang Iser failed, if I remember correctly, exactly because of this: Iser insisted—rightly, I think—that comparative literature become a school subject, but he couldn't move the Berlin Senate to agree.

**SR**: There was a group of students at the institute who would have preferred to see you as Szondi's successor. Derrida's posthumous papers even contain a report on you that the FU's hiring committee had officially requested.

**SW**: It was very clear to me that nothing would come of that. For two reasons: first, formally, it was extremely rare, almost a taboo for anyone to be granted a professorship at the university that had awarded them their habilitation—not at least directly. But also substantively: I had, of course, too many enemies! And there were probably people who in their *désarroi* assigned me partial responsibility for Szondi's suicide, because I had indirectly contributed to the tensions we have been discussing. . . . Of course no one ever said that to me directly. But there was no doubt that I was always an outsider to many. From the beginning I had understood the function of a "wissenschaftlicher Assistent" as comparable to that of an American assistant professor. At an American university, an assistant professor does not depend on any one tenured professor or endowed professorship, whereas an "Assistent" in Germany is directly tied to a "Lehrstuhl," a tenured professor with an endowed professorship. That was the fatal part of the one-man institute construction. Szondi could accept what Derrida did, up to a point at least, but many of his students were never comfortable with Derrida's work. Whereas those of us who were inspired by it felt that we might be able to replace and renew a depleted tradition, thereby offending those who still clung to it. I was certainly not always particularly diplomatic in this respect, but I was more concerned to explore the different horizons that were opening at the time, horizons that I felt might really make an important difference to literary studies and more generally.

**IA:** Was Szondi regarded in mythical or heroic terms, as a great father figure or superego? Was there a guilty conscience due to the growing divergence within the institute?

**SW:** Szondi certainly enjoyed a special status and prestige, which, although based in large part on his work, also was nourished by a certain feeling of guilt. An anecdote: many new students or even colleagues who encountered Szondi for the first time at Kiebitzweg tried to transfer his name from an allegedly German phonetics to an imagined, but false, Hungarian pronunciation by addressing him as "Herr Shondi." . . . This situation had, from my point of view, partly quite negative consequences on the work climate among the Ph.D. students. Since Szondi was known as a perfectionist, many students had extreme difficulties reaching this degree of perfection, if they could reach it at all. Szondi once told me that he felt physically "ill" when he had to read a bad term paper. I couldn't quite understand that: my feeling was that a bad term paper didn't hurt anyone except for the one who wrote it. . . . We were of course worlds apart in this regard. One of Szondi's favorite words was *prüfen*, "to examine." If one absolutizes the standpoint of examination, one assumes a position of examiner that in the end is theological for me. One can examine something only if one has an encompassing overview of it. By contrast, in physics it was discovered a while ago that any observation, any attempt at measurement, inevitably influences that which is observed, and vice versa. Heisenberg called this the "uncertainty principle." One changes the things to the degree that one wants to observe them, and consequently one is changed oneself. Szondi was known for his meticulousness; he could carry it to a very impressive degree, but at the same time, I'm afraid, this intimidated a not insignificant number of students. Egoideal or superego, or something of both.

**IA:** Everyone who experienced the time after Szondi's death mentions conflicts and the formation of various factions; some speak of deconstruction—in the singular—as a "sect" or "private mythology." We are less interested in which people were involved in these conflicts than in the substantive struggle. Was Szondi's "legacy" still at stake? A legacy that one wanted to understand differently depending on which "party" one belonged to? Or did a break with hermeneutics and "philological insight" take place?

**SW:** Whether "deconstruction in the singular" at Kiebitzweg, or anywhere else, had the character of a "sect" I'll gladly let others decide. I would only ask that one keep in mind that reducing a multifaceted and heterogeneous movement of thinking and writing to a monolithic unity—deconstruction in the *singular*—itself seems to me a sectarian gesture. Concerning Szondi's legacy, it might consist in the serious attempt to let the tensions between history and language, between generality and singularity play themselves out in the study of literature—but elsewhere too—without wanting to force them into harmony.

**IA:** Why did you decide in 1975 to leave Berlin and the FU?

**SW:** Three reasons: (1) Since I had received my habilitation in Berlin I had few opportunities to receive a tenured post there—at least at the FU. But I also didn't want to go elsewhere in Germany, which in any case wouldn't have been easy with my profile. (2) At the time the application of official "exclusions from the profession"—*Berufsverbote*—began, directed against many critical leftists. I had experienced something similar as a child in New York City during the early fifties, when anticommunist sentiments were being officially encouraged as part of the developing cold war mentality, and I had no particular desire to go through a similar experience again. While I was a visiting professor at Johns Hopkins, I received a letter from the FU administration asking me to name people who had participated in political gatherings at the university et cetera. The letter was signed anonymously "on behalf of" [*im Auftrag*]. While I cannot remember the exact circumstances, I remember being particularly disturbed by the dissolving of any responsibility in this bureaucratic "i.A." (3) By contrast, I found the intellectual climate in American universities and in particular at Johns Hopkins at the time quite exciting. After twelve years abroad I was curious to see what was happening "at home." But I did feel badly about leaving Germany and the FU, especially given the hierarchical structure of the university, in which there were not many "habilitated" professors who would support students working in a poststructuralist and deconstructive mode.

**IA:** Did you follow the further development of the Berlin AVL Institute (with Lämmert, Menninghaus, Mattenklott)?

**SW:** No, I didn't. Or only very little.

**IA:** How do you see the institute and its history today (insofar as you have a general sense of it) in relationship to the development of comparative literature at other places?

**SW:** Since I haven't been at the FU since 1975 I cannot say much about the development of the institute, at least not from firsthand experience.

**IA:** To return to the beginning of our conversation and your disappearing from the history of the institute: How did you make sense of your not being part of the official history of the institute until now? If you had to paint a picture of the founding time, where would be your place?

SW: Since I have partly had this experience not just at the FU but also at the Humanities Center at Johns Hopkins, I don't think that the reasons are to be found solely in or around Kiebitzweg. My work, and perhaps my personality, have been shaped by a movement that regards a certain kind of disappearing—the fading of the trace, for instance—as ineluctable. If one is lucky, such disappearing, however, can leaves traces, at least sometimes. What does Freud write with regard to the committing of a murder? "The difficulty lies not in the execution of the deed but in doing away with the traces."[7]

**Translated by Jonas Rosenbrück**

## Notes

1. This interview originally appeared as "Samuel Weber: Deckerinnerungen. Gespräch mit Irene Albers und Sima Reinisch," in *Nach Szondi: Allgemeine und Vergleichende Literaturwissenschaft an der Freien Universität Berlin 1965–2015*, ed. Irene Albers (Berlin: Kulturverlag Kadmos, 2015), 299–309. The Institut für Allgemeine und Vergleichende Literaturwissenschaft (Institute for General and Comparative Literature) at the Freie Universität-Berlin, commonly abbreviated as AVL, is now named the Peter Szondi-Institut. All notes to the interview are those of the editors of this volume, and the English version differs slightly from its German counterpart.

2. "I am very pleased with the interest provoked in the students, around ten, gathered in our workshop. I'm even under the impression that the atmosphere here is very favorable to a reception of a thought like yours, especially with the young students."

3. The Rostlaube is the colloquial name given to the main building housing the departments of literature, which, since they prepared for a position in secondary teaching, were frequented by large numbers of students, as distinct from comparative literature, which was not taught in high school.

4. In "Vous voulez rire" Derrida several times promises to recount the story of the first time he met Weber at Tegel Airport in West Berlin: "There was (we're still laughing about it, and everyone with us, but why?) an original and theatrical *quiproquo* and we're still trying to figure out which *deus ex machina* providentially staged it when I got off the plane thirty-five years ago in Berlin. Sam Weber first mistook someone else for me, *qui pro quo*. Can that ever be straightened out?" (214). Even as the interviewer presses him to tell the story, Derrida demurs, perhaps because, as he says, "a ten-hour interview would be indispensable" (231). And in the end, as a final note, Derrida encapsulates the meeting in a single fragment: "I replaced someone who had taken my place at S.W.'s place, in his car" (234). Even as it runs counter to the direction of Derrida's reflections, the editors of this volume hereby provide an account of their meeting that is longer

than a single sentence yet shorter than a ten-hour discussion: In the summer of 1968 Weber drives to Tegel Airport to pick up Derrida and take him to the AVL in Dahlem, where he is scheduled to give a lecture. Weber catches sight of a man who is impatiently waiting for a ride and ushers him into his car, only to discover soon thereafter that the rider is not Jacques Derrida but a rather well-known Italian actor. Weber turns around, drops off the actor, and approaches Derrida, explaining the mix-up and suggesting that there is at least one reason for the confusion: as a theoretician of violence—"La violence de la lettre" had recently been published in *Tel Quel*—he could perhaps be mistaken for an actor known for his violent roles. To which Derrida responds, "Violence, yes, but not brutality." As a coda: it is reported that Derrida would continue the story with an account of his return flight to Paris, where the Italian actor was also on the plane, surrounded by a coterie of fans, and the actor would gesture back to him, laughing at the suggestion that he (the actor) should be mistaken for Derrida.

5. "I hope that you will come to Berlin, and I am convinced that your work will have an extremely favorable influence on the unfortunate stagnation of the humanities in Germany."

6. "If I see it correctly, there exists a certain 'style,' half-Szondi, half-Derrida (which I find more and more interesting and dangerous at the same time)."

7. Sigmund Freud, *Moses and Monotheism*, trans. Katherine Jones (New York: Vintage Books, 1967), 52.

# CONTRIBUTORS

**Isabelle Alfandary** is a professor of American literature at the Université Sorbonne Nouvelle Paris–3 and a program director at the Collège international de philosophie. She is the author of *e. e. cummings ou la minuscule lyrique* (2002) and *Le risque de la lettre* (2012). The author of numerous articles and essays on American poetry, critical theory, continental philosophy, and psychoanalysis, she is completing a study entitled "Derrida/Lacan: Entre psychanalyse et déconstruction."

**Susan Bernstein** is a professor of comparative literature and German studies at Brown University. She is the author of *Virtuosity of the Nineteenth Century—Performing Music and Language in Heine, Liszt and Baudelaire* (1998) and *Housing Problems—Writing and Architecture in Goethe, Walpole, Freud and Heidegger* (2008). She has published articles on Nietzsche, Wagner, Kant, Avital Ronell, and the uncanny and is currently working on a book project entitled "The Other Synesthesia."

**Marc Crépon** is a director of research at the CNRS center Archives Husserl. He is also currently the chair of the Department of Philosophy of the École Normale Supérieure (Paris) and the dean of the transdisciplinary Graduate School in Literature and Science. His publications address issues of moral and political philosophy and focus most notably on the question of violence. Among his publications are *Vivre avec, la pensée de la mort et la mémoire des guerres* (2008; translated into English as *The Thought of Death and the Memory of War* [2013]); *La guerre des civilisations* (2010); *Le consentement meurtrier* (2012); *Elections, de la démophobie* (2012); and *La vocation de l'écriture, la littérature et la philosophie à l'épreuve de la violence* (2014).

**Jacques Derrida** (1930–2004), one of the greatest philosophers of the twentieth century, taught at the École Normale Supérieure and the École des Hautes Études en Sciences Sociales in Paris and at the University of California at Irvine. He is the author of over forty books. His seminars are now being published posthumously, beginning with *The Beast and the Sovereign* (2008) and *The Death Penalty* (2012).

**Astrid Deuber-Mankowsky**, a professor of media studies and gender studies at the Ruhr-University Bochum and an associate member of the Institute for Cultural Inquiry Berlin, has published extensively on topics in feminist theory, media theory, and continental philosophy as well as religion and modernism. Her first book, *Der frühe Walter Benjamin und Hermann Cohen: Jüdische Werte, Kritische*

*Philosophie, vergängliche Erfahrung* (2000), was awarded the Humboldt University prize for best dissertation. She is also the author of *Lara Croft: Cyber Heroine* (2005) and *Praktiken der Ilusion: Kant, Nietzsche, Cohen, Benjamin bis Donna J. Haraway* (2007).

**Peter Fenves** is the Joan and Serepta Harrison Professor of German, Comparative Literary Studies, and Jewish Studies at Northwestern University. He is the author of several books, including *Late Kant: Towards Another Law of the Earth* (2003) and *The Messianic Reduction: Walter Benjamin and the Shape of Time* (2011).

**Béatrice Jongy-Guéna,** *maître de conférences* in comparative literature at the University of Bourgogne, is the author of *L'Invention de soi: Rilke, Kafka, Pessoa* (2011), the editor of *L'Automédialité contemporaine* (*Revue d'Etudes culturelles*, no. 4, 2009), and the coeditor of *Transmission / Héritage dans l'écriture contemporaine de soi* (2009). Her research is oriented toward theater and contemporary forms of self-representation, while her current work concerns hybrid genres that combine autobiography, fiction, and essay.

**Dragan Kujundžić** is a professor of Jewish, Germanic, and Slavic studies and film and media studies at the University of Florida. He has edited *Deconstruction: A Merry Science* (1985), *Khoraographies for Jacques Derrida on July 15, 2000* (2000), *Who or What—Jacques Derrida* (2008), and two volumes on J. Hillis Miller, *J* (2005) and, with Barbara Cohen, *Provocations to Reading* (2005). He is the author of *Critical Exercises* (1983), *The Returns of History* (1997), *Tongue in Heat* (2003), and *Out of Interculturality* (2016), as well as the documentary films *The First Sail: J. Hillis Miller* (2010), with the film-book by the same title (2015), *Frozen Time, Liquid Memories* (2012), and *Cinemuse: Selfie with Sokurov* (2016).

**Kevin McLaughlin** is the dean of the faculty and the George Hazard Crooker University Professor of English, Comparative Literature, and German Studies at Brown University. He is the author of three books: *Writing in Parts: Imitation and Exchange in 19th-Century Literature* (1995), *Paperwork: Literature and Mass Mediacy in the Age of Paper* (2005), and *Poetic Force: Poetry after Kant* (2014). He is also the translator with Howard Eiland of Walter Benjamin's *Arcades Project* (1999).

**Nikolaus Müller-Schöll** is the chair of theatre studies and head of the M.A. program in dramaturgy at the Goethe-University in Frankfurt am Main. Among the numerous books he has written and coedited are *Das Theater des "konstruktiven Defaitismus": Lektüren zur Theorie eines Theaters der A-Identität bei Walter Benjamin, Bertolt Brecht und Heiner Müller* (2002) and *Performing Politics: Politisch Kunst machen nach dem 20. Jahrhundert* (2012).

**Marc Redfield** is the chair of the Department of Comparative Literature and a professor of English and comparative literature at Brown University. His publications include *Phantom Formations: Aesthetic Ideology and the Bildungsroman* (1996), *The Politics of Aesthetics: Nationalism, Gender, Romanticism* (2003),

*The Rhetoric of Terror: Reflections on 9/11 and the War on Terror* (2009), and *Theory at Yale: The Strange Case of Deconstruction in America* (2015). He coedited *High Anxieties: Cultural Studies in Addiction* (2002), edited *Legacies of Paul de Man* (2007), and guest-edited special issues of the journals *Diacritics*, *Romantic Praxis*, and *Wordsworth Circle*.

**Peter Szendy**, a professor of philosophy at the University of Paris Ouest Nanterre and a musicological advisor at the Cité de la musique, has also been a visiting professor at Princeton and Brown. He has extensively written on listening, organology, and (musical) prosthetics; reading Melville; and the aesthetics of surveillance. Recently translated books include *Apocalypse-Cinema: 2012 and Other Ends of the World* (forthcoming) and *Kant in the Land of Extraterrestrials: Cosmopolitical Philosofictions* (2013).

**Samuel Weber** is the Avalon Foundation Professor of Humanities at Northwestern University and directs Northwestern's Paris program in critical theory. He studied literature with Paul de Man and philosophy with Theodor Adorno and Jacques Derrida. He has published on Balzac, Sterne, Hölderlin, and Kafka, among others, as well as on Kant, Freud, Heidegger, and Derrida. He worked for a time in Germany as a dramaturge, an experience that produced a book, *Theatricality as Medium* (2004). His most recent major publication is a collection of essays in French, *Inquiétantes singularités* (2014). He is currently working on a book with the tentative title "Towards a Politics and Poetics of Singularity."